THE COMING OF AUSTRIAN FASCISM

Martin Kitchen

CROOM HELM LONDON

McGILL-QUEEN'S UNIVERSITY PRESS
MONTREAL

©1980 Martin Kitchen
Croom Helm Ltd, 2-10 St John's Road, London SW11

British Library Cataloguing in Publication Data

Kitchen, Martin
    The coming of Austrian Fascism.
1. Austria — Politics and government — 1918-1938
1. Title
943.6'05   DB97

ISBN 0-7099-0133-X

McGill-Queen's University Press
1020 Pine Avenue West, Montreal H3A 1A2
    :
ISBN 0-7735-0520-2

Legal deposit 2nd quarter 1980
Bibliothèque Nationale du Québec

Printed and bound in Great Britain

CONTENTS

ACKNOWLEDGEMENTS

I am most grateful to the generous support of the Canada Council, without which this book could not have been written. The staffs of the Allgemeines Verwaltungsarchiv, the Haus- Hof- und Staatsarchiv, the Kriegsarchiv and the Verein für die Geschichte der Arbeiterbewegung, all of which are in Vienna, were unfailingly helpful. I owe a particular debt of gratitude to Frau Dr Isabella Ackerl of the Wissenschaftliche Kommission des Theodor-Körner-Stiftungsfonds und des Leopold-Kunschak-Preises zur Erforschung der österreichischen Geschichte der Jahre 1918 bis 1938 for her friendly help and assistance. I am deeply saddened that I am unable to give this book to Ilona Duczynska whose generosity, enthusiasm and encouragement I shall not forget. Her death was a great loss to her many friends throughout the world. Bernice Ferrier and Wilma Wiffin typed the manuscript without losing their good humour.

INTRODUCTION

On 12 February 1934 fighting broke out in Linz between government forces and the Social Democratic Party. Within hours Vienna was up in arms, and the fighting soon spread to other parts of Austria. A few days later the party was destroyed, and Austria seemed to many observers to have joined the ranks of the fascist states. The violence of the fighting, particularly the shelling of the vast workers' housing complex, the Karl-Marx-Hof, and the summary execution of a number of the leading figures in the fighting, horrified the civilised world. The struggle of the Austrian workers against the systematic destruction of democratic freedoms, their desperate, frustrated and hopeless fight against overwhelming odds, and their determination that their country should not go the same way as Italy and Germany was an inspiration to many to form an anti-fascist front in which the struggle for socialism became subordinated to the defence of democracy. Yet from the very outset there was a feeling that this effort was too late. The attitude of the Western democracies towards the fascist states and the Stalinist purges in the Soviet Union, and the failures of the popular front governments in Spain and France reinforced this sense of hopelessness. As time went by 12 February ceased to be an inspiration and became a myth, but a myth that could be interpreted in several different ways. Was it an example of determined proletarian class consciousness betrayed by incompetent or even sinister leadership? Did it show the hopelessness of armed struggle against government forces, and thus the need for compromise with extreme right-wing governments? Was it a revolution, or merely a mindless brawl? Was the Social Democratic Party destroyed by its own internal weaknesses, or was it crushed by the government? These questions were not merely the result of various exiles banging their heads against various ideological walls, but they involved fundamental issues of socialism, democracy and fascism. It is largely for this reason that 12 February still excites strong responses, as the discussions at a symposium held in Vienna on the 40th anniversary amply demonstrate.[1] Old political

1

resentments certainly linger on, but they now seldom stand in the way of an objective analysis of the failures of the Austrian republic.

The Social Democratic Party of Austria was formed relatively late but it soon earned a deserved reputation for its contribution to socialist thought and for the strength of its organisation and its imaginative educational and artistic activities. 'Austro-Marxism' was soon to become the dominant ideology of the Second International. Like the party on which it was modelled, the German SPD, it suffered from a fatal inability to reconcile demands for revolution with the need for reform, a central difficulty for social democratic parties on which Rosa Luxemburg wrote her most powerful pamphlet, *Reform or Revolution?* A party with so many outstanding intellectuals was not slow to find solutions to this problem, but in every instance the cure was worse than the disease. The most prevalent attitude was one of revolutionary fatalism, a blind faith in the inexorable laws of historical development that would lead inevitably to socialism. It was thus hardly surprising that Lenin was to hurl some of his most poisonous darts at the Austrian socialists and the philosophical tradition on which it was based.[2] This fatalism paralysed the party leadership, the belief in the automatic arrival of socialism combining with a false sense of optimism. Dr Pangloss in Marxist clothes was hardly a figure likely to deal with determined political opponents in a social and economic situation that greatly favoured the right. Austro-Marxism thus served both as a pep pill and a tranquilliser, giving double comfort to a patient who seemed no longer aware of the disease from which he was suffering.

The rhetoric of the party leadership helped to hold the different strands together, although by 1934 internal tensions had reached breaking point. At the same time it convinced many on the right that the party really was a revolutionary menace that had to be destroyed. Other more cynical and realistic politicians deliberately used the radical phraseology of their opponents to justify their attacks on the party. A party that was acting purely in self-defence could thus be presented as preparing for civil war, the Austro-fascist state as the only possible alternative to 'bolshevism'. In fact the party had already been politically defeated by 1934: the Palace of Justice affair of 1927 and the closing of parliament in 1933 were both striking evidence of its inability to combat the rising tide of right-wing extremism. The Communists could demand more determined action, but they were too small a sect to have any influence.

The main force on the right, the Christian Social Party, had its origins in the radical right of the 1890s, with its anti-semitism and confused anti-capitalism. During the republic it became more respectable and more closely associated with the mainstream of Catholic Social philosophy. It never accepted the principles of liberal democracy, and at best it merely tolerated the republic as an unpleasant and hopefully temporary nuisance. The democratic faction within the party was without influence and did little but raise false hopes among the Social Democratic moderates. From 1930 fascistic tendencies within the party became increasingly pronounced, and many longed for a 'March on Vienna' or an authoritarian *coup d'état*.

The Social Democrats did not take the threat of fascism in Austria at all seriously until it was too late. The Heimwehr, the paramilitary force of the extreme right, was hopelessly muddled and confused. Endless wrangles between the shallow prima donnas who led the movement, rivalries and quarrels, uncertainty about the aims of the movement, organisational weakness and the temptation to make deals with the Nazis or the Italian Fascists behind the backs of other leaders all served to render the movement politically ineffective. Almost until Hitler became Chancellor of Germany in January 1933 the Austrian Nazis appeared to be a small sect of misguided cranks and adventurers, the lunatic fringe of the radical right. After 1933 there was a tremendous growth in the size and influence of the party which could now count on the support of a great power and basked in the reflected glory of the spectacular success of the German party.

Political radicalism was in large part a result of the economic problems of the republic, which in turn were made considerably worse by political decisions and attitudes. The dislocations caused to the economy by the lost war were particularly severe in Austria, for a small German state was all that was left of a large multinational empire. To most Austrians merging with Germany, an Anschluss, was the obvious and only solution to Austria's economic problems. All arguments to the contrary were dismissed as propaganda by the Entente to justify the peace settlement. Thus the problems of how to deal with inflation, to stimulate investment for industrial expansion, overcome the chronic balance of payments deficits and decrease unemployment were all too often tackled in a halfhearted manner pending an Anschluss with the more vigorous German economy. Governments adopted strictly deflationary policies, thus making the chronic unemployment problem even worse, and doing little to restructure the economy. In such a situation wild speculation, particularly by the banks, became the favourite economic activity of the republic, and capital that was needed for industrial development was frittered away in frivolous adventures on the stock exchange and currency speculation. The persistently high levels of unemployment severely weakened the labour movement that found it increasingly difficult to undertake effective industrial action. In many instances the unemployed, who saw little prospect of a future job, and who felt that they had nothing to lose, formed the left-wing within the Social Democratic Party, while those with regular employment favoured compromise and caution. The Christian Socials found their strongest support in the agricultural regions which were consistently favoured throughout the republic. The radical right was largely recruited from the urban petty bourgeoisie who felt threatened by both big business and by the organised working class, and who had often lost their modest savings by imprudent speculation and saw their earning power eroded by inflation. Thus the economic problems of the republic were to aggravate the political tensions that were already intense in a state that few accepted or wished to see survive in its present form.

In the early years of the republic the Social Democrats were confident that they had sufficient influence over the army and the police so that they could never be used against the party. Thanks to the determined efforts of the Christian Social Party this influence was systemmatically reduced. By 1927, at the latest, it was clear that the executive (the army and the various police forces) could be used against the Social Democrats without the slightest concern that it might not obey orders from the government. To counter the Heimwehr, and to compensate for this loss of influence over the army, the Social Democrats built up their own paramilitary force, the Schutzbund. The Schutzbund was weakened from the beginning by a number of factors. Almost all the leading Social Democrats had a horror of violence and a sense of moral decency which was in marked contrast to their often rather bellicose public utterances. As a result the precise role of the Schutzbund was unclear and the rank and file became increasingly confused and frustrated. Unimaginative planning by the Schutzbund leadership, who wanted it to be organised on traditional military lines, added to the confusion. In a head-on collision between the Schutzbund and the executive there could be no doubt that the Social Democrats would be defeated. Warnings to this effect from Körner were ignored, and the government was confident that it had little to fear in the event of a showdown with the Social Democrats.

When Dollfuss became Chancellor in 1932 he had no clear programme of action, but he was determined to move step by step towards an authoritarian regime.[3] Faced with this salami tactic the Social Democrats were at a loss to know what to do. At which precise point should they rise up in defence of democracy? Part of the trouble was that it was exceedingly hard to find anyone who was a truly committed democrat. The Social Democratic left was for 'socialism', some feeling that this would involve a temporary phase of proletarian dictatorship and all agreeing that it would involve something radically different from bourgeois democracy. The right of the party was prepared to compromise its position on democracy to defend the régime against National Socialism. Dollfuss could thus be supported as the 'lesser evil', just as the German Social Democrats had supported Brüning.

Dollfuss's attitude towards the Nazis was far from straightforward. Outwardly he appeared to be determined in his opposition to the party, but at the same time he was always ready to negotiate. Within his government Fey was more militantly anti-Nazi, and yet he was also the most vigorous proponent of a fascistic régime. The Italian government continually insisted that the only way to deal with the problem of Nazism in Austria was to destroy the Social Democrats, thus convincing the misguided Austrian Nazis that the régime was truly anti-Marxist and worthy of support. It is uncertain to what extent Dollfuss accepted this argument, although it was most convenient for him apart from the fact that the Italians were asking him insistently to act more quickly than he wished. There can be no doubt at all that he saw the Social Democrats as the main enemy, and that he had a certain ideological sympathy for the National Socialists. He tried to postpone the ban on the Nazi Party, arguing that it was ridiculous to take action against the Nazis without taking similar action against the Social Democrats. It was Fey who insisted that the Social Democrats and Communists were innocent of terrorist acts and that immediate action against the Nazis was essential. This did not mean that Fey had any sympathy for the left, simply that he preferred to wait until they were provoked into action so that they could then be destroyed by the government forces once and for all.

Few realised that in the long run Dollfuss was cutting off the branch on which he was sitting. Only with the help of the Social Democrats could the independence and domestic peace of Austria be preserved. The alternatives were democracy or Nazism. A fascist Austria would not prevent an Anschluss, and as Karl Winter argued, it was a question of the 'swastika on the Brenner or democracy in Austria'. On 12 February 1934 democracy was finally destroyed in Austria, and the way to the Nazi Anschluss was left wide open.

In spite of many disastrous errors by the Social Democratic leadership there can be no question about the responsibility for the tragedy. It was neither an 'uprising of the Austrian workers' nor was it the outcome of a carefully prepared strategy by Dollfuss. It was the desperate defence of democratic freedoms in the face of endless provocations by a government which was determined utterly to destroy an opponent that had already been politically defeated. The actions of the Dollfuss government were both morally indefensible and politically inept. The government lost its strongest supporters in the struggle against National Socialism in an act of mindless vindictiveness. 12 February 1934 led directly to 12 February 1938 when Schuschnigg capitulated to Hitler at Berchtesgaden and the fate of the 'Christian, German, authoritarian Austria based on the estates' was sealed. In the final hours before the Anschluss some finally realised that the workers had died in 1934 not only for freedom and democracy but also for Austria itself. The cause was already lost and the leadership feeble, but their efforts and heroism remain one of the great episodes in the history of the European working class.

Notes

1. Ludwig Jedlicka and Rudolf Neck, *Das Jahr 1934: 12. Februar* (Vienna 1975).
2. V.I. Lenin, *Materialismus und Empirokritizismus; kritische Bemerkungen über eine reaktionäre Philosophie* (Berlin 1964).
3. Some still argue that Dollfuss was really a democrat. See the article by John Rath in Rudolf Neck and Adam Wandruszka, *Beiträge zur Zeitgeschichte: Festschrift für Ludwig Jedlicka* (St Pölten 1976).

1 AUSTRO-MARXISM IN THEORY AND PRACTICE

The Austrian Social Democratic Party was constituted as a united and supranational party with a broadly Marxist programme at the party congress which met on New Year's Eve of 1889 at Hainfeld, the 'Bethlehem of Austrian Socialism'.[1] There are a number of reasons why the party was formed at such a relatively late date. The economic backwardness of Austria had retarded the formation of a large and class-conscious industrial working class. Unity had been hampered by national differences and by regionalism, a problem that was not helped by the natural admiration of the German Austrians for the SPD in the Reich. The determination of many German Austrians to follow the model of their northern comrades gave the movement a certain Greater German bias, later to be found in the enthusiasm of Austrian Social Democrats for the Anschluss in the years before 1933, which was hardly attractive to socialists from the other nationalities of the Dual Monarchy. The repression of the working-class movement, particularly after the anti-socialist laws in Germany in 1876, exacerbated the already very marked tendency towards factionalism, making the formation of an effective and united party all the more difficult. Followers of Lassalle quarrelled with admirers of Schulze-Delitzsch, Proudhonists quarrelled with anarchists, nationalists quarrelled with internationalists. There had been considerable progress in the years before Hainfeld, particularly in the field of workers' education, and in 1869 there were 13,350 Austrian members of the First International.[2] But previous attempts to form a united party, such as the Neudörfl conference in 1874, had achieved very little. It was the combined effects of the depression from 1873 which made the Austrian labour movement far more receptive to Marxist ideas, and the undoubted diplomatic skills of Viktor Adler that made Hainfeld possible.

The Hainfeld programme, which remained in force with a few modest changes until the Linz conference in 1926, combined long-range aims such as the abolition of the private ownership of the means of production and exchange, with condemnations of the state as an instrument of class oppression, denunciations of the progressive emiseration of the working class, and short-term demands for freedom of speech, universal suffrage, free education, the separation of church and state and progressive labour legislation. As was the case with many parties in the Second International the party was committed to a programme that was essentially reformist, but spiced with Marxist notions of the contradictions between capital and labour and of the historic mission of the proletariat, without seriously confronting the problem of attaining its long-term aims or tackling the fundamentally revolutionary aspects of Marx's thought. Hainfeld achieved unity, but the price that was paid was a loss of revolutionary *élan*. Immediate reforms seemed more important than distant goals so that 'revolution' became increasingly remote from daily political practice to the point that it was little more than an article of faith, a promised land towards which the inexorable laws of capitalist development were inevitably leading. By failing to confront the dialectical relationship between reform and revolution the party could all too easily fall prey to a confident passivity and fatalism.

In the years immediately after Hainfeld these problems seemed remote and scholastic, for there were many immediate problems to face. Much of the party's efforts were directed towards a reduction of the length of the working day and a reform of the franchise. The opportunities afforded by the Russian Revolution of 1905 were skilfully and courageously exploited so that universal suffrage was granted, making the party the second largest party in the Reichsrat at the election of 1907. This was a great victory, but it further strengthened the reformist tendencies within the party, and ideas of a fundamental and revolutionary restructuring of society were pushed aside as the party became increasingly concerned with immediate tasks, thus tacitly accepting the existing system as at least providing enough scope for effective political action. This tendency was further strengthened by the privileged position of the Austrian workers within the Empire. They formed a labour aristocracy who tended to look down on their less fortunate comrades in Bohemia, Moravia, Hungary or the Balkans, and many feared that the end of the monarchy, which as socialists they passionately advocated, might very well mean the end of their own special status. The party's nationality programme, adopted at Brunn in 1899, attempted to overcome these difficulties by calling for the creation of a 'democratic federation of nationalities' in place of the old Empire. But this was hardly a solution, for nothing was said of ways of overcoming the crass regional disparities and widely different levels of development which lay at the heart of the problem. When it was suggested that such a fundamental reform could be achieved by administrative decrees, it seemed to many that this was simply a means of continuing German domination within the Empire. It was only in 1918 when it was clear that the Empire was falling apart, and when the Soviet call for the self-determination of peoples had a tremendous impact on the nationalities, that the dream of a socialist Austria-Hungary was abandoned.

It was the American socialist writer Louis B. Boudin who coined the phrase 'Austro-Marxism' to describe the ideology of the party and its principal thinkers, Karl Kautsky, Rudolf Hilferding and Otto Bauer, and the expression was soon widely used.[3] Austro-Marxism was the specific Austrian form of reformism, stressing gradual reform within the existing system and neglecting the revolutionary aspects of Marx's thought. The Austro-Marxists were the most coherent and subtle representatives of the dominant ideology of the Second International. Their centralist position was strongly opposed not only to the leftist position of Lenin and Rosa Luxemburg, but also to the abandonment of Marxism by Bernstein and his revisionist followers. In theory they hoped to save the party and the International from adventurism, fractional strife and the rejection of fundamental socialist aims, but in practice their attempts to overcome the fundamental differences between left and right greatly strengthened the revisionist position. They hoped to apply Marxist methods in order to understand the fundamental changes that had occurred within society in the age of monopoly capitalism and imperialism. The result was a number of outstanding works, of which Hilferding's *Finanzkapital* was the most significant, which made major contributions to Marxist literature. But although many of these works were radical in tone and far-reaching in their conclusions, they all too often provided elaborate Marxist justifications for reformist practice and were characterised by a pious faith in blind laws of historical development towards socialism which could be used to support a fatalistic wait-and-see attitude by the party leadership. From its inception Austro-Marxism was plagued by a contradiction between its apparent radicalism and its attentist practice. In the long run its position as arbiter of the fractional strife within the International could not be maintained. It was too radical for the revisionists, who objected to its Marxist rhetoric, and was roundly denounced by the left for its denial of revolution.[4] Even more important was its failure to understand the imminent danger of an imperialist war and to realise the revolutionary possibilities that existed in the age of imperialism. The Austro-Marxists were traumatised by the fear of the disintegration of the party into the countless waring factions that had existed before Hainfeld. Party unity was to be preserved at all costs by radical phrases to appease the left, reformist practice to satisfy the right and a blind faith in the 'objective' laws of history that insured that everything would turn out all right in the end.[5]

The party leadership was able to maintain this balancing act in the pre-war years without serious difficulty. The party grew in size and influence and modest reforms were achieved. The outbreak of the war was the most serious test of the party's convictions and sincerity, and the party failed miserably. The Reichsrat had been closed in March 1914, but there can be no doubt that the party would have voted for the war credits in spite of the resolutions of the International in 1907 and 1912 against an imperialist war. The party press echoed the arguments of the German party against bloody Russian aggression and called for all-out support of the war effort. Although Viktor Adler tried to restrain some of the more bellicose of his colleagues, it appeared to the rank and file of the party that the leadership was solidly behind the war, and they were thus left confused and often angry. The party had taken a strong stand against any possible war, and had a large pacifist faction; now it appeared to be swept away by an excessive chauvinism that was not shared by the average worker, who had been rendered relatively immune to such hysteria, largely due to the efforts of the party which now seemed to have abandoned its principles. The result was a rejection of the party by many faithful members, and there was a similar decline in trade union membership. In Vienna and Lower Austria, the heartland of the party, membership dropped by 65 per cent between 1914 and 1916; in some parts of Austria membership fell by 80 per cent. It only began to pick up again when the party abandoned its support of the war and assumed a more critical role.[6]

The attitude of the party towards the war was the direct cause of the growth of a left-wing opposition within the party. Led by intellectuals such as Viktor Adler's son Friedrich, Robert Danneberg, Otto Bauer, Julius Deutsch and Gabriele Proft, it was but a small faction. Viktor Adler, who liked to use medical analogies taken from his experience as a doctor, and who saw socialism as a question of hygiene, felt that such factionalism was merely a typical symptom in a society that was suffering from fever.[7] The left opposition followed the example of the centre of the German USPD, which were dominated by the Austrians Kautsky and Hilferding, and denied that the war was defensive but rather an imperialist and aggressive war. However, they were anxious to maintain party unity and avoided any revolutionary actions which would have been the logical consequence of their analysis of the nature of the war. Many left-wing socialists, particularly the students, became increasingly impatient with Friedrich Adler's moderation and frequent inconsistency, and formed a left radical group which was strongly influenced by Leninist ideas. Friedrich Adler found himself trapped between the party establishment led by his father, and the increasingly attractive and vociferous left. On 21 October 1916 in an act of desperation he assassinated the Minister President, Stürgkh. Surprisingly, although Friedrich Adler was motivated more by the need to find a way out of his own intellectual and emotional problems, the assassination turned out to be a turning point in the history of the party. Friedrich Adler overnight became a folk hero. In a dramatic speech at his trial he attacked the ruling class and its war policy as well as the 'social patriotism' of the Social Democratic Party. The bullet that hit Stürgkh was also aimed at the entire social system which included his own father, prompting one historian to speak of 'patricide by proxy'.[8]

By 1917 social tensions within the Dual Monarchy were becoming so acute that the government was obliged to make considerable concessions. The Reichsrat was reconvened. The Social Democrats were allowed to hold a party conference, and also to attend the meeting of the International at Stockholm. The position of the left was greatly strengthened. The February revolution in Russia made it even less plausible to see the war as a struggle against Russian despotism. President Wilson's high-minded talk about democracy was a powerful propaganda weapon for the anti-war faction. The Petrograd Soviet's call for an end to the war without reparations or annexations found a loud echo throughout Austria. At the party conference Otto Bauer, who had just returned from a prisoner-of-war camp in Russia, was the main spokesman of the left, attacking the party leadership for its chauvinism and reformism, but at the same time insisting that the party should set its own house in order and avoid any splits. The party leadership accepted much of the criticism of the party's 'Crown Prince', Otto Bauer, and in doing so was able to absorb and to a large extent neutralise the effects of the sharp leftward swing of the party. The speeches and writings of the left made it appear that the party was on a radical course, but the practical politics of the party remained much the same. The old contradiction between revolutionary rhetoric and cautious practice that had characterised the party since Hainfeld remained, although in a new and more subtle form.[9]

During the January strike in Austria, in which almost one million workers were involved, and in which far-reaching political demands were made, including the immediate end to the war, the party played a skilful role as mediator between the strikers and the government. The party was thus able to defeat the radicals but also to gain certain concessions for the strikers so as to satisfy the party members. Much the same role was played by the party during the Austrian 'revolution' of 1918-19.

It is extremely doubtful whether it is permissable to use the term 'revolution' to describe the events in Austria at the end of the war, and it is certain that the collapse of the monarchy and the establishment of the republic were not the work of the Social Democrats, but rather the result of a process of internal decay. Whether or not a revolution was possible is still hotly debated among historians and publicists, but there can be no doubt that the party actively restrained the movement towards revolution. Otto Bauer's suggestions for extensive national-isation were countered by Renner's sarcastic remark that it was no good nationalising debts, a phrase that was soon elevated to the level of a cliché by right-wing Social Democrats. The party insisted that a revolution in Austria would be countered by a blockade by the Entente, and that it would not be tolerated outside the industrial areas and would thus lead to the disintegration of German Austria. Once again 'wait and see' took the place of determined political action. The revolution in Austria was to be postponed until there were revolutions in the Entente countries and in Czechoslovakia. The left continued to make revolutionary noises but the party followed a policy of cautious and gradual reform as suggested by Renner and Hanusch. In the long run this policy could win little support from outside the ranks of the party faithful. Dramatic speeches in support of the Soviet govern-ments in Munich and Hungary, and illegal shipments of weapons to Bela Kun's supporters, horrified the right. The insistence that the objective situation in Austria would not permit a similar experiment in Soviet democracy disgusted the left.[10] But the party was able to maintain its strength and influence by its very real achievements in social reform, which included the introduction of unemployment benefits in November 1918 and the long-awaited eight-hour day in December of the same year. In the following year a law introducing works councils was drawn up as part of a scheme of educating the workers in management and preparing the way for greater workers' control and even of nationalisation of sectors of industry.

The demand for an Austrian republic on 30 October 1918 by the party was not the result of a determined effort to seize power, but because the party was forced into action by the workers of Vienna who were growing increasingly impatient with the passivity of the Social Democrats. The party accepted a National Assembly made up of deputies who had been elected before the war and which acted as a further hindrance to significant and fundamental changes in the structure of society. This feeble policy was excused on the grounds that German Austria was merely a provisional state that no one really wanted, and that within a short time an Anschluss with Germany, a Germany that appeared to be dominated by the workers' and soldiers' councils, would create a totally different situation. On 2 November 1918 Friedrich Adler was set free from prison and was welcomed as the greatest hero of the Austrian left. The radicals asked him to join in the formation of an Austrian Communist Party, but Adler refused. By rejecting the left and by returning to the Social Democrats Adler did more than any single individual to strengthen the position of the Social Democratic Party among the working class.[11]

The rejection by the party of a revolutionary Soviet solution was clearly seen in the formation of the first republican government. Under the leadership of Renner, the outstanding spokesman of the right, the party joined in a coalition with the Christian Social Party and the Greater German Party. This coalition continued after the elections of February 1919 which left the Social Democrats as the largest party in parliament, although the bourgeois parties had a majority. The right-wing parties needed the Social Democrats to contain and control the radicalised working class and to save Austria from bolshevism. Otto Bauer was ready to admit that Ferdinand Hanusch's social legislation and the granting of votes to women was designed in part to assuage the working class that had become dissatisfied with the policies of the leadership, and appeared eager to emulate the revolutionaries in Budapest and Munich. Once the Hungarian and Bavarian Soviets had been smashed there was a marked lack of enthusiasm among the bourgeois parties for further social reform and some of the existing legislation was hastily modified.[12]

Verbal radicalism and practical reformism served to assuage the working class and to protect the bourgeoisie. The right was not too alarmed at the sight of a law which envisaged the possible future nationalisation of certain sectors of industry, including coal, electricity, iron and forestry with full compensation for the present owners, for the prospect seemed a somewhat remote possibility. Radical workers were all too ready to believe that the debate was a victory for their demands. Social Democratic control of the workers' and soldiers' councils was also effective in containing the demands for socialisation. The councils were vitally important in 1918-19 in controlling prices, providing social assistance, and in many cases saving people from starvation. The Communist demand for 'all power to the Soviets' could easily be met by the Social Democrats who effectively controlled the Soviets. In the elections for the workers' councils in Vienna in 1919 the Communists were only able to gain five per cent of the vote.[13] As the revolutionary wave ebbed, the factory councils, which were concerned with purely economic questions, and which worked closely with the trade unions, gradually began to replace the more radical and political workers' councils, a process that was speeded up by the coalition government granting the factory councils increasing power and influence. By such means considerable reforms were made within the capitalist system, the system thus being strengthened against the threat of revolutionary overthrow.

By 1920 the danger of revolution had passed and the economic situation appeared to be relatively stable. As far as the bourgeois parties were concerned the Social Democrats had performed their task and could now be dropped. In June 1920 the coalition fell apart, and the elections in October returned the Christian Socials as the largest party, to form a new government supported by the Greater Germans. As their right-wing coalition partners moved further to the right, the Social Democrats were relieved to abandon the coalition, and the move was warmly supported by the rank and file. In opposition the purity of Austro-Marxism could be preserved and the unity of the party maintained. The pragmatism of the party as a partner with the bourgeois parties had alienated many loyal socialists. But now the Christian Socials could be denounced as traitors and imperialist agents, as the party appeared to go on a left-wing course.

Even in opposition the party was ready to compromise. The Geneva Treaty of 1922, under which the League of Nations granted Austria a large loan, was strongly attacked by the party. Under the terms of this agreement foreign capital was able to make massive profits at the expense of the Austrian people, the country lost financial sovereignty and was forced to carry out drastic austerity measures which further depressed the living standards of the working people, and the treaty was used as an excuse to undo many of the achievements of 1918. The introduction of a value added tax was a further burden on lower income groups, and by 1925 78 per cent of state income came from indirect taxation.[14] The Social Democrats put forward an imaginative alternative programme designed to restore the economy without depending on outside financing. Yet when the matter was voted in parliament the party abstained on the grounds that there was only a choice between loss of freedom or economic catastrophe. This abstention enabled Ignaz Seipel's government to obtain the necessary two-thirds majority to ratify the treaty. For many Social Democrats the party's policy of 'neither the one thing nor the other' was a serious setback, and Seipel summed up the right's feelings when he said that politically Otto Bauer was a man with two left hands.[15] Bauer was to write that 4 October 1922 was Seipel's revenge for 12 November 1918, but he should have added that Seipel's triumph was made all the easier by the attitude of the Social Democratic Party.[16]

In spite of the inept policies of the party during the debates over the Geneva Treaty the harsh economic effects of the government's policy rebounded to the party's favour, and in the parliamentary elections in October 1923 the party increased its number of seats by ten per cent, although this was not sufficient to enable it to form a majority. The bourgeois parties maintained their coalition and Seipel stayed in office. The party which claimed that it had created the republic was excluded from power, and it was only in Vienna that it was possible to strive for a 'partial realisation of socialism within the womb of bourgeois society'.[17] In the 1920s Vienna was the model of Austrian Social Democracy, an example of what socialism could achieve, the ideal of social democrats throughout the world, an inspiration to poets and town planners, painters and social workers, dreamers and men of action. Contrary to Seipel's taxation system, particularly after Geneva, Vienna's municipal taxes were redistributive. Heavy taxes were levied on automobiles and servants, luxury apartments and race-horses, whereas the modest pleasures of the less fortunate were lightly taxed. The income from these taxes was used to build workers' housing such as the Karl-Marx-Hof which was an outstanding piece of urban architecture all too soon to become the tragic symbol of the defeat of the working class in 1934. The schools, hospitals and welfare services of Vienna were without equal in Europe. The mayor of Vienna, Karl Seitz, and his financial councillor, Hugo Breitner, by actively promoting public expenditure, particularly on council housing (65,000 new apartments were built between 1923 and 1933) did much to maintain employment levels well above the national average, and thus to reduce the demand for the social services which were ready to meet the needs of the less fortunate.

For the bourgeoisie massive expenditure on housing, schools, hospitals and the social services were denounced as 'taxation sadism' and 'council house bolshevism'; Vienna was a constant aggravation and provocation, a thorn in the flesh of the Austrian bourgeoisie, an example of socialist profligacy and utopianism, the capital city of punitive taxation and the class war. For the Social Democrats 'Red Vienna' was the living symbol of socialism, to be defended at all costs against the attacks of the reactionaries. Thus in the republic the old dichotomy between Vienna and the provinces became increasingly acute as it took on an intense political form. The right was determined to smash Red Vienna, the left to defend it against a 'March on Vienna' which they were convinced would be the first step to establish fascism in Austria.[18]

The constant attacks on Vienna placed the Social Democrats increasingly on the defensive thus further cramping their political activities at the national level. The remarkable achievements of Red Vienna could all too easily be used to disguise the miserable failures of the party in the rest of Austria, and the applause of foreign visitors helped to assuage the frustrations of a party that had been out-manoeuvred by its opponents. The growing tension between Vienna and the provinces, and the determination of the Austrian bourgeoisie to kill this socialist hydra, was one of the main causes of 12 February 1934. The continually defensive attitude of the Social Democrats the main reason for their defeat.

Throughout the 1920s the steady increase in the popular vote for the party hid the fact that its effective political power was gradually fading. Trade union membership dwindled away even before the mass exodus after 1929. The achievements of 1918-19 on the shop floor were never consolidated and were slowly erroded. In the army the party lost its influence and the traditional conservative officers re-established their authority. The weakness of the party prompted the reactionaries to further acts of violence that were seldom punished in the courts, and Seipel continued to chip away at the foundations of the liberal democratic state. The working class became increasingly discontented with the lack of action by the party and demanded vigorous defence of republican freedoms against mounting reaction. The party realised that action was needed, but the course they took was typical of Austro-Marxism. Words were deemed an adequate substitute for deeds. A new party programme was felt to be the obvious solution.

The Linz programme of 1926 appeared to make the party the most determined and revolutionary of all social democratic parties. A stern warning was issued to the bourgeoisie that should it try to frustrate the transition from capitalism to socialism 'the working class would be forced to smash the opposition of the bourgeoisie by means of dictatorship'. The use of the word 'dictatorship' in the party programme was hotly debated, but Otto Bauer was able to ensure its inclusion. The right immediately seized the opportunity to denounce the party as bolshevik, naturally overlooking the fact that dictatorship was seen as a defensive policy to defend a socialist state created by popular vote. 'Dictatorship' once again did much to satisfy the increasingly radicalised and alienated left wing of the party, served to 'épater les bourgeois', and disguised the fact that it meant little more than the determination to defend the constitution of the republic against violence from the right. Hardly a revolutionary statement, and certainly not 'bolshevik'. If dictatorship proved a magic formula to assuage the radicals, Bauer's talk of the 51 per cent of the vote needed to achieve socialism was warmly approved by the right wing. Indeed the programme used the popular Austro-Marxist phrase 'the balance of power' (between bourgeoisie and proletariat) to once again entertain the possibility of a coalition with the bourgeois parties.

The balancing act of the Linz programme was typical of Otto Bauer who in one breath could talk of dictatorship in a way that inspired the left and then talk of the horrors of violence and civil war in such blood-curdling terms as to horrify his audience. If the Hainfeld programme was above all the work of the 'socialist doctor' Viktor Adler, with its determination to overcome party factionalism and create a united party, Linz was Bauer's characteristic effort. Otto Bauer, born in 1881, was the outstanding and also most typical representative of the party during the republic. His considerable intelligence could all too often lead him to arrogance, his brilliance into empty mandarin discourses of the sort so brilliantly satirised by Karl Krauss. Like so many Austrian statesmen from Seipel to Kreisky it often seemed that Bauer was too big a man for so small and insignificant a state. As an intellectual well versed in Marx's writings, as well as those of his bourgeois critics, Bauer saw himself as a leading, if not *the* leading, spokesman of the Marxist school of the whole world (to whom he dedicated with characteristic pathos his book on the Austrian Revolution), attacking what he termed the 'vulgar Marxism' of the Communists and the radical left, as well as the revisionism of Renner and his followers. As an intellectual in a party that was remarkably open to new intellectual currents Bauer was profoundly influenced by the empirio-criticism of Ernst Mach and by the philosophy of the 'Vienna Circle' of Carnap and Schlick. Lenin had already attacked the scepticism and fatalism of this philosophical approach, and there can be little doubt that the study of these philosophers reinforced Bauer's own mechanistic and deterministic reading of Marx that left little room for conscious and determined political action. Bauer was indeed the true standard-bearer of Austro-Marxism.

Bauer had come to Marx and Engels through Kant, as had so many Central European Marxists, including Georg Lukacs, and there was a marked ethical and humanistic element in his Marxism that was curiously at odds with his often blind faith in the objective forces of historical development. He hoped that somehow 'history' would come to the rescue, and obviate the need for bloody revolution, civil war and dictatorship. At times it would seem that his Marxism provided him with protection against the need to compromise with the real world of suffering and violence of which he had such a deep and profound disgust. Bauer once said: 'I am the teacher of the proletariat, not a political leader', a remark that is typical of his perpetual self-criticism and self-doubt and an acknowledgement of his inability to undertake decisive political action.[19] Yet Bauer sought to compensate for this lack of decisiveness by revolutionary rhetoric about the dictatorship of the proletariat, the class struggle and imminent civil war. He certainly had no illusions about bourgeois democracy, but in spite of his frequent use of the word 'revolution' he shrank back from the consequences of his words. He attacked the subjectivism of the reformists and expounded at length on objective factors, but his critics were often correct when they charged him with using these 'objective factors' as an excuse for inaction.

Bauer's counterpart within the party was Karl Renner, the great reformist pragmatist, although he too was an intellectual of great distinction. His book, *The Social Function of Legal Institutions, Particularly of Property* (1904), is a classic of legal theory. Renner saw himself as a social democrat in the tradition of Lassalle rather than Marx. Unlike Bauer, who had certain reservations about democracy, he was emphatic in his belief in the virtues of majority rule, of compromise and respect for minorities. Society could only progress through the give and take of political democracy, through toleration and the debate between the parties. Democracy, he believed, should also be extended to the workplace, but nationalisation was no magic formula for success, merely the first bureaucratic stage towards the *Gemeinwirtschaft* (social economy) which was his ideal. Small producers could be excluded from the need for nationalisation for Renner claimed that 'general nationalisation is general nonsense'. Renner was one of the first socialists to denounce the Soviet Union as 'state capitalism', for him the natural outcome of a blind faith in nationalisation and a bureaucratic road to socialism. He warned that the simple 'expropriation of the expropriators' did not necessarily lead to the end of exploitation, and he rejected the Marxist contention that there was a fundamental contradiction between the bourgeoisie and the proletariat. He believed that these conflicts could be overcome by the rise of the new managerial and technocratic class, and by the common aims of the *Gemeinwirtschaft*. Similarly Renner rejected the revolutionary aspects of Marxism and was scornful of Bauer's lip service to them. He believed passionately, as did Lassalle, in the relative neutrality of the state and in its moral function, and in the use of the law as a means of achieving social justice. Thus for him Marxist talk about 'basis' and 'superstructure' had little meaning, and he preferred the Hegelian notions of 'state' and 'society' which the young Marx had so violently and scornfully attacked. He stood for individual freedom against the demands of the 'Soviet Jesuit state' and for an 'empirical socialism' against 'Marxist deductive tactics.' Regarding Bauer's theories about the collapse of capitalism as being little more than theology, he warned of the dangers of everlastingly talking about revolution while at the same time saying that it is impossible to make one. In spite of his instinctive understanding of the realities of political power Renner never enjoyed the same prestige within the party as Bauer. He was respected, and his influence after 1945 was considerable, but in the First Republic he had little impact on the party's policy although the achievements of the party in the field of social policy are in large part due to his influence, although one should add that he was building on foundations laid by the old bureaucracy and by Karl Lueger, hardly suitable godparents of a truly socialist policy.[20]

The rhetoric of the Linz programme was skilfully exploited by Seipel to form a 'bourgeois bloc', the unification of the right-wing parties, including some National Socialists and monarchists, behind an anti-socialist programme. In January 1927, during a clash between Social Democrats and fascist war veterans in Schattendorf in Burgenland, an eight-year-old boy and an invalid were shot. A fifteen-minute general strike was called in protest at this outrage. A few weeks later army units tried to disarm a section of the party's parliamentary organisation, the Schutzbund, but the determined resistance of the Viennese workers frustrated this attempt.

In an atmosphere of mounting political tension elections were held in April 1927. The result was a further victory for the Social Democrats who gained 42 per cent of the popular vote. Seipel was able to continue in office, but he was obliged to bring the Landbund (Agrarian League) into his coalition. The failure of Seipel's anti-socialist course led many on the right to demand an end to parliamentary democracy and the creation of a fascistic state. Meanwhile the Schattendorf murderers were tried and acquitted. A spontaneous demonstration of the Viennese workers, led by the workers in the electricity works, could not be controlled by the police. The demonstrators marched on the Palace of Justice, the hated symbol of class injustice, and set fire to the building. The police were armed and attacked the crowd. The result was 86 dead and 1,100 wounded. The violence of 15 July 1927 was in many ways a turning point in the history of the republic. It was a dramatic illustration of the impatience and the radicalisation of the working class. It showed that the leadership of the Social Democratic Party, which had played no part whatever in these recent events, was losing touch with the rank and file of the party. It also showed that the right had no scruples in using the utmost violence against its opponents. 15 July was not a revolutionary situation that a determined party leadership could have exploited to overthrow Seipel's government; if anything it was precisely the opposite. The party leadership suffered from a total paralysis of the will and had completely lost control over the rank and file. It showed up the pseudo-leftism of the Linz programme which was so completely out of step with party practice. Otto Bauer was always talking of the 'decisive battle' when the Schutzbund would take up arms in defence of democracy, but after July 1927 there were many who doubted that this was much more than a bold threat to add weight to verbal protest. Bauer's liking for revolutionary phrases was equal to his horror of civil war and his respect for legality. Viktor Adler had described himself in a letter to Engels as a 'privy councillor [*Hofrat*] of the revolution'. Much the same can be said of Bauer and his colleagues.[21] The leadership failed on 15 July 1927 and was never to make good its mistakes. Its failure was an encouragement to the right who could make skilful use of the party's revolutionary phraseology to justify its violently anti-socialist position, while at the same time realising that it had nothing really to fear. It discouraged the working class and gave fresh confidence to the ultra-right.

From 15 July the government continued its efforts to undermine the power of the working class and to undo the achievements of 1918. The real strength of the socialist movement was on the factory floor, and it was here that the most determined efforts of the right were directed. Social Democratic and even Christian unions were driven out of major factories, and frequent violations of the factory council laws were allowed to pass without determined resistence. 'Factory Fascism' was first fully established as early as July 1927 in *Alpine-Montangesellschaft*, Austria's largest industrial concern, which was controlled by German interests. All workers were forced to join the 'independent union' which was directly controlled by the works management. Special premiums and privileges were given to workers who joined the Heimwehr. Workers who resisted these moves were dismissed and lost their homes. Talk of 'works patriotism' and of 'pro-works community' were clear indications of the fascistic nature of these measures.[22]

Further opportunities were offered to the government by the economic crisis of 1929. Extremist demands for a complete revision of the constitution and for a drastic curtailment of the independent rights of Red Vienna were not satisfied, but the Social Democrats entered into negotiations with the government and accepted a weakening of the power of parliament and the strengthening of the exceptional powers of the president. For the time being it seemed that parliament still had adequate control over the president, and that the 'depoliticisation' of the constitutional court would strengthen its independence and authority, when in fact it placed it firmly in the hands of conservative and authoritarian elements. Many Social Democratic leaders, including Braunthal, imagined that the negotiations between Chancellor Schober and Danneberg for the party was a decisive defeat for fascism. It is true that the immediate demands of the extreme right had not been granted, but it is also clear that the Social Democrats had been forced to make a number of significant concessions that could hardly be fêted as a victory for democracy.[23]

The Social Democrats had further successes in the elections of 1930, the last elections that were to be held during the First Republic, and in the summer of 1931 Seipel approached the party with the suggestion of forming a coalition government. At this time even Renner, who had always spoken in favour of co-operation with the bourgeois parties, refused the offer. The party would not risk the odium of becoming involved with austerity measures to overcome the economic crisis that were bound to be exceptionally unpopular.

After 1930 the party seemed almost helpless in the face of the steady erosion of democracy. The industrial area of Upper Styria became completely controlled by Factory Fascism. In 1931 an attempted putsch by the Heimwehr led by Dr Pfrimer failed, but the leader escaped punishment. The National Socialists steadily grew in strength and audacity. The Dollfuss government, formed in May 1932, soon showed its determination to crush Social Democracy and to establish an anti-democratic and authoritarian regime. Within less than a year parliament had been dismissed and Dollfuss ruled by means of the 'wartime emergency economic law' (*Kriegswirtschaftlichen Ermächtigungsgesetzes*), the result of a series of highly dubious constitutional moves. At the same time the Schutzbund was outlawed, and party meeting places were constantly raided in the search for hidden weapons. The Communist Party was banned, May Day celebrations forbidden and the Patriotic Front formed as an anti-socialist coalition. The death penalty was reintroduced. The leading Social Democratic paper, the *Arbeiter-Zeitung* of Vienna, was no longer allowed to be freely circulated.

In the face of this right-wing offensive the Social Democratic Party became increasingly defensive. In spite of the ringing words of the Linz programme and stirring speeches warning the government of the dire consequences of any further restriction of democratic rights, the party prepared to negotiate with Dollfuss, excusing their timidity with talk of the 'lesser evil' and the need to protect the last remaining vestiges of republican democracy. In many parts of Austria the workers were growing impatient with the conciliatory attitude of the party leadership and were demanding action in defence of their freedom; but the leadership constantly warned them of the dangers of provoking the government and the need to keep the powder dry for the day when the government would go too far.

The policies of the Social Democratic Party during the Dollfuss era, which are analysed in greater detail in a later chapter, were thus very much in keeping with the traditions of the party. An unquestioned and passionate desire to preserve the democratic freedoms of the republic was crippled by a fateful paralysis of the will. The leadership recoiled from the final consequences of their own rhetoric and was never short of ingenious explanations for its inactivity. Meanwhile the rank and file grew increasingly impatient and radical so that by 1934 the leadership was dangerously isolated from the mass of the party.

When the blow was finally struck in February 1934 the party was unprepared, disorganised and lacked a coherent strategy with which to defend the republic. Moral indignation, stoical resignation and isolated incidents of extraordinary heroism were not enough against a determined and ruthless opponent.

The weaknesses of the party were often concealed by the fact that it enjoyed considerable international prestige, particularly for its achievements in socialist theory. In the years before the First World War the leading figures of Austrian socialism had openly proclaimed their Marxism, and there was a general agreement on first principles, so that it is possible to see them as a distinct group of Austro-Marxists. With the war and the Bolshevik Revolution this sense of common direction was lost, and individual members began to take distinct positions on fundamental issues, so that the term 'Austro-Marxism' ceased to have a precise meaning.[24]

In 1903, the Zukunft (Future) Society was formed in Vienna which became the organisational centre of the group to which Otto Bauer, Karl Renner, Rudolf Hilferding, Julius Deutsch and Max Adler, to mention the best-known members, belonged. Shortly afterwards the two great theoretical journals of Austro-Marxism were founded: *Marx-Studien* (1904) and *Der Kampf* (1907). The main concern of the group was to bring Marxism up to date so as to understand the problems of a world that had changed considerably since Marx's death, and particularly to tackle the intractable problems of the Austro-Hungarian Empire. They did not wish to reject Marxism, as did Bernstein and the German revisionists, but rather to tackle the immediate problems of the day, using Marxism as a guide. It is therefore hardly surprising that much of their important early work was on the question of the nationalities, of which Otto Bauer's book of 1907, an attempt to overcome some of the problems left by the Brünn programme, was the outstanding example.[25]

Belief that nationalism was an atavistic sentiment, and that the Empire could be reformed so as to ensure genuine national equality, led some of the Austro-Marxists to argue for the preservation of the integrity of the Empire during the war, a position quickly denounced by the left as 'social patriotism'. Karl Renner was particularly outspoken in his view that Social Democrats should support the war effort and fight for the preservation of the territorial integrity of the Empire, an argument which enraged Lenin, who condemned the Austro-Marxists as 'bandits' accomplices'.[26] Renner continued to insist that the war had to be fought to preserve Austria, and that the

Zimmerwald left's 'revolutionary capitulationism' was in fact capitulation before a harsh and unpleasant reality, and that their policy could well lead to the victory of Tsarism — hardly a desirable aim for socialists.

Renner, always a fiercely independent thinker who was never afraid to take an unpopular position, was in a minority in the party, his social patriotism condemned by the left-wing majority. After the war the Austrian Social Democrats refused to join the Communist International, being unable to swallow the 21 points demanded as a precondition of entry, and which would have led to the full bolshevisation of the party. On the other hand they rejected the social patriotism of the remnants of the Second International. An attempt to form yet another International in Vienna in 1921 was a failure. The only support for this move came from the German Independent Socialists (USPD), a party which was strongly influenced by Austro-Marxist ideas but which was soon to collapse, its members joining either the Social Democrats or the Communists. The '2½ International', as Radek contemptuously dubbed it, was an example of the Austro-Marxists' attempt to find a third way between bolshevism and a luke-warm reformism. Lenin had said that it was easy for the Austro-Marxists to fall between two stools, and the history of the party certainly shows that their position was exceptionally difficult to maintain in practice.

The party left feared that Austro-Marxism would degenerate into well-meaning social work, propping up a moribund bourgeois society, its efforts rewarded by a few ministerial seats. The right, whose most perceptive spokesman was still Karl Renner, argued that the classic capitalism of Marx's day had been replaced by the 'organised capitalism' that Hilferding had analysed, and that this made it possible for socialists to seize state power by democratic means in order to achieve socialism. Marx had argued in his polemics with Lassalle that the object of the socialist movement was not to attain state power but to destroy the state. Renner insisted that as the state in the higher form of advanced capitalism regulated and controlled all aspects of human existence it should be used for socialist ends.[27]

When faced with the practical choice in 1918, the Social Democrats unhesitatingly supported the new republic, their theoretical objections to collaboration with the bourgeoisie forgotten as they saw no possible alternative but the total disruption of everyday life and civil war. There were strong elements in the working class who wanted revolution and the creation of a Soviet republic, but the party was opposed to this suggestion partly because of its rejection of violence as a means of attaining political goals, and partly because it feared that a socialist coup would promptly provoke the intervention of the Entente and a violent reaction from the rural areas.[28] Such an attitude prompted Lenin and the bolsheviks to step up their denunciations of the Austro-Marxists as agents of the bourgeoisie and gravediggers of Austrian socialism. The distance between the Austrian Social Democrats and the bolsheviks thus became increasingly pronounced, but the vast mass of the working class remained faithful to the party, the Communists being little more than a sect.

The material gains for the working class in the early years of the republic were substantial, and the policy of collaboration seemed to pay off. The creation of the basis for a welfare state, the eight-hour day and the dramatic improvement of housing and working conditions, all efforts associated with the name of Ferdinand Hanusch, certainly gave an enhanced sense of dignity to the working class, but the central problem of the formation of a socialist society was no closer to solution. Otto Bauer tried to find a way out of this awkward situation by his assertion that Austria was in a state of equilibrium between the class forces, and that therefore, according to his reading of Engels, it was no longer a class state.[29] As compensation for the failure to establish a socialist state in 1918-19 Bauer stated that 'our revolution ... has implanted the nuclei of the socialist mode of production, which only need to be developed in order gradually to undermine the domination of capital and eventually to abolish it'.[30]

The nuclei of the socialist mode of production were implanted in a singularly hostile environment. Although socially and economically little had changed and it was absurd to celebrate 12 November 1918 as a day of revolution, a large sector of Austrian society bitterly resented the republic and was determined to destroy it. In part the Social Democrats were responsible for this hostility towards the republic. They made loud noises about nationalisation and then did little about it, thus frightening the bourgeoisie while leaving them the instruments of economic power. Thus the *Oesterreichische Alpine-Montangesellschaft*, the country's largest corporation, was threatened with nationalisation, was left untouched and became the incubator and patron of the Heimwehr, and the bastion of Factory Fascism.

It is hardly surprising that Bauer's claim that Austria had become a 'peoples' state' was sharply criticised. From the right Kelsen, the father of the republican constitution, correctly accused Bauer of misinterpreting Marxism by suggesting that the state could at any time be neutral in the class struggle, and he added that Bauer had misread Engels' writings on this topic in *The Origins of the State, the Family and Private Property*.[31] On the left it was pointed out that the 'equilibrium' was merely a pause in the class struggle, not a genuine and lasting balance of power. Nobody saw fit to quote from Clausewitz's *Vom Kriege*: 'A total equilibrium cannot result in a standstill, because in this situation he who has the positive purpose (the attacker) will remain ahead.'[32] By 1920 the 'equilibrium' was a thing of the past, and the coalition with the bourgeois parties dissolved. The left rejoiced that this unnatural marriage had been annulled, the right regretted that the machinery of government had been handed over to the bourgeoisie.

The Palace of Justice affair in July 1927 showed that the instruments of state power were firmly in the hands of the bourgeoisie. Renner's proposed solution was to renew the coalition with the bourgeois parties and thus avoid the civil war which seemed to be likely, but in the circumstances of the day it is difficult to see how such a policy would have worked.[33] With the acute economic problems of the republic compounded by the worldwide depression, the working class was seriously weakened and the bourgeoisie in no mood for concessions. On the other hand, the mood of the rank and file was increasingly militant, and a policy of co-operation could well have resulted in a mass exodus to the Communist Party. The party's militant rhetoric provided ample ammunition for the right, which knew perfectly well that the Social Democrats were determined to remain within the law and that the leadership could be relied upon to curb the ardour of the party militants. Any remaining doubts on this issue disappeared after the dissolution of parliament on 15 March 1933, when the party refused to move, even though Dollfuss was clearly determined to destroy the democratic constitution.[34]

There was a further dimension to Austro-Marxist thought that paralysed the will of the leadership, and that was a profound belief in historical inevitability that had been so characteristic of the Marxism of the Second International, in which the Austro-Marxists had played such an important role. A philosophical conviction of the relative futility of individual action, except in certain rare historic conjunctures, reinforced the unwillingness of the leadership to take decisive action and provided a justification for passivity and submissiveness in the face of a determined opponent. The profound humanism and passionate belief in the unfolding of human potential and freedom is a magnificent legacy of Austro-Marxism, but where this stood in the way of decisive action, when such action could not be avoided, the consequences were disastrous.

The dilemmas of Austro-Marxism in the interwar period are central to Social Democracy. How to find a path to socialism without resorting to violence and the violation of individual freedom, how to create the 'new man' in a new society, how to meet the immediate material needs of the masses without relinquishing the long-term goal of a socialist society, how to preserve democracy by democratic means against a determined opponent, and how to steer a path between confrontation and compromise are all critical problems for democratic socialists. It is the great achievement of the Austro-Marxists that they confronted these issues, and if their answers were not always correct, and never unanimous, at least they have provided ample food for thought.[35] To 'Euro-Communists', particularly in the Italian Communist Party, the experiences of the Austrian Social Democrats are of considerable interest, and there is already the beginnings of an Otto Bauer renaissance. To contemporary socialists the possibility of a genuine democracy without socialism seems increasingly remote, as the power of the giant monopolistic corporations increases. Marxists like Kautsky had abandoned the idea that democracy could only exist in a socialist state, and most Social Democrats agreed with this position. Nowadays the situation is not so clear. Democracy can only be extended and strengthened by a massive restructuring of the foundations of society so that the people can have real control over their own destinies. But socialism without democracy is equally undesirable, leading to a non-capitalist but non-socialist bureaucratically controlled form of state power that has yet to be satisfactorily explained and analysed. In the search for a synthesis of democracy and socialism Austro-Marxism provides some indication of possible routes to follow. Otto Bauer's theory of 'integral socialism', developed in *Between Two World Wars?*, in which he suggested a combination of the virtues of Communism and Social Democracy, and a positive yet critical attitude towards the Soviet Union, has lost nothing of its actuality as the left looks for ways out of its present impasse. Bauer's hopes that the Soviet Union would become more democratic as it grew in economic strength have been dashed, in spite of the high hopes aroused at the time of the Twentieth Congress in 1956, and Communists have still to free themselves from the dangerous illusion that present Soviet reality can be equated with socialism. Yet to criticise Soviet society should not lead to anti-Communism, or to a complacent acceptance of the status quo in the capitalist world. Austro-Marxism is still relevant in pointing the way forward, its failures in practice being often as instructive as its considerable theoretical achievements.

On the whole, the Austro-Marxist balancing act between left and right was enormously successful; the revisionists were kept under control, the left restrained from indulging in excessive revolutionary zeal. The party was determined to combat bolshevism in Austria, being critical from the outset of the authoritarian and bureaucratic aspects of Soviet Communism, without lapsing into a crude anti-Marxist position, and it realised that this could only be done by making concessions to the left, even if those concessions more often than not were theoretical rather than actual. The rhetoric of the party thus helped to keep members from joining the Communists, for the party appeared to many to be further to the left than it was in fact. So effective was this policy that it was not until after the debacle of 12 February 1934 that Communists were able to make serious inroads into the Social Democratic Party. It is thus understandable that the Communists kept up a constant attack on the pseudo-radicalism of the Social Democrats who, they argued, pulled the wool over the workers' eyes and served to prop up the bourgeois régime which they claimed to wish to destroy.

The main reason for the formation of a Communist Party in Austria was the disillusionment of the radical left with the policies of the Social Democratic Party during the war.[36] There were those who could not accept the party's justification of the war as a defensive war against Tsarist tyranny and who took the anti-war resolutions of the Second International seriously. As the war continued this fiction became all the more difficult to accept, and the militarisation of the workplace, the prohibition of strikes, the lengthening of the working day to 13 hours, the abolition of jury courts, the restriction of fundamental freedoms such as freedom of the press, and the use of military courts for civilian offences, all served to increase the disenchantment with a party that seemed to be too closely associated with those responsible for the militarisation of public life. At first this discontent was expressed in a mass exodus from the party and from the trade unions, and it was not until much later that an organised alternative to the still immensely influential Social Democratic Party was attempted.

The party left was often perceptive in its criticisms of party policy, but they had no mass support and shied away from revolutionary activity. They could easily be dismissed by the leadership as 'intellectual troublemakers'. A small group of radicals, organised in the study group 'Karl Marx', had established contact with Lenin at the Kienthal conference in 1916, but this was a very small number of militants with very little influence. By 1917 the government was obliged to relax some of its more stringent measures in order to avoid serious disruption on the home front. At the same time the Social Democrats stepped up their pacifist propaganda. By these means the wind was taken out of the sails of the radical left. At the party conference in 1917 Otto Bauer repeated the resolutions of the International against war, issued a *mea culpa* on behalf of the party leadership, and stated that the party would do nothing to support the war and would fulfil its historic role by means of the class struggle. The party leadership, which by 1917 was discredited in the eyes of many members, was thus able to restore its position by the traditional means of radical phrases combined with reformist practice. Verbally the Austrian party was the most radical of all Social Democratic parties, in practice it differed very little from the rest. That the rank and file was growing increasingly impatient with the leadership can be clearly seen in the response of the strikers in January 1918 to the demand by the party to return to work. In Wiener Neustadt, an industrial centre that had always been at the forefront of political activity, Karl Renner was arrested by militants when he tried to persuade the workers to go back to work. Some workers began to feel, in the words of one pamphlet, that the Social Democrats were trying to 'force the yoke of capitalist exploitation' upon the working class, and demanded a new political organisation that would not compromise with the existing system.[37]

The Communist Party of Austria (KPÖ) was founded on 3 November 1918. It was a minute group that failed to include all the radical factions of Social Democracy. The party was formed too early and with too little preparation to be really effective. It was a gesture of frustration against the policies of the Social Democrats, not the result of a serious debate on the means and aims of a revolutionary Marxist party. Its leaders were men who lacked experience and had little or no influence among the working class. The proclamation of the Soviet republic in Hungary resulted in a sudden increase in party membership, from a mere 3,000 in February 1919 to 40,000 in June, but once again the Social Democrats were able to hang on to their radical supporters by declarations of solidarity with Hungary, and the failure of the experiment could be used to discredit those who supported the idea of Soviet power for Austria. Lacking either mass support or skilful leadership, the attempt to seize power on 15 June 1919 by a group of Communists led by the Hungarian emissary Ernst Bettelheim was a miserable failure which did much to discredit the party at a time when significant political gains could have been made. The whole episode was so poorly managed that it would be a mistake to see it as an attempt at a putsch, although the Viennese police published a forged document which was designed to show that a sinister plan to seize public buildings and arrest the government existed. The defeat of the Hungarian Soviet government on 1 August marked the end of the radical period of post-war politics in Austria and further weakened potential support for the party.

The party was further hampered by violent internal dissent between those who supported the sectarian theory of the 'revolutionary minority', which neglected the need for careful and thorough organisation of the masses, and those who felt that the time had come for systematic organisational work among the working class. The left continued to maintain the foolish position of boycotting all elections, but the right was able to insist on a programme that stressed trade union work and a concentration on strengthening the position of the party in the works' councils. At the Third Party Congress in 1919 the notion that one could dispense with revolutionary mass action was condemned and the slogan was adopted 'Onward to the Masses'. Pushed by Lenin's condemnation of left-wing sectarianism the party decided to put forward candidates for the parliamentary elections in October 1920.[38] The result was a fiasco. The party gained only 23,000 votes and not one deputy was elected. Even the successes of the party had very little immediate effect. Thus the party condemned the idea of an Anschluss with Germany, a demand that was shared by all parties except the extreme nationalist right, but although this policy was realistic, given the determined opposition of the Entente to the Anschluss, and meant that the party did not have to go through an embarrassing revision of its policy in 1933 as did the Social Democrats, the anti-Anschluss stand of the party did nothing to win it further support.

The greatest successes of the party in these early years were in the trade union movement and in the army. By 1923 the Communists within the trade unions formed a 'Red Trade Union Opposition' and in the following year published their own works newspapers which were effective propaganda instruments. In 1921 the Communists gained 21 per cent of the votes for the soldiers' councils, and their newspaper, the *Red Soldier*, had a circulation of 4,000.[39] However, largely due to the efforts of War Minister Vaugoin, Communists and Social Democrats were gradually weeded out of the army, although the task proved rather more difficult than had at first been imagined.

Outspoken opposition to the Geneva Treaty, which had resulted in a marked increase in unemployment, and a sixteen-fold increase in food prices, according to government statistics, gained the party some support and advances were made in the factory council elections in July and August of 1923. But in the parliamentary elections in September the party lost votes, gaining a mere 22,000 votes in the whole of Austria. An unrealistic programme denouncing any coalition government and calling for a government of workers and peasants was hardly likely to win much support from workers who were encouraged by the improvement of the position of the Social Democrats after the fiasco of the Geneva Treaty.

With the failure of the party at the elections and with the relative stabilisation of the world economy, the Communist Party went through a period of severe crisis in the course of which it came dangerously close to breaking apart. A right-wing faction under Josef Frey called for a close co-operation with the Social Democrats, a suggestion that was denounced as capitulation by the extreme left under Karl Tomann and Franz Koritschoner who called for an active revolutionary policy. For almost two years the party was paralysed by bitter dissent and personal feuds. The party conference in 1924 degenerated into a series of fist fights, and the Communist International had to intervene to impose a provisional leadership on the party from members who belonged to neither of the warring factions. At the end of the year an extraordinary conference elected Johann Koplenig as party leader and it seemed that the immediate crisis had been overcome. Although factional squabbles continued (Tomann was eventually to become a Nazi, Frey a Trotskyite), 'Kop' did much to restore a degree of unity to the party and to recover some of the ground that had been lost in the course of two years of self-destructive bickering. Thus the party conference for 1926 had to be postponed for fear that it would dissolve into factional fights, the opposition within the party having brought out its own newspaper.

After the Schattendorf affair, but before the elections of April 1927, the Central Committee of the party suggested a common front against fascism with the Social Democrats, and promised that Communists would support Social Democratic candidates in the forthcoming elections. The offer was refused by the Social Democrats on the grounds that the party was, in Otto Bauer's words, '90 per cent bolshevik', that there was little immediate danger of fascism, and, confident of success at the elections, the party was determined to continue its efforts to win a parliamentary majority.

The Communists decided to test the 'bolshevism' of the Social Democrats by demanding the arming of the workers in July 1927 to nip fascism in the bud. The Social Democrats argued that such a course of action would precipitate a bloody civil war, strengthen the position of the fascists in the rural areas and cause chronic economic disruption. It was not until after 12 February 1934 that some Social Democrats began to argue that the Communists had been correct in 1927, and that a golden opportunity to beat back the forces of reaction had been missed.[40]

If the Social Democratic Party was unable to contain the steady move towards the extreme right because of its refusal to take resolute action, the Communists were equally ineffectual because of their frequent lapses into ultra-left positions that were completely out of touch with the reality of the situation in Austria. Their warnings about the dangers of fascism were often perceptive, and the radicalisation of the political situation with the onset of the depression enabled the party to win more members. But the party was still minute and there were no gains in electoral support. In November 1930 it could only win just over 20,000 votes in an election where the Nazis got more than 110,000.

By 1932 the Communist Party was stuck between its determination to expose the Social Democrats as the 'main social support for the dictatorship of the bourgeoisie', and the desire of many members to co-operate with them in a united struggle against fascism. As part of the tactic of the 'united front from below', anti-fascist committees were formed in which the Communists kept a low profile. At the same time the attacks on the 'Social Fascists' in the party press were moderated. This right-wing policy prompted stern rebukes from the Communist International which felt that the Austrian party was being remiss in exposing the Social Democrats. Although the Communists had modified their tone, the object was still to undermine the Social Democratic Party by means of the united front from below, and to expose the leadership. After the outlawing of the party, attacks on the Social Fascists were begun once again, particularly from the Communist International which tried to argue that the party ban was in part the result of the machinations of the Social Democrats, and further evidence of their complicity with Dollfuss.

The Communist Party was also uncertain how to deal with the left-wing opposition within the Social Democratic Party. It was easy enough to dismiss them as a group of Trotskyites, but it was also felt that they might be won over to the Communist Party, for they were a clear sympton of disillusionment with the right-wing course of the party leadership. Although by late 1933 there were an increasing number of joint efforts by Communists and Social Democrats, the left-wing opposition remained loyal to the party, and it was not until the destruction of the Social Democratic Party in February of the following year that the policy of the united front from below began to have a real effect when many Social Democrats joined the Communist Party.

The party thus made frequent but often ambiguous attempts to push the Social Democrats into determined action to halt the steady erosion of democratic freedoms, but all offers of support were rejected by a party which felt that it had little need of advice from such a small and seemingly ineffectual group. The Communist Party was thus left in a dangerously isolated position. Dollfuss banned the party in May 1933 partly as a demonstration to his right-wing hangers-on that he was determined to crush Marxism, and partly because he feared that Communist activity might in the long run spur the Social Democrats into action. The annual conference of the Vienna section of the Social Democratic Party protested against the outlawing of the Communist Party, and the *Arbeiter-Zeitung* declared itself to be in solidarity with the party members, but the Social Democrats refused the Communist suggestion of mass demonstrations and strikes in protest against this misuse of the emergency wartime laws. Few Social Democrats realised that their party would be next on the list, and that Dollfuss was waiting for his opportunity to strike.[41]

Notes

1. *Verhandlungen des Parteitags der Oesterreichischen Sozialdemokratie in Hainfeld* (Vienna 1889). There has been considerable debate among socialists as to how 'Marxist' the programme was. Opinions range from an insistence that the programme was solidly based on the *Communist Manifesto*, to the assertion that it was the work of reformists and opportunists. There can be little doubt that the programme was a victory for the moderates. For further details see Norbert Leser, *Zwischen Reformismus und Bolschewismus. Der Austromarxismus als Theorie und Praxis* (Vienna 1968), p. 203.

2. Hans Hautmann and Rudolf Kropf, *Die österreichische Arbeiterbewegung vom Vormärz bis 1945* (Vienna 1974), p. 57.

3. Leser, *Zwischen Reformismus*, p. 173. Louis B. Boudin, *The Theoretical System of Karl Marx in the Light of Recent Criticism* (Chicago 1907). Boudin also wrote a number of articles for the German Social Democratic journal *Die neue Zeit*. Kautsky lived in Germany before Hainfeld, and Hilferding moved to Berlin in 1906, but their effect on the Austrian party was considerable so that it is hardly stretching a point to include them among the Austro-Marxists.

4. 'The Proletarian Revolution and the Renegade Kautsky' in V.I. Lenin, *Selected Works* (Moscow 1971), vol. 3, p. 76: 'The proletarian revolution is impossible without the forcible destruction of the bourgeois state.'

5. Norbert Leser, 'Der Austromarxismus als Strömung des marxistischen Zentrums', *VIII Linzer Konferenz der Historiker der Arbeiterbewegung* (Linz 1972).

6. Hautman and Kropf, *Arbeiterbewegung*, p. 118.

7. Ludwig Brügel, *Geschichte der österreichischen Sozialdemokratie* (Vienna 1925), vol. 5, p. 257.

8. Adam Wandruszka in Heinrich Benedikt, *Geschichte der Republik Oesterreich* (Munich 1954), p. 440.

9. Hans Hautmann, 'Die Kriegslinke in der Sozialdemokratischen Partei Oesterreichs zwischen 1914 und 1918', *Die Zukunft*, 13-14 (Vienna, July 1971).

10. F.L. Carsten, *Revolution in Central Europe 1918-1919* (Berkeley 1972), pp. 78-126, 238-46.

11. Hans Hautmann, *Die verlorene Räterepublik* (Vienna 1971), p. 78.

12. C.A. Gulick, *Austria from Habsburg to Hitler* (2 vols., Berkeley 1948), vol. 1, pp. 235-55.

13. Hautmann and Kropf, *Arbeiterbewegung*, p. 137.

14. Karl Ausch, 'Genfer Sanierung und der 12 Februar 1934' in *Vom Justizpalast zum Heldenplatz* (Vienna 1975), pp. 32-5.

15. Leser, *Reformismus*, p. 367.

16. Otto Bauer, *Die österreichische Revolution* (Vienna 1923), p. 285.

17. Wandruszka in Benedikt, *Geschichte der Republik*, p. 461.

18. Felix Czeike, 'Wirtschafts- und Sozialpolitik der Gemeinde Wien in der Ersten Republik (1919-1934)', *Wiener Schriften*, vols. 6 and 11 (Vienna 1958/9) for a discussion of the achievements of 'Red Vienna'.

19. Rudolf Litschel, *1934 — Das Jahr der Irrungen* (Linz n. d.)

20. The best modern discussion of Bauer and Renner's political thought is in Leser, *Reformismus*.

21. Adler to Engels 1892; ibid., p. 401. On 15 July 1927 see *Die Ereignisse des 15 Juli 1927* (Vienna 1979).

22. Hautmann and Kropf, *Arbeiterbewegung*, pp. 158-9.

23. Leser, *Reformismus*, pp. 440-8.

24. Ibid. Leser's book is the outstanding study of Austro-Marxism. For English readers Tom Bottomore and Patrick Goode (eds.), *Austro-Marxism* (Oxford 1978), is a useful introduction.

25. Otto Bauer, *Nationalitätenfrage und die Sozialdemokratie* (Vienna 1907).

26. Leser, *Reformismus*, p. 179.

27. Karl Renner in *Protokoll der Verhandlungen des Parteitages 1917*, p. 122.

28. Bauer, *Revolution*, p. 91.

29. Ibid., p. 246.

30. Ibid., p. 161.

31. Hans Kelsen, *Marx oder Lassalle — Wandlungen in der politischen Theorie des Marxismus* (Leipzig 1924), p. 285.

32. Clausewitz, *Vom Kriege*, Book 1, Ch. 1.

33. Leser is undoubtedly correct in denouncing the 'tub thumping party hacks who used exalted revolutionary rhetorical phraseology to compensate for their loss of real power' (Norbert Leser, 'Austro-Marxism: A Reappraisal', *Journal of Contemporary History*, vol. 11 (July 1976), p. 145) but his argument that Karl Renner's policy was a viable alternative is open to serious doubt. Brilliant in the discussion of party ideology, Leser tends to divorce this from the concrete economic and social situation in which it was developed. He also tends to overlook the effects of political struggles within the party. See section 4 of Ilias Katsoulis, *Sozialismus und Staat*, (Meisenheim/Glan 1975), for further discussion of this point.

34. Everhard Holtmann, *Zwischen Unterdrückung und Befriedung. Sozialistische Arbeiterbewegung und autoritäres Regime in Oesterreich 1933-1938* (Munich 1978), p. 67. Holtmann tends to underestimate the radicalism of the rank and file and the hostility of the bourgeois parties which were major factors in determining the position of the party.

35. An Otto Bauer symposium was held in Vienna in November 1978 under the auspices of the Austrian Young Socialists, at which the Italian Communists Lombardo Radice and Giacomo Marramao were key speakers.

36. See Herbert Steiner, 'Die Kommunistische Partei Oesterreichs von 1918 bis 1933. Bibliographische Bemerkungen', *Marburger Abhandlungen zur Politischen Wissenschaft*, vol. 11 (Meisenheim/Glan 1968); Friedl Fürnberg (ed.), *Geschichte der Kommunistischen Partei Oesterreichs* (Vienna 1977); Hans Hautmann, *Die Anfänge der linksradikalen Bewegung und der Kommunistischen Partei Deutschösterreichs 1916-1919* (Vienna 1970); Hautmann, *Räterepublik*.

37. Fürnberg, *Kommunistischen Partei*, p. 25.

38. 'Left-Wing Communism — An Infantile Disorder' in V.I. Lenin, *Selected Works*, vol. 3.

39. Fürnberg, *Kommunistischen Partei*, p. 57.

40. This is the argument of 'Georg Wieser' (Otto Leichter), *Ein Staat Stirbt. Oesterreich 1934-1938* (Paris 1938).

41. Fürnberg, *Kommunistischen Partei*, p. 126.

2 THE CHRISTIAN SOCIAL PARTY

Although the ideological origins of the Christian Social Party lie far back in Austrian history, it was Karl Lueger who first created a mass movement, the Christian Social Peoples' Movement (*christlichsozialen Volksbewegung*), that was to form the organisational basis of the most important political party of the First Republic.[1] Lueger realised that classical liberalism had run its course, and that free-trade capitalism which had promised wealth and prosperity to the majority had failed to satisfy the aspirations of the little man. Lueger's answer was a rejection of democracy, the preservation of the small producer against big capitalism, anti-semitism and a moderate amount of social reform. He was elected to the Reichsrat in 1885 and shortly afterwards became associated with the Catholic Social reformer Prince Alois Liechtenstein. Through Liechtenstein he met a number of other Christian Social reformers, among the most important of whom was Vogelsang. The group would meet in the restaurant *Zur goldenen Ente* and it was during these famous 'duck evenings' that the ideological and organisational nucleus of the new movement was formed.

The movement began to gather momentum at about the same time as the formation of the Social Democratic Party at Hainfeld in 1888, but for the time being the main enemy were the free-thinking, highly educated and often Jewish capitalists with their somewhat smug belief in 'Manchester-liberalism', materialism and positivism. With the rise of Social Democracy the movement had to fight a two-pronged battle against capitalism and socialist anti-capitalism. Prominent Jews in the liberal as well as the socialist camps made anti-semitism a powerful political weapon in this struggle, and although the Christian Socials never sank to the depths of the virulent racial anti-semitism of later fascists, and although some Christian Socials were quite immune to anti-semitic feelings, anti-semitism was an inherent part of Christian Social ideology and a clear prefiguration of fascist racism.

The aristocracy, the upper bourgeoisie, the civil servants and army officers had little sympathy for a movement which they felt to be vulgar and lower class. That a great prince like Liechtenstein could be associated with it was explained away by the fact that he had married a bourgeois girl and was simply slumming.[2] Catholic bishops who tended to come from the same exalted social background also had no desire to become involved. The resistance of the ruling class to Lueger and the movement can best be seen in the fact that the Emperor Franz Josef refused to accept his election as mayor of Vienna, even though he had been elected three times with steadily increasing majorities in 1897. Eventually the Kaiser had to give way to the determination of the Viennese to appoint Lueger, and even Pope Leo XIII, who had attacked Lueger for his attempts to undermine the authority of the Austrian bishops, eventually gave him his blessing and approval of the movement's social programme. The encyclical *Rerum Novarum* of 1891 was, after all, very close in spirit to the kind of thing that Lueger was proposing.

The first great success of the party had been in Vienna, but gradually it began to win support away from the conservatives in the rural areas of the country. At the same time the movement was becoming more respectable and less revolutionary in tone. In 1907 the Christian Socials and the conservatives amalgamated to form the Christian Social Reich's Party. But Lueger was keenly aware that the danger of this amalgamation was that the party might become too conservative, too much dominated by agrarian interests and thus lose the all-important support of the urban petty bourgeoisie and disaffected intelligentsia. When Lueger died in 1911 the party lost a leader who was one of the most striking figures of his times. The city hall in Vienna was to fall into the hands of the Social Democrats to form the power centre of Red Vienna. Lueger's fears seemed confirmed. His party had become respectable, had lost its quasi-revolutionary vigour and was now on the side of the state and the preservation of the existing system.

The party had close contacts with the Archduke Franz Ferdinand, who shared many of the party's views including its anti-semitism, and also with Kaiser Karl. But in 1918 the dynasty was discredited, the mood of the country republican, and it would have been political suicide for the party to continue its close association with the royal house. Its radical and populist traditions from the days before its amalgamation with the conservatives were quickly remembered, although many party leaders fought fiercely for the monarchy, among them the future president of the republic, Miklas, and the party was plunged into a profound crisis that continued well after the proclamation of the republic in November 1918. It was Seipel who managed to find a way out of this impasse. He suggested that the republic was a compromise, and should be respected as such with all its weaknesses. Of course the extreme monarchists thought that this was naked republicanism, and the left accused Seipel of sneakily plotting a restoration. But on the whole the formula, which was typical of Seipel's refusal to take a clear stand on most issues, helped to hold the party together and satisfied the majority.

Seipel was the outstanding figure in the Christian Social Party in the republic and was almost immediately recognised as leader.[3] He was a priest and an intellectual, author of a number of works on social and constitutional theory, and had never intended to take up a political career. He was a man of considerable intellectual ability, extreme political cunning and occasional wit. The true Seipel is hard to define, and this accounts partly for his continued fascination to later generations, but the search for the real man is bound to be misleading. Seipel was a politician who always left his options open, who refused to be tied by any over-hasty commitment to a particular political line. There is, however, in his political life a consistency and a direction that made him much more than a political opportunist. The main source of his political thinking was reactionary authoritarian Catholicism, of the sort that influenced Franco and Salazar, and, *mutatis mutandis*, Vargas in his first period as president of Brazil. This Seipel adapted to the situation in Austria. The approach has sometimes been termed 'clerical fascism' but, as will be discussed later, this term is of questionable heuristic value.

Seipel was certainly not a modest man, but he preferred to remain somewhat in the background, playing the role of grey eminence. The trouble was that his front men, Streeruwitz, Schober and Vaugoin, were not of sufficient format. Partly for the same reason, and partly through political necessity, he was content to rule through a coalition, the Bürgerblock of the 'anti-Marxist' parties, and he was prepared to make considerable concessions to maintain this coalition. Between 1922 and 1930 the Christian Social Party and the Greater Germans were in a coalition in which Seipel gave little away to his partners, while at the same time appearing to do so. Concessions to the Greater Germans on the question of Anschluss were of little significance given the attitude of the Entente, particularly after the Geneva Treaty, while the Greater Germans' concessions of non-interference in issues of the church and state were of considerable importance to the clerical party.

Anti-socialism was the essential ingredient of Seipel's politics and the driving force behind the Christian Social Party. Born into the working class (his father drove a cab), Seipel had the snobbish dislike of that class of a man who had made his own way into better circles. Socialism represented everything that he disliked; it was the ideology of a class he despised, it was atheistic and anti-clerical, materialist and, in its radical democratic demands, the enemy of the bourgeois republic that Seipel felt himself called upon to defend. Social Democracy was the enemy, and an enemy that was to be fought to the death, not the respected opponent of the great bourgeois democracies. The concept of a loyal opposition would have seemed madness to Seipel. Socialism had to be crushed, if not by constitutional means then by violence.

The total rejection of Social Democracy, which was at times the largest party in the republic, could all too easily lead to a rejection of party politics and of the bourgeois democratic republic itself. Words with socialist overtones like 'class' were replaced in party writing by vague concepts of 'estate', and ideological rubbish from Italian Fascism began to seep into the political language of the Christian Socials. By the late twenties, with a marked radicalisation of the political situation and a growing influence of the Heimwehr on the party, this tendency became more pronounced. A need was felt to provide an alternative and coherent ideology to Marxism. Othmar Spann's turgid writings seemed to fit the bill with their vague promises of an 'organic state' that would be neither fascist nor Marxist nor even capitalist. These ideas were spiced with a strong dose of reactionary Christian Romanticism, a hankering after the complete pre-industrial world where it was thought, in spite of massive evidence to the contrary, each knew his place. It needs considerable imaginative power to understand how men of intelligence and practical experience can possibly have taken this nonsense seriously, but it was all part of the intellectual baggage of the far right and seemed to have great appeal, particularly to the academic youth. Few now have the stomach to wade through Spann's dreadful prose, yet at the time his books were bestsellers, his lectures packed. These ideas appeared to have been given the approval of the Pope with the publication of the encyclical *Quadragesimo Anno* in 1931.[4]

The first significant moves towards the creation of an authoritarian state were made by Vaugoin's minority government in 1930.[5] Vaugoin hoped that by building on the authoritarian traditions of his party he would be able to win support in the elections of November. The plan included effectively stopping parliamentary control over the army, strict measures against opposition newspapers, an intensive hunt for the weapons of the Social Democratic Schutzbund, and the ending of Social Democratic control over the railways. Vaugoin hoped that this policy would lead to a crushing defeat of the Social Democrats and turn the voters away from the Nazis. In 1930 the Nazis in Germany had made their first great electoral breakthrough, and Vaugoin was anxious that the same should not happen in Austria. But Vaugoin's scheme was fundamentally unrealistic. His candidate as director of the railways, the director of the Graz tramways Dr Strafella, had been found guilty of corruption, and the suggestion that he should be appointed triggered off an affair that had brought down the previous government of Schober. But Vaugoin stubbornly hung on to his candidature. His alliance with the Heimwehr was also highly dubious. The Heimwehr leaders Starhemberg and Pfrimer were on a radical course, and it seemed to many Christian Socials to be a betrayal of the conservative traditions of the party to ally with such elements. It was also a dubious tactic to combat the fascism of the Nazis with the fascism of the Heimwehr. Vaugoin's policy was a failure and split up the party. There were those who continued to support his authoritarian line, but a strong section of the party led by Ender from the Vorarlberg opposed the alliance with the Heimwehr. President Miklas, using the constitutional powers granted to his office in 1929, replaced the Vaugoin government with a new government under Ender, a course of action that was not supported by Seipel who refused to join the new cabinet which he felt to be too moderate.

Seipel was bitterly disappointed that he had not been able to push the party as far to the right as he would have liked. After the publication of the *Quadragesimo Anno* he began to talk in rather vague terms about the formation of a new society based on the estates and professions and in which the political parties would cease to exist in their present form.[6] Discussions about a proposed 'Christian state of the estates' (*christlichen Standestaates*) continued. But the realisation of this scheme was made all the more difficult by the loss of popular support in the election of 1932 and by the need to form a new coalition government. Dollfuss was unable to form a coalition with the Greater Germans who feared that if they became too closely associated with him the Lausanne loan question would lose still more support, and at this time the party was already on the rocks. Discussions with

Heimwehr leaders about the possibility of ruling by emergency decree, like the Brüning and Papen governments in Germany, were more promising, but did not reach any positive conclusions.[7] The main result of these talks in Portschach was that the Heimwehr leader Fey was appointed state secretary for security, which placed the police and gendarmes under his control thus giving him enormous political power and keeping up the momentum towards the formation of an authoritarian state.

In October of 1932 the 'wartime emergency economic law' was used against those functionaries deemed responsible for the collapse of Austria's most important bank, the *Creditanstalt*.[8] As this move came some 16 months after the event the object was quite clear, and Dollfuss was ready to admit that it was simply a step towards the creation of a form of authoritarian government. The emergency law was convenient in that it could be invoked without discussion in the Nationalrat and was not even supervised by a parliamentary committee. The disadvantage, as far as Dollfuss was concerned, was that the law was restricted in its application and could not be used as widely as paragraph 48 of the Weimar constitution which gave the German President quasi-dictatorial powers. Dollfuss believed that he had found a way of governing without making the slightest concessions to the Social Democrats, and felt sure that he could count on the Heimwehr to support his anti-socialist and anti-democratic course.

On 4 March 1933 parliamentary business could no longer be conducted, three successive presidents of the Nationalrat having resigned. The leadership of the Christian Social Party agreed that the time had come for an authoritarian government, for a change in the constitution and an end to parliamentary compromise. Those who doubted the propriety or political wisdom of such a move were on the whole convinced by the argument that there was a strong anti-parliamentary feeling in the country as a whole, and that decisive action of this kind would stem the tide of National Socialism. A ban on political demonstrations and censorship of the opposition press was followed by general agreement by the party that the Nationalrat should not resume its business until the opposition parties agreed to constitutional changes. The fact that a few Social Democrats and Greater Germans slipped into the Nationalrat before the police cordon had been formed around it and insisted that the parliamentary session had not been formally ended was an empty gesture. Had it been backed up with a general strike, as the government feared might be possible, the story might well have been different.[9]

Dollfuss was aware of the possibility of a general strike and was determined to use force in such an eventuality. This at once gave rise to rivalry in the government. Fey wished to use the Heimwehr as the military arm of a new authoritarian regime, much as the Fasci had been used in Italy. Vaugoin wanted to use the army which was known to be sympathetic to the Christian Social Party and its new course.[10] A solution to this problem was found with the creation of a Voluntary Defence Corps (*freiwillige Schutzkorps*) under Fey which seemed to Dollfuss to be a rather more reliable organisation than the Heimwehr, which had sourly pointed out that it was not 'married to the government'.

By this time it was clear that Dollfuss had gone far beyond the limits of legality in establishing the foundations of his new regime. The city government of Vienna brought in a number of actions in the constitutional court questioning the legality of some of the government's decrees. It seemed obvious that the constitutional court would rule against the government and therefore Dollfuss mounted a massive attack on the court, virtually forcing judges to resign until there were not enough judges left to try the cases. By 27 May 1933 this aim had been achieved.

The destruction of the Austrian constitution by these means was warmly applauded by most party members who now wanted to achieve their supreme goal, the destruction of Social Democracy. Neustädter-Stürmer, a Heimwehr member of the coalition, put the matter succinctly. 'Marxism' should be destroyed and at the same time National Socialism could be defeated by 'out-Hitlering Hitler' (*überhitlern*).[11] The first step would clearly be the destruction of the Schutzbund, and it was suggested that with the Schutzbund out of the way the Social Democrats would be willing to negotiate some sort of a compromise with the government. Dollfuss did not believe that the dissolution of the Schutzbund would lead to violence, but Vaugoin assured him that if it did the government was well prepared and it would simply mean that the whole affair would be over quicker. Dollfuss was convinced that if he were to do what Hitler had done in Germany he would win massive support, particularly in the countryside, and that when the Social Democratic Party was destroyed many disillusioned socialists would join the government side.

Dollfuss had claimed that the attack on the Schutzbund would put a greater political distance between the Christian Socials and the National Socialists. In fact precisely the opposite happened. The attempt to out-Hitler Hitler was as disastrous in Austria as it was in

Germany under Papen. The Heimwehr partners in Dollfuss's government had already begun to negotiate with the National Socialists behind his back. Shortly afterwards Dollfuss did exactly the same, hardly the action of a man determined to crush the National Socialist movement. The fact that the Vatican was beginning negotiations for a concordat with Nazi Germany showed a degree of toleration for National Socialism by the Catholic church that concerned even Dollfuss, and the attitude of Cardinal Innitzer of Vienna towards the Nazis was problematical. Indeed Dollfuss's entire behaviour makes it obvious that his concern at this time was more with the Social Democrats than the Nazis, and that his talk of attacking the Social Democrats in order to win support away from the Nazis was little more than a debating point. When Hitler's envoy Habicht told Dollfuss in May that he was delighted with the Chancellor's work because Social Democrats were now joining the Nazis, Dollfuss replied: 'I am so anti-Marxist, that I can perfectly well accept that!'[12] Dollfuss was fully prepared to consider a coalition government with the National Socialists, but the determined opposition of the party caucus put an end to this suggestion. Dollfuss's subsequent anti-Nazi course was determined by foreign political considerations and the growing hostility between Germany and Austria, and not by a fundamental rejection of compromise with them.

In June 1933 the Nazi Party was banned after long and difficult debates as to how this was to be done. The kind of salami tactics that had been used against the Social Democrats were obviously not appropriate — there would have to be an outright ban on the party. The more determined anti-Marxists argued that it was absurd to allow the Social Democratic Party to continue its work, even without the Schutzbund and without its May Day celebrations while at the same time banning a party that was nothing if not anti-socialist. Anschluss supporters also had sympathies for the Nazis even if they did not always approve of their methods. It was precisely these methods that provided the excuse for closing down the party. The murder of army volunteers by Nazis in June and the subsequent determined anti-Nazi actions by Vaugoin finally pushed the government into action.

Radical anti-Marxists now demanded swift action against the Social Democrats, but Dollfuss urged caution saying that a long process of negotiations and re-education was preferable to armed confrontation. Dollfuss insisted that he and the Christian Social Party represented the true Austria, and that this message should be drummed into the heads of the doubtful and undecided. In more exalted moments he saw himself as the representative of true German culture and insisted that Nazi efforts abroad to claim a monopoly in this field should be countered.[13]

Such talk merely underlined how isolated Dollfuss and the Christian Social Party had become. The grand strategy of winning mass support by attacking the Social Democrats had failed miserably. The very suggestion by the Nazis that there should be new elections threw the party into panic. Schuschnigg had long doubted whether there was much point in even continuing the life of the party, suggesting an alternative Patriotic Front of Catholic and ultra-conservative factions. A *Vaterländische* Front was indeed formed on 20 May 1933, but this action also backfired. The Christian Social Party continued to exist, but there was uncertainty among people at large whether or not the Patriotic Front and the party were the same thing, so that what was designed as a dramatic political action that would mobilise all Catholic and conservative forces turned out to be a damp squib. To most people it seemed that the name had been changed, and that was all.[14]

The party leadership, particularly the chairman Vaugoin, began to fear that Dollfuss would soon dispense with the party. On 11 September their fears seemed to be confirmed. In a major speech given at the trotting-racetrack in Vienna the Chancellor condemned the parliamentary and party system and announced his intention to create a new state based on the estates. Shortly afterwards he reorganised the government and Vaugoin lost his cabinet post. On 3 October Dollfuss called a meeting of the party caucus to justify this drastic course of action that had in fact been dictated in large part by the attitude of the Heimwehr.[15] He made a stirring appeal for support, painting a dramatic picture of his foreign political successes with Britain and France, and warning of the danger from the Social Democrats and Nazis. He told the party that Vaugoin had taken his dismissal 'from head to toe like a gentleman'.[16] When asked how he envisaged a new constitution, Dollfuss could spread little light. Vague talk about the constitution being in accordance with Austria's intellectual history, without discounting the experiences of Italy, was not very illuminating. Yet his performance was remarkable. Hardly a voice was raised in defence of Vaugoin, there were no complaints that the party had been totally ignored, and there were fervent expressions of confidence in his leadership. As one speaker, Aigner, phrased it, Dollfuss was putting into practice the political wishes of the Holy Father and as such would enjoy the support of all Catholics. Another speaker referred to the tremendous enthusiasm of the clergy for the new course. Underlying these remarks was the vain belief that the church would keep the Heimwehr in line and counteract the propaganda of the National Socialists. As was later to happen in Franco's Spain, the church was to provide the ideology for an authoritarian régime that had nothing whatever to offer but authority, and in the case of Austria even that was questionable.

Relations with the Social Democratic Party were also discussed at the meeting of the party caucus on 3 October. Dollfuss was very concerned that news of a Social Democratic offer of co-operation with the government should not leak out, because it would offer the Nazis a golden opportunity to attack the sincerity of the government's anti-Marxism. He promised that the independence of Vienna would end and that if there was any resistance martial law would be proclaimed within five minutes. Vaugoin and his small group of supporters were almost alone in thinking that the best way to attack National Socialism was to attack National Socialists, and he had even been prepared to allow negotiations between the army and the illegal Schutzbund to talk of a possible alliance in the eventuality of an attack on Austria by the Nazi 'Austrian Legion' stationed in Bavaria.[17] With Dollfuss talking of attacking the Nazis by smashing the Social Democrats and at the same time negotiating with the Nazis there was no hope whatever for Vaugoin's policy, particularly as the vast majority of the Christian Social Party was solidly behind the Chancellor.

By now the party was little more than the propaganda organ of Dollfuss. It split up into small groups on provincial lines, according to professions (such as the Farmers' Association) and other sections like the Catholic Women's Organisation. The party had no influence whatever on discussions of the new constitution and was kept chronically short of money. By demanding the end of party politics the party had committed suicide.

The Christian Social Party's main coalition partner was the Greater German Party. In many ways this seemed to be an obvious relationship. Both parties were conservative, both supported the idea of an Anschluss, both shared anti-semitic prejudices and a belief in the possibility of creating a true national community that would spell an end to the class struggle. But it soon became apparent that the Greater Germans had little to offer in the way of support. The party was an uneasy and unstable collection of different groups and was rapidly losing its popular support. Moreover, a coalition partner was only necessary within the framework of a parliamentary democracy. As the

Christian Socials set about the destruction of Austrian democracy they had less and less need for the support of the Greater German Party.

Nationalism in Austria had always been a complex issue. German nationalists in the Dual Monarchy had little sympathy for the patriots who supported the Habsburg state. A strong sense of regional particularism undermined both positions. Above all there was the problem of the future relations between German Austria and Germany, would it be an association of states (*Staatenbund*) or a federal state (*Bundesstaat*), was the best solution *grossoesterreichische, grossdeutsche* or *kleindeutsche*? Schwarzenberg and Bruck had dreamed of the 'Great Austria' from the Baltic to the Adriatic and the creation of a cosmopolitan Central Europe centred on Vienna. This utopian vision was contrary to the economic and political realities of the day, particularly the rise of Prussia as a great industrial and military power.[18] The idea lived on in the romanticised form of a hankering after the old dynasty, in a reactionary Catholicism and in a profound respect for the paraphernalia of the old monarchy.[19]

The *grossdeutsche* solution had been put forward by Schmerling in 1848, a close association between the two German states without the automatic abandonment of the non-German states of the monarchy. This was also hardly a realistic programme and could easily be attacked by its opponents for its refusal to accept the profound differences between the Prussian and the Austrian states, and by others as treason against the 'Austrian state idea'. After 1918 the problem of the non-German states had been resolved by the Entente so that one great stumbling block on the way to a *grossdeutsche* solution had been removed, and the fact that an Anschluss with Germany had been forbidden made it in some ways all the more attractive. The Greater Germans could appeal to the national liberal traditions of 1848 which rejected the old dynasty and called for a popular united Germany under a sympathetic Emperor like the Archduke John. But these revived *grossdeutsche* ideas had lost their liberal flavour and were tinged with a mean chauvinism. The old dynastic state was condemned as 'Jewish', 'Asiatic' and 'un-German'. German nationalism had lost its humanism and cosmopolitanism and was increasingly spiced with racial doctrines and imperialist ambitions. It had become a form of German nationalism that was often associated with anti-clericalism. The most extreme form of this nationalism was the suggestion of Schönerer and his followers who believed that the Empire should be allowed to fall apart and German Austria simply become a part of Prussia-Germany.[20] It was an expression of frustration and weakness, a condemnation of the rotten Babel of the Dual Monarchy, a desire to submit to the powerful German state to the north. The influence of this kind of thinking on Hitler is obvious.

In February 1919, 26 nationalists were elected to the constituent assembly. Under the leadership of Dinghofer, who was one of the three presidents of the assembly, the nationalists were brought together to form the Greater German Association (*Grossdeutsche Vereinigung*). In September of the following year, after difficult negotiations between some 17 different nationalist groups the *Grossdeutsche Volkspartei* was formed. The Farmers' Party (later Bauernbund) and Riehl's National Socialists refused to join the new party.[21] The party's programme called for Anschluss with Germany, the ending of the class war and the creation of a sense of community (*Volksgemeinschaft*), the support of private property without 'capitalist excesses', the removal of the 'Jewish yoke' and a condemnation of the Habsburgs and their empire. The party accepted the democratic republic on the grounds that it was the best guarantee of keeping out the Habsburgs, but they were concerned about the sinister machinations of the Jews within such a system, and warned party members to pay particular attention to this problem.

From the outset the party lacked real organisational unity. The constituent organisations continued their own individual existence. Alpinist clubs, student associations, gymnasts and the like were never fully controlled by the party leadership. The leadership itself was singularly incapable of exploiting a growing nationalism to the advantage of the party. Popular outbursts against the peace treaty, and the struggles in Carinthia and the Burgenland were never directed and used by the party. First the Heimwehr was successful in mobilising nationalist resentments for political purposes, and then the National Socialists were able to create a mass movement on the ruins of the Greater German Party.

In the Schober cabinet of 1921 the Greater German, Waber, was appointed Minister of the Interior. The coalition was an uneasy one, the Greater Germans being always suspicious that their colleagues were betraying the national interest. Waber's only significant piece of legislation forbad East European Jews from obtaining Austrian citizenship, a bill that was celebrated as 'the first real anti-Semitic act in the whole history of anti-Semitism'; an act that was proudly quoted by the Greater Germans when attacked by other anti-semitic groups for being soft on the Jews.[22]

Constant stress of the need for Anschluss coupled with anti-semitic outbursts were the major contributions of the Greater Germans to various coalition governments. Their support for the Geneva Treaty seriously compromised their position on the Anschluss in the eyes of many, and their opponents accused them of having sold the country to the League of Nations. The unpopularity of Seipel's austerity measures after Geneva further weakened the party's position. Much of the party's support came from the civil service, and the civil service was particularly hard hit by measures for which the party was at least partially responsible. It is hardly surprising, therefore, that the party lost half its seats in the Nationalrat elections of 1923.

It became increasingly clear that the Greater German Party had nowhere to go. Anti-semites could find more radical parties. Everyone was in favour of the Anschluss, apart from the tiny Communist Party and a few Austrian nationalists. Its coalition with the Christian Social Party had done nothing to increase its popularity. An attempt to win over a section of the working class and to form its own trade unions was a miserable failure, and any workers who sympathised with the idea were soon to join the 'independent unions' of the Heimwehr. The party had nothing that the other parties could not offer in a more distinct form. The more radical the political situation became, the duller the Greater Germans appeared. Even the central idea of the party, the Anschluss, was a source of some confusion. To some it might involve the Prussianisation of Austria, the loss of a sense of national identity and difference. The idea was not only impractical, given the attitude of the Entente, it was also perhaps not quite as attractive as it first seemed. The *Gleichschaltung* of 1938 was certainly not what they wanted. Meanwhile, the party had no leaders capable of firing the enthusiasm of the Austrian people. The party seemed to be slowly dwindling away, without a sense of direction and with little chance of a revival.

The party had voters, but few members. Finance came in large part from Germany and from some Austrian industrialists, but income was dependent on the party's influence. As it began to diminish funds were slowly cut off, so that by the beginning of the 1930s the financial position of the party was very serious. The party also lacked a newspaper, unlike all the other major parties in Austria at the time, although they did get a sympathetic hearing in some lesser papers.[23] The disappointing performance of the party in the elections of 1930 led to a slow erosion of supporters who began to join the more promising ranks of the National Socialists. The National Socialists were delighted to get this support which they badly needed against the

Heimwehr, but on the other hand they did not want an alliance with the Greater Germans whom the Gauleiter of Vienna, Frauenfeld, denounced in 1932 as 'old and feeble'. During the 1932 provincial election campaign there were continual insults hurled between the Nazis and the Greater Germans, and the results were a disaster for the latter who lost all their seats in the provincial parliaments. Some pessimists even talked of disbanding the party. The party was almost bankrupt, the membership was leaving either to the Nazis or to the Christian Socials, and there was an obvious need for a new orientation by the party to save what could be saved.

In spite of this perilous position, the party seriously misjudged the Nazis. They felt that the Nazis were slipping towards socialism, and they also imagined they were a temporary phenomenon. The party thus began to see its task as forming a non-Nazi front that would step into the breach once the Nazi Party collapsed. Some signs that the German nationalists in Germany were making advances at the expense of the Nazis gave a certain encouragement to this totally unrealistic analysis of the situation in Austria. As the Christian Social Party went on an increasingly authoritarian course which aimed at doing away with parliament, an alternative route of parliamentary activity and possible alliance with the Christian Socials was closed off. Now the poor Greater Germans found themselves as the unwilling defenders of a parliamentary democracy for which they had never had much real sympathy. The Nazis were delighted at the collapse of the Greater Germans, and Frauenfeld, who fancied himself as something of a wit, remarked that they were neither great nor German and were hardly even a party.[24]

By 1933 the Greater Germans could either disband or enter into an alliance with the Nazis. On 15 May the dramatically titled 'fighting community' (*Kampfgemeinschaft*) between the Greater Germans and the Nazis at last took place. In what appears to have been a secret section of the agreement, the Nazis accepted that the Greater German Party should be destroyed once the Nationalrat was dissolved. The alliance was thus purely temporary, and only postponed the death agonies of the party.[25]

Even after the ban on the Nazi Party the Greater Germans were unable to restore their fortunes. Many members disliked their new partners, were unable to accept the leadership principle and disliked the Nazis' enthusiasm for violence. They wanted a greater degree of independence for the party and for Austria against Germany. Greater Germans like Foppa and Langoth played an important role in the negotiations between the government and the Nazis, and they began to dream that their vision of a truly national front was near to realisation. But with the failure of these talks such dreams were also shattered. As far as the government was concerned this merely showed that there was little to choose between the Nazis and the Greater Germans. They were united in their opposition to the government and should therefore both be persecuted. Greater Germans were accused of terrorist actions committed by the Nazis, respectable nationalist civil servants were painted as violent revolutionaries. Many Greater Germans lost their jobs in the civil service and as schoolteachers, and as a result they gravitated towards the Nazis, radicalised by treatment that they felt to be grossly unfair.

By now the party had virtually ceased to exist. It continued to provide useful services for the Nazis by providing middlemen between arrested Nazis and the authorities, but these efforts gained them little thanks from the Nazis. Through their alliance with the Nazis the 'respectable' Greater Germans, the party of civil servants and schoolteachers, had given the Nazis a certain respectability, but at the same time they lost their own. This loosely organised party was constantly short of money and lacked any clearly defined political goals. Just like the German National Party it could not survive the embrace of the Nazis, and its collapse gave the National Socialists new and important support from the 'respectable classes'.

Notes

1. There is unfortunately no modern study of Lueger. Rudolf Kuppe, *Karl Lueger und seine Zeit* (Vienna 1933), is outdated.

2. Heinrich Benedikt, *Geschichte der Republik Oesterreich* (Munich 1954), p. 311.

3. Klemens von Klemperer, *Ignaz Seipel — Christian Statesman in a Time of Crisis* (Princeton 1972).

4. *Quadragesimo Anno: Encyclical Letter of His Holiness Pope Pius XI.*

5. A. Staudinger, 'Bemühungen Carl Vaugoins um Suprematie der Christlich-sozialen Parteien in Oesterreich (1930 bis 1933)', *Mitteilungen des Oesterreichischen Staatsarchiv*, vol. 23, 1970 (Vienna 1971).

6. Alfred Diamant, *Austrian Catholics and the First Republic* (Princeton 1960), p. 190.

7. Benedikt, *Geschichte der Republik*, p. 196.

8. The most detailed account of the wartime emergency economic law is P. Huemer, *Sektionschef Robert Hecht und die Zerstörung der österreichischen Demokratie* (Vienna 1975).

9. Benedikt, *Geschichte der Republik*, p. 201.

10. *Vom Justizpalast zum Heldenplatz* (Vienna 1975), p. 70.

11. Ibid., p. 72.

12. *AVA*, Christlichsozialer Klubvorstand, 2 May 1933.

13. These attempts were not successful. During the depression Austrians living abroad usually had more pressing problems. See *NPA*, Fasz. 313, for further details.

14. I. Bärnthaler, *Die Vaterländische Front — Geschichte und Organisation* (Vienna 1971). See also Chapter 8 below.

15. C.A. Gulick, *Habsburg to Hitler* (2 vols. Berkeley 1948), vol. 1, p. 1123.

16. *Vom Justizpalast zum Heldenplatz*, p. 79.

17. A. Staudinger, 'Die sozialdemokratische Grenzländerkonferenz vom 15. September 1933 in Salzburg — Ein sozialdemokratisches Angebot militärischer Kooperation mit der Regierung Dollfuss gegen den Nationalsozialismus', *Festschrift für Franz Loidl*, vol. 3 (Vienna 1971).

18. Martin Kitchen, *Political Economy of Germany 1815-1914* (London 1979).

19. Schuschnigg and Miklas were not immune to such ideas. See Benedikt, *Geschichte der Republik*, p. 370.

20. *Grossdeutsche* and *kleindeutsche* are confusing terms at the best of times, and the problem is compounded by the fact that the words have a different meaning in an Austrian context. Schönerer's *kleindeutsche* ideas would be considered *grossdeutsche* in Germany!

21. Benedikt, *Geschichte der Republik*, p. 384.

22. Ibid., p. 386.

23. Isabella Ackerl, 'Das Kampfbündnis der Nationalsozialistischen Deutschen Arbeiterpartei mit der Grossdeutschen Volkspartei vom 15. Mai 1933' in *Das Jahr 1934: 25. Juli* (Vienna 1975), p. 23. See also her PhD disseration, 'Die Grossdeutsche Volkspartei 1920 bis 1934 — Versuch einer Parteigeschichte' (Vienna 1967), an invaluable source of information.

24. F.L. Carsten, *Faschismus in Oesterreich* (Munich 1977), p. 178.

25. Ackerl, 'Kampfbündnis', p. 30.

3　THE EXTREME RIGHT

The ideology of the extreme right in Austria was made up from the beginning of two powerful ingredients: German nationalism and anti-semitism.[1] Within the Austro-Hungarian monarchy the Germans formed a minority, slightly over 35 per cent in 1910, and although they were by far the most influential and successful of the national groups they felt constantly threatened, particularly by Slav nationalism. Many German Austrians looked with envy and admiration at Germany and felt that they could only survive as a powerful national group through Anschluss with the Reich. This arrogant and over-bearing chauvinism was strengthened by a heavy dose of anti-semitism, the 'socialism of fools' that was particularly attractive in Vienna, a city in which the Jews played such a prominent role in cultural and intellectual life.

The first politician to combine German nationalism and anti-semitism into a successful political platform was Georg Ritter von Schönerer who was born in 1842, the son of a successful engineer who had been enobled as a result of his efforts as a railway builder.[2] Schönerer's politics were a strange mixture of Greater German nationalism, an increasing element of anti-semitism, and radical liberalism in his demands for freedom of the press and assembly, rights for the trade unions and co-operatives, limitation of the power of the church and nationalisation of the railways.

These liberal demands brought Schönerer very close to the position of the Social Democratic leader Viktor Adler and the great liberal historian Heinrich Friedjung.[3] For a time they served to disguise the profoundly reactionary thrust of his politics, and, conversely, the famous Linz programme of the Austrian liberals of 1882 was marked by a shrill nationalism — many of its supporters were truly 'German' in their anti-semitism. Three years later a paragraph was added to the Linz programme calling for the ending of 'Jewish influence in public life'. Schönerer, although more outspoken than many in his anti-semitism, was not outside the mainstream of Austrian politics at the time. Gradually, however, his anti-semitism became more violent and

developed into the racial anti-semitism characteristic of the new
extreme groups. But he did not abandon the liberal and 'social'
aspects of his programme, and was much more successful than
Stoecker in Berlin in winning support from a wide section of society
including members of the working class, a fact of great concern to
socialists who were quick to see that anti-semitism was a powerful
manipulative ideology to win working-class and, particularly, lower-
middle-class support away from 'Jewish' and 'un-German' socialism.
Patient effort by the Social Democratic Party, particularly its
outstanding educational programme, countered the effects of this
propaganda, and Schönerer's increasing excesses and frequent lapses
into vile and vicious behaviour discredited his position, so that he was
unable to exploit this potential support. In 1888 he was sent to jail for
leading an assault on a newspaper office and was deprived of the right
to vote or stand for election for five years. His pro-German and anti-
Habsburg position did not increase his popularity, nor did his attacks
on the Catholic church. Many German nationalists found his
obsession with German calendars, German religion and Germanic
folk customs, many of which were of dubious authenticity, to be
merely silly. With the introduction of universal suffrage in 1907
Schönerer's movement suffered a severe setback, and he was unable to
retain his seat in the Reichsrat. On the eve of the war he came close to
admitting defeat, claiming that Austria had become a Slav state and
that the Germans had done nothing to preserve their cultural heritage
and their racial dignity.

Schönerer was the leading spokesman of those Austrians who
rejected the multinational Empire, who feared that the Germans
would be pushed aside by the 'lesser' nationalities, and who admired
the Germany of Bismarck, not only for its power and prestige, but also
because of its social legislation which seemed to offer an alternative to
socialism. It was a negative, pessimistic and even fatalistic stance. It
found supporters among student associations, gymnastic clubs and
youth groups. There was little support for such ideas among those who
had direct experience of the Empire, in the bureaucracy and in the
army, for there was something infantile and immature in a movement
that fed on hysteria and mystical rhetoric. It was only after 1918, when
the Empire had collapsed, that these ideas were revived in a new and
potent form, when they were to have a sinister influence on Hitler and
the National Socialists.[4] It was via Schönerer and his movement that
the Nazis were to find many of the ingredients of their witches' brew of
nationalism and racism, the perverted liberal-democratic notions of

1848 that had degenerated into a reactionary anti-capitalism, an ultra-reactionary anti-conservatism and anti-traditionalism. It was from this source that German fascism was to get its pseudo-revolutionary rhetoric which was to make it a popular mass movement, and which was to cause such problems once the movement gained power.[5] The ideology was a mass of contradictions from the outset, as Bismarck was quick to point out to a group of Schönerer supporters who visited him in his retirement, for their hero had little sympathy for their radicalism and their lack of political realism, telling them that their prime duty was to be good Austrians.

Schönerer died in 1921, but he paid no part in the political life of the republic. He stayed at home muttering of betrayal and of Jewish conspiracy, his political ineptitude having done much to split the national camp. Small parties like the German Workers' Party, the National Democratic Party and the German Agrarian Party were mere sects with little influence, but they carried within them the seeds of fascism which were soon to develop to become one of the most powerful forces in Austrian politics.

The trauma of a lost war, the collapse of the Empire and the shortages and hardships of the immediate post-war period could all be used by the extreme right to discredit the republic and its leading party, the Social Democrats. Anti-semites were quick to denounce the 'Jewish black market', reactionaries in the provinces complained about the parasitism of Red Vienna, and the fear of a Communist uprising became very real in April and June of 1919. The right was determined to arm itself in defence of private property and as a guarantee against revolution. Throughout Austria paramilitary organisations sprang up spontaneously calling themselves Heimatwehr or Heimwehr, names which signified their determination to defend the fatherland and the home against sinister foreign and alien influences. These organisations were encouraged and financed by the government, a government that was led by the Social Democrats, on the grounds that they were needed to preserve law and order, protect private property and control demobilised soldiers who were running amok. For months after the war the Heimwehr was engaged in fights with Yugoslav units in southern Austria.[6] It soon began to look as if the Heimwehr was out of control. It grew steadily in size and was heavily armed, some units even had airplanes. In spite of its repeated insistence that it was apolitical and merely interested in the preservation of law and order, these assurances could hardly be reconciled with the speeches and reports of many Heimwehr officers,

which showed their determination to stop the influence of the soldiers'
and workers' councils, stem the tide of Social Democracy and pursue
extreme nationalist goals. Very soon the Heimwehr came into conflict
with the Volkswehr, the republican army which at that time was still
very much under the influence of the Social Democrats. The
Heimwehr was regional rather than national in flavour, the uniforms
having the coat of arms of the provinces, and the leaders of the
movement, such as Starhemberg, Pfrimer and Steidle, were anti-
centralists who appealed strongly to local patriotism, defending traditional and provincial values against the un-German cosmopolitanism
and socialism of the capital. The leaders of the movement were ex-
officers, professional men and often aristocrats. The rank and file
were mostly of peasant stock, although the most radical and violent
members came from extremist student groups. From them came
slogans such as: 'Struggle against Marxism and Bourgeois Democracy,
for the Construction of an Authoritarian State and the Anschluss.'
The use of the swastika showed that their claim to be apolitical could
hardly be taken seriously.[7] Many Heimwehr units were not allowed to
join political parties, but this was simply a reflection of the fact that
none of the existing parties met with their approval, for they all
seemed either to be Marxist or dangerously sympathetic to bourgeois
democracy.

The Heimwehr attracted war veterans who found it impossible to
settle down to normal civilian life, and adventurers who looked for any
chance to fight and who joined forces with the Oberland Freecorps
against the Munich republic, or fought in the Sudetenland along with
German nationalists. They were a dissatisfied and angry lot who
seemed to be looking for a fight rather than acting as politically
neutral special constables. The Heimwehr was unable to be really
effective on the national level because of its lack of central organisation, its regionalism and its lack of any coherent ideology beyond an
ill-considered and virulent anti-Marxism.

Close contacts between the Heimwehr in western Austria and the
Bavarian Orgesch, the best organised of the anti-socialist paramilitary
organisations in Bavaria, gave this section of the Heimwehr a stronger
sense of direction and a more outspoken position against international
Jewry and its agents in Vienna, against the Habsburg monarchists and
in favour of the Anschluss. The Bavarians were able to win over the
Heimwehr in Tyrol and Salzburg for a common struggle against
'Asiatic influences' and 'Jewish bolshevism', and for the preservation of
'Germanic culture'. Close organisational links were formed between

the Orgesch and the Heimwehr, but there were limits to the effectiveness of this attempt to unify the Heimwehr. Many Heimwehr leaders had little sympathy for the idea of an Anschluss and were fervent Austrian nationalists. Some were sympathetic to the Christian Social Party and were not prepared to join in a blanket condemnation of all parties. As the Bavarians became increasingly radical, particularly after the murder of Erzberger in 1921, which was greeted as a tremendous triumph for the Ultras, the divisions between the Greater Germans and the Christian Socials within the Heimwehr became more pronounced, even in the provinces that bordered on Bavaria and which had hitherto been most sympathetic to the Orgesch. On the German side of the border there were similar divisions and rivalries among the extreme right, particularly after the failure of the Kapp putsch in 1920, so that the formation of a strong, tightly organised and united paramilitary force in which Germans and Austrians could work side by side became an increasingly remote possibility. In such a situation the inevitable claims of betrayal and lack of national spirit only served to divide the movement still more, and as the 'Red Peril' seemed increasingly remote, there was little to inspire a sense of common purpose and a need for decisive action. Attempts by Ludendorff's right-hand man, Colonel Bauer, to support Ludendorff's bid to become the dictator of Germany with the aid of paramilitary forces in Budapest and Austria failed largely due to the divisions within the Austrian camp. Bauer was quickly to find that not all the Austrian right was Greater German and that the movement was full of clericals and separatists.[8] The situation was made all the more complex because of sympathy in some sections of the Heimwehr for an Anschluss with Bavaria rather than with the Reich, and yet some Christian Socials, for reasons that are totally obscure, sympathised with Ludendorff in spite of his lunatic religious ideas which were totally irreconcilable with the professed Catholicism of the party.

Attempts were made to achieve a certain degree of unity within the Heimwehr by the use of financial pressure. In 1922 the Austrian Industrialists' Association agreed to finance the Heimwehr by paying 150 million crowns per month. The money was to be paid to the leader of the Christian Social Party, Dr Seipel, who was thus given enormous influence over the Heimwehr. Seipel was determined to make the Heimwehr an effective and united force against what he was pleased to call anarchy, and as a defence against foreign enemies, whoever they might be. For many Heimwehr leaders the idea of placing the movement under the 'reactionary and clerical' Christian Socials was quite unacceptable. In the eyes of these men Seipel was un-German, tarred with the same brush as 'Erzberger, Wirth and comrades'.[9]

After 1923, when Ludendorff and Bauer were discredited after the failure of the Hitler putsch, the problem of attitudes towards Bavaria and Germany were less important. Now the Heimwehr looked increasingly to Italy as its model, and there were demands that the Heimwehr, like its Italian comrades, should set about putting its own house in order, not only Red Vienna but also the Jewish bureaucrats in the provinces. Discussions were thus held as to how the Heimwehr could be reorganised along fascist lines. With the formation of the Schutzbund by the Social Democrats it seemed that Austria was rapidly approaching a situation of near civil war. But in fact an improvement in the economic situation after 1923 and the failure of the Social Democrats to make any significant gains resulted in a cooling of passions on the right. The 'Red Peril' seemed remote and cries of the 'Fatherland in Danger' found little echo.

The Heimwehr now appeared to be in decline, short of money and uncertain as to its aims. In Tyrol there was bombastic talk of a 'national revolution'. But the phrase had lost much of its sting after the failure of its realisation in Bavaria in 1923. In Styria the Heimwehr voiced its determination to save the country from the rule of party or class, in other words from Social Democracy, and there were increasingly close ties between the Styrian leader Dr Pfrimer and Hitler, reflected in talk about Greater Germany and in the use of the swastika. In other provinces the Heimwehr was divided between Austrian nationalism and a hankering after the Anschluss, held together by occasional battles with Social Democrats and rousing but somehow slightly unconvincing talk of the dangers to Austrian culture of Asiatic Marxism.

A new lease of life was given to the Heimwehr on 15 July 1927 when the Palace of Justice affair was made to seem the beginning of the socialist revolution. The Heimwehr enthusiastically set about breaking the strike and acting as auxiliary police. In many areas the Social Democrats and the Schutzbund were forced to retreat and the strike had to be called off. In the industrial area of Styria Pfrimer issued an unequivocal ultimatum to the Social Democrats who, because of their relative weakness, were forced to back down.[10] The Heimwehr was thus able to stop a general strike, and the workers of Vienna were left hopelessly isolated. July 1927 was a triumph for the Heimwehr at a time when morale was beginning to run very low. Its prestige in government circles was greatly enhanced. New recruits from all walks of life were eager to join. What had seemed to be a somewhat tiresome and ineffective organisation now showed itself to be far more useful than its critics had imagined. The Heimwehr leaders were quick to seize the opportunity to bury most of their differences and create a national organisation. They elected Steidle from Innsbruck as national leader, with Pfrimer as his deputy and Field-Marshal von Pichler as military leader.

The successes of July 1927 and the reorganisation of the Heimwehr in the following year fuelled Steidle's political ambitions. He began to see himself as a statesman of European mould and began negotiations with the Hungarian Prime Minister, Bethlen, for financial and military support in order to force the Austrian government to go on an extreme right-wing course. Bethlen had already discussed similar proposals with Mussolini in April 1928 in the course of a meeting in Milan. The Italian dictator expressed his willingness to send weapons to the Heimwehr provided that they would agree to act quickly, and promised some concessions in the South Tyrol question to show his sincerity. Once Steidle gave his word that the Heimwehr would not press the South Tyrol issue, Mussolini began to send money via Budapest to finance the purchase of arms.

For Mussolini the Heimwehr was to be used to strengthen the axis from Rome to Budapest, but Steidle's ambitions were much more grandiose, and soon began to run counter to those of the dictator. He hoped to use Italian support to launch a 'March on Berlin' and thus to become the Greater German Mussolini. To this end Steidle began negotiations with the German National Party leader, Hugenberg, and with the Stahlhelm, although Steidle's envoy (Rosa Luxemburg's murderer, Pabst) was careful to talk in general terms about the need for a common anti-Marxist front. Of course Steidle could not realise these exotic ambitions without substantial financial support, and this could only come from Mussolini or Bethlen. Mussolini, however, wanted less talk and more action, and thus demanded a guarantee that the Heimwehr would keep its promises. In August 1929 Steidle and Pfrimer therefore promised that the Heimwehr would overthrow the Austrian constitution not later than 15 March 1930. Even this was not enough for Bethlen, who acted as intermediary between Heimwehr and the Italian government. He demanded a further declaration that Vienna would be rid of its Social Democratic government. Bethlen was satisfied with Steidle's reply, but somewhat concerned as to how the putsch was to be organised, unless it could be provoked by the Social Democrats, which unfortunately seemed unlikely. Shortly afterwards the Hungarian government began to send money, although not nearly as much as Steidle requested.[11]

The Heimwehr was now financed in part by fascist Italy and its ideology became increasingly fascist in tone. Its programme, published in November 1929, called for the creation of a fascist state, but there were still serious divisions within the movement as to what this involved. There were those who wanted a march on Vienna, and those who still dreamed of a march on Berlin. The movement was also seriously divided on the South Tyrol issue, a question which also plagued the National Socialists. Could *völkisch* nationalists ignore their blood brothers in South Tyrol, or should sympathy for fascist Italy come first? At least there was general agreement that the Heimwehr's main enemies were 'Jewish-Marxism', 'union terror' and the 'tyranny of the parties'. Reform of the franchise and the introduction of a parliament based on the estates rather than the parties was also generally deemed desirable. Disagreement came as to how this was to be achieved. There were those who argued that it would be possible through pressure on the right-wing parties, whereas the radicals insisted that a violent coup was the only possible way of obtaining fundamental change.

The immediate problem facing the Heimwehr leadership was how to meet the promise they had made to Mussolini that they would act soon and decisively. Massive demonstrations were held in the working-class districts of Vienna, Wiener Neustadt, Innsbruck and elsewhere, but although the Social Democrats held counter-demonstrations violence was avoided in part through the intervention of the police which kept the two sides apart.

Violence seemed to be the quickest and most effective way of reaching the Heimwehr's political goal, but it seemed almost impossible to precipitate in favourable circumstances. Political persuasion also seemed tricky. Seipel skilfully used the Heimwehr in his campaign against the Social Democrats, but he was also careful to keep them at arms' length and would not consider allowing them to share political power. He was sympathetic to many of the Heimwehr's aims and had no love whatever for the political parties or for parliamentary democracy. His concern was to bring the Heimwehr more in line with his own brand of ultra-conservatism and to curb their more eager leaders.[12]

At the end of 1929 the Heimwehr was at the height of its powers and seemed close to achieving its aims. The new Chancellor, Dr Schober, had been police chief of Vienna and was responsible for the bloody repression of the workers in July 1927. The Heimwehr was convinced that he was their man, although Steidle warned against excessive optimism, muttering that he was at heart a bureaucrat. They were soon bitterly disappointed with Schober's constitutional changes which, although they were distinctly anti-democratic and authoritarian, were a far cry from the full-scale fascism that the Heimwehr was demanding. The spectacle of the Chancellor negotiating with the Social Democrats on constitutional changes was more than some Heimwehr leaders could stomach. Before long, hopes in Schober turned into disappointment, and murmers of betrayal of the national cause were to be heard at many a Heimwehr meeting.

Mussolini's views on the matter were quite the contrary.[13] He had greater confidence in Schober than in the Heimwehr. He was growing impatient with the Heimwehr's endless excuses for their inaction, and thought that Schober could be persuaded to bring in reforms along broadly fascist lines, particularly as the Duce was dangling the carrot of an Italian loan in front of the Chancellor's nose. Disappointment with the Schober government placed further strain on a movement that had never been united in its purpose. Steidle in Tyrol was no longer on speaking terms with Pfrimer in Styria. The nationalists brought up the South Tyrol issue and warned of too close an association with Mussolini. Greater Germans denounced the radical Heimwehr leaders as troublemakers who were diverting the movement away from its original intention of guaranteeing 'bourgeois order'. There were others who felt that the Heimwehr was too soft and narrow-minded, altogether too *spiessbürgerlich*. The leading figure in this last group was Count Ernst Rudiger von Starhemberg.[14]

Starhemberg came from a distinguished aristocratic family, was rich, ambitious, and an often frivolous adventurer. He decided to form an elite corps of some 50,000 men within the Heimwehr, if necessary at his own expense, that would show up the posturings of the pseudo-radicals. His famous name and his fashionable good looks were successful in strengthening the prestige of the Heimwehr and in bringing in new recruits. In July 1929 he was elected Heimwehr leader in Upper Austria. Starhemberg rapidly became the most popular and admired of the Heimwehr leaders. Some felt that 'feudal barons' like Starhemberg, Czernin or Hohenberg would turn the Heimwehr away from the avowed though totally unrealistic and fraudulent goal of creating a society that existed beyond class, organised in Professor Othmar Spann's much quoted phrase, along vertical lines rather than the loathsome horizontal of the Marxists. In a movement as divided as the Heimwehr Starhemberg was bound to have his critics, and in spite of his undoubted ability as a public speaker he lacked the really forceful personality that alone might possibly have united the various factions.

The rise of Starhemberg served to emphasise the differences and divisions within the Heimwehr. Starhemberg was at this time a fervent admirer of Hitler, his political ideas very close to National Socialism, and he was given to outbursts of radical anti-semitism. Steidle therefore made a valiant attempt to give the movement some semblance of unity and to outline some common political goals. In May 1930 the Heimwehr leaders met at Korneuburg and were addressed by Steidle on the political aims of the movement. He argued that the Heimwehr could either use its influence to push the parties in the direction that they desired, or it could become an outright fascist movement. Steidle argued strongly for a disavowal of parliamentary government, the reorganisation of the state along corporatist lines — a nebulous idea that combined notions from Spann's book *The True State* and vague borrowings from Italian fascism — and the acceptance of the leadership principle. Following the speech the delegates were called upon to swear an oath, the 'Korneuburger Oath', in which they promised to work for the overthrow of the existing state, its replacement by a state based on the estates, and for a two-pronged attack on the 'Marxist class-war' and 'liberal-capitalist economics'. Even members of the parties, including Julius Raab, Seipel's envoy from the Christian Social Party, accepted the oath.[15]

In the weeks after Korneuburg Steidle gave a series of speeches that were peppered with references to fascism, to democracy as a ghastly child of the French Revolution, and for the need to go back to truly German forms of political organisation. Understandably enough, this caused considerable confusion in the rank and file of the Heimwehr and did nothing to create the ideological unity which had been prematurely celebrated in May. Many nationalists felt that fascism was a foreign importation that was dangerously un-German. Some were concerned at the blatantly anti-constitutional position of the movement, a matter of particular concern to members of parliament. Starhemberg, who had not been consulted about the Korneuburg programme, was opposed to Steidle on personal as well as ideological grounds. Some had qualms about reconciling the oath they had made to the constitution with the Korneuburg oath, although the Christian Social Party came to the extraordinary conclusion that there was no real conflict between the two. The Heimwehr had managed to survive as a loose confederation of anti-Marxists, now it seemed to be in danger of falling apart over ideological issues.

Many members refused to swear the oath, and the attempt to persuade right-wing members of parliament to undermine the parliamentary system misfired. Most important of all, Schober refused to tolerate the attempts by the Heimwehr to become a second government challenging the authority of his own cabinet. As a gesture of his determination to stand up to the Heimwehr Schober extradited Pabst, a German citizen, a man who had played a decisive role at Korneuburg and who, it seemed, was negotiating with the Italian government to make the acceptance of a loan to Austria dependent on concessions to the Heimwehr. The loss of Pabst was a serious blow to the Heimwehr and to the Steidle faction for he was a man of enormous energy and considerable organisational talent.[16] In fact Pabst was allowed to return to Austria shortly afterwards under the new government, having spent the interval in Italy where he was treated as a fascist hero. By the time he returned the Heimwehr had come under a new leadership.

Starhemberg had profited from the dissension within the movement over the Korneuburg oath to further his own political ambitions. He began negotiations with Schober, and through the Chancellor won the support not only of the Christian Social Party but also of the Industrialists' Association which began to finance the Starhemberg faction.[17] Starhemberg, with the support of his new allies, became national leader of the Heimwehr, but he was no more successful than his predecessor in achieving unity of aim and purpose. In Vaugoin's short-lived government Starhemberg was appointed Minister of the Interior, the Heimwehr having fielded candidates in the elections of November 1930 and having achieved six per cent of the popular vote.

This brief episode of sharing parliamentary power triggered off a fresh round of recriminations. The National Socialists, who had made a poor showing in the November elections, began to break up Heimwehr meetings. Starhemberg, who had offered the Nazis an electoral alliance, and who had made direct appeals to Nazi voters by his talk of the Jews as 'flat-footed foreign parasites', was now obliged to cut off all links with them. But it was not only the Nazis who condemned Starhemberg. Radicals in the Heimwehr, and those who took the Korneuburg oath seriously, were horrified at his compromises with a hated parliamentary system. Others were understandably confused by his wildly contradictory remarks and frequent changes of course. Thus the golden boy Starhemberg was unable to achieve any degree of unity, and indeed the Heimwehr became more fractionalised than ever. By fielding their own candidates in November they helped the Social Democrats to become the largest party in the Nationalrat, a position they had lost in 1920. Even as an anti-Marxist movement the Heimwehr had proved a failure.

Starhemberg retired to his estates to try and put them in order, his financial resources having been drained by his political adventures. Steidle had lost much of his influence in Tyrol, largely because of his endless talk about dictatorship, which had little real appeal even to the most authoritarian of the Tyrolese who feared a loss of local autonomy, and also because he was generally regarded as indolent. Pabst left Austria again, this time in disgust at endless factional bickering. Pfrimer came increasingly close to the National Socialists. Starhemberg's personal and political rival in Vienna, Fey, continued his attacks on the national leadership.

In September 1931 Pfrimer, having made constant appeals to the Nazis to support all efforts to do away with Marxism and parliamentary democracy, and having become utterly disillusioned with the leadership of the Heimwehr, attempted a coup. At first he was successful in some towns in Styria, and Graz was surrounded. It was almost bloodless, power seeming to fall effortlesssly into Pfrimer's hands. However, the coup was ruined by the very divisions within the Heimwehr that it was partly designed to overcome. Pfrimer got no support from any of the other leaders, and even the most theoretically bellicose among them stayed cautiously at home. The government allowed the Styrian Heimwehr to surrender without handing over its arms. Pfrimer was tried and acquitted, the jury expressing their solidarity by giving him the fascist salute. In the movement as a whole there were fresh recriminations, and Pfrimer was particularly angered by the lack of support from his erstwhile friends in the Nazi Party.

The Pfrimer putsch was a further defeat for the Heimwehr, and disillusioned right-wing activists turned towards the National Socialists as the party most likely to realise their aims. The elections in April 1932 showed increased support for the Nazis and a marked decline in votes for the Heimwehr's *Heimatblock*. The main issue dividing the Heimwehr was now its attitude to parliament. Starhemberg still had considerable prestige in the movement, particularly when he was able to get a large number of weapons from the Italian government, but to many it seemed that he was dangerously compromised with the corrupt parliamentary system. Those who demanded violent action against the constitution, and who were attracted by *völkisch* and anti-semitic ideas, found it very difficult to think of any viable alternative to close co-operation with the Nazis who appeared to be on the threshold of power in Germany. Even Pfrimer swallowed his pride and offered the unconditional support of his men to Hitler. When Hitler became Chancellor, Starhemberg travelled to Berlin and offered his services to the Führer, but Hitler would not accept his conditions for entering the party, which included the removal of some key figures in the Austrian Nazi Party in whom Hitler still had full confidence.[18]

After his rebuttal in Berlin, Starhemberg's attitude towards the Nazis became even more contradictory. On the one hand he denounced the Austrian party as being run by a bunch of Czechs whose unracial activities included working hand in glove with the bolsheviks in the Democratic Party; yet on the other hand he continued to try and negotiate an agreement with the National Socialists. The more frustrated he became the more he denounced the Nazis as a foreign party, adding that Austria's national renewal should come from Vienna and not from Berlin. Berlin was Prussian, and to be Prussian for a good Austrian was to be un-German. Starhemberg shared Hitler's dreams of colonisation in the East and the creation of a great German Empire, but he saw such an empire centred on Vienna, possibly with himself on the throne.[19] With leaders voicing opinions such as these it is hardly surprising that the Heimwehr was in disarray.

Starhemberg's annoyance with the Nazis was due in part to the fact that his arch rival, Fey, was busy intriguing with the Gauleiter of Vienna, Frauenfeld, and although he was Dollfuss's Vice-Chancellor he was eager to overthrow the Christian Social government and replace it with a new régime under the Heimwehr and the National Socialists. Pabst, Hitler's representative Habicht, and the Lower Austrian Heimwehr leader Alberti were involved in these discussions. Hitler expressed his interest, but the Nazis were never quite certain how serious the overtures from the Heimwehr were, or whether factions were trying to use the support of the Nazis to discredit their opponents within the movement. The longer the talks went on the more the Nazis became impatient with the lack of decisive leadership and sense of purpose among the Heimwehr.

The formation of the Dollfuss government in May 1932 was an encouragement to those who felt that the Heimwehr could again play its traditional role of pushing a right-wing government further to the right. This view was shared by Mussolini who hoped that between them Dollfuss, Starhemberg and Fey would be able to form an Austrian brand of fascism that would be allied with Rome rather than Berlin. Mussolini's desire to have greater influence on Austrian politics became all important after Hitler's appointment as German Chancellor. The major obstacle was that Dollfuss and the Heimwehr were uneasy and treacherous partners, both sides being quite prepared to negotiate with the Nazis behind the other's back. The Heimwehr concentrated its efforts in early 1934 on restructuring the provincial parliaments on authoritarian lines. Little did they know that in February their main aim would be achieved, the smashing of Social Democracy.

Although the Heimwehr, in its confused way, claimed to be a uniquely Austrian form of fascism, and as such the true home for devout patriots, the Nazis also had some reasonable claims for the allegiance of right-wing Austrians. The extreme right could never be really effective unless there was co-operation between the Heimwehr and the Nazis, but both movements were plagued by internal dissent and were often locked in bitter rivalry. The decline of the Heimwehr coincided with the growth of National Socialism, which became particularly dramatic after Hitler's rise to power in Germany, when the small Austrian party could count on the support of the resources of a great power hellbent on establishing its hegemony in Central Europe.

The early history of the National Socialist Party is a familiar story, and need not be repeated in detail.[20] Its antecedents were in the anti-Czech labour movement in Bohemia, in which German workers were determined to protect their own earning power against the threat of cheap Czech labour, turning to arguments from Schönerer's racist vocabulary, denouncing Marxism and a government that was selling out German workers to the Czechs.

The first German Workers Conference was held in 1899 in Eger, the delegates expressing their determination to push back the Czechs and proclaiming their admiration for Schönerer. On the eve of the war there were 45,000 members of the association, but most workers remained faithful to the Social Democratic unions which were far more successful in looking after their interests. The German Workers Party (*Deutsche Arbeiterpartei*), founded in 1904, was an offshoot of the earlier movement. The programme was a curious mixture of liberal demands for freedom of the press and universal suffrage with violent racist attacks on the Czech workers. Like almost all reactionary parties it claimed to rise above the squalid struggle of classes and to represent truly national interests. In 1911 the party was able to get three candidates elected to the Reichsrat, defeating Social Democratic candidates in northern Bohemia. The party lashed out at the Social Democrats, accusing them of being the Jewish lackeys of German capitalism. By 1918 this pseudo-socialism was acknowledged in the new name of the party, the German National Socialist Workers Party (DNSAP). With the collapse of the Dual Monarchy the party split up into a number of small groups; one remained in Bohemia, another was formed in Vienna and a third in Polish Silesia. Unlike the later Nazi Party the DNSAP was loosely organised and its leadership was democratically elected. Ideologically it was close to the later party, particularly to the Nazi 'left'. There was the same ill-articulated anti-capitalism, the condemnation of 'interest slavery', the demand for the abolition of the great trusts and cartels, the rejection of 'non-productive capitalism' which was condemned as 'Jewish', and demands for a massive German colonisation effort that would drive out the lesser races of Slavs and Jews and give the German race its rightful place as a great creative culture.

In the years immediately after the war the National Socialists in Austria were just another extremist and racist group with few members and little influence. They appeared to be part of the flotsam and jetsam left behind after the collapse of a great empire, a set of cranks and extremists no different from a number of other similar groups. Fortunately, violent nationalism and hysterical anti-semitism had little appeal to the electorate, and in 1919 it was only in Salzburg that a couple of National Socialists were elected to the Landtag (provincial parliament).[21] In the elections for the Nationalrat in the following year the party received less than 34,000 votes in the entire country, and was not able to get a single member elected. Meetings of the representatives of the National Socialists of Greater Germany were held in Austria after the war, where representatives of the Austrian party, the Munich group and the North German 'German Specialists' gathered together. Hitler made his first appearance at the Salzburg meeting in 1920 where he impressed the delegates with his abilities as an orator. But for the moment the National Specialists of Greater Germany were a collection of small groups who were unwilling to lose their autonomy and accept central leadership, and the conferences achieved little except to provide platforms for men like Gottfried Feder to deliver yet another diatribe on 'interest slavery'; hardly enough to inspire the movement to unite in a determined and common struggle.

With the economic crisis of 1923 the party made some progress and they claimed 34,000 members.[22] By this time Hitler had established his unquestioned authority over the Munich party which had become the best organised and by far the most influential of the National Socialist parties. The Austrian party came increasingly under the influence of Hitler's faction, taking his advice on critical questions of political strategy, and creating an Austrian SA that was soon busy at work beating up socialists and engaging in the odd political assassination.

It was Hitler's influence that forced the Austrian National Socialist leader, Riehl, to leave the party and form his own insignificant sect. At the Salzburg Party Conference in 1923 the party accepted Hitler's view that there should be no electoral alliance with the Greater German Party in the forthcoming elections, as the Greater Germans had suggested, on the grounds that the Nazis were anti-parliamentary and should refuse to take part in the party political game. Riehl felt that his objections to this view were confirmed in the electoral results in which the Greater Germans did very poorly, and shortly afterwards he resigned from the party. For the time being this mattered very little. The failure of the Hitler putsch in 1923 discredited the movement both in Germany and in Austria, and the party was further hurt by a period of relative, though uncertain, economic stability. Soon it seemed that the party might simply fade away. In the long run, however, Hitler's victory over Riehl in 1923 was to pay off handsomely, and the Austrian movement was to come increasingly under his control once such independent leaders had left. After the split in 1923 the Austrian party dwindled away and lacked the leadership that alone might have saved it. The anti-Marxist forces were now unquestionably led by the Heimwehr, certainly not by the National Socialists. The party was virtually bankrupt and lost members rapidly. The rump swore their allegiance to Hitler, but they were not a very impressive bunch.

The small Austrian party was rent with dissent. Workers for the party newspaper, *Deutsche Arbeiterpresse*, went on strike against the editorial board and accused the party leadership of grabbing all the money and exploiting their labour. Members of the SA made ominous references to corruption in high places, foreshadowing the split between left and right which was to plague the party in the 1930s.[23] The result was the resignation of a number of leaders and further divisions within the party. By 1926 two separate parties were formed in Austria, both of which accepted Hitler as their Führer. To Hitler this was further evidence of the incompetence of his Austrian followers. In August 1926 he gave a stern lecture to both factions at a meeting in Passau, boasting of the great achievements of the German party and contrasting them to the pathetic showing of the Austrians. Hitler's message was clear. The Austrians should place themselves under his leadership, Austria would become a *Gau* and would be treated no differently from the Rhineland or Bavaria. Hitler appealed to the activists who dominated the Austrian party, with his condemnation of parliamentary methods, and insisted, somewhat unconvincingly, that his putsch attempt in 1923 had been an enormous success for the movement. Hitler's speech had a great impact. Some Austrians disliked the German party, feeling that its leadership was too bourgeois and that it had no roots in the working class, but the majority were carried away by Hitler's rhetoric, and certainly there was no one within the Austrian party who could match Hitler in prestige and in demagogic ability; and, after all, he was an Austrian.

1926 marks the end of a vaguely reformist National Socialism with a broadly democratic internal structure that was in its own curious way loyal to the Austrian state, at least as a geographical concept. This was replaced by the Hitler movement which placed the Austrian Nazis under the direct control of the German party and which subordinated its needs and aims totally to those of its partner. This was the first Anschluss, a taste of things to come. By 1931 the Austrian party had lost the last vestiges of its organisational independence.[24]

At first it seemed that the reorganised party was even more ineffectual than its predecessor. Hitler's choice as Gauführer, a retired colonel by the name of Jankovic, turned out to be totally inept. In 1926 the party only had about 200 active members and was without money. In the following year the party only received 27,000 votes in the Nationalrat elections, a showing which even the most sanguine had to admit was a disaster. The organisation of the party was chaotic, meetings poorly attended, party dues seldom paid punctually. Jankovic resigned in disgrace and the party had to be directed from Munich. Frantic anti-semitic outbursts sometimes met with some popular response, but on the whole they were an excuse for effective political action. In spite of the efforts of the Munich headquarters, by 1929 the Austrian party only had 5,000 members, at a time when the German party had 178,000.[25] The party was still rent with factions and there were constant disagreements between the party and the SA, the Hitler Youth and the Nazi student association, disagreements that sometimes led to violent confrontations. The Gauleiter would not co-operate with one another and behaved in an irresponsibly egotistical manner. The constant changes in the top leadership of the party caused further confusion.

The Austrian party was fired with enthusiasm after the increasing success of the German party after 1930 and mounted a massive propaganda action to attract support. The effort was partially successful, though certainly not on the same scale as the German party. In July 1931 the party was reorganised once more. The six Austrian Gauleiter were placed under a central organisation for Austria, the Landesleitung. The Landesleiter for Austria, Alfred Proksch, was soon manipulated by the Landesgeschäftsführer, Theo Habicht, a former Communist German from Wiesbaden, who became the effective leader of the party. Even Habicht was not able to achieve complete unity within the party, and was constantly crossing swords with the Gauleiter particularly with the somewhat wilful Gauleiter of Vienna, the bank clerk Alfred Frauenfeld.[26] The reorganisation of 1931 had a number of important consequences. The party was certainly more effectively organised, but it was also becoming bureaucratised, losing much of its original dynamism, falling into the hands of political bosses who were soon to be opposed by those who believed that they alone encorporated the true spirit of the party. The reorganisation did not mean that the Austrian party was the mindless instrument of the German party. Habicht was Hitler's representative in Austria, but at this time Hitler had little interest in Austrian affairs, he had more important battles to fight in the Reich. Habicht thus had a great deal of independence, and could also make sure that Hitler only heard what he, Habicht, wanted him to hear about Austrian affairs.

Certainly the party was greatly strengthened by these developments and was attracting new members, particularly from the Heimwehr. But this again created problems. How close could the party get to the Heimwehr without being accused of sympathy for reactionary legitimists, as Habicht accused Frauenfeld, the most outspoken of those who favoured co-operation with the Heimwehr? The best answer seemed to be a kind of popular front from below, between the Nazis and the Heimwehr rank and file who were to be won away from their Habsburg-nationalist leaders. The Heimwehr itself was so divided that a coherent policy towards it was almost impossible.

Gradually the National Socialists picked up support. First of all from the small *völkisch* groups, only the most bizarre of which remained independent. Some of the Greater Germans changed sides, particularly those who were frustrated at the party's lack of impact and those who felt that the leadership was far too bourgeois. Many Heimwehr members joined the party, so that in some parts of Austria the Nazis were already more important than the Heimwehr. Although precise data on the social composition of the party are not available, it would seem that, like the German party, its main support came from the disgruntled petty bourgeoisie.[27] Unlike the old Riehl party, the Nazis had virtually no support whatever from the working class, which remained loyal to the Social Democrats. In the countryside the majority remained faithful to the Christian Social Party. It was in the urban areas that the Nazis were to make their big gains. In the civic elections in Vienna in 1932 the party obtained 201,000 votes and 15 per cent of the seats, whereas eighteen months previously they had only got 27,000 votes.[28] The German experience seemed to be repeating itself in Austria. The small parties of the middle were being swept away and were joining the Nazis. It remained to be seen whether the Christian Social Party and the left would be able to contain the Nazi movement. As the Christian Socials seemed to be on what the Nazis perceptively called a 'Brüning course' — the establishment of a form of authoritarian government that would dispense either temporarily or permanently with parliament — the fate of Austrian democracy depended more and more on the Social Democratic Party.

Engelbert Dollfuss, who became Chancellor in May 1932, was uncertain how to deal with the National Socialists. He saw them as a threat to his position, he disliked their violent anti-semitism and as a devout catholic he had no sympathy for their hankering after a Germanic religion. As an Austrian patriot he looked upon them as a foreign party. On the other hand he admired their 'idealism' (a popular word of the day that was used to disguise a multitude of sins) and their energy, and he hoped that by decisive action on his part against the left he could win over a sizeable number of National Socialists and strengthen his own régime. Dollfuss, as he was the first to admit, had little talent for party political intrigue, and his attempts to come to some sort of arrangement with the Nazis all failed.

Immediately upon being appointed Chancellor Dollfuss negotiated with Habicht, offering the Nazis two cabinet appointments if they would stop their propaganda for new elections. Habicht demanded five ministerial positions, immediate elections and the exclusion of the Heimwehr and the Landbund from the government. In spite of this rebuff Dollfuss continued to negotiate. In the autumn of 1932 it appears that he was willing to make considerable further concessions to Habicht, but determined resistance from the Heimwehr put a stop to any further negotiations between the two men. Habicht had every reason to demand a high price from Dollfuss. The Nazis had constantly denounced the parliamentary way to political power and needed a compelling reason to compromise this principle. There was also indication that the party was winning support from the Christian Social Party and thus the Nazis could affort to wait. In the meantime, the Nazis were determined to show up the government's failure to deal with the menace of Marxism by mounting a series of violent terrorist attacks on the Social Democrats, attacks which became increasingly frequent and bloody just before the party was outlawed in June 1933.

Dollfuss's decision to outlaw the party, as we shall see, was determined more by foreign political considerations than by the activities of the party in Austria. There can be no doubt, however, that his refusal to allow elections encouraged the rowdies in the party to engage in further acts of violence, and there were those who began to fear the possibility of a coup by the Nazis in Austria.

Although there had been clear signs that Dollfuss was likely to act against the party, the Nazis seem to have been ill prepared for the move. In May 1933 the Ortsgruppenleiter were ordered to appoint deputies in case of their arrest, but little else was done to meet this eventuality.[29] In June some Nazi leaders, including Frauenfeld, were arrested and sent to the Wollersdorf concentration camp. Most of the leaders crossed the German border to set up their offices in Bavaria. An 'Austrian Legion' was formed, with various camps throughout Bavaria, and was given rigorous military training. The Dollfuss government was accused of breaking the constitution, of high treason and of bloodthirsty cruelty against the National Socialists. Any attempts to form a new Nazi party in Austria were condemned. Party members were ordered to continue their propaganda efforts by word of mouth, by painting swastikas and by building up an illegal press.

The exiled leadership was determined to keep close control over the party in Austria. Political control rested in the 'Landesleitung Oesterreich'. A 'Kampfring der Deutsch-Oesterreicher im Reich' was responsible for propaganda in Austria, and for making the sorry plight of the Austrian Nazis known to the world press. The Austrian Legion, the main centre of which was at Dachau, was trained by the SS, SA, the regular army and by the police. Attracting the rootless and the unemployed the legion soon had about 10,000 members.[30] The legion had two main functions: to keep the government in Vienna constantly worried about the possibility of an attack from across the border, and to smuggle propaganda material and weapons into Austria. In both respects it was effective. However, the quality of the propaganda was on the whole very low. Primitive insults of Dollfuss and his government, blood-curdling accounts of the horrors of life in Austria, and endless praises of the achievements and glories of the Third Reich. At a somewhat higher level, radio talks from Munich, particularly speeches by Habicht, gave a semi-official account of German policy towards Austria and were taken seriously by political analysts in the Foreign Ministry in Vienna. Meanwhile, throwing stink bombs and painting swastikas provided some substitute for political action, particularly in a party which had a youthful membership which enjoyed such pubescent pranks.

By the autumn of 1933 hand-made grenades were taking the place of stink bombs as the party began a systematic terror programme to try and show the inability of the Dollfuss government to maintain law and order. Hitler had actually forbidden terrorist actions in August, but he did nothing to stop Habicht who stepped up the terrorism in Austria to reach a peak in February 1934.[31] Habicht was skilfully able to exploit the divisions within the Nazi movement to strengthen his own position to the point that he was even able to stand up against Hitler, and in most instances to get his own way.

The movement was seriously divided between those who favoured terror and those who were opposed to it — Riehl was the leader of this latter group. Rivalries between the SA and the SS, which were becoming increasingly acute in Germany, were also reflected in Austria, and are vitally important to an understanding of the murder of Dollfuss by an SS unit in July 1934. The 'Kaiser' — the Austrian Gauleiter — continued to quarrel with one another as they struggled for positions of greater power and influence. Yet in spite of these divisions the party was a constant thorn in the flesh of the Dollfuss government. Massive propaganda against the Chancellor, backed by the entire German press, was bound to have an effect.[32] The constant threat of military action of some sort by the Austrian Legion was a major preoccupation in the cabinet. Endless violence by the Nazis in Austria served to further discredit the régime.

At first it seemed that 12 February 1934 had solved the Nazi problem. Those like Riehl who argued for compromise could now insist that the government had shown its determination to deal with Marxism and had moved a step closer to National Socialism. But in fact the reverse happened. With the defeat of the Social Democrats the Nazis gained strength, some disillusioned activists in the Social

Democratic Party joining the Nazis in the mistaken belief that their 'socialism' was to be taken seriously. Even Habicht called for a truce in February 1934, only to start a fresh wave of terror the following month. It was thus immediately clear that Dollfuss's gamble of winning support from the extreme right by determined action against the left had failed, and indeed it merely strengthened the determination of the Nazis to smash his régime.

Notes

1. For a useful introduction see F.L. Carsten, *Faschismus in Oesterreich* (Munich 1977).

2. The excellent dissertation by J.C.P. Warren, 'The Political Career and Influence of Georg Ritter von Schönerer', London 1963, has unfortunately not been published. Andrew G. Whiteside, *The Socialism of Fools — Georg Ritter von Schönerer and Austrian Pan-Germanism* (Berkeley 1975), is a useful study.

3. Carsten, *Faschismus*, p. 13.

4. Heinrich Benedikt, *Geschichte der Republik Oesterreich* (Munich 1954), p. 377, for examples.

5. Reinhard Kühnl, *Die nationalsozialistische Linke, 1925-1930* (Meisenheim 1966), for an excellent discussion of this problem.

6. Carsten, *Faschismus*, p. 41.

7. The slogan comes from the Graz Heimwehr; ibid., p. 43.

8. Material on Bauer's activities will be found in his papers, BA Koblenz, 30a.

9. Carsten, *Faschismus*, p. 60.

10. Ibid., p. 105.

11. L. Kerekes, 'Akten zu den geheimen Verbindungen zwischen der Bethlen-Regierung und der österreichischen Heimwehrbewegung', *Acta Historica*, XI, no. 2 (Budapest 1965).

12. Klemens von Klemperer, *Ignaz Seipel* (Princeton 1972).

13. L. Kerekes, 'Italien, Ungarn und die österreichische Heimwehrbewegung 1928-1931', *Oesterreich in Geschichte und Literatur*, IX (1965).

14. Ernst Rudiger Prince Starhemberg, *Between Hitler and Mussolini* (London 1942). These memoirs are frequently dishonest but often revealing.

15. Carsten, *Faschismus*, p. 161.

16. Benedikt, *Geschichte der Republik*, p. 365.

17. Carsten, *Faschismus*, p. 167.

18. Ibid., p. 199.

19. Ibid., p. 200.

20. See: K-D. Bracher, *Die deutsche Diktatur* (Cologne 1969); A. Ciller, *Vorläufer des Nationalsozialismus* (Vienna 1932); Andrew G. Whiteside, *Austrian National Socialism before 1918* (the Hague 1962).

21. Rudolf Brandstötter, 'Dr. Walter Riehl und die Geschichte der nationalsozialistischen Bewegung in Oesterreich', unpublished PhD thesis, Vienna 1969, p. 150.

22. Carsten, *Faschismus*, p. 73.

23. Ibid., p. 134.

24. Gerhard Jagschitz, 'Zur Strucktur der Nationalsozialistischen Deutschen Arbeiterpartei in Oesterreich vor dem Juliputsch 1934', *Das Jahr 1934: 25. Juli* (Vienna 1975).

25. Carsten, *Faschismus*, p. 144.

26. Jagschitz, 'Nationalsozialistischen', p. 10.

27. Ibid., p. 11.

28. Carsten, *Faschismus*, p. 186.

29. Jagschitz, 'Nationalsozialistischen', p. 13 (note the printing error of the date).

30. Figures from ibid., p. 14.

31. Jens Petersen, *Hitler-Mussolini. Die Entstehung der Achse Berlin-Rom 1933-1936* (Tübingen 1973), p. 197.

32. This can clearly be seen in the caricatures in contemporary copies of satirical papers such as *Simplizissimus* and *Die Brennessel*, most of which are merely scurrilous.

4 THE ECONOMIC PROBLEMS OF THE AUSTRIAN REPUBLIC

Austria-Hungary had never been one of the great economic powers, and certainly was no match for Imperial Germany, but in the years before the First World War it had enjoyed a certain prosperity, and appeared to have a reasonably healthy and expanding economy. With 52 million inhabitants, of whom 28 million lived in the Austrian part of the Empire, it was the third largest state in Europe.[1] Yet even in the Austrian part of the Dual Monarchy only 23 per cent of the population were employed in industry, and 53 per cent worked in agriculture. In Hungary 69 per cent were still employed in agriculture. By comparison, in France 42 per cent were engaged in agricultural pursuits, in Britain only 13 per cent. Austrian industry was heavily concentrated in certain areas: Bohemia and Moravia, Silesia, Styria and the area around Vienna. The monarchy was thus in many respects a backward agrarian country, but with pockets of flourishing industry. With adequate supplies of raw materials and a high degree of industrial concentration, the economic situation of the country was rather more favourable than might at first be supposed.

With the collapse of the Empire in 1918 the new Austrian republic and Czechoslovakia were in relatively favourable positions. Czechoslovakia, with 34 per cent of the population, produced 45 per cent of the national income, and Austria, with 22 per cent of the population, produced 30 per cent of the national income. The remaining 44 per cent of the population of the Empire had only produced 25 per cent of the national income.[2] Vienna, as the capital city of a vast empire, was in a particularly privileged position. It was the centre of an immense bureaucratic apparatus, and the head offices of the great banks and insurance companies were mostly to be found there. Thus, although there were sizeable industrial enterprises on the territory of the Austrian republic, the fact that Vienna was no longer a major European capital caused severe dislocations and hardships.

Agriculturally the territory of the republic was by no means backward. The forests and the dairy farms of the alpine provinces were highly productive, and the grain production of Lower Austria was well above the national average. Thus the republic, with the exception of the backward Burgenland, inherited the most developed part of the old Empire, although Czechoslovakia had some of the most modern and capital intensive industrial plants. The republic had 90 per cent of the motor vehicle production, 83 per cent of locomotive production and 75 per cent of the production of rubber. But there were serious problems. The republic was desperately short of supplies of coal and oil, and could only meet about one-tenth of its fuel requirements. Austrian industry was almost totally dependent on Silesian coal which was now protected by high tariffs. Obviously hydro-electric power was the answer to Austria's energy requirements, but this could only be a long-term project, and was in any case an almost impossible undertaking for a country that was suffering from an acute lack of capital.

Although agriculture in the republic was well above the average of the old Empire it could not produce enough to feed the population. The war had disrupted agricultural production, which had fallen by 53 per cent since 1913. By 1919 the country was virtually starving. Most of the farms were too small to be effective productive units. Only 0.6 per cent of the farms were larger than 500 acres (200 hectares). But perhaps an even greater problem was what to do with Vienna. Talk of 'hydrocephalic Vienna', the Austrian equivalent to 'the great wen', was not entirely without justification. The republic had only 6.5 million inhabitants, but of these 615,000 were civil servants and their families, most of whom lived in Vienna. As Gustav Stolper said, German Austria was the 'bourgeois' among the peoples of the monarchy, providing the judges, civil servants, professors and officers, most of whom could find no employment in the small remnant of an empire of 52 million.[3] Old habits died hard. In 1919-20 state revenues were 6,295 million crowns, but expenditures were 16,873 million crowns. In such a situation it is hardly surprising that there was loud denunciation of Vienna and all that it stood for, and nationalists and racists found rich material for their campaigns of hate. '*Los von Wien*' became a popular cry. Multinational Vienna, the capital of a multinational empire, was now denounced as a seething mass of Jews, Croats, Hungarians, Italians and Slovenes which threatened the true

Austrian values of a peasant and petty bourgeois provincial way of life. Traditional animosity towards the capital was thus compounded in this new and explosive situation.[4]

A country that seemed to be but the pathetic remnant of a great empire, that was unable to feed its own population, whose industry was cut off from its traditional sources of raw materials and from its established markets, and whose great financial institutions had lost most of their investment outlets, seemed doomed. Shortages of coal and oil affected not only industry but also transportation and home heating. The demobilisation of a vast army and the inability of the economy to switch back rapidly to peacetime production further compounded the problems facing an economy that was near to collapse. These economic problems inevitably heightened the political crisis, as men were driven to desperation by starvation, cold and a sense of hopelessness. The situation was made still worse by a dramatic rate of inflation caused by the demand for scarce commodities, the economic dislocations caused by the war and the chronic indebtedness of the state. By January 1919 Austria's largest steel firm had to shut down because of lack of fuel. Until 22 March 1919 the Entente maintained an economic blockade against the Central Powers, making the import of goods from abroad almost impossible. It was only the exceptional efforts of the coalition government to control the economy and to lay the basis for a welfare state that saved the country from complete collapse, and the working people from utter degradation.

In this situation it is hardly surprising that there was a vigorous debate about the economic future of the new state. The simple and popular answer to all economic problems was that the republic could not continue to exist as an independent state and that an Anschluss with Germany was the only answer. Some thought of a Danubian confederation, but those who argued, in the fashionable parlance of the day, that Austria was 'viable' were usually dismissed as hopeless romantics. All states had considerable problems in adjusting to peacetime conditions, and these problems were greater in Austria than anywhere else. Austria had neglected its own natural resources for too long, and had been content to live off the other provinces of the Empire. Coal for Austrian enterprises had come from the coalfields of Bohemia, Moravia and Silesia, but now Czechoslovakia and Poland were demanding high prices for their coal. In the textile industry spinning had been done in Austria, the weaving in Bohemia, and the clothing manufacturers were in Vienna. Structural problems such as these made it all the more difficult to return to a peacetime economy.

During the republic the metal industry was only partly able to do so, and as a result there was chronic unemployment in this sector and many firms fell into foreign hands. Thus in 1919 a consortium of Italian banks bought Austria's largest company, the *Alpine-Montangesellschaft*, and two years later it fell into the rapacious clutches of Hugo Stinnes.

In the debate on the text of the Treaty of Saint-Germain Otto Bauer argued that Austria could not exist as an independent state and that Anschluss with Germany was the only possibility of overcoming the chronic economic problems of the new state. The vast majority of the writers on the economic viability of the republic agreed with Bauer, although their political positions were mostly totally different.[5] Indeed, it needed considerable intellectual courage for an economist to even tentatively suggest that the country had much chance of survival. Gustav Stolper, Austria's most widely read and respected economic journalist, never tired of proclaiming the gloomy prognosis that his country could not possibly survive.[6] Almost the only voices raised in opposition to this prevailing view came from foreigners. Thus the distinguished economists W.T. Layton and Charles Rist, in their report for the League of Nations published in 1925, argued strongly that the Austrian economy was distinctly viable.[7] The Czech economist, Antonin Basch, strongly supported this view, pointing to the very considerable economic assets of the country.[8] These views in turn were denounced as anti-Austrian and anti-German propaganda, the result of total misunderstanding of conditions in Austria.[9] To a certain extent this flood of literature proclaiming Austria's inability to survive as an independent state was a self-fulfilling prophecy. With the experts painting such a gloomy picture of Austria's prospects it was hardly suprising that confidence in the Austrian economy was lacking. Investments were inadequate, short-term speculation seeming to be a more attractive prospect. The statistics of industrial growth are misleading. Austrian industrial production grew faster than in Germany in the early 1920s, and faster than England in the second half of the decade, but the starting point was so much lower that these figures are hardly indicative of a healthy economy.[10] With low levels of investment and unsatisfactory industrial growth, unemployment became an acute problem. Only England with its harsh deflationary policy, and Germany with its obsession with rationalisation, had comparable records. In 1929 the unemployment figures were 3.7 per cent for Austria, 3.5 per cent for Germany and 3.7 per cent in

England. By comparison Czechoslovakia had 0.4 per cent and France less than 0.1 per cent.[11]

Another persistent problem was the balance of trade deficit. As late as 1929 only 67 per cent of imports were covered by exports. In Germany the figure was 97 per cent, in England with its massive invisible exports that are not covered in these figures it was 69 per cent, and in Czechoslovakia 103 per cent. To Otto Bauer this problem of the balance of payments was the key to Austria's inability to survive as an independent nation. He did not believe that the situation could be solved by a drastic cut in imports and an increase in domestic production because he was convinced that Austria would never be able to stand on its own two feet. He also realised that the social consequences of a strict deflationary programme would be disastrous. In fact Bauer was only partly correct. By 1937 Austria had solved the balance of payments problem by cutting back imports, increasing some invisible exports and improving the tourist industry. But at this was not achieved by any substantial increase of exports, which would have been exceedingly difficult during the depression, the social costs were very high. In fact the value of exports fell by 41 per cent between 1929 and 1937. It is thus hardly surprising that by 1933 unemployment reached a peak, with 400,000 workers desperately looking for jobs. The political consequences of this deflationary policy for the labour movement were profound, and strictly limited the possibilities of effective political action.

From the very outset the republic regarded itself as an integral part of the German state. On 12 November 1918 the National Assembly announced that Austria was part of Germany, and on 21 March 1919 the German constitutional committee accepted Friedrich Naumann's motion that Austria should be considered as an integral part of the new German state. The Treaty of Saint-Germain put an end to this dream, and also took little notice of the economic problems of the Austrian republic. Some sections of the treaty dealt with customs arrangements between Austria and the succession states, problems that were also mentioned in the peace treaty with Hungary. But from the outset it was clear that the succession states were determined to assert their independence from Austria and that the Entente powers would not tolerate an Anschluss with Germany. Article 80 of the Treaty of Versailles said that an Anschluss would be permissible if the League of Nations agreed, but it was clear that this would never happen. The argument that Austria could not survive as an independent nation was widely accepted, and was a major reason for the willingness of the League of Nations to provide loans. The victorious allies had decided that Austria should remain independent, and were thus prepared, up to a point, to pay the price.

There can be no simple answer to the question of the economic viability of the Austrian republic in the interwar years. That most Austrians favoured an Anschluss cannot be denied. It is less easy to determine how far the economic arguments were merely justifications for the desire for Anschluss, however sincerely they might have been felt. Most experts agreed that Austria faced enormous difficulties. A truncated country, cut off from its traditional area of economic activity which had been largely self-sufficient, ruined by a long and costly war, surrounded by states that were facing severe hardships, and forced to meet the harsh demands of a peace treaty, was bound to have to face tremendous difficulties. A bold and radical economic plan was needed to restructure the economy, yet no one was willing to tackle this problem. Rather than face the problems it was decided to try to maintain levels of consumption as far as possible, and to do so with foreign loans. The Entente realised that in order to kill the Anschluss idea they would have to do something to prop up the economy. In the first two years after the war $120 million were given in credits to buy foodstuffs, without which the population would have starved.[12] These early attempts were limited in their effectiveness, and governments were hesitant to become too involved. Sir William Goode's programme failed when the British government refused to grant further credits to Austria. The Frenchman, Loucheur, called for considerable control over the Austrian economy in return for credits, but these guarantees were not considered enough by the international financiers who were to advance the loan. Another scheme by Ter Meulen, in which the League of Nations was to be involved, was abandoned when the Austrian crown was further devalued.[13]

The most immediate and obvious problem was that of inflation, a problem that plagued all the states in the immediate post-war period to greater or lesser degrees. The situation was made worse by the government's attempts to overcome the difficulty by printing money. Within a very short space of time dealings with Hungary, Poland and Czechoslovakia were on the basis of barter agreements. Even the credits, such as the 800 million shillings from the 'International Committee for Relief Credits' in Paris in 1920, brought only temporary relief, and the political price paid was high.[14] Many Austrian firms in the succession states were hastily sold, from shipping companies in the Adriatic to steel works in Bohemia. Foreigners bought Austrian companies on favourable terms. The Ministry of Finance was able to use the money paid for the *Alpine-Montan* to pay for the import of coal and foodstuffs. In spite of slight improvements in industrial and agricultural production, and further foreign loans, the budget deficit continued to increase at an alarming rate. Wild speculation and a complete imbalance between domestic production and consumption was the major cause of inflation which resulted in a 7,000-fold devaluation of the crown against its 1913 value by August 1922. The government tried to lessen the harmful effects of inflation by subsidising food prices. By 1921 58 per cent of government expenditure was devoted to food subsidies, but by 21 December that year it felt obliged to stop these payments. The result was an immediate rise in prices and demonstrations by workers against the rapid decline in their standard of living. Attempts to offset this effect by indexing wages to prices failed. By 1924 the average real income of workers and employees was 25 per cent below the 1914 level.[15]

Excessive government expenditure was thus both cause and effect of the inflation. But most experts argued that inflation was caused solely by excessive government expenditure, and demanded drastic reductions in welfare payments that cushioned many Austrians against the worst effects of the inflation. Even the Social Democrats were unwilling to tackle the problem seriously, for although the party congress in 1919 pointed out that the root of the problem lay in the difference between domestic production and consumption, a remedy was likely to be unpleasant for the working class, at least in the short term. Rapid inflation brought spectacular profits to financial manipulators, thus providing ample ammunition to reactionary anti-capitalists and anti-semites, who blamed the workings of 'Jewish capitalism' for Austria's sad predicament. Inflation also destroyed the savings of the middle classes, making them more receptive to radical political ideas from the prophets of the extreme right.

There was general agreement that Austria would have to rely on foreign loans in order to expand the economy, and would have to cut back government expenditure, including the food sudsidies. Even the Social Democrats agreed in principle to these suggestions, as can be seen in Bauer's economic plan published in October 1921.[16] Although the Social Democrats called for tighter controls on foreign currency and increased taxation on those best able to pay, and hoped to link the reduction of the food subsidies to increase in industrial production, it is difficult to see how the plan could have been realised without further depressing the living standard of the working class. But at least the plan was a serious, comprehensive and intelligent attempt to deal with the problems of the Austrian economy. No other party or individual made such an effort.

By 1922 the inflation reached its height. Speculation against the crown became increasingly frenzied. In January the Swiss franc was worth 1,135 crowns. By July it was worth 5,750 crowns when bought in Vienna.[17] The government seemed incapable of taking decisive action. Seipel's finance plan of June 1922 called for the formation of a new bank of issue, a halt to the printing of money, an increase in taxation and a reduction in government expenditure. The Seipel government and its advisors from Britain, France and Geneva believed in the magic effect of covering one-third of the value of circulating money by gold. Thus the bank of issue took foreign currency, estimated its value in crowns at an inflated rate, and issued new currency. Gold and foreign credits that came from the liquidation of the old Austro-Hungarian bank, rather than forming the secure basis for a new bank of issue, simply increased the rate of inflation. Within a few weeks of the announcement of the plan the franc rose to 16,000 crowns. At the beginning of July 1922 the cost of living index stood at 3,672 (January 1921 = 100), but by August it reached 16,548. There was hardly any foreign currency to pay for necessary imports. Many firms did not have the money to pay their workers. The economy seemed on the verge of collapse, and the government had no solution.

On 7 August the government sent an *appel désespéré* to London. Lloyd George replied on behalf of the allied governments that the Austrians should approach the League of Nations, and added that there was little hope that the Entente powers would be able to help.[18] Seipel then visited Prague, Berlin and Verona showing that his skill as a diplomat was greatly superior to his ability as a financial expert. The Germans had their own problems and could do little to help Austria, but they were alarmed that Austria might be forced to rely on support from Czechoslovakia. Thus they urged Seipel to try to get help from the League, and failing that, from Italy. The Chancellor knew that he could play the Czech card against the Germans when necessary. To the Italians, Seipel proposed an extensive customs and monetary agreement that was worked out in some detail by Austria's foreign trade specialist, Dr Schüller. Given the rivalry between Czechoslovakia and Italy, and the close ties between Prague and Paris, this was a skilful move. Benes, the Czech Minister President, was horrified when he heard of the Austrian *démarche* in Verona and promptly informed his friends in Paris. Within a very short space of time the British and French governments announced that they would support an attempt by the League of Nations to salvage the Austrian economy. In September 1922 the League established a special committee to examine the Austrian problem. By October the plan was complete.

In the first of the Geneva Protocols, which Seipel signed on 4 October 1922, Austria agreed to uphold Article 88 of the Treaty of Saint-Germain and not give up its independence. In return the governments of Britain, France, Italy and Czechoslovakia, alarmed no doubt by Seipel's trip to Berlin, agreed to guarantee the political independence, territorial integrity and sovereignty of Austria. In the second protocol Austria was granted a credit of 650 million gold crowns. The third protocol made the granting of this credit dependent on major internal reforms, and the use of revenues from customs and the tobacco monopoly as a guarantee for the loan. Even though the income from these sources was greatly in excess of the yearly payments required by the League they were to be paid into a special account controlled by the League Commissioner, Dr Zimmermann, the mayor of Rotterdam. Austria had to agree to the supervision of its budget by the commissioner, to ensure that revenues were increased and expenditure reduced. The commissioner and his staff were to be given far-reaching powers, and were to be paid by the Austrians. If the Austrian government did not do exactly what the commissioner required he could cut off the loan. Above the commissioner was the Control Committee whose powers were never clearly defined, but it was clear that it could interfere in almost all aspects of Austrian economic life, should it so desire.

The protocols formed the framework within which the reform of the Austrian economy was carried out by the government in close consultation with experts from Geneva. The plan for balancing the budget could only be realised by draconian measures and was extremely ambitious, as can be seen in the projected figures.

	Oct. 1922	1923	1924	1925
Expenditure	672.5*	552.7	458.4	370.0
Revenue	215.1	332.3	448.2	489.3
Deficit/Credit	− 457.4	− 220.4	− 10.2	+ 119.3

*figures in millions of crowns.[19]

The Seipel government suggested that indirect taxes should be drastically increased, particularly on sugar, alcohol and tobacco, that a value added tax should be introduced, and customs duties, postage and railway rates also increased and 100,000 positions in the civil service abolished. Direct taxes were hardly affected and agriculture continued to enjoy a privileged position. Plans to build an extensive hydro-electric plant, which was essential for the economy, had to be abandoned due to the opposition of Czechoslovakian coal interests who feared a drop in exports.

A major problem with the Seipel plan was that increased taxation, high tariffs, price increases of bread, electricity and transportation all increased the production costs of industry, making it more difficult than ever to increase industrial production and to overcome the balance of payments problem by increased exports. From a political point of view the Geneva Protocols involved a serious diminuation of the powers of parliament. Parliament was obliged to give the government, and any subsequent government, full powers to implement the reconstruction programme without consulting parliament. This clause was particularly welcome to Seipel with his extreme authoritarian views.

The Geneva protocols and the reconstruction programme triggered off a violent debate which still rages in the pages of contemporary historians. Greater German nationalists saw the reaffirmation of Article 88 of the Treaty of Saint-Germain as a betrayal of the German cause. Social Democrats saw the whole scheme as an attempt to destroy parliamentary democracy, to undo the social achievements of the republic and to sell out the country to foreign capitalists. There can be little doubt that the plan can be severely criticised. The government showed little understanding of economic problems, did much to fuel the inflation that was at the root of the problem and refused seriously to discuss alternative plans from men such as Alexander Spitzmüller, governor of the Austro-Hungarian Bank, Gustav Stolper, the liberal economist, to say nothing of Otto Bauer. The loan was at the exceptionally low rate of 80 per cent, so that for a loan of 790 million gold crowns, Austria only received 632 million, and was obliged to pay ten per cent interest on the full sum. It is thus hardly surprising that the League found little difficulty in finding investors. The social costs were very high. The austerity programme caused increased unemployment and a drastic reduction in welfare services. Seipel had found a perfect alibi for his anti-social and anti-democratic policies. The Geneva Treaty was thus a further step towards the radicalisation of Austrian politics, and did much to increase the appeal of the radical right. At best it improved the rate of exchange of the crown, but it did nothing to improve the fundamental structural problems of the economy. Balancing the budget was one thing, maintaining satisfactory levels of employment was another. Austerity resulted in a fall in production in some sectors and rationalisation in others, both caused unemployment or underemployment. In 1922 there were 41,000 workers receiving unemployment benefits, by 1923 there were 110,000. The problem was particularly acute in the metal industry where 30 per cent of the workers were unemployed in 1925.[20] The disparity between the profits of the banks and the stock exchange and the poor performance of industry became worse after Geneva. It is no wonder that it became increasingly difficult to find enthusiasts for capitalism either on the right or the left, and that political polarities became even more marked.

Although it is easy to criticise the Geneva Treaty, it is equally easy to forget the extraordinarily difficult situation in which Austria was placed. A Danubian confederation that some proposed was a political impossibility. Anschluss with Germany would have been an unacceptable violation of international treaties. Franckenstein, the Austrian ambassador in London, proposed a private loan in the City, but given the attitude of the British government this was hardly realistic. The only remaining solution was a loan from the League.[21] Austria, as a small country suffering from the drastic effects of a lost war and a lost empire, could not possibly hope to set its own house in order, particularly in a world that was undergoing a prolonged stagnation with high rates of inflation. Different terms could almost certainly have been negotiated, and the effects of the treaty need not have been so severe, but there would have to have been some other Chancellor than Seipel.

The most immediate and salutory effect of the Geneva Treaty was a stabilisation of the Austrian currency. The bank no longer fuelled inflation by indiscriminate use of the printing press. Foreign confidence in the economy was at least partially restored, and Austria seemed once again to offer an attractive investment potential. By 1924 it was impossible to balance the budget, but the foreign trade deficit, although reduced, was still substantial. Government expenditure was only reduced by four per cent in 1923 although the plan called for a 70 per cent reduction — a totally unrealistic figure. Unemployment had risen substantially, but many of the 100,000 civil servants whose jobs were doomed were still at work. The Austrian civil service was grossly overstaffed largely because of a policy of equal opportunities for the nationalities of the old Empire, and also because many German-speaking civil servants had returned to Austria after the war. By 1925 the civil service was reduced by 84,362, but many of these were pensioned off with 90 per cent pensions.[22]

As Layton and Rist pointed out in their report on the Austrian economy for the League of Nations in 1925, the major problem in Austria was the low productivity of industry and the high level of unemployment. This could only be overcome by finding new markets, which in turn was dependent on better trade relations with the succession states. In the atmosphere of mistrust and neomercantilism that marked the post-war era this was an exceptionally difficult problem, and it was perhaps easier to dream of an Anschluss as the answer to all Austria's problems than to seriously tackle the question of expanding foreign trade within the given situation. Stabilisation thus did not lead to any marked improvement in industrial output, but it did set off a wild bout of stock exchange speculation. Speculators were prepared to pay two per cent per week interest rates on money borrowed for speculation, and as some shares rose tenfold within three weeks this hardly seemed too high a price to pay. Capital that could have been used to improve Austria's industry was thus frittered away in non-productive speculation. The interest rate was driven up to such an extent that it was reported that firms were paying up to seven per cent per month for bank loans.[23] Banks were borrowing from the National Bank at nine per cent and were loaning the money to their clients at up to 50 per cent. When the government attempted to reduce these absurd rates of interest in order to encourage industrial expansion, the banks used their capital for speculation rather than for direct loans to industry. When the Austrian banks did invest in industry it was more often than not in foreign concerns.

Rising prices and unemployment drastically reduced the living standards of most Austrians, but even the little man was busily engaged in stock exchange speculation. In December 1923 the leading financial journal, *Volkswirt*, sternly warned that looking upon stock exchange profits as an integral part of income was 'strengthening the deeply rooted tendency of the Austrian people towards frivolity'.[24] This speculative fever reached a height in January 1924, but by March there were ominous signs that the bubble might soon burst. By this time it seemed that substantial new profits could no longer be made on the Vienna stock exchange. Investors began to look for a new source of quick profits, and were convinced that they had found a sure winner in the French franc. Substantial profits had been made by speculating on a massive fall in the Austrian, Hungarian and Polish currencies. Between December 1923 and March 1924 the French franc had fallen by 50 per cent against the Swiss franc, and many experts were convinced that it was about to nosedive. In fact the opposite happened. A large loan from the Morgan Guarantee Trust to the French government reversed the tendency, and between March and April the franc rose by 83 per cent. Within a few weeks Austrian speculators lost an estimated 500 billion crowns, thus triggering off the stock exchange crash. In order to pay for these staggering losses, speculators sold their shares as quickly as possible thus ruining all the small investors who had not been involved in the more complex speculations against the French franc. Foreign investors withdrew their capital as quickly as possible, placing a tremendous strain on the crown. The collapse of the *Allgemeine Depositenbank* was the first of a series of bankruptcies that was to lead eventually to the collapse of Austria's largest bank, the *Creditanstalt*, in 1931.

The collapse of the stock exchange undid many of the benefits of the Geneva Treaty. Unemployment rose to over ten per cent. The balance of trade deficit was still excessive, and could only be kept down to 650 million gold crowns by higher tariffs and by the reduction in domestic demand caused by the crash. The inflation rate continued to climb, and the government was obliged to borrow money to pay the salaries of the greatly reduced civil service. Foreign credits became increasingly difficult to obtain. Montague Norman, the governor of the Bank of England and a stern believer in good financial house-keeping and deflation was horrified at the spendthrift habits of the Austrian National Bank. Such was the power of the Bank of England that Norman was able virtually to stop all foreign loans to Austria, and could force the Austrian government to maintain a ridiculously high bank rate of 13 per cent. Industrial recovery under these conditions was almost impossible. It took months of hard bargaining for the Austrian government to get the League to agree to a modest loan to modernise the railways. Eventually it was possible to reduce the bank rate to eleven and then to nine per cent.

In January of 1925 the new currency, the shilling, was introduced, with one shilling equal to 10,000 paper crowns. The new currency brought some order to the financial life of the country, for accounts often showed sums in crowns of different values, but the opportunity was not taken to collect back-taxes on gains on the profits of inflation by means of the currency reform. For the ordinary Austrian it meant that prices and wages were simply divided by 10,000. For industrialists and bankers it often meant additional tax relief.

Credit restrictions triggered off a fresh round of inflation, which in turn provoked a series of strikes. The wage increases that resulted from these strikes failed to keep up with the rate of inflation. Higher tariffs brought in additional revenues to the state but placed an even heavier burden on the consumer and made Austria's export position more difficult than ever. Foreign Minister Mataja, who supported the French idea of a Danubian confederation rather than the popular demand for Anschluss, tried desperately to persuade Austria's trading partners to reduce their tariffs, but to no avail. Austria's inability to increase exports was seen as the root of its economic problems, and the situation was made all the more difficult by the fact that sharp inflation had brought Austrian prices up to, and in some cases beyond, those of its trading partners. Blame was also placed on what were considered in some quarters to be the intolerable cost of the social services, inflated wages and ridiculously high rates of taxation on the rich, successful and enterprising. Layton and Rist, neither of whom were in any sense radical in their views, pointed out in their report to the League that the cost of the social services was in fact lower than in Germany and roughly the same as in Czechoslovakia. Wages were also lower than in Germany, and taxes on the entrepreneur were lower than in Germany, Italy and France. They agreed that Austria had to improve its exports, but quite how this was to be done in the atmosphere of the time was hard to tell.

The government continued to pursue a deliberately deflationary policy, maintaining a high bank rate. The power of the banks, in spite of seemingly endless bankruptcies and squalid cases of political corruption, was such that they were able to extract rates of interest far above the bank rate, even from their most solid respectable clients.[25] This policy kept inflation within bounds and did something to maintain the competitive edge of Austrian products, but it made investment for modernisation and improvement of industry extremely difficult. A distrust of the state itself made this situation even worse. As the republic seemed to many to be a temporary affair until the Anschluss question could be settled, many industrialists preferred to wait for political developments before making any major commitments. Various plans for customs unions, with Germany or with other neighbouring states, most of which were hopelessly utopian given the climate of the times, and which preoccupied politicians throughout much of the 1920s, only served to create further uncertainty and made it impossible to develop a viable economic plan for the country's future. In 1924 46 per cent of Austrian exports went to Czechoslovakia, Poland, Romania, Yugoslavia and Hungary, but high tariffs in the countries that once had been part of the old Empire placed a strict limit on expansion in this area.[26] Exports to these countries became less significant, dropping to 39 per cent of total exports by 1929. New markets were found in the United States and other overseas countries.

Austria countered the high tariffs of the succession states with high tariffs of its own. This protectionist policy suited the purposes of the agricultural sector, the most loyal supporters of the government. The farmers used this opportunity to improve productivity. New land was brought under cultivation, modern methods were applied, particularly the increased use of artificial fertilisers, resulting in high yields. Farmers' co-operatives were particularly important in helping the smaller farmer to increase his productivity and to reach a wider market. Some farmers were quick to exploit the new market for special crops, such as sugar beet which traditionally had been grown in Czechoslovakia, thus reducing the country's dependence of expensive imports. Agriculture was able to meet an increasing percentage of the country's needs and thus made a major contribution to improving the balance of trade.

In spite of the deflationary policy real advances were made between 1924 and 1929. Gross national production rose by 19 per cent, and industrial production by 40 per cent.[27] This was largely achieved by rationalisation and modernisation, which in turn often involved an intensification of labour and further unemployment. The economy was still two per cent below the 1913 level on the eve of the depression, and it would be a mistake to think that these were years of general prosperity and steady growth. Private consumption increased markedly; by 1929 it had reached 117 per cent of the 1913 level, a figure that was not to be surpassed until 1954. But this prosperity was very unevenly distributed and lacked sound foundations. With the exception of 1925 Austria had a permanent trade deficit which necessitated further foreign loans which were all too easy to obtain given the high rates of interest. These loans were usually short-term as investors were uncertain about the future prospects of the country and much of the money was looking for a quick return. Short-term loans were then invested in long-term projects through the intermediary of the big banks. When the depression struck and these funds were withdrawn this caused additional havoc.

Dependence on foreign loans was not the only form of external domination of the Austrian economy. In 1926 Austria joined the international steel cartel, and thus agreed to abide by its production norms. German steel firms were hardly interested in the overall welfare of the Austrian economy. After the collapse of the Stinnes empire, the *Vereinigte Stahlwerke* took over most of the company's Austrian holdings. Its concern was to get its hands on Styrian iron ore, not to promote the steel industry in Austria. In spite of this demand for ore by Germany, production was still below the 1913 levels. Industry was working well below capacity, in some branches of heavy industry as much as 50 per cent below. Industry seemed to be stagnating, and the country rapidly becoming a source of cheap raw materials. This trend meant that little was done to offset rising unemployment. Trade union membership dropped steadily throughout these years, in spite of electoral gains by the Social Democrats. Thus, in the best years of the republic, the labour movement was further weakened, entering the depression years divided and debilitated.

Some economists welcomed the inflation and the Geneva Treaty in that it drove little and inefficient companies to the wall, leaving the large and powerful companies to lead the way in a more efficient and effective economy. Countless small banks had disappeared, either by bankruptcy or by takeovers, so that by 1927 only four large banks were left: the *Creditanstalt*, the *Bodencreditanstalt*, the *Wiener Bankverein* and the *Niederösterreichische Escompte-Gesellschaft*. The *Länderbank* was controlled from Paris. The remaining banks were too small to be of great importance. Although the large banks had cleared the field of competition their position was far from strong. They had lost about three-quarters of their capital since 1913 through the effects of war, inflation and excessive speculation. And they were heavily in debt to foreign investors. By 1925 the relationship of domestic to foreign capital in the big banks was between 1:3.4 and 1:5.7.[28] The large banks were thus desperately short of capital, although this did nothing to restrain their speculative urges. For the moment this hardly seemed to matter. 1927 was a good year as the world market improved, and Austria profited particularly from the growing demand from Germany. In almost all sectors of the economy there were satisfactory improvements. But Austria still had a serious balance of payments deficit of 20 billion shillings which could only partly be met by invisible exports. Further foreign loans were needed to cover this deficit, and once again short-term loans were invested in long-term projects. The president of the National Bank, Reisch, although urging caution, suggested that his bank had sufficient reserves of foreign currency to pay back these loans, and that there was thus no need for concern. What he did not realise was that there was a shortage of shillings to pay the National Bank for the foreign currency should the loans be called in.

The relative prosperity of 1927 had almost no effect on unemployment. The number of the unemployed only fell by 1,000 and the rate of unemployment was four to five times higher than in Germany. Yet in spite of an overall improvement and a budget surplus the government continued its rigid deflationary policy, so that nothing was done to combat the chronic unemployment. Credit remained tight, so that many of the new share issues were simply to pay off current account debts, and many of these shares were brought up by the banks. There was very little new investment.[29] This relatively satisfactory performance by the Austrian economy continued into the summer of 1929, the hard winter of 1928-9 having been withstood without too much additional hardship. The collapse of the *Bodencreditanstalt*, one of the four large banks, shortly before 'Black Thursday' in New York, was the first striking sign that beneath the outward appearance of apparent prosperity all was not well. The *Bodencreditanstalt* was very closely connected with the Christian Social Party and also with the Heimwehr, so the affair was both a political and a financial scandal. The government sent the police in search of Rothschild, who was on a hunting expedition, and he somewhat reluctantly agreed to provide funds to help the ruined bank to merge with the *Creditanstalt*. Chancellor Schober proudly announced that he had used a machine-gun rather than a pistol to convince Rothschild to acquiesce. Some of the directors of the *Creditanstalt* tried to stop the merger, for they knew that their own bank was in serious difficulties, but in October 1929 the bank swallowed its bankrupt rival. The fundamental weakness of the *Creditanstalt* was that it was tied too closely to Austrian industry, its success or failure depended almost exclusively on the performance of industry. As the capitalist world entered its most severe and dramatic depression it should have been clear that without drastic and decisive action the bank was doomed. The bank had to keep industry provided with sufficient credits to keep going, particularly as it was the principal shareholder in a number of important companies, but it found itself increasingly unable to do so. The bank also lived too much in the past, seeing itself as the court bank of a vast empire. Its investments in the succession states were far too high, and often frivolous. As one example, the bank lost 600 million shillings financing the Rumanian sugar industry that had stockpiled sugar that could not be sold because its price was well above world levels and domestic demand was too low.[30] The bank had become too large, financing three-quarters of Austria's industry. It was poorly organised and badly managed. The industry that it controlled was in need of fundamental reform. On 8 May 1931 the bank announced its balance for 1930 which showed a deficit of 150 million shillings. After a long and often fierce debate parliament agreed to grant the bank a credit of 500 million shillings, for it could not allow the bank to collapse with the resultant almost total disruption of the Austrian economy.[31] In the course of the reorganisation of the bank it came under the control of an executive committee of foreign bankers, at the suggestion of Sir Otto Niemeyer who led a delegation of British bankers to investigate the situation, even though Sir Otto, as a director of the *Creditanstalt*, was in part responsible for the unfortunate situation in which it found itself. A Dutchman, Van Hengel, was made chairman both of the executive committee and the board of directors. Austria's main bank was thus now controlled by men whose main concern was with foreign creditors rather than with the overall interests of the Austrian economy.[32]

The failure of the *Creditanstalt* caused a run on the shilling. Negotiations for a custom union between Austria and Germany had caused a violent reaction from France and Czechoslovakia, and the case had been taken to the International Court at the Hague and to the Council of the League of Nations. In such a situation the French demanded a ridiculously high price for a loan to Austria, and the government, although in an exceptionally weak position, felt obliged to refuse the French terms. The British, anxious to protect the independence of Austria and their own investments, particularly those of the British Rothschilds, agreed to grant a loan of foreign currency to tide the Austrians over the immediate crisis, and complained of the 'blackmail tactics' of the French government. There is some evidence that the French decided to get their own back on the Bank of England for interfering in their Austrian policy, and began a massive sale of their sterling holdings, a major contributing factor to the devaluation of the pound in September 1931.[33]

As early as August 1931 the Austrian government made an approach to Geneva asking the League for help to overcome the crisis precipitated by the failure of the *Creditanstalt*. The advice from Geneva was familiar: save money and balance the budget. In the 1932 budget the government made drastic cuts in government expenditure, and continued propping up the shilling at a ridiculously high rate of exchange. The result of this policy was a catastrophic rise in unemployment which reached 24 per cent in 1933 when 480,000 workers were out of work. Many of these workers had been unemployed for a year or more. The attempt to find partial relief from this situation by means of a customs union with Germany was squashed by the International Court at the Hague by a vote of eight to seven, and this did nothing but strengthen France's determination to use the League and any forthcoming loan as a means of upholding the Treaty of Saint-Germain.

Credit restrictions, the reduction of wages and salaries, cuts in government expenditure and increases of taxation did little to alleviate the crisis. By December of 1931 the National Bank could only cover 25 per cent of the circulating money. Foreign capital was withdrawn. Production continued to fall. A conference in Innsbruck in 1932 attempted to grapple with the problems of the Danubian countries, but with little success. The Stresa conference repeated the conventional wisdom of the day: the crisis could only be overcome with even stricter deflation. Taxes should be increased still further, and government expenditure pruned to the limit. A moratorium on foreign debts was the only positive outcome of the conference. Austria was able to secure a further loan, the Lausanne loan, which in many ways was a repeat performance of the Geneva loan of 1922. Austria was once again subjected to the financial scrutiny of the League of Nations, and had to promise that its first obligation was towards its foreign creditors.[34] The loan was not difficult to obtain. The French wanted another guarantee against an Anschluss, having been badly shaken by the customs union scheme and by the not very decisive decision of the International Court. The British were worried about getting their money back from Austria. The League felt that Austria needed a shot in the arm so as to be able to keep paying back the original Geneva loan. A special envoy of the League, another Dutchman, Rost van Tonningen, who had worked previously with Zimmermann, was given wide powers to control the economy. His views were orthodoxly deflationary, and he called for further taxes, cuts, economies and substantial increases of indirect taxation.

It took some time to collect the money for the loan, given the parlous state of international finance. Half of the loan went immediately to pay the British and other foreign creditors. The other half went to pay off debts to the banks that the government had been obliged to incur because of its short-term deficits, particularly those of the railways. Thus the loan brought no positive stimulus to the economy, and no money was invested to improve the country's productive potential.[35]

Between 1929 and 1932 production fell by 39 per cent, exports by 47 per cent and unemployment rose by 97 per cent. Industrial production was more than 39 per cent below the 1913 level.[36] The measures taken by the government to overcome the crisis placed an intolerable extra burden on the working class. As unemployment benefits were only paid for a limited time, continued mass unemployment caused frightful hardships. Austria had unnaturally high levels of unemployment even before the depression, because of its inability and unwillingness to strengthen its industry, so that the effects of the depression were worse in Austria than almost anywhere else. From 1931 wages were systematically reduced, and cheap female labour was used wherever possible in place of male labour.

The Lausanne loan did nothing to save Austrian democracy. The experts from Geneva agreed with Dollfuss that the country's economic problems could only be overcome by authoritarian government. Rost van Tonningen, who was later to become one of the founders of the Dutch Fascist Party, wrote in his diary: 'The chancellor, Kienbock [Minister of Finance in a number of Seipel's governments, at this time president of the National Bank] and I agreed that it was necessary to close down the Austrian parliament, as this parliament was sabotaging the work of reconstruction.'[37] Rost van Tonningen energetically supported Dollfuss's anti-democratic policies, but he was an untrustworthy ally. After the assassination of the Chancellor he quickly joined the ranks of the murderers.

A persistent deflationary economic policy combined with an anti-democratic determination served to demoralise and weaken the working class while radicalising some elements within it. Dollfuss was determined to use the opportunities offered by the depression to the full. Once parliament had been closed down and the government began to rule by emergency degree, a series of measures were taken to further weaken the organised working class. 'Economic necessity' was used as an excuse for such political moves. Social security payments were reduced. Strikes were forbidden. The rights of workers to even discuss wages and working conditions were drastically reduced. The worker's councils elections of 1933 were postponed and in January 1934 they were bought under government control.[38]

Thus by February 1934 the condition of the Austrian working class was miserable, in spite of a slight improvement at the beginning of the year. With massive unemployment, the erosion of political rights and wretched living conditions the vast majority of the workers were demoralised, tired, hungry and lacking in a sense of common purpose and direction. On the other hand, a minority was becoming increasingly militant, enraged at the anti-social economic measures of the government and the conciliatory attitude of the Social Democratic Party leadership. They demanded action before it was too late. In the face of a pronounced swing towards fascism they had had enough. But the conditions in which the militants had to fight were hardly favourable.

Notes

1. 1910 figures.
2. K.W. Rothschild, 'Wurzeln und Triebkräfte der Entwicklung der österreichischen Wirtschaftsstruktur' in W. Weber, *Oesterreichs Wirtschaftsstruktur gestern — heute — morgen* (Berlin 1961), vol. 1, pp. 52-3.
3. L. Kerekes, 'Die wirtschaftliche und soziale Lage Oesterreichs nach dem Zerfall der Doppelmonarchie' in Rudolf Neck and Adam Wandruszka, *Beiträge zur Zeitgeschichte: Festschrift Ludwig Jedlicka* (St Pölten 1976), p. 86.
4. Ibid., p. 91.
5. Otto Bauer, *Die Wirtschaftskrise in Oesterreich* (Vienna 1925); Friedrich Hertz, *Ist Oesterreich Wirtschaftlich Lebensfähig?* (Vienna 1921); Erich Gebert, *Flammenzeichen* (Vienna 1927).
6. See Gustav Stolper, *Deutsch-Oesterreich als Sozial- und Wirtschaftsproblem* (Munich 1921).
7. W.T. Layton and Charles Rist, *Die Wirtschaftslage Oesterreichs* (Vienna 1925).
8. A. Basch and J. Dvoracek, *Austria and its Economic Existence* (Prague 1925).
9. The latter view in S. Schilder, *Der Streit um die Lebensfähigkeit Oesterreichs* (Stuttgart 1926). Schilder was a *Privatdozent* in Vienna at the time.
10. K.W. Rothschild, 'Staatengrösse und Lebensfähigkeit. Das Oesterreichische Beispiel', *Zeitschrift für Nationalökonomie*, 19 (1959), p. 305.
11. Figures taken from the *Statistical Yearbook of the League of Nations*.
12. Karl Ausch, *Als die Banken fielen* (Frankfurt 1968), p. 12.
13. Grete Klingenstein, *Die Anleihe von Lausanne* (Vienna 1965), p. 19.
14. Heinrich Benedikt, *Geschichte der Republik Oesterreich* (Munich 1954), p. 492.
15. For wages and prices see B. Kautsky, *Löhne und Gehälter* (Vienna 1926).
16. For details see Ausch, *Banken*, pp. 29-35.
17. Ibid., p. 43.
18. Klingenstein, *Anleihe*, for further details.
19. Ausch, *Banken*, p. 79.
20. Rothschild, 'Wurzeln', pp. 79-80.
21. See the remarks by Kerekes in: *Vom Justizpalast zum Heldenplatz* (Vienna 1975), p. 246.
22. For details see Viktor Kienböck, *Das öesterreichische Sanierungswerk* (Stuttgart 1925), p. 55.
23. Ausch, *Banken*, p. 121.
24. Quoted in ibid., p. 124.
25. For the bank scandals see ibid. Although a rather journalistic and one-sided book it gives invaluable information and partly makes up for the lack of scholarly works on the economic history of the republic.

26. Rothschild, 'Wurzeln', p. 85.
27. Gustav Otruba, *Oesterreichs Wirtschaft im 20. Jahrhundert* (Vienna 1968).
28. Ausch, *Banken*, p. 304.
29. Benedikt, *Geschichte der Republik*, p. 495.
30. Ausch, *Banken*, p. 345.
31. Klingenstein, *Anleihe*, p. 38.
32. Ausch, *Banken*, p. 383.
33. Karl Erich Born, *Die deutsche Bankenkrise 1931* (Munich 1967), p. 66.
34. Klingenstein has a much more favourable attitude towards the loan, but her arguments are not always convincing.
35. Ausch, *Banken*, p. 407.
36. Rothschild, 'Wurzeln', p. 88.
37. Klingenstein, *Anleihe*, p. 98. On Rost van Tonningen see E. Fraenkel (ed.), *Correspondentie van Mr. M.M. Rost van Tonningen* (Gravenhage 1967).
38. Hans Hautmann and Rudolf Kropf, *Die öesterreichische Arbeiterbewegung vom Vormärz bis 1945* (Vienna 1974), pp. 157-8.

5   THE ARMY AND THE POLICE

The creation of a new Austrian army to replace the old imperial army was the work of the Social Democratic Party and Julius Deutsch, who was Secretary of State for Defence in the first two years of the republic.[1] Deutsch argued that the army should be demobilised and replaced by a new volunteer republican army. Soldiers' councils were encouraged in order to stop the formation of Red Guards under Communist influence who might well have spearheaded a serious attempt to instigate a revolution in Austria. Like Noske in Germany, Deutsch wanted to steer a middle path between left and right and at all costs preserve law and order. In the interests of preserving domestic peace and preventing a revolution both were prepared to co-operate closely with the old elites; Noske with the army high command, Deutsch with the police chief of Vienna, Dr Schober. Unlike Noske, Deutsch was determined that the officer corps of the republican army should be quite different from that of the old army, for he realised that a sympathetic army was essential to the success of a Social Democratic 'revolution' in Austria. The Red Guards were incorporated into the new Volkswehr (people's army), much to the alarm of the bourgeoisie, and the new army was thus a strange mixture of revolutionaries, adventurers and even criminals, almost impossible to discipline and of dubious military value. Deutsch skilfully kept the Red Guards under control and jokingly remarked that they brought a little 'change and life' to the Austrian 'revolution'.[2] Unlike his colleague in Germany, Deutsch realised that the danger from reaction was far greater than the danger of bolshevism, and he was certainly not prepared to be the 'Bluthund' of the left as Noske was pleased to call himself. He was prepared to allow the formation of local defence units in the provinces, hoping that they would be in accordance with Social Democratic ideas of a militia; but in fact they were to form the nucleus of the paramilitary organisations such as the Heimwehr that were to plague the Social Democrats throughout the life of the republic.

The Volkswehr proved to be a fierce defender of the territorial integrity of the new state, fighting against the Yugoslavs in Carinthia, but in domestic politics there was less unanimity. Units of the Volkswehr, particularly the radical 41st battalion in Vienna, gave active support to the Hungarian Soviet republic, causing the direct intervention of the Entente.[3] After June 1919, when it seemed that the Communists might seize power in Vienna, the 41st battalion was disbanded and Communists were purged from the army. The Social Democrats could then do little but wait for the decision of the Entente and the outcome of the peace treaty and its military provisions. They wanted to have a voluntary militia, whereas the Entente insisted on a long-service professional army. Deutsch said: 'We want to make sure that the class struggles are not carried out by armed men. We want to make sure that quarrels between the classes, which are necessary, do not become a bloody civil war.'[4]

Deutsch, and his military advisor Körner, were determined that the new Austrian army, even if it could not be a militia, should be truly in tune with the political ideas of the new republic. Political education was thus strongly emphasised, not as in the case of the German Reichswehr in order to shut the army off from the main political currents of the day and maintain a strongly conservative and 'unpolitical' stance, but rather to make the army sympathetic to Social Democracy. Both Deutsch and Körner also favoured the creation of a trade union for military personnel to replace the soldiers' councils which seemed to have little effective use in the more settled times after the summer of 1919. Deutsch hoped that the union would emphasise the democratic nature of the new army, help the task of political education and mark a definite break with the traditions of the past. He argued that a union in the army was as logical as a union in the postal service or in the railways.

As the political power of the Social Democrats slowly eroded there seemed little hope that their military programme could provide the legal basis for the new army. Events in Germany, however, convinced many who were sceptical about the need to ensure that the army was thoroughly committed to the republic, and who felt that too radical a break with military tradition was dangerous, that such guarantees were indeed necessary. The Kapp putsch opened the eyes of many Austrians to the possibility of a reactionary coup and they realised that what they had tended to dismiss as Social Democratic hysteria was a very distinct possibility. Deutsch was convinced that without the help of the impact of the Kapp putsch the army bill would never have passed.[5] It would be a mistake to imagine that this new army, the Bundesheer, was created without severe political struggles. Indeed the coalition fell apart over the issue of the role of the soldiers' councils on 10 June 1920, and was only patched up again a month later in a provisional government, without a Chancellor, until the results of the elections, to be held in October, were known.[6] For this reason the army bill was a compromise, although the Social Democrats imagined that they had won a great victory with the soldiers' councils and with the close association they had established with the army in the first two post-war years.

The bourgeoisie was scared that the army was too much of a 'party army', the armed wing of the Social Democrats. The Christian Socials were determined to break the hold of the Social Democrats over the army, and Carl Vaugoin, War Minister from 1922 to the end of 1933, methodically set about ridding the army of its associations with Social Democracy. In 1921 the *Militär-Wochenblatt*, the professional journal of the German army, wrote of the Austrian army: 'The politically completely disrupted, communistically infected, and union-organised army is a reflection of the tragic condition of German Austria, and the soldiers' councils have completely destroyed the idea of the power to order and command. With its thirty thousand men, as allowed by the Entente, the army in its present form has not the slightest value for the military strength of the state — it is more of a danger.'[7] Yet in spite of these attacks, and the basically hostile attitude of the officer corps, the Social Democrats were able to maintain their influence over the rank and file, and skilfully used the soldiers' councils to stop the officers from too open an expression of reactionary and monarchist sympathies. The party was thus able to keep the army politicised in spite of determined efforts by the right to make the army unpolitical like the Reichswehr.

Carl Vaugoin, a protégé of Lueger's and a man of distinct organisational talent, realised that an unpolitical army was not possible. From this he drew the obvious conclusion that the existing political institutions of the army should be used by the Christian Social Party to establish its control, thus replacing the Social Democrats as the controlling political force over the Bundesheer. His close associate, the legal expert Dr Robert Hecht, was able to make a number of subtle changes in the army bill that greatly facilitated Vaugoin's task.[8] He could also count on the support of a number of senior officers, including the chief of the general staff, Jansa.

The army was thus directly involved in the political struggles of the day, a field where the Social Democrats and the Christian Socials tested their relative strength. In 1924 the most brilliant military mind of his day, a convinced republican and dedicated Social Democrat, Theodor Körner, resigned his position as inspector of the army. Körner found it impossible to work with Vaugoin, not only because of political differences and his determination to keep the army republican and closely associated with the Social Democrats, but also because he wished to protest against the deliberate cutback of funds to the army. As a result of the Geneva Treaty of 1922 the government was required to balance its budget, and the man who had been appointed to enforce these conditions, Dr Zimmermann, a Dutchman whose country at that time only had an army of 15,000 men, suggested that there should be a drastic reduction of the size of the army and that the War Ministry should be subsumed in another ministerial department. Körner estimated that as a result of these provisions the number of soldiers allowed by the peace treaty had been reduced by seven per cent of the officer corps, 19 per cent of the NCOs and 28 per cent of the rank and file. Of the remaining soldiers many were in fact civil servants and thus had little direct military use. For Körner the army had ceased to be an effective military instrument and had become a mere administrative organisation designed to look after military installations and equipment. Its sole military purpose seemed to be to put on official parades which were, for Körner, the result of an unfortunate hankering after a glorious past and a means of concealing the true misery of Austria's military situation. The Burgenland crisis and the fighting in Carinthia were clear evidence that Austria needed an effective army to defend its borders, and Körner argued that Switzerland had only been able to preserve its neutrality during the war because it had an effective militia. Körner complained that the politician Vaugoin had refused to listen to his military arguments against the reduction and reorganisation of the army with its emphasis on such useless luxuries as the cavalry, and against the refusal of the War Ministry to listen to practical military advice. The ideal of an army that was close to the people, a democratic and republican army, was sadly far from realisation, and Körner protested that the present government was frustrating all efforts in this direction. He wanted an army in which officers and men co-operated and were not divided by caste distinctions as had been the case in the old army, but the present political course was making this exceedingly difficult, if not impossible.[9]

Vaugoin used the opportunity of the debate on the army estimates to make a conciliatory speech in which he accepted in principle some of Körner's criticism and promised an increase in the size of the army as soon as it was economically possible. But Körner's resignation marked the end of an era. The Social Democrats knew that they had lost control over the army and that there was clear indication of it falling under the direct influence of the right. Increasing emphasis was now placed on the paramilitary organisations of the political organisations. The Social Democrats, fearing that they might lose the struggle for the army, concentrated on building up the Schutzbund. In spite of Vaugoin's promises, virtually nothing was done to increase the size of the army or to spend more money on new equipment. The army was becoming increasingly demoralised, uncertain of its role and resentful of becoming the object of party political controversy.

The growth of the paramilitary organisations was bound sooner or later to lead to conflict. On 23 January 1927 the Schutzbund marched through the streets of Schattendorf, a village on the Hungarian border in Burgenland. A counter-demonstration by war veterans, many of whom came from outside the village, led to fights in which a 40-year-old Social Democratic war invalid and a nine-year-old child were killed. Those charged with the offence were tried before a jury court in Vienna and were acquitted. Even the minor charges of manslaughter and of causing a disturbance were dismissed. The Social Democrats found themselves in a somewhat difficult situation. They had been loud in their demands that the cases should be heard in a jury court, but this tactic had misfired. On 15 July the *Arbeiter-Zeitung* published an article by Friedrich Austerlitz in which the acquittal was described as 'a dangerously frivolous game' and he asked: 'Is not this unconditional, provocative acquittal of men who killed workers itself civil war?'

The Schattendorf affair was not an isolated incident, but one in a series of political murders in which Social Democrats were killed by members of extreme right-wing organisations. A trial also followed the seizure of a collection of weapons hidden in a Vienna arsenal by the Social Democrats, the existence of which had been betrayed to Vaugoin by a Social Democratic captain, Marek. The Schutzbund was prepared to defend the arsenal against a unit of the Bundesheer that was sent to collect the weapons, and at the same time the electricity workers threatened to go on strike. The army was forced to retire, as it was again in a second attempt six days later on 8 March. Then, in an extraordinary about-turn, the Social Democrats agreed that the weapons should be handed over to the army on the grounds that

Marek was threatening to take the whole affair to the Entente. Having first threatened violent resistance and strike action, the party meekly gave way, leaving the rank and file frustrated and perplexed.[10]

In Vienna the situation was electric. The acquittal of the Schattendorf murderers was to many workers the final straw. The country was almost on the verge of a civil war. Only the reluctance of the Social Democratic leadership to become involved in a massive demonstration against the decision of a jury court, and the serious weakening of the Vienna Schutzbund after the seizure of the weapons in the arsenal prevented the outbreak of large-scale fighting. On the morning of 15 July the electricity workers went on strike and marched along the ring road. They were soon joined by other workers. As they approached the parliament building a small group of policemen tried to stop their advance but they were swept aside by the workers. The police chief, Schober, then ordered the mounted police to stop the procession. A number of workers were injured by sabre wounds. The crowd grew increasingly angry, marched towards the Palace of Justice, and built barricades. The police entered the Palace of Justice and began to fire on the demonstrators. The building was then set on fire and the hated symbol of class justice was destroyed. The crowd refused to allow the firemen to reach the Palace of Justice, even though the Social Democratic mayor of Vienna, Seitz, pleaded with them, and they would not accept any intermediaries from the party. Schober asked Seitz to allow the military to come to the aid of the police who were no longer able to control the situation, but the mayor refused. At this point the Schutzbund was alerted. Armed with clubs its task was to stand between the police and the workers, to allow the fire brigade to put out the fires, and to maintain the peace. But the Schutzbund was quite unable to control the situation and merely earned the contempt of both sides in the conflict. Schober then obtained permission from Chancellor Seipel to arm the police. Six hundred policemen arrived at the Palace of Justice. There followed several hours of bloody fighting in many parts of Vienna in which the police vented their violent hatred of the demonstrators.[11]

Had the workers been armed, a civil war would certainly have broken out in July 1927. Otto Bauer proudly announced that the party had saved the country from further violence, but in fact it had suffered a shattering defeat. The general strike on 16 July seemed to be a triumphant demonstration of the power of the party, but Seipel had no doubt that he was the real victor. Otto Bauer was able to disguise the impotence of the party with a new theory of the 'pause'. The party, according to this notion, stood between two revolutions, the revolution in the immediate post-war years and the revolution that was yet to come. The theory provided an excuse for the party's inactivity and it was only saved from total resignation by a romanticised vision of the struggles to come.[12] By keeping the army out of the fighting it was still possible to hope that the army was sympathetic to the working class. The police, aided in some instances by units of the Heimwehr, had broken the general strike, but the army had not intervened. In October 1927 elections were held for representatives (*Vertrauensmänner*) in the army. Among the men the Social Democratic Army Association (*Wehrverband*) got just over 50 per cent of the vote but received a minority of the positions due to peculiarities in the electoral system. 610 officers supported the Social Democrats, 1,700 opposed them.[13] From these results, which were immediately affected by the events in July, the Social Democrats had no reason to be optimistic about the army. As both the Heimwehr and the Schutzbund grew in strength and determination, the army became increasingly important as a counterweight to these paramilitary organisations. In 1928 in Wiener Neustadt, a town famous both for its working-class militancy and for its military acadamy founded by Maria Theresa, the army was called upon for the first time to keep the Heimwehr and the Schutzbund apart, and to avoid clashes that were anxiously expected.

As the army seemed increasingly to be needed to maintain peace at home and stop the various paramilitary organisations of the political parties from going for one another's throats, the call for an unpolitical army became louder and more convincing. There was some confusion about how, and in precisely what circumstances, the military could come to the assistance of the civil authorities.[14] The question of the power of command over the army was also somewhat vague, resting with the War Minister rather than with the President as was the case in Germany. The role of the Parliamentary Commission for Army Affairs created further problems, for the members functioned both as civil servants and as politicians, a combination that seemed appalling bastardy to the Austrian mind. Hecht's idea in pointing out these problems was to set the stage for a major reform of the army which would bring it more in line with the German model. An unpolitical army was to be created, free from close control by parliamentary bodies, such as the Parliamentary Commission (which was in fact abolished in 1932), and with political instruction devoted to propagandising the need for the army to remain above politics. Under the terms of the constitutional reform of 1929 the President was given supreme command over the army, a move designed by Hecht and Vaugoin to move the army further away from the political control of parliament. For the time being economic concerns were of paramount importance and the government was unable to devote its full attention to the question of army reform. The Schober government preferred to seek the support of Fascist Italy against the upsurge of radical nationalism in Germany and against the Little Entente with its sympathies for Social Democracy, rather than strengthen the army. On the other hand as long as the Heimwehr and the Schutzbund continued to play significant roles in the political life of the country — in 1930 the Heimwehr was represented in Vaugoin's government, with the Chancellor continuing as Minister of War — it was almost impossible to separate the military from the political. Both the Heimwehr and Schutzbund were determined to extend their influence as far as possible into the army and the police force to neutralise the effect of both in the event of a clash between the armed forces of the left and the right. As the army became more and more under the control of the Christian Socials, thanks to almost ten years of effort by Vaugoin, both the Social Democrats and the Greater Germans argued that funds should be cut back; the fact that these demands were made in the midst of a crippling depression made them all the more convincing. At the beginning of 1931 even Deutsch demanded a 30 per cent reduction in the military budget.[15]

On 12 and 13 March the Heimwehr attempted their putsch in Styria. The leaders of the Social Democratic Party were informed of what had happened by Koloman Wallisch and immediately told the Minister of the Interior, Winckler, who dismissed the whole affair as a 'drunken brawl'. The Schutzbund was placed on the alert, and the government was warned that unless something was done against Pfrimer and his men it would be forced to go into action against the Heimwehr. The army eventually moved, but on the advice of Starhemberg (who was closely associated with the putsch) it moved as slowly as possible to allow the Heimwehr time to disband, and for Dr Pfrimer to cross the Yugoslav border. The only casualties were from sporadic fighting between the Schutzbund and the Heimwehr. The actions of the government and of the army in March were thus hardly encouraging to those who hoped that the army was still staunchly republican and a determined defender of the constitution. But at least the army had acted, and there was no obvious sympathy for the putsch among the officer corps, even though many officers moved in right-wing circles.

As the political situation in Austria became increasingly tense, the army became more politicised. Army officers were involved in training paramilitary organisations in spite of a clear ban on such activity. In 1932 active officers ran for political office and were elected to provincial parliaments. The Social Democrats were alarmed at the growth of National Socialism within the army, and demanded the resignation of Vaugoin who, in their view, had allowed the army to be undermined by such reactionaries.[16]

In 1933 Dollfuss dismissed Vaugoin. As chairman of the Christian Social Party he was not particularly enthusiastic about Dollfuss's intention to create a new constitution along the lines suggested by Mussolini at their meeting at Riccione. Within the cabinet Vaugoin was in sharp conflict with Fey, in part because Fey wanted the army to give the Heimwehr the weapons that they had seized from the Schutzbund. Dollfuss's reliance on Italian support in the event of outside aggression tended to make him neglect the army. Thus both as Minister of War and as a Christian Social politician Vaugoin found himself out of sympathy with Dollfuss's politics. His successor, General Count Alois Schönburg-Hartenstein, was a 74-year-old professional soldier who had been born in Germany and had been an officer cadet in the Saxon army. He believed that the army should be completely unpolitical, isolated from daily political struggles, unthinkingly obeying the commands of superior officers. He reluctantly had to accept the system of elected representatives in the army but insisted that the best representatives of the men's interests were the officers. He was successful in demanding a substantial increase of more than 25 per cent in the army estimates, and promptly began upgrading the arms and particularly the transportation of the army, in order to make it a more effective and modern military weapon.

By February 1934 the army consisted of 25,000 men, which was still 5,000 below the maximum allowed by the Treaty of Saint-Germain. It was just about adequately equipped to deal with civil disturbances, given the fact that the paramilitary organisations with which they would have to deal had no artillery and inadequate transportation and were not as highly trained, but the army was quite incapable of dealing with an invasion by a foreign power. The most powerful gun in the Austrian army could only fire a distance of fifteen kilometres.[17] Most of the guns had a range of seven kilometres. Politically the army was still seriously divided. Formally all soldiers made an oath to the republic, but there were few wholehearted republicans in the army, and very few in the officer corps. Traditionalists looked back to the good old days of the Empire and hankered after the restoration of the monarchy. The more modern-minded were full of admiration for the Reichswehr, tended to the Greater German in their sympathies and often had a sneaking admiration for Hitler and his régime.

By 1934 there can be no question that the army could be counted upon as a safe defence against Social Democracy. Legally the army was required to come to the aid of the civil powers if asked to do so by the federal government, the provincial governments or by local police chiefs. Exercises had been carried out before February 1934 to ensure that such assistance would be swift and effective. In every manoeuvre the Social Democrats were seen as the obvious enemy. No plans were made for dealing with a serious putsch by the Heimwehr, even though this had already been attempted in Styria, nor were the Nazis thought to be a potential cause of civil unrest, in spite of constant terror attacks by the outlawed party.[18] On the other hand it must be emphasised that the army was lucky that the Schutzbund had been seriously weakened by frequent raids and by the arrest of many of its leaders, that the general strike was a total failure and that many Social Democrats were unwilling to follow the militants in a life-and-death struggle for the preservation of democracy in Austria. Had the Social Democrats been able to mobilise fully all their resources in February, an army of 25,000 men would have had extraordinary difficulty in mastering the situation.

The Social Democrats had hoped that the police force of the new republic, like the army, would be sympathetic to the party and uphold republican virtues. In the early years of the republic there was some grounds for hoping that this might well be the case. The police co-operated with party officials and with the Schutzbund, policemen were organised in a trade union, and the old animosity of the police towards the Social Democrats seemed to have disappeared. The Palace of Justice affair on 15 July 1927 was a dramatic and shattering demonstration that the Social Democrats could no longer count on the sympathy of the police.

Previous to 15 July 1927 the police had carefully avoided interfering with Social Democratic demonstrations. Party officials had always kept the police chief, Schober, well informed of their plans, and the police always remained discreetly in the background. Even on 1 December 1921, when the inner city of Vienna had been ransacked, the police remained out of sight, although a few Communists were rounded up.[19] On 14 July 1927 Schober was assured by party leaders that no demonstrations had been planned to protest against the decision in the Schattendorf case. Thus the police were highly alarmed when faced with a crowd which the Social Democrats were unable to control, even when the Schutzbund was called in to stop the crowd going on the rampage. The demonstrators were equally enraged at the sight of armed policemen blocking their path, for this had never happened before. The ensuing riot was thus as much an attack on the police as it was a protest against the court's decision on the Schattendorf affair.

After the burning of the Palace of Justice the government was determined to strengthen the powers of the police, and also to bring the police under the closer control of the central government. Schober hoped that it would be possible to include a reform of the police, which would include the formation of a federal police force, in the proposed constitutional reforms of 1929. For two years there had been a hotly debated question of the constitutionality of the Vienna street police being under the control of the federal government, an issue that had tried the legal skills of the constitutional court and which had still not been satisfactorily answered.[20] The Social Democrats for their part were determined to resist this move, hoping that at least part of the police force would be under the jurisdiction of Social Democratic mayors.

Gradually the police force became the executive of the political wishes of the government. Rumours of an impending putsch by the Heimwehr in Styria led the acting police president, Pamer, to mobilise the force. Starhemberg brought such pressure to bear on Pamer that he was forced to resign. Immediately after the trial of Pfrimer the police raided the Ottakring Worker's Home, seizing some hidden weapons. As this came immediately after an attempted coup by the Heimwehr, and as none of the units of the Heimwehr had been disarmed by the authorities, this was a clear indication to the Social Democrats of the bias of the police force and of the extent to which the government could count on the police in its struggle against the left.

The day after the Simmering affair in which Nazis had fought Social Democrats in a working-class district of Vienna, on 17 October 1932, Fey was made State Secretary for Public Security, and was thus responsible for the police. Fey made use of the government's emergency powers to increase the powers of the police, giving them the right to levy substantial fines, to usurp some of the powers of the judiciary, and at the same time drastically diminishing the rights of the people to appeal against police actions. In July 1933 the police could give jail sentences of up to six months for 'terrorist acts', and these sentences did not count towards any eventual sentence handed down by a normal court. In the provinces local security directors were appointed who reported directly to the Chancellor's office. They took over the responsibility which had previously been that of the provincial governments to 'maintain public law, order and security' and this included the right to control all meetings and assemblies and to censor the press as well as to seize weapons and munitions. In September 1933 the government began to open detention camps for political opponents, a significant step in the direction of establishing a new authoritarian régime clearly distinguished from liberal democracy.[21]

The same process that was noticeable in the army and the police was also characteristic of the administration of justice. Equality before the law was guaranteed in the republican constitution, but the practice of the law soon became a mockery of that principle. Particularly after the collapse of the coalition in 1920 the Social Democrats were increasingly critical of the administration of justice. As in Germany, right-wing offenders were usually given very mild punishments, whereas the full severity of the law was meted out on offenders from the left.[22] The Schattendorf trial of 1927, and the trials of those involved in the Pfrimer putsch in 1931-2, appeared to many Social Democrats as classic examples of class injustice, and they began a campaign for reform both within parliament and without. Their demands were for democratisation of justice, an increase in the power and authority of the juries, and the election of judges by the people as well as the use of lay judges as foreseen in Article 91 of the constitution. Seipel summed up the feeling of the right when he wrote in the *Reichspost* in 1929 that jury courts were Soviet institutions that were the first step towards setting up the Checka in Austria, and for this reason they could not be tolerated.[23] After 15 July 1927 the bourgeois parties began a massive attack on 'peoples' justice' with the fraudulent demand for the depoliticising of the administration of justice. The problem was obviously not quite as simple as that. Jury courts proved incapable of dealing effectively with political crimes. The Schattendorf murderers were after all tried by a 'Soviet' jury court. Jury courts tended to be mild, whatever the offence, and it just so happened that most of the offences were committed by the right.[24] Representing a seriously divided people, the juries were often confused and uncertain, easily manipulated by skilful lawyers and judges, most of whom came from right-wing circles. The Social Democrats were at a loss to know how to deal with this situation. They supported juries as democratic institutions, but they were appalled at many of the decisions of jury courts. They felt that a juryman's sense of common justice was a guarantee against a cold and bloodless application of the law. Yet at the same time they felt that a strictly formalistic approach to the law would stop judges from being given too much room to interpret the intentionality of it. Thus the Social Democrats could never decide if their interests would best be served by a strict adherence to the letter of the law, or by a generous interpretation of legal norms.

The Dollfuss government had no doubts about its attitude towards the jury courts. In March 1933 the number of jurors was reduced from twelve to six. Judges were no longer bound by the decision of the jury if they felt that it was favourable to the defendent, and could in such instances refer the case to the Supreme Court, which in turn could appoint a new jury.[25] In June the Constitutional Court was emasculated, so that any judges who resented the new course of the government and its policy of ruling by emergency decree had no means of appeal. By the end of 1933 the process whereby the opposition had ceased to be 'loyal' and become criminal, the classic characteristic of authoritarian régimes, was almost complete. In November 1933 courts martial were used for cases of murder, arson and severe damage to property. On 3 February a further step was taken to end the 'unnatural division' between judge and jury by forcing the jury to deliberate in the presence of judges, and each juryman was to give a full account of his reasons for supporting the judgement.

The government was not fully successful in ensuring a submissive collection of judges and state prosecutors. Many lawyers were Greater Germans, and had reservations about government policy. Some were sympathetic to the National Socialists. Extremely mild sentences against Nazis who were found guilty of terrorist acts were a source of considerable concern to Schuschnigg as Minister of Justice. A way round this problem was to use the greatly increased powers of the police to fine and imprison those suspected of political crimes. Schuschnigg thus ordered that the police should make sure that all those who were arrested for such crimes should be given the maximum punishment before being handed over to the courts, where they might very well be let off scot free.[26]

To make absolutely certain that the courts would be the willing servants of the government Dollfuss was strongly in favour of a constitutional amendment whereby judges could be removed if they were not submissive to the will of the government. The example of the Third Reich in this respect was considered to be particularly admirable. Unlike the Germans, however, the Austrians were concerned to preserve as far as possible the appearance of maintaining the rule of law. Posting of judges to other courts was preferred to outright dismissal, and courts martial were used rather than establishing special courts for political offences which would have been clearly unconstitutional. An order of 9 February 1934 gave Schuschnigg further powers to interfere in the operation of the courts, and in a number of clearly unconstitutional moves the government was given almost complete political control over the courts so that by February 1934 Dollfuss had been able to establish what Otto Leichter was to call a 'semi-dictatorship'.

Notes

1. See Ludwig Jedlicka, *Ein Heer im Schatten der Parteien* (Graz 1955); Kurt Peball, *Die Kämpfe in Wien im Februar 1934* (Vienna 1974); Anton Staudinger, 'Die oesterreichische Wehrgesetzgebung 1919-1934', *Oesterreichische Militärische Zeitschrift* (1971), pp. 151-5, 219-24.

2. Heinrich Benedikt, *Geschichte der Republik Oesterreich* (Munich 1954), p. 42.

3. Jedlicka, *Ein Heer*, p. 17.

4. Julius Deutsch, *Ein weiter Weg. Lebenserinnerungen* (Vienna 1960), p. 82.

5. Jedlicka, *Ein Heer*, p. 25.

6. Benedikt, *Geschichte der Republik*, p. 109.

7. Jedlicka, *Ein Heer*, p. 57.

8. For details of Hecht's activities see P. Huemer, *Sektionschef Robert Hecht* (Vienna 1975).

9. Jedlicka, *Ein Heer*, p. 64.

10. 'Pertinax' (Otto Leichter), *Oesterreich 1934. Geschichte einer Konterrevolution* (Zürich 1935), p. 44.

11. C.A. Gulick, *Austria from Habsburg to Hitler* (2 vols., Berkeley 1948), vol. 1, pp. 717-71.

12. Norbert Leser, *Zwischen Reformismus und Bolschevismus. Der Austromarxismus als Theorie und Praxis* (Vienna 1968), pp. 429-48.

13. Jedlicka, *Ein Heer*, p. 76.

14. See Hecht's comments in *Militärwissenschaftliche Mitteilungen* (1929), p. 391.

15. Jedlicka, *Ein Heer*, p. 89.

16. Ibid., p. 92.

17. Peball, *Kämpfe in Wien*, p. 8.

18. Ibid., p. 9.

19. Gulick, *Hapsburg to Hitler*, vol. 1, p. 737.

20. Ibid., p. 785.

21. Gerhard Jagschitz, 'Die Anhaltelager in Oesterreich (1933-1938)' in *Vom Justizpalast zum Heldenplatz* (Vienna 1975), pp. 128-51.

22. Gerhard Botz, *Gewalt in der Politik* (Munich 1976). A detailed study of the judges has yet to be made.

23. Ignaz Seipel, *Kampf um die österreichische Verfassung* (Vienna 1930), p. 235.

24. For a spirited discussion see Viktor Liebscher, 'Die österreichische Geschworengerichtsbarkeit und die Juliereignisse 1927' in *Die Ereignisse des 15. Juli 1927*, pp. 60-99.

25. Everhard Holtmann, *Zwischen Unterdrückung und Befriedung. Sozialistische Arbeiterbewegung und autoritäres Regime in Oesterreich 1933-1938* (Munich 1978), p. 55.

26. Ibid., p. 60.

6 THE SCHUTZBUND

Socialist parties were usually confused in their attitude towards the military, and the Austrian party was no exception. All condemned militarism as a fundamental evil of capitalist society, without having a precise idea of what militarism involved, and they were uncertain as to what should take its place in the new socialist society.[1] Some saw the answer in pacifism, others felt that as long as armies were regretfully necessary they would have to be highly professional and disciplined. Most socialists had a rather naîve faith in a 'people's army', in which the entire people would be armed in a vast militia that could never be used as an instrument of class oppression by the minority, as could the hated standing armies of the past.[2] It is thus hardly surprising that the Hainfeld Party Congress of 1888-9 called for the replacement of the standing army by a universal arming of the people, a demand which echoed the party's first programme of 1868.[3] Even so there was confusion as to what this involved. The radicals around Viktor Adler insisted that it was a revolutionary proletarian policy bitterly opposed to bourgeois pacifism, whereas others saw it as a means of national self-defence that avoided the dangers of a socially exclusive and politically reactionary professional army.

In the months immediately after the war the Social Democrats, under the leadership of their military expert Julius Deutsch, set about creating a new republican army, a militia made up officers and men who were loyal to the new state and who were able to function effectively within new forms of military organisation.[4] The Treaty of Saint-Germain put an end to this experiment, for the army was limited to 30,000 men and the idea of a people's army had to be abandoned. But the Social Democrats were determined not to give up hope and devoted considerable effort to drafting an army bill that would neutralise as far as possible the bad effects of a small professional army. The new law, passed in March 1920, gave soldiers the right to engage in political activity and kept the soldiers' councils and unions which had been one of the major achievements of the upheavals of 1918. The army was sworn to protect the constitution and to maintain law and order at home. As long as the Social Democrats formed the government such an army might have been ready to support the party, but men like Bauer and Deutsch were well aware of the fact that a bourgeois régime would quickly be able to turn the new army into a reliable instrument against Social Democracy. On 10 June 1920, when the Social Democrats left the government, it was clear that the party had failed to solve the problem of the role of the military within the bourgeois democratic state, and that given the alarming growth of paramilitary organisations, both within Austria and in the neighbouring states, it would not be long before the Social Democrats would be forced to rethink their position.

The new Austrian army, the Bundesheer, was thus neither a reliable instrument of Social Democratic policy, nor did it bear any relation to the people's army of the socialist theorists. Indeed it rapidly threatened to become yet another standing army, with only a few constitutional restraints holding it back from becoming an effective anti-socialist institution. In its search for an alternative military organisation the party looked back to the experience of the various self-defence units of 1918. With the chaos of a lost war and the collapse of the Empire, farmers and workers formed armed units to protect property and maintain law and order against undisciplined armed bands of soldiers returning home. Weapons were easily obtained, either from the returning soldiers or from government arsenals. Within a few weeks the country was brimming over with arms, and paramilitary organisations mushroomed everywhere.[5]

The farmers were the first to organise, particularly in Carinthia, Tyrol and Vorarlberg. Before long ex-officers were playing a leading role in organising these groups into an increasingly effective and politicised movement, the Heimwehr. Self-defence against marauding hoardes of half-starved soldiers thus became defence against socialism, and even against the legitimate authority of the state. The workers were quick to follow the example of the farmers, in part because they were alarmed at the prospect of armaments from the arsenals falling into the hands of their enemies, but also because they were anxious that the factories should keep functioning to provide work for their demobilised comrades. But the workers' corps was also formed of the most radical elements of the working class who were often inspired by the example of the October Revolution to work for the creation of a new Austria from which all those men and institutions whom they held responsible for the war would be expropriated. As both the workers' and farmers' military organisations grew in strength and in political awareness, each felt threatened by the other, until Austria increasingly became divided into two armed camps.[6]

From the outset the Social Democrats adopted a tactic of defending what had been achieved rather than launching an offensive strategy to rout the enemy. Thus there is clear evidence that the great January strike of 1918 could well have been the beginning of the Austrian revolution were it not for the fearful and cautious attitude of the Social Democratic leadership.[7] The refusal to help Bela Kun's régime in Hungary against violent reaction was as much a rejection of the idea of an Austrian revolution as it was of the experiment in Budapest. Similarly the Social Democrats were determined to control the workers' councils, in which the militants were strongly represented, so that far from being a means of pushing the Social Democrats forward they became instruments for the suppression of Austria's infant Communist movement.[8] In such circumstances it was obvious that the workers' corps would also become purely defensive organisations, leaving all initiatives to their opponents on the right.

Sympathy for the Hungarian revolutionaries was far greater than support for the left within the Austrian labour movement. In July 1919 the Vienna Workers' Council (*Kreisarbeiterrat*) voted in favour of a one-day strike in sympathy for Bela Kun's government. This gesture did nothing to help Bela Kun, but it certainly strengthened the determination of the Austrian right to crush any threat from the Social Democrats.[9] To many, even parliamentary democracy appeared to be such a threat. The violent repression of the Hungarian left in a terror campaign which began in August 1919, coupled with the growing strength of the organised right at home, made it obvious that the enemy was on the right, and that a threat from a revolutionary soviet movement seemed increasingly remote. In the following weeks new military formations were formed in the major industrial centres, the 'workers' battalions' and 'alarm battalions' which were closely associated with the local workers' councils. The result was the formation of an Ordnerwehr (special force) controlled by the workers' councils.[10] As the workers' councils were not party organisations, the Communists tried hard to exert maximum influence over this new military organisation, but they were hopelessly isolated and outnumbered, as were other left groups. Frustrated at every turn, the left could do little but abstain from voting, and thus abstain from exercising any influence over the military organisation of the working class.

In 1921 the Ordner placed themselves under the command of the Bundesheer during the Burgenland crisis, and units took part in the fighting against the Hungarians. Shortly afterwards the arrival of the Emperor Karl in Oedenburg posed the threat of a monarchist coup against the republic, and the Ordner were once again placed on the alert. The constant activity of fascistic groups in Bavaria, Hungary and Italy was also perceived as a serious threat, and the Ordner grew both in numbers and in determination. At the party conference in 1922 the importance of the Ordner as a guarantee against any further attempts at a putsch was stressed, but it was also argued that the army should be increased, on the somewhat dubious grounds that the larger it got the more like a militia it would become.[11] But the party was still uncertain about its attitude towards the arming of the proletariat, and many on the right had serious reservations. As a result, the party leadership did nothing to hinder the growth of a paramilitary organisation, but on the other hand it did little to encourage it.[12]

The refusal of the party's offer to join a coalition government in 1922 in order to help solve the economic crisis, and the negotiation of a substantial loan from Geneva by the Seipel government, were further setbacks for the party's attempt to influence military policy. The growth of the paramilitary organisations of the Austrian right, and the sharpening crisis in Italy, were further reasons prompting Deutsch to again stress the importance of strengthening the military capabilities of the party in his speech to the 1922 conference, held only a few days before Mussolini's March on Rome. But this stress on the importance of military virtues should not be taken as evidence of a radicalisation of the party. A party document on the role of the Ordner, written in May 1922 before the Seipel government was formed, and which was edited by Rudolf Löw, gives a clear indication of the party's views.[13] It was argued that the principal role of the Ordner should be to preserve 'iron quiet and conscious discipline', so that the party should not be provoked into foolish action, either by the provocations of the extreme right or by the *radikalinskis* within the party. By these means it should be possible to preserve the 'equilibrium of class forces'.[14] Thus the Ordner were supposed to act as umpire between the proletariat and the police, its very existence was to guarantee the equilibrium, while the proletariat was to follow meekly the orders of what amounted to a party police force. Yet at the same time it was argued that such a policy was part of the raising of the 'military consciousness' of the working class. The party was trapped in a hopeless contradiction. Nor could it decide exactly how the proletariat could be 'militarised'. Some thought that the Ordner should be a highly disciplined and apolitical group, others that it should be closely associated with the rank and file of the party, forming a militant elite. It was a struggle between the traditional ideas of conventional ex-officers and those who tried to formulate a new military philosophy appropriate for a socialist party. This debate was to be crucial for the future of the Schutzbund and the outstanding spokesmen of the two sides were Major Alexander Eifler and General Theodor Körner.[15]

The triumph of fascism in Italy and the mounting tension between the workers and the Heimwehr, which was first to come to a head in the Judenburg affair in November 1922, were further evidence that the Social Democrats had to prepare for an increasingly bitter struggle.[16] It became clear to many Austrian socialists that fascism could only be stopped by the determined and united effort of the entire working class, and that if necessary fascist terror would have to be met with appropriate military action by party militants. Individual acts of violence would not be enough, only the organised mass action of a highly trained party army could stem the tide of fascism.[17] The failure of the military actions of the Communist Party of Germany (KPD) in 1921 and 1923 showed that weapons and courage were not enough to make an effective military force. Careful strategic planning and training were essential.[18] For the time being the debate over the nature of such a force was conducted at a very basic level — Eifler arguing that the party should, in effect, create an army that was well disciplined and trained as any other; the opposition rationalising their fears that such an army would be a provocation to the right and lead to an 'arms race' by condemning Eifler's ideas as old-fashioned militarism dressed in red. It was not until 1924, when Körner joined the party, that the debate was to become a fundamental discussion of the military strategy of the Social Democratic Party, in which Körner was soon to prove himself one of the outstanding military theorists of the socialist tradition.

By early 1923 the decision had been taken to reorganise the Ordner and to form a more effective military organisation to be called the Republican Defence League (*Republikanischer Schutzbund* or '*Resch*'). On 19 February the Vienna Schutzbund was formally constituted. The new organisation was placed under the direction of the local workers' councils, and when these councils ceased to exist in 1924 it was controlled by the Social Democratic Party.[19] On 12 April 1923 the statutes of the Schutzbund were formally approved by the federal Ministry for Internal Affairs and Education. In the statutes the purpose of the Schutzbund was clearly stated. Its aim was to defend the constitution, to help the authorities maintain law and order and to protect the government against any attempted putsch, to provide assistance in the event of natural catastrophes and to protect meetings held by republican organisations. The statutes further claimed that the Schutzbund was a non-military organisation devoted to the development of the minds and bodies of its members, placing a particular emphasis on marches and band music, 'in order to preserve march and folk music'. In short, the Schutzbund sounds in the statutes like an organisation of overgrown boy-scouts, with a typically Austrian love for marching bands.

In the course of the year Schutzbund units were formed in all the federal states, with the exception of the Burgenland where all paramilitary organisations were forbidden due to the sensitive political situation. The provincial organisations enjoyed considerable autonomy. Through the means of a complex organisational structure the Schutzbund was gradually to become the private army of the Social Democratic Party, and in the process was to lose many dedicated members, particularly from the Communist Party, and much of its original spirit.

The new organisation was soon involved in an endless series of confrontations with the military organisations of the right. In November 1923 the Schutzbund was placed on a general alert when it was feared that Hitler's attempted coup in Munich might trigger off similar attempts in Austria. Had the Schutzbund been put to the test there is probably little that it could have done with its infant organisation and lack of arms and equipment, but it was a useful test of the command structure and a political gesture that could not be ignored. In this period the links between the Schutzbund and the unions were also strengthened. The unions gave substantial financial support to the Schutzbund, which in turn acted as a kind of proletarian police force to maintain discipline during strikes.

The Schutzbund was also particularly anxious that 'tradition', that powerful and emotive word in interwar Austria, should not become the exclusive province of the army and the organisations of the right. The Schutzbund consciously propagated the idea of the 'republican tradition', and even went as far as to support the foundation of a curious hybrid, the 'Republican Deutschmeister', in an attempt to use the glamour and nostalgia of a great regiment to win recruits for socialism.[20] As no other such organisations were formed it may be assumed that this remarkable experiment was a failure. On the other hand there can be little doubt that the Schutzbund was particularly attractive to those who liked the rigmarole of uniforms, parades,

bands and military festivities. Julius Deutsch argued strongly that
fascists should not be allowed to have a monopoly of such activities and
argued for an 'intelligent exploitation of naïve popular sentiments'.[21]
In more practical terms he suggested that such exploits would provide
inspiration for the rank and file and impress the opposition. Marches
and festivals were of course excuses for excessive drinking, and the
Schutzbund leadership was careful to stress the harmful effects of
alcohol on 'proletarian discipline'. Drinking was thus strictly forbidden on all such occasions, although it is hard to believe that such a
draconic measure was ever strictly enforced.

It would be a mistake to imagine that the Schutzbund, even in these
early years, was a kind of socialist carnival club. Three Social
Democrats were killed by Nazis in Vienna in 1923. In the following
year the Nazis tried to break up a workers' gymnastic meeting in
Korneuburg. In the course of the fighting eleven members of the
Schutzbund were seriously wounded.[22] Leopold Miller, a Social
Democratic leader in Mödling, was killed in the course of a further
confrontation between Nazis and the Schutzbund. The reaction of the
right to these episodes was to claim that the Schutzbund was planning
a *coup d'état*, a belief that was supported by totally spurious evidence
of a massive conspiracy that would involve the plunder of churches
and monasteries, the disarmament of the army, the smuggling of
weapons from Czechoslovakia and the seizure of farmers' crops.[23]
Another charge was that the Schutzbund was an instrument of French
policy designed to keep Bavaria in check, and that Social Democratic
support for the idea of an Anschluss was thus a cynical fraud designed
to fool the Austrian people. The Nazis further claimed that the
Schutzbund was to be used to protect the Zionist Congress held in
Vienna in 1925, a charge which prompted the Social Democrats to
point out that they did not support 'bourgeois-nationalist elements'.
In spite of the denials of the Vienna police chief, Schober, the
Schutzbund was accused of the murder of a young man killed in the
course of a street fight in the Praterstern in Vienna. The more the
Schutzbund protested against such unfounded charges, the more the
right was convinced that they had something to hide.

Although the government frequently joined in these attacks on the
Schutzbund, mounting tension between Austria and Italy, caused by
the rather scatter-brained suggestion that Austria should form a
federation with Yugoslavia, Czechoslovakia and Rumania, prompted
the government to suggest that the Schutzbund should support the
army in the Tyrol against a possible Italian attack. After some

awkward preliminary negotiations, General Wittas and Colonel Cless, representing the War Ministry, met with Julius Deutsch, Körner and the Tyrol Schutzbund representative, Michael Viertler, in the Schutzbund's Vienna offices on 21 December 1925.[24] Deutsch assured his visitors that one of the Schutzbund's prime concerns, as stated in its statutes, was the defence of the republic, and promised 1,000 men from the Tyrol with further reserves if necessary from other parts of Austria. The army in return agreed to arm, equip and feed the men. In the course of further meetings in the Tyrol and in Vienna general agreement was reached in a remarkably cordial atmosphere; however, as the crisis with Italy died down, these arrangements were never put to the test. But at least relationships between the Schutzbund and the army seemed to be settled for any similar future occasion. The attitude of the authorities was now hopelessly contradictory. On the one hand they saw the Schutzbund as a patriotic militia that was willing to provide invaluable support to Austria's minute army, on the other hand they persisted in regarding it as a band of socialist ruffians devoted to violence, murder and the dictatorship of the proletariat. In part this was a consequence of a similar lack of unified purpose within the ranks of the Schutzbund. Some were anxious to stress its purely defensive role and its respectability, others saw it as the vanguard of the proletariat, an instrument for the creation of a new society. The Schutzbund was, however, essentially a defensive institution, both tactically and ideologically.

The defensive nature of the Schutzbund was further emphasised at a meeting in Vienna in July 1926 of Schutzbund leaders. At the conclusion of the meeting the foundation of an 'International Commission for Defence against Fascism' was announced. The formation of the commission was the result of a long process dating back to the Matteotti murder in 1924 when the French socialist Paul Faure had suggested to Friedrich Adler, the secretary of the Socialist International, that a concentrated international effort to combat fascism was essential. International fascism would be combated by international anti-fascism, and perhaps in this manner the traumatic failure of the Second International in 1914 could be atoned. The commission was a loose organisation with its offices in Vienna. Julius Deutsch was appointed chairman.[25] The commission collected material on fascism and published leaflets warning against the dangers of fascism, but it had no real understanding of the nature of fascism and no clearly defined policy on how to deal with a serious threat from fascistic movements; it was therefore unable to make any major contribution to the anti-fascist struggle.[26]

In October 1926 Seipel became Chancellor and began a skilful and systematic attack on Social Democracy. A few days later in Linz the party held its conference at which the Linz programme was approved. This programme is one of the key documents of Austro-Marxism. It stressed the need for 'defensive violence' which was clearly to be the province of the Schutzbund, for the Linz conference established close organisational links between the party and what was now in effect its military arm. Otto Bauer, the architect of the Linz programme, realised the need for violence in the defence of basic democratic rights, and yet as a humanist of profound moral convictions he had a deep horror of violence and would never give an order that might result in the loss of human life, however worthy the cause. Körner was one of the very few who realised that it was impossible to fight a war, however morally justified it might be, with an army of pacifists.[27] It was the tragedy of Austrian Social Democracy that the leadership had such a clear vision of the forthcoming struggle between the bourgeoisie and the working class, and urged that civil war was necessary if democracy were to be threatened with destruction by the right, and yet they were paralysed by the thought of the consequences of such a policy, even though so many of the rank and file had no such reservations. The bourgeois parties did not share these inhibitions, so that when the final clash came they were bound to triumph.

Under these circumstances, talk of a civil war in defence of democracy could be used by the bourgeois parties to argue that the Schutzbund was an organisation that was systematically preparing for civil war. Incidents of violence continued to occur between the Heimwehr and the Schutzbund, reaching a climax in the Schattendorf affair of January 1927.[28] The violence of the right caused a marked increase in the number of Schutzbund volunteers, in some cases entire factories either joining or giving financial support to the organisation.

Of greater political significance was the arsenal affair of March 1927.[29] During the 'revolution' of 1918 the Social Democrats had been quick to take over control of all arsenals and munitions depots in order that the reactionaries would be denied this major source of weapons. To make doubly sure that this would not happen, many of the weapons were carefully hidden in underground passages that were then bricked up. The secret of these concealed arms was known exclusively to trusted Social Democrats. But the fear that the Entente powers might start making awkward demands obliged the Social Democrats to come to an agreement with the Christian Socials. Under the terms of this agreement weapons could not be moved from one place to another without the consent of both parties. The Christian Socials, however, had no knowledge of the hidden weapons, which were now regarded as belonging to the Social Democratic Party. By 1922, when the Social Democrats were no longer in the government, it was clear that further concessions would have to be made. Vaugoin, as War Minister, managed to gain further concessions for the Christian Socials, but until the end of 1926 the officer in charge of the arsenals was a Social Democrat, who in effect acted as a representative of the party. In 1926 the 1922 pact was revised so that a Christian Social representative now shared the responsibility of supervising the weapons in these depots. By this time it was clear that the object of this new pact was for the Christian Socials to find out the full details of the hidden weapons, a task that was made all the easier by the fact that the Social Democratic officer proved to be amenable to bribes. The only immediate problem was that the Social Democratic officer, Marek, had only a vague idea where the weapons were hidden.

The election campaign of 1927 gave the Christian Socials a golden opportunity to press forward. If they could find the hidden weapons they could discredit the Social Democrats' campaign for honest and open government and win a trump card in their effort to show that the Schutzbund was preparing in an underhand and dishonest way for civil war.

The party and the Schutzbund were indeed in a curious position. The party now had effective control over the Schutzbund, but local units were desperately short of weapons. The weapons held in reserve were controlled in a peculiar condominium with the class enemy, and the Social Democrats' chief representative was corrupt. The attitude of the army and the police was also uncertain. About half of the soldiers supported the Social Democratic Military Association (*Militärverband*) and most of the police force were members of socialist trade unions.[30] Thus, when on 2 March 1927 a group of Christian Social soldiers entered the Vienna arsenal and took away some of the hidden weapons that had been discovered, the Schutzbund was uncertain how to react. The response of the rank and file in the 10th district of Vienna, who were given responsibility for the Vienna arsenal, was immediate and violent. They called for a declaration of civil war, saying that if the Social Democrats backed down now there would never be a second chance, as the relative strength of the Christian Socials was increasing every day. The Schutzbund leadership, however, was anxious to avoid any violence and hoped to find a negotiated solution to the problem.

Workers from all parts of Vienna surrounded the arsenal. An armed unit of the Schutzbund arrived on the scene. After some tense hours the army was withdrawn from the arsenal, and a relative calm was restored. Negotiations between the two sides began, starting with a conversation between Seipel, the Chairman of the Social Democratic Party and the mayor of Vienna. The next move was dictated by Marek. It appears that the Christian Socials refused to pay the bribe that he demanded for betraying the whereabouts of the weapons, and that he then threatened to inform the Entente if he was not paid in full. This both the Christian Socials and the Social Democrats wished to avoid, and it was therefore agreed that the weapons should be moved to another location and that the condominium should be preserved. The Social Democrats were able to get a considerable number of 'their' weapons out of the arsenal before the bulk was moved. Many also remained hidden in the arsenal, but the government was unwilling to risk another explosive incident and no further searches were made.

The arsenal affair was undoubtedly a setback for the Social Democrats, and Seipel had handled the situation cautiously but firmly. The Social Democrats had shown their teeth. The threat of an electricity strike had been a major reason why the troops had been withdrawn from the arsenal. The Schutzbund had been mobilised, and the government was clearly as afraid of a possible civil war as was the leadership of the Social Democratic Party. The Social Democrats had kept most of their weapons, and the condominium stayed intact. But Seipel and Vaugoin had discredited the party in the eyes of the bourgeoisie, which was now more than ever prepared to believe the story that the Linz programme was a call for civil war. Perhaps even more important was the fact that the party militants began to feel increasingly isolated from the leadership. The theory of 'defensive violence' was contradictory to the defensive conciliation of party practice. An increase of 228,000 votes for the party in the subsequent elections was some compensation, but this was still a long way off from the majority for which they hoped. Seipel lost votes, and the campaign against 'Social Democratic terror' clearly had not paid off at the polls. Seipel suffered a moral defeat. The Social Democrats celebrated an electoral victory. But the class forces remained the same. The party had been put to the test and had failed to crush the reactionaries, as it promised it would do in its recent programme.

For Vaugoin there was no doubt that the convenient villain of the piece was Marek. In a curious conversation with Deutsch, one month after the arsenal affair he described Marek as 'the greatest scoundrel I know'. Vaugoin argued that he would have taken all the weapons that were hidden in the arsenal were it not for the fact that he was scared of an armed confrontation with the Schutzbund, adding that he knew perfectly well that weapons were still hidden in the arsenal. He knew that Marek's disreputable behaviour would place Deutsch on the defensive, and he used this knowledge for all its worth. The 'sick idiot', 'criminal' and 'vagabond' Marek was thus a godsend to Vaugoin throughout the entire affair. He knew that he had scored against the Social Democrats, but being far from an extremist he had no desire to risk driving the advantage home.[31]

On the evening of 14 July 1927 the verdict of the Schattendorf murder case was handed down. The accused were found not guilty, a decision that outraged the workers of Vienna and which resulted in spontaneous demonstrations against what was felt to be a flagrant example of class justice. At three in the morning on 15 July the electricity workers of Vienna decided to call a protest strike which began three hours later. The party leadership was determined not to become involved in any strike or demonstration, and hoped that rousing editorials and protest notes would be enough to placate the rank and file.[32] The suggestion that the Schutzbund should be mobilised was turned down on the grounds that it might be seen as an attempt to provoke the authorities.[33] The police chief of Vienna was told that there were no demonstrations planned against the court decision, and Deutsch and Seitz did their utmost to stop the strike.[34]

By the early morning of 15 July it was clear that the party leadership was unable to control the spontaneous indignation and outrage of the Viennese workers. It was suggested that units of the Schutzbund should be used to control the crowds, but once again this was rejected on the grounds that this might be seen as evidence that the demonstration had been planned by party headquarters. It was only when news of violence between the demonstrators and the police on the ring road reached party headquarters was it decided to mobilise part of the Schutzbund in an attempt to control a situation that appeared to be getting out of control. By this time it was too late. Many of the key members of the Schutzbund were among the demonstrators, and thus could not be found. Meanwhile the Palace of Justice, the police station in the Lichtenfelsgasse and the editorial offices of the *Reichspost* were already in flames.

The Schutzbund was now placed in an exceedingly difficult situation. It was called upon to protect the workers from the excesses of the police, but also to hold back the demonstrators from any further acts of violence. As a result they found themselves hopelessly alienated from both sides in the clash. They were able to clear the way so that firemen could fight the flames. A small group under General Körner entered the blazing Palace of Justice, and rescued a number of policemen and civilians who preferred to stay in the building rather than risk what they imagined was a lynching mob outside. Medical units of the Schutzbund also treated wounded policemen. But such acts of disinterested heroism were ignored by the police. When the police began firing at the crowds they took careful aim at the uniformed Schutzbündler, even though they were unarmed. Their situation was thus hopeless. They could not support the police against the workers, but neither could they give fullhearted support to the workers, for then it would appear that the burning of the Palace of Justice had been planned by the party. Unable to find any way out of this cruel dilemma, the Schutzbund was ordered to withdraw.

During the evening of 15 July party leaders met with prominent trade unionists to discuss further action. There were those, among them Dr Wilhelm Ellenbogen who was ideologically on the right of the party, who argued that the time had come to fight. But the majority of those present rejected such a radical proposal and it was decided to call a one-day general strike, mobilise the Schutzbund and at the same time ban all demonstrations. On the following day there were isolated incidents of violence and clashes with the police, particularly in the outer districts of Vienna, but the immediate crisis appeared to be over.

After the events of 15 July it was obvious that the party had to reconsider its position. A severe defeat had been suffered which clearly showed that the political situation had been misunderstood. Bauer's formula of the 'equilibrium of class forces' could no longer be seriously upheld.[35] The notion that the police sympathised with the workers was clearly a myth, although some socialists persisted in arguing that the fact that the army had not taken part in the violence which had resulted in some 90 fatalities showed that the army, unlike the police, was basically behind the workers. Seitz suggested the formation of a special Gemeindeschutzwache (proletarian police force) which would separate the police from demonstrators in the event of further riots liable to leave the workers helplessly exposed to the police. The Gemeindeschutzwache was instantly denounced by the bourgeois press as a 'red praetorian guard', and the inter-allied military committee that was supposed to see that the terms of the Treaty of Saint-Germain were enforced, complained to the Chancellor that the new force was incompatible with the treaty. Seitz quickly gave way to this pressure, dissolved the organisation within a few days and created a new force of about 1,000 men called the Gemeindewache, with limited functions and without the close ties to the Schutzbund that was central to the concept of the Gemeindeschutzwache.[36] The new organisation was too small to be particularly effective, and had limited authority, but it was continually denounced by the right as the 'cadet school of the Schutzbund' and seen as further evidence of the sinister intents of the government of Red Vienna. There can be little doubt that, in spite of vigorous denials, there was a close association between the Gemeindewache and the Schutzbund, but the precise role intended for the Gemeindewache is unclear. According to the testimony of the traitor Eduard Korbel at the Schutzbund trial, the new organisation was given special training in sabotage, using the sewage system to place explosive charges under police stations, barracks and other important public buildings. But Korbel was such an unreliable and self-serving witness that little credibility can be given to his testimony.

The first official statement by the party on the events of 15 July was issued after a meeting of the national leadership of the Schutzbund with senior officials of the organisation from Vienna. It was agreed that the Schutzbund had acted correctly and that everything possible had been done to protect the workers.[37] But at the national conference of the Social Democratic Party, a kind of unofficial party rally, held immediately afterwards, there were some harsh criticisms of the Schutzbund. It was pointed out that it was absurd to arm the Schutzbund with clubs and expect them to restrain the heavily armed police. Julius Deutsch came under attack, and it was suggested that he was an incompetent who was merely playing at soldiers. There was a general feeling that the Schutzbund had failed and that a new strategy was needed, but there was too wide a range of suggested solutions. There were those who demanded a more effective military policy, although there were many different suggestions how this should best be achieved, and the right wing, whose outstanding spokesman was Karl Renner, argued that the weakness of the Schutzbund was further evidence for the need for a compromise with the bourgeois parties and an end to the policy of confrontation. At the conference Oskar Trebitsch, who was close to Renner, called for 'inner disarmament', a realisation of the appalling risks of a civil war, and serious negotiations with the government.[38] The right suggested that the Schutzbund should be disbanded, for its very existence was pushing the country towards civil war.

Bauer and his supporters could not accept these arguments. To them disarmament could only be considered from a position of strength. When the Schutzbund was as powerful as the military formations of the opposition it might be possible to negotiate, but for the moment such an offer would simply be seen as a sign of weakness by the government. The Bauer group believed that the Schutzbund should be reorganised and that a new strategy should be evolved so that from a new position of strength it might be possible to gain some concessions from Seipel. But Bauer's strongest argument was that the Christian Social government would not consider a coalition, and he argued consistently that 15 July had been a putsch attempt by the Social Democrats to gain state power. On behalf of the government Vaugoin said: 'Herr Doktor Renner, we don't make a coalition with the men of July and their protectors ... We do not want a coalition with people for whom amnesty of those guilty of arson and other crimes is more important than the weal of the peaceful citizens.'[39] Talk at this time of a coalition was so clearly unrealistic that Bauer had little difficulty in countering the attack on his leadership.

On 15 and 16 October, exactly three months after the Palace of Justice affair, the Fifth Schutzbund Conference was held at which a new programme, written by Alexander Eifler, was adopted unanimously.[40] The fundamental idea behind Eifler's programme was that the Schutzbund should become fully militarised to become an obedient, and even unthinking, executive organ of the party leadership. Officers were no longer to be elected but appointed. There were to be no political discussions within the Schutzbund which was unquestioningly to follow the directives of the party leadership. The Schutzbund was thus to become the unpolitical instrument of the party. It would protect the democratic republic against fascist or monarchist threats, it would ensure that the rank and file did not indulge in spontaneous demonstrations of the sort that had resulted in the tragedy of 15 July, and it must be prepared to resist any violent attacks on the state even if they came from the ranks of the proletariat.

From the outset Körner was concerned that the reformed Schutzbund would fall prey to a kind of social democratic militarism, and that 'proletarian discipline' might become a serious hindrance to individual initiative and political far-sightedness without which he was convinced the Schutzbund would become militarily useless. The

Schutzbund remained a political organisation inasmuch as it was a democratically organised association under the political direction of Julius Deutsch and Karl Heinz, but it was predominantly a military organisation under Körner and Rudolf Löw. Körner insisted that the political dimension was vital, saying at the conference that 'The Schutzbund must not only be the most determined section of the proletariat, it must also be the furthest thinking.' Alexander Eifler on the other hand stressed the technical military aspects of the Schutzbund and wanted to keep politics out of the organisation. Curiously enough Eifler, who at this time was the technical leader of the Schutzbund in Vienna, was supported in this view by the politician Deutsch. Here were the seeds of the future conflict between Körner and Eifler that was to have such a fatal effect in the years to come.

In the spring of 1928 Theodor Körner presented his paper, 'Principles for the Use of Violence and Civil War', to the Schutzbund leaders.[41] Körner was a passionate democrat who believed that violence was only justified in the event of a flagrant violation of democratic principles by the government in power. State power should be achieved by democratic means, violence only used in the defence of democracy, civil war only justified when the vast majority of the people were prepared to support such a struggle as an ultimate expression of the popular will.

Körner's democratic convictions were in perfect accordance with his profound and professional understanding of military affairs. He was convinced that the people could never win a victory against the military in street fighting unless other significant factors undermined the power of the state. Thus a direct confrontation with the military had to be avoided at all costs. The troops could only be defeated by slowly wearing down their will to continue the fight. This could be achieved by moral persuasion and by constant pin-pricks that would weaken their resistance and cause the officers to lose control over their men. 'Passive defence' was thus the key to success, for a direct fight with well-armed and well-disciplined troops was bound to lead to failure. The greatest possible mistake would be to copy the methods of the opponent, and thus fight according to his rules. Almost any weapons would be used, provided that they were in the hands of determined men who use them skilfully. The secret for success was to exploit to the full the great strength that lies dormant within the working class, to study all possibilities and to encourage self-discipline, self-reliance and self-esteem.

This insistence on the political and psychological dimension of civil war shows that Körner had moved a long way from the Eifler programme of the Fifth Conference. Körner was now convinced that the Schutzbund had to be politicised, so that it was in complete accord with the party, and that it could not be an effective military force if it became merely the apolitical military apparatus of the party. The Schutzbund should welcome innovative and original ideas and encourage creative thinking about the strategy and tactics of modern civil warfare. Far from being a mere executive organ of the party, it could well become its backbone, attracting the most determined and far-sighted elements of the socialist movement.

Eifler and General Friedrich Mayer were horrified by these ideas. Eifler refused to admit that the Schutzbund had suffered a defeat on 15 July, and claimed that it had been immensely strengthened by the reforms of the last few months. The new depoliticised Schutzbund, he claimed, was a greatly improved military force, and he violently disagreed with Körner that it would not be possible to fight the army in an open street battle. He also disagreed that the Schutzbund should try to politicise the army and the police, for he felt that this was the task of the unions, even though 80 per cent of the Viennese police force was unionised — a fact that had done nothing to discourage them on 15 July. Eifler had no patience whatsoever with Körner's insistence that the military and the political had to be seen as a whole. As a professional soldier, who had resigned his commission in July, Eifler could only think in purely military terms and was unable to grasp the significance of the political and psychological dimension of civil warfare.

For the time being it was agreed to overlook the fundamental differences between Körner and Eifler's views on the future of the Schutzbund. In a memorandum which concluded the conference it was agreed that an open confrontation with the enemy should be avoided and that Körner's delaying tactics should be used. The importance of a general strike in the event of civil war was stressed, and it was underlined that all possible methods were to be used in the struggle. This emphasis on the moral aspects of civil warfare and on the need to avoid conventional fighting against the army and police was certainly a victory for Körner, but he was fighting a losing battle. Eifler had far stronger support from the party leadership. Körner had the tacit support of many of the rank and file, but behind Eifler stood Deutsch and Bauer. The result was a deadlock. Eifler, Deutsch and Bauer wanted a strictly disciplined paramilitary force that was unquestioningly obedient to the party, but at the same time they were unwilling to give the decisive leadership that such an organisation needed. On the one hand the leadership demanded blind obedience, on the other it waited passively for the masses to act. The rank and file grew increasingly impatient, but waited for orders from above. A better recipe for political inaction could hardly be found. Once again militant phrases thinly disguised political impotence.

For the next few months there were some halfhearted attempts to negotiate internal disarmament in which the Schutzbund offered to convert itself into a sports club if the Heimwehr disarmed. Such a proposal was unacceptable to the Heinwehr, and Seipel, who wished to make use of the Heimwehr for his own political purposes, demanded such a high price from the Social Democrats that the negotiations were bound to fail.[42] As one journalist remarked, the conditions that Seipel laid down had 'as little to do with internal disarmament as with the average age of penguins'. It seems likely that Seipel felt that offers of negotiations from the left were a sign of weakness. In December he gave a speech in Graz in which he openly supported the Heimwehr, saying that they and not the Social Democrats should control the streets in demonstrations and marches. At the same time Seipel was talking of a reform of the constitution. Such was the background to the police raid on the Social Democratic Party's headquarters in Vienna on 14 February 1929 in the course of which a number of weapons were seized.[43]

This razzia was an ominous sign of things to come and a clear provocation of the party, and yet the leadership refused to act, arguing that the time was not yet ripe. Seipel's resignation at the beginning of April, a calculated move to retreat and await the time to strike hard at the left, was interpreted by the Social Democrats as a sign of weakness and the beginning of a new and more moderate era. Some modest measures by the new government, under the industrialist von Streeruwitz, designed to curb the martial ardour of the Heimwehr, confirmed this view.

A clash between the Schutzbund and the Heimwehr in Sankt Lorenzen in Styria in August 1929, a fight that resulted in four deaths and some sixty injured, was taken by the Schutzbund leadership as triumphant proof that even when outnumbered the Social Democrats were more than a match for the Heimwehr, and that any attempt to launch a 'March on Vienna' was bound to fail.[44] This was a somewhat exaggerated version of an essential truth. It is almost certain that the Heimwehr, along with the Styrian Landeshauptmann, Rintelen, hoped to provoke an incident that would at least lead to the downfall of the Streeruwitz government which might possibly be the first act of a Heimwehr putsch.

It soon became apparent that the optimism of the Social Democrats was misplaced. Seipel was determined to change the constitution so as to undo the democratic achievements of the republic, but ever conscious of the dangers of alienating the Western powers he hoped to achieve these ends not by a coup, but by pseudo-democratic means. He was thus to continually prod the Heimwehr into actions calculated to create a climate of uncertainty and unrest that would make it all the easier to realise his plan. The Heimwehr was to weaken both the Streeruwitz government and the Social Democrats, and prepare the way for Seipel's triumphant return. By September 1929 it was widely believed that the Heimwehr was preparing a coup, and the Social Democrats boldly announced that Austria would become neither a Hungary nor an Italy.[45] For the moment Seipel still preferred to remain out of office and to play the role of kingmaker. On 25 September Seipel told Streeruwitz to resign and to appoint Schober as his successor.[46] The new government immediately set to work on the reform of the constitution, in an atmosphere that was made all the more tense by the failure of the *Bodencreditanstalt*, and by serious economic dislocations as a result both of the worldwide depression and of the activities of the Heimwehr. In spite of furious denunciations of the proposed constitutional changes, the Social Democrats negotiated with Schober and agreed on a formula that became the basis for the new constitution on 7 December 1929. For the Social Democrats, Danneberg proved to be a shrewd negotiator, and he was able to stop the attempt to create a presidential régime that the Heimwehr hoped would be the first step towards the creation of a fascistic state in Austria. The President was given certain additional powers, but he could not act without the consent of parliament. The great constitutional theorist, Kelsen, argued that although the powers of parliament were somewhat limited, democracy had been saved.[47] The compromise ended the constitutional crisis, but the Social Democrats made the fatal mistake of celebrating the final defeat of fascism. The Heimwehr had been frustrated, but Austrian fascism was far from dead.

Since the autumn of 1928 the Schutzbund had begun training for a confrontation with the Heimwehr, for until the compromise of December in the following year the party feared that a Heimwehr putsch was imminent. The task was to make an organisation that had little military training beyond some basic drill into an effective force. To this end manoeuvres were held in the vicinity of Vienna and the

Schutzbund was given basic infantry training, although at the insistence of Deutsch they were not given real weapons for drill.[48]

In early 1929 the Schutzbund developed a plan for the defence of Vienna, a scheme that bears the unmistakable imprint of Eifler's thinking, although at his subsequent trial Eifler claimed that it was written with the close co-operation of Körner. Since the plan was diametrically opposed to everything that Körner stood for, and was bitterly attacked by him, Eifler's statement is clearly absurd. The basis of the plan was that if the Heimwehr attempted a putsch they would try to seize the important government buildings in the centre of the city. The Schutzbund and all forces that remained true to the constitution would then control the outer districts of Vienna from whence they would be able to force the Heimwehr out of their positions in the inner city. This at least was the version of the plan that Eifler gave at his trial, adding that he assumed that the army and the police would be on the side of the constitution and that thus the Schutzbund would probably be able to remain neutral in the struggle. He further claimed that the Schutzbund would remain passive for twelve hours to await the outcome of a general strike, would arm gradually if the party leadership deemed this necessary, and would ensure that law and order was maintained in the area under its control.

There are no reasonable grounds for doubting that Eifler's account of his plan for the defence of Vienna given at his trial is substantially correct. Ilona Duczynska assumes that the anonymous *Tactics for Streetfighting* is Eifler's plan for Vienna.[49] The wild and terroristic tone of much of the document is such that it cannot possibly be the work of Eifler, who was known for his right-wing views and his old-fashioned manner of tackling military problems. In this document there is no question that the enemy included the army, the police and 'fascist units of the Heimwehr'. The plan called for an all-out offensive in which the barracks, police stations, military buildings, police headquarters, the Ministry of Justice and the Chancellory should be blown up. The post office, radio station and all printing shops were to be seized. All officers in the army and the police were to be rendered 'harmless'. The bourgeoisie would thus be confronted with open 'class terror' in a series of rapid and independent actions. On the other hand the plan does talk of forming a 'defensive ring', which was the basis of Eifler's plan, and there is talk of converting the outer city into a 'stone labyrinth' in which the enemy would be lost and destroyed. This version of the plan is thus hopelessly confused, combining wild offensive plans with the strategy of the defensive ring. It would seem therefore that it was a clumsily revised version of Eifler's plan by some extreme left-winger within the Schutzbund.

That *Tactics for Streetfighting* cannot be taken very seriously is also suggested by the fact that the police did not use it as evidence of a premeditated putsch attempt by the Schutzbund. The blood-curdling language of much of the document would have been most valuable to the prosecution's case had they been able to establish its authenticity. With massive evidence to the contrary, it was felt that it could not be used to prove that the official policy of the Schutzbund was to prepare for a violent revolution.

Körner played no part in the development of the Eifler plan. Eifler, who could count on the support of Deutsch, had managed to push Körner onto the sidelines and refused to attend a meeting that Körner called to discuss strategy for Vienna. The resulting plan was clearly rushed, badly thought out, and was later to be devastatingly criticised by Körner. It was truly tragic for the Schutzbund that at this critical juncture one of the outstanding military thinkers in the history of socialism should have been pushed aside by a second-rate, conventional and unimaginative career soldier. When Körner saw part of the draft plan he dismissed it as 'rubbish' and added that he thought that the whole Schutzbund in Vienna was a 'swindle'.[50]

On 19 October the Sixth Schutzbund Conference was held in an optimistic atmosphere, occasioned by the marked increase in membership and the supposed effectiveness of the recent reorganisational measures.[51] In a powerful speech to the conference, Bauer warned of the dangers of a fascist takeover by means of Schober's proposals for constitutional reform and stressed that the Social Democrats must be ready to fight at any time in defence of democratic freedoms. A representative of the German Social Democratic Reichsbanner, Karl Höltermann, promised the support of 100,000 German workers who were prepared to fight for democracy in Austria when necessary. The theme of the conference was familiar. The party was prepared to disarm if the opposition would do the same. It was determined to remain within the bounds of democratic legality, but should the democratic state be challenged they were prepared to fight. Most delegates were confident enough in the strength of the Schutzbund to be convinced that the government would never risk a showdown. They could thus afford to indulge in radical rhetoric without pausing to assess the consequences of their words. This fatal overestimation of their own strength was increased when the Schober government was forced to compromise over constitutional reform.

Under Eifler's leadership the Viennese Schutzbund undertook a series of manoeuvres in early 1930, in part to discipline and train the members but also as a warning to those who, under Seipel's outspoken leadership, denounced the constitutional compromise and demanded further drastic action. In February some 700 Schutzbündler took part in a ski exercise in the Vienna woods at the end of which they were treated to another rousing speech from Otto Bauer. In April a much larger exercise took place in which the Vienna Schutzbund trained with units from the area around Vienna. Nearly 19,000 men took part in this exercise, and many others were alerted.[52]

Shortly after these events Schober announced that he was determined to pursue a policy of internal disarmament. That this policy had little chance of success was obvious after the 'Korneuburg oath' of the Heimwehr with its avowed intention to create a fascist state in Austria. Furthermore, the Heimwehr was nothing without its paramilitary organisation, whereas the vast Social Democratic Party stood behind the Schutzbund. As Fey rightly remarked, internal disarmament would be suicide for the Heimwehr. The Social Democrats announced their support for disarmament, in part no doubt because they knew that it was very unlikely ever to be effected, but at the same time they were afraid that disarmament was very likely to be a one-sided affair. The close co-operation between the authorities and the Heimwehr, particularly in the provinces, was a well-established fact, and any disarmament provisions were therefore bound to be more strictly applied against the 'enemies of the state' on the left than against the 'true Austrians' on the right. A new and meaningless law on the right to carry weapons was passed in June 1930 which was designed largely for foreign consumption and certainly helped to create a climate favourable to obtaining a further loan from the League. The situation of the paramilitary forces remained unchanged. There were isolated instances of violence between the Heimwehr and the Schutzbund, but the situation was somewhat ameliorated by bans on demonstrations in Lower Austria, Burgenland and Vienna.

On 25 September 1930 the Schober government fell, once again in large part due to the machinations of Seipel. A new government under Vaugoin, which included the two Heimwehr leaders, Starhemberg as Minister of the Interior and Hueber as Minister of Justice, was established as a caretaker government. Elections were called for 9 November.[53] With two outspoken opponents of parliamentary democracy in key positions in the new government the Schutzbund was deeply concerned. By late October rumours began to circulate that the Heimwehr was planning a coup, but it was felt that this was only likely if the right suffered a severe electoral defeat.

At the beginning of October rumours became increasingly persistent that the government was planning to outlaw the Schutzbund.[54] The party decided not to make this an issue over which it was prepared to fight, but planned to convert the Schutzbund into a kind of party police force of Ordner. This plan was published in the party newspaper, including the detail that uniforms would be replaced by red armbands which were dutifully prepared by the party.[55] In fact Starhemberg dropped the plan to ban the Schutzbund, and instead the government ordered a series of hunts for hidden weapons in party buildings, including co-operative stores, printing shops and council houses. Vaugoin's attempt to discredit the party in the eyes of the voters by unearthing hordes of weapons was a miserable failure. In spite of frantic efforts by the police and the army (the working-class town of Wiener Neustadt being placed virtually under military occupation) little was found except a few small-arms. The results were thus out of all proportion to the efforts. In Linz the army had even brought in artillery in a demonstration of the seriousness of the situation. The Social Democrats refused to be provoked, much to the disgust of the Heimwehr, and the total passivity of the party served to underline the futility of the whole effort. The Social Democrats, with more than 41 per cent of the popular vote, gained the most seats at the election, so Vaugoin's tactics had misfired. Vaugoin remained in office for a few weeks, his government being replaced by a cabinet under Otto Ender, with Schober as Vice-Chancellor and Foreign Minister.

For the next few months economic problems and the instability of the new government were the major concerns of Austrian politics, and the Schutzbund seemed to be more concerned about the workers' olympic games held in Vienna than in the possibility of a fascist coup. Then in September 1931 came the Pfrimer putsch. The party warned the government that unless swift action was taken the Schutzbund would be forced to act on its own. The dilatory behaviour of the government obliged the Schutzbund to order the mobilisation of the units in Styria, the centre of the putsch, and all other units throughout the country were placed on the alert.[56] Great care was taken that the Schutzbund should not become involved in the fighting, the move being simply designed to place pressure on the government to act decisively. In Bruck-an-der-Mur, the stamping ground of the militant Koloman Wallisch, the Schutzbund had little sympathy for this policy of restraint and fighting almost broke out between the government forces and the Social Democrats who were anxious to act immediately. The party leadership justified its inaction by claiming that had the Schutzbund acted against the putschists, the government forces would have joined in with the Heimwehr against the Social Democrats. As it was the government had been forced, even if somewhat reluctantly, to act against Pfrimer and his supporters.[57]

The argument of the leadership at the time of the Pfrimer putsch was a declaration of complete bankruptcy, and made a mockery of the arguments of the Schutzbund leadership in such documents as the Eifler plan. If the police and the army were to support a fascist coup that was opposed by the Schutzbund, and if the Schutzbund was incapable of handling such a situation, then clearly a drastic revision of policy was required. If the Schutzbund was nothing more than a bargaining counter for Bauer and Deutsch in their negotiations with the government, then plans such as Eifler's were meaningless. It was all very well to talk of 'proletarian discipline' and 'iron patience', but more and more members of the Schutzbund were forced to ask themselves what purposes such virtues served.

Shortly after the abortive Pfrimer putsch, Alexander Eifler, in consultation with local Schutzbund leaders, worked out a rough plan of action for Upper Styria. The plan was a typical example of Eifler's military thinking, and was later adapted for other parts of Austria. It was this plan that prompted the final break with Körner, who had already left the Schutzbund, having been continually frustrated that the party leadership supported Eifler's ideas which he regarded, in the words of his comments on the plan for Vienna, as 'hair-raising rubbish'.

Until 15 July Eifler had acted as a part-time adviser to the Schutzbund, working under a pseudonym. After the Palace of Justice affair he played a critical role in the reorganisation of the Schutzbund, and almost immediately came into conflict with Körner.[58] Eifler was soon complaining to Deutsch that Körner was refusing to work with him and offered his resignation. Deutsch, who consistently favoured Eifler rather than Körner, and thus made one of the most fateful errors of judgement in the history of Austrian Social Democracy, refused to accept this offer of resignation and strengthened Eifler's position. Körner continued to complain that the divisions among the Schutzbund leadership were seriously weakening the organisation, and that it was impossible to develop adequate strategy and tactics when so many people were involved. There was also a clash of personalities involved. Körner was a cool intellectual behind the warm human exterior; Eifler was a man of action who had little sympathy or understanding for military theory and was totally lacking in political understanding. Eifler regarded Körner as an aloof mandarin lacking in common sense; Körner saw Eifler as an unimaginative and second-rate junior officer. From Deutsch's brief biographical sketch of Eifler it is clear that he too felt that Körner was an unpractical idealist with a blind faith in the ability of the masses to find the right solutions in moments of crisis.[59] Nothing could be further from the truth. Körner was as much a master of the practical minutiae of tactics as he was of the broad outlines of strategy.

Although Körner had resigned from the Schutzbund in 1930, this fact was not widely known, and he still enjoyed the respect of many of the provincial leaders. Thus, after the Pfrimer putsch, he was invited by the Styrian Schutzbund to give his reasons for his disagreement with the national leadership and also to comment on the plans for Styria.[60] Eifler's plan for Upper Styria is a brief sketch, largely concerned with the relative strength of the Schutzbund and the Heimwehr, and contains only a rough outline of possible action.[61] Körner's criticisms are far more detailed and mercilessly expose the weaknesses of Eifler's concept.[62]

The basis of Körner's criticism was that Eifler was a typical militarist, as unimaginative as Pfrimer and the Heimwehr, who thought that a putsch was a purely military affair in which only the Schutzbund and the Heimwehr would be involved, and in which neither the army nor the people would be in any way interested. He also could not resist the comment that even as a military man he was incompetent, for he did not know the difference between the 'little war', guerrilla war, and civil war. If the plan was ever put into practice Körner was convinced that the Schutzbund would suffer another debacle like the Palace of Justice incident.

Even assuming that the struggle would simply be between the Schutzbund and the Heimwehr, Eifler's own figures showed little reason for optimism. In Upper Styria the Heimwehr had twice the number of men, nearly 13,000 rifles as against under 2,000, and 163 machine-guns to 25. These figures are clearly false. In the 1930 elections the Social Democrats polled nearly 35,000 votes, the Heimat-block only 12,500. That the Heimwehr should have had 11,350 men is thus highly unlikely. The precondition for any military planning is a clear and accurate analysis of relative strengths and weaknesses. The result of such sloppy work as Eifler's was to spread uncertainty throughout the Social Democratic movement, and to undermine the fighting spirit of the working class.

For Körner the notion that the Schutzbund alone should protect the democratic constitution was typical of arrogant pre-war militarism, with its confidence in the superiority of the military over the civilian. Since the party and the unions left everything to the Schutzbund the entire Social Democratic movement was weakened and potential strengths were not exploited. Furthermore, Körner argued, the republic could not be saved by directions from party headquarters in the Wienzeile in Vienna, but by individuals throughout the country who were well aware of what was at stake and who were prepared to act.

As many officials, such as local mayors, were Social Democrats, Körner felt that it would be perfectly possible to use the police, the gendarmerie and even the army to protect the republic against an attempted putsch by the Heimwehr. Where this was not the case the unions and the party should use all the powers available to them, and the Schutzbund form a reserve for use in the last instance. The Schutzbund lacked the experienced military leaders and the weapons to be an effective military force in the conventional sense. As a military force it was greatly inferior to the army or the police, and it would be folly to try to create a force that would attempt to fight the army on its own terms, as Eifler seemed to think was possible. The strength of the Schutzbund lay, in Körner's view, in its political convictions and in its relationship with the labour movement. These had to be strengthened, rather than attempting to turn it into a pseudo-army.

As the events of 12 February were to show, Körner was perfectly correct in saying that Vienna was the key to the whole situation, and that the decision in any attempted coup would be made in the capital. He dismissed the idea of a Heimwehr 'March on Vienna' as idle chatter, typical of 'dilettantes like Eifler and ignoramuses like Pfrimer and Steidle', for it was far beyond the technical ability of the Heimwehr to follow through with such a complex operation. The whole key to the situation lay in seizing state power, and that could only be decided in Vienna. Thus a new plan for the capital was urgently needed to replace Eifler's 'nonsense'.

Körner's fundamental conviction was that unless the people were convinced by the political stand of the party the Schutzbund would have no hope of success in an armed confrontation. In this sense it was

to be considered primarily as a political organisation. It was for this
reason that he distrusted ex-officers in the Schutzbund, of whom Eifler
was the prime example. Körner believed that they were blinkered by
their past experience and were unable to think in anything other than
purely military terms. He was equally distrustful of revolutionary
hotheads whom he feared shared much the same mentality as some of
the more outspoken Heimwehr leaders. In this category he placed
Koloman Wallisch, whom he described as 'a big mouth'.[63] Just as
Engels had argued in his introduction to the 1895 edition of Marx's
Civil War in France, Körner insisted that the time for heroic storming
of the barricades and pitched battles with organised state power had
passed. The secret for success now was to unleash the slumbering
power of the working class and to use that strength in every possible
way. The Schutzbund should exploit those situations where it enjoyed
local superiority, remain highly flexible and rely on the support of the
masses. Careful collection and analysis of information about the
enemy was essential so that effort would not be wasted against a
superior opponent and so that the factor of surprise could be used to
the full. His carefully considered and detailed criticisms of the Eifler
plan place Körner among the great theorists of guerrilla warfare, with
the important difference that he was concerned with saving the democratic state from a right-wing coup rather than attempting the violent
seizure of state power.[64] It was not until after the catastrophe of 12
February 1934 that Deutsch came to agree with Körner that the
Schutzbund could augment the strength and organisation of the
working class, but never replace it.[65]

Körner's efforts to persuade the party leadership that Eifler's
approach was leading the Schutzbund to certain failure had no effect.
Eifler was, after all, faithfully carrying out the directives of Deutsch,
who in turn was respected by Bauer and the other leaders, even though
there were some who thought him to be a lightweight. Thus Körner
came to be regarded by many as a 'bottle-green philosopher' who had
lost his sense of practical realities.[66]

Meanwhile the police continued its raids on party centres, the most
sensational being in the working-class district of Vienna, Ottakring, in
January 1932 when more than 7,000 rifles were discovered and eight
machine-guns. This was reported in the right-wing press as proof that
the Social Democrats were preparing for civil war, and denounced by
the *Arbeiter-Zeitung* as illegal provocation. The strongest argument
for the Social Democrats was that the government had done nothing to
seize the weapons of the Heimwehr, which appeared to be much more

strongly armed, and which had only recently been involved in the abortive Pfrimer putsch. The Ottakring affair strengthened the determination of the party to strengthen the Schutzbund, and with Eifler now in uncontested charge of military planning, and having been given the appropriately militaristic title of 'chief of staff', it became increasingly similar to an ordinary army in training and tactical planning. But even in these terms Eifler's programme was contradictory. The Schutzbund was ordered to practice map reading, drill and field duty, but, perhaps out of fear of reactions from the authorities, they were given no weapons training. Certainly most Schutzbündler were given elementary instruction in the use of small-arms, but they were given so little practical training that it was absurd to imagine that they could ever be the match of the government forces in an outright confrontation. Massive manoeuvres, involving up to 16,000 men were also held in the summer of 1932.[67] In October the growing tension between the Schutzbund and the increasingly militant Nazis broke out into open violence in Simmering when two Nazis and a policeman were killed as the Schutzbund defended the local party centre from a Nazi attack.[68]

The Dollfuss government forced the Schutzbund on the defensive by its increasingly authoritarian policies. The closing of parliament in March 1933 obliged the Schutzbund to think seriously in terms of using force, for many argued that this was precisely the kind of violation of the constitution that the Linz programme held to be a justifiable cause for armed resistance. Militants, like Koloman Wallisch, ordered their men to get their weapons from the hiding places and to be prepared to fight at a moment's notice.[69] Throughout the country there were many units who believed that the time had come to fight, for otherwise Austria would go the same way as Germany where the full horrors of fascist tyranny were already clearly apparent. In general it was the rank and file who were pressing the leadership to act, the local leaders waiting for news from Vienna. Some, like Wallisch, were prepared to go it alone, and to ignore orders from the Wienzeile. Such men were probably right that the time had come to fight, but it is also undoubtedly true that the training and mentality of the Schutzbund and the political stance of the party was such that it would have led to a crushing defeat. The time was ripe, but the Social Democrats were hopelessly unprepared.

Immediately after the closing of parliament the government of Tyrol banned the Schutzbund, arguing that it had been preparing for a coup. Two weeks later, on 30 March 1933, Dollfuss issued a decree abolishing the Schutzbund throughout Austria. Three years previously the party had decided that the banning of the Schutzbund should not be taken as a reason for armed resistance, and an order was issued to all units to accept the Chancellor's decree peacefully. In some districts there was isolated violence between Schutzbündler and Heimwehr or Nazi units, but in general the abolition of the organisation passed without incident.[70] The party countered this move by announcing the formation of a new organisation, the Ordnerschaften, which it hoped would be twice the size of the Schutzbund. The government tried to ban this as well, and many local leaders were arrested on charges of forming a secret society. The supreme court, however, decided that the Ordnerschaften was not a continuation of the Schutzbund, but police harassment and uncertainty over the legal situation certainly hampered the formation of the new organisation. The party promptly called for the formation of yet another organisation, the 'Propaganda Division', a name that had a less obvious connection with the Schutzbund.

The Propaganda Division was made up of all members of the Young Front, to which party members between the ages of 20 and 30 belonged, the Youth Organisation made up of boys between the ages of 16 and 20, and lastly the Ordnerschaften which was, of course, the Schutzbund under a new name. The Ordner were to form the military nucleus of the Propaganda Division, the Young Front was to be largely responsible for anti-Nazi work, and the Youth were to form a reserve.[71] The whole was placed under the direction of Julius Deutsch, with Eifler as the military expert, and Bauer responsible for liaison with the party. From the available evidence it would seem that there was very little military training of any kind undertaken by the Propaganda Division, and its new title seems to be an accurate reflection of its activity.

It is clear that the illegal Schutzbund was merely a shadow of its former self. Many militants had left, disgusted with its failure to act in March. Others were fearful of being involved with an illegal organisation. Many were afraid that they might lose their jobs if their employers discovered that they were active members of the Propaganda Division. The party had hoped that it would be twice the size of the Schutzbund; in fact it was far smaller and it had lost many valuable members, among these the most important single group being the railway workers who were totally demoralised after the failure of their strike in the autumn of 1933.

The Propaganda Division saw the main danger in late 1933 as

coming from the Nazis, and as they were still smarting under the humiliation of illegality they made overtures to Vaugoin suggesting that they might provide the men for a force to be armed by the government to guard the sovereignty of Austria. Vaugoin showed some interest in this suggestion, but he was dismissed from his cabinet post before the discussions had developed.[72] Continuing searches for weapons, arrests of prominent socialists, and the slow erosion of democratic rights by the Dollfuss government, made it obvious that there could be no further question of negotiations. The four preconditions for the use of violence by the party had been agreed upon in September at a meeting of party and union leaders, and had been reaffirmed at the extraordinary party conference in October. With the Nazis and the Heimwehr becoming increasingly violent and outspoken, and the government more hostile to the Social Democrats, the illegal Schutzbund feared that they might soon have to fight. At a meeting on 5 January 1934 the Eifler plan for Vienna was reaffirmed as official strategy, a general strike being taken as the signal for action.[73] From the evidence presented at the Schutzbund trial it would seem that the meeting was an expression of fear that the Schutzbund would have to act against an intransigent and anti-democratic government, and that therefore the organisation had to be on the alert. There is no evidence that any of the leaders at this meeting pressed for action against the government. Party policy was still to react to the government's actions rather than to take any initiative.

On 3 February Eifler and Rudolf Löw were arrested, and in the following few days other leading Schutzbündler were rounded up. Thus by 12 February the Schutzbund had been crippled by the ban, its leaders were mostly under arrest or close police supervision, and the rank and file were either frustrated or resigned. It had an ill-considered plan of action whose author was in jail. The Schutzbund was to fight with great bravery against overwhelming odds, but acts of great personal courage could not overcome years of faulty planning, insufficient training and a determined and ruthless opponent.

Notes

1. V.R. Berghahn, *Militarismus* (Cologne 1975), for a useful bibliography and an excellent discussion of the problems of defining the term.

2. For an introduction to Engels's criticism of the idea of a 'people's army' see Martin Kitchen, 'Friedrich Engels' Theory of War', *Military Affairs*, XLI, no. 3 (October 1977).

3. *Die österreichische Sozialdemokratie im Spiegel ihrer Programme* (Vienna 1964), p. 28.

4. For the early history of the army see: Ludwig Jedlicka, *Ein Heer im Schatten der Parteien* (Graz 1955).

5. Julius Deutsch, *Aus Oesterreichs Revolution* (Vienna 1923).

6. Christine Vlcek, 'Der Republikanische Schutzbund in Oesterreich. Geschichte, Aufbau und Organisation', unpublished PhD thesis, Vienna 1971.

7. Roman Rosdolsky, *Studien über revolutionäre Taktik — Der österreichische Januarstreik 1918* (Berlin 1973); Otto Bauer, *Die oesterreichische Revolution* (Vienna 1923).

8. Bauer, *Revolution*, p. 151.

9. Ilona Duczynska, *Der demokratische Bolschewik. Zur Theorie und Praxis der Gewalt* (Munich 1975), p. 63; Hans Hautmann, *Die verlorene Räterepublik. Am Beispiel der Kommunistischen Partei Deutsch-Österreichs* (Vienna 1971), p. 197.

10. Precise names are difficult. The Arbeiterwehr originated in the period immediately after the war. The Ordner protected party members. In 1920 the two were combined to form the Ordnerwehr which many party members still persisted in calling the Arbeiterwehr.

11. *Parteitagsprotokoll 1921*. The conference was held between 25 and 27 November, when it was clear that Kaier Karl's putsch attempt had failed and when the Burgenland crisis was over.

12. Duczynska, *Bolschewik*, p. 71. Julius Deutsch argued at the party conference that even if the workers were not armed they should be 'militarised' (*Wehrhaftmachung*).

13. Ibid., p. 72. Löw had been a captain in the Austro-Hungarian army. He became a close associate of Körner and an expert in guerrilla warfare. He was later to fight with the Haganah in Palestine. He was one of the most dramatic personalities in the Austrian party.

14. The 'equilibrium of class forces' was a favourite notion of Bauer and is discussed in detail in *Revolution*.

15. On Eifler see Julius Deutsch, *Alexander Eifler, ein Soldat der Freiheit* (Vienna 1947). On Körner see Duczynska, *Bolschewik*; Eric C. Kollmann, *Theodor Körner, Militär und Politik* (Vienna 1973).

16. For the activities of the Heimwehr at this time see Julius Deutsch, *Die Faschistengefahr* (Vienna 1923) and *Wer rüstet zum Bürgerkrieg?* (Vienna 1923).

17. See Julius Deutsch's arguments in *Antifaschismus* (Vienna 1926).

18. Deutsch spoke of 'organised readiness for action' (*organisierte Tatbereitschaft*).

19. Vlcek, 'Schutzbund', p. 70 for organisational details.

20. Ibid., p. 93.

21. Deutsch, *Antifaschismus*, p. 87.

22. For the problem of violence in the republic see Gerhard Botz, *Gewalt in der Politik* (Munich 1976).

23. This 'plan', purporting to come from Julius Deutsch, was first published in the *Innsbrucker Volkszeitung*, 8 November 1924, by the Tyrol Heimwehr leader Dr Richard Steidle.

24. Details of this curious affair in *Dokumente zum Wiener Schutzbundprozess* (Karlsbad 1935), pp. 14 ff. Seipel was furious when he heard of the scheme, and the Minister of War, Vaugoin, denied having any knowledge of the negotiations, claiming that it was an affair of the Tyrol government. Vlcek, 'Schutzbund', p. 493 for the text of Vaugoin's letter to Seipel.

25. Vlcek, 'Schutzbund', p. 126-8.

26. See Chapter 11 for a discussion of theories of fascism.

27. Duczynska, *Bolschewik*, p. 91.

28. Botz, *Gewalt*, pp. 107-11 for details of the Schattendorf affair.

29. For full details see Josef Gerdenitsch, 'Das Wiener Arsenal in der ersten Republik', unpublished PhD thesis, Vienna 1967.

30. Duczynska, *Bolschewik*, p. 96.

31. Ibid., pp. 97-100 for excerpts of the Vaugoin-Deutsch discussion.

32. See *Arbeiter-Zeitung*, 15 July 1927.

33. Julius Deutsch, *Ein weiter Weg. Lebenserinnerungen* (Vienna 1960), p. 166.

34. Vlcek, 'Schutzbund', p. 148.

35. Duczynska, *Bolschewik*, p. 112.

36. Vlcek, 'Schutzbund', p. 155.

37. *Arbeiter-Zeitung*, 24 July 1927.

38. Vlcek, 'Schutzbund', p. 161. Trebitsch's (and Renner's) views are summed up in Oskar Trebitsch, *Der 15 Juli und seiner rechte Lehre* (Vienna 1927).

39. C.A. Gulick, *Austria from Habsburg to Hitler* (2 vols., Berkeley 1948), vol. 1, p. 765.

40. 'Verhandlungsbericht der fünften Reichskonferenz' in *Der Schutzbund*, November 1927.

41. Norbert Leser, *Zwischen Reformismus und Bolschewismus. Der Austromarxismus als Theorie und Praxis* (Vienna 1968) p. 487; Duczynska, *Bolschewik*, pp. 120-32, for discussion of this paper.

42. Gulick, *Habsburg to Hitler*, vol. 1, pp. 797-806, for details.

43. Vlcek, 'Schutzbund', p. 189.

44. Ibid., pp. 204-21.

45. *Arbeiter-Zeitung*, 19 September 1929.

46. Gulick, *Habsburg to Hitler*, vol. 1, p. 854.

47. Leser, *Reformismus*, p. 446.

48. The full details in *AVA*, Schutzbundprozess.

49. Vlcek does not mention this curious text in her excellent thesis. It is to be found in *AVA*, Februar 1934, Box 5 and is reprinted in Duczynska, *Bolschewik*, pp. 349-62. Her comments are on pp. 125, 153, 188, 222, 229 and 345.

50. Vlcek, 'Schutzbund', p. 228.

51. *Der Schutzbund*, November 1929, for details of the conference.

52. Vlcek, 'Schutzbund', p. 242.

53. Gulick, *Habsburg to Hitler*, vol. 1, pp. 901-14.

54. Vlcek, 'Schutzbund', p. 256.

55. *Arbeiter-Zeitung*, 5 October 1930.

56. Gulick, *Habsburg to Hitler*, vol. 1, pp. 951-8 for a summary of events.

57. *Arbeiter-Zeitung*, 14 September 1931.

58. On Eifler see Helmut Tober, *Alexander Eifler, vom Monarchisten zum Republikaner*, unpublished PhD thesis, Vienna 1966; Deutsch, *Eifler*, is too uncritically laudatory in tone. Eifler was sent to Dachau after the Anschluss, where he died in 1945. A man of great courage and energy, he was one of the outstanding men among the prisoners and an inspiration to many of his comrades.

59. Deutsch, *Eifler*, p. 28.

60. Vlcek, 'Schutzbund', p. 279.

61. Text in ibid., pp. 512-24.

62. Text in ibid., pp. 525-47. Vivid commentary in Duczynska, *Bolschewik*, pp. 157-65.

63. In his letter to Deutsch and Bauer, 8 Februar 1932. Vlcek, 'Schutzbund', p. 553.

64. This is substantially the argument of Duczynska.

65. Julius Deutsch, *Putsch oder Revolution?* (Karlsbad 1934), p. 26.

66. Bottle-green was the colour of the pre-war K-u-K general staff uniform.

67. Vlcek, 'Schutzbund', p.301.

68. Rudolf Neck in *Vom Justizpalast zum Heldenplatz* (Vienna 1975), pp. 94-102 for details.

69. Paula Wallisch, *Ein Held stirbt* (Graz 1964), p. 178.
70. Vlcek, 'Schutzbund', p. 311.
71. Ibid., p. 316.
72. Richard Bernaschek, *Die Tragödie der österreichischen Sozialdemokratie* (Prague 1934), p. 19.
73. Vlcek, 'Schutzbund', p. 328.

7   FOREIGN POLICY: DOLLFUSS BETWEEN MUSSOLINI AND HITLER

Even before Hitler came to power in Germany, Mussolini was concerned about the possibility of an Anschluss. It had long been the policy of the Italian government to keep Austria as a buffer state, for, as the saying went in Rome, 'When the Germans have breakfast in Innsbruck they will dine in Milan.'[1] Although the inalienability of Austrian independence was guaranteed by Article 80 of the Treaty of Versailles, and this had been reaffirmed in the Geneva Treaty of 1922, the Italian government was well aware of the strong movement for an Anschluss both in Austria and in Germany. Seipel's refusal of Stresemann's overtures for a customs union in November 1927, by which Stresemann hoped to torpedo the French scheme for a Danubian confederation, did not disguise the fact that most Austrians favoured a close association with Germany, and only a handful of Communists and extreme Austrian nationalists and monarchists opposed the idea.

The Italian Foreign Minister Grandi hoped that it might be possible to counter the threat of an Austro-German customs union with a customs agreement between Austria and Italy.[2] But given the parlous state of the Austrian economy this was not an immediately attractive prospect, and Grandi had little opportunity to pursue the scheme. In July 1932 he was dismissed by Mussolini for his 'pacific and internationalist policy'. Mussolini took over the post of Foreign Minister himself, but the formulation of foreign policy, particularly the Austrian question, was largely the province of the newly appointed Under-Secretary of State, Fulvio Suvich. Suvich came from Trieste and had a certain residual sympathy for Austria which strengthened his intellectual rejection of the idea of an Anschluss. As a Jew he had no sympathy for National Socialism. Supported by the chief of the cabinet, Baron Pompeo Aloisi, the Palazzo Chigi launched a much more agressive policy in South-East Europe, a policy that was likely to run up against French schemes for a Danubian confederation and German schemes for a customs union with Austria. Mussolini saw the dilemma when he said: 'We can march together with Germany on the Rhine, but not on the Danube.'[3]

Suvich's aim was to create a strong triangle of Rome-Vienna-Budapest in which Grandi's scheme for a customs union would be strengthened by close political ties. He hoped that Starhemberg and the Heimwehr could become the main instruments of Italian policy in Austria. In June 1932 Mussolini had told Starhemberg that he would never allow Austria to become part of Germany, for this would simply mean that Italy had fought the war in vain and that 'Trieste would cease to be Italian.' Thus for the Italian government an independent Austria was one of the main aims of foreign policy.[4] In February 1933 Mussolini repeated this theme to Starhemberg, saying that a German Danube was as bad for Italy as a French one. Starhemberg desperately needed Italian support. His finances were ruined and the Heimwehr appeared to be in danger of falling apart. It would seem that he was able to use his charm to convince the Italians, although certainly not entirely. They wanted him to show results, which was understandable enough. What is surprising is their failure to see through Starhemberg to reveal the mediocre and politically naîve man that hid behind the facade of the suave aristocrat. Nor did the Italians seem to know anything of Starhemberg's strong sympathies for the Nazis and of his dealings with them.

When Gömbös came to power in Hungary in September 1932 it seemed that the time had come to press forward with the new policy. For the time being, however, Austria had no desire to break off its friendly relations with Germany, Anschluss sentiments still being very strong, for Hitler had not yet come to power. The Germans knew perfectly well what Mussolini was up to, but they were convinced that his scheme was bound to fail and were not particularly concerned. Their relative lack of interest was partly due to the fact that they were unaware of the secret trade agreements that had been negotiated between Italy, Austria and Hungary in 1931 and 1932, the Semme-ring-Brocchi treaties. This system of cheap credits, transport premiums, customs reductions and preferential duties was immensely complex. Eighteen different certificates were needed to export industrial goods from Austria to Hungary. Few people in the countries involved really understood the treaty, which involved all kinds of fraudulent bookkeeping to get round other existing trade agreements, and it is thus hardly surprising that the Germans did not really know what was afoot.[5] For the Italians the treaties seemed to offer the chance of a degree of economic penetration that could be used to strengthen their political influence over Austria and Hungary.

In January 1933 Hitler became Chancellor, thus the more agressive Italian policy had little time to achieve any positive results before the situation was radically altered by the creation of a second fascist state. As early as January 1933 the German Foreign Minister Neurath told the Reichstag Committee on Foreign Affairs that an Anschluss with Austria was one of the main aims of German policy.[6] Neurath also warned that relations with Italy were bound to become difficult because of German policy towards Austria. It would seem, however, that the traditional diplomats had little sympathy for any radical change of policy and did not feel that an Anschluss was worth too high a price. Thus the German ambassador in Vienna, Rieth, did not even wish to support the Austrian Nazi Party. Hassell, the German ambassador in Rome, believed that friendly relations with Italy were possible in spite of Austria, and he implied that the Anschluss should not become a priority of German policy.[7]

The position of Austria in Italo-German relations became all the more pressing as the Dollfuss government appeared to outsiders to be on the verge of collapse in early 1933. At the end of 1932 Mussolini honoured the agreement he had made with Starhemberg in the summer and sent weapons for the Heimwehr. These weapons were a part of the war booty that Italy had captured from Austria at the end of the war. They were to be stored in the Austrian arsenal at Hirtenberg, 50,000 rifles and 200 machine-guns to be given to the Heimwehr, the remainder to be sent on to Hungary. The movement of such a large quantity of arms could not be kept secret, and on 8 January 1933 the leading Social Democrat newspaper, the *Arbeiter-Zeitung*, published an article uncovering the whole affair, an article based on accurate information given by workers who realised the political implications of the scheme and who were determined to stop the arming of their enemies in the Heimwehr.

The article was a bombshell. For the Czechoslovakian, Yugoslavian and Rumanian governments this was clear evidence that Italy was behind a determined effort to undo the Treaty of Trianon and to rearm Hungary, thus strengthening the revisionist bloc. The Little Entente was determined to take the matter to the Council of the League of Nations, for they knew that they had proof of a breach of the peace treaty. England and France, however, were equally determined to stop this move, for they had no wish to compromise their relations with Italy. They tried to placate their allies in the Little Entente by promising to take the matter up directly with the Austrian and Hungarian governments, and the French assured them that they would not hand over their share of the Lausanne loan, more than 300 million shillings, until a satisfactory explanation was provided by Vienna.

The Italians and the Hungarians tried to get out of the affair by issuing flat denials of any knowledge of it, and by attributing the scandal to malicious socialist propaganda. Vienna was thus left having to bare the brunt of the attack. The Little Entente suggested that as a first step the weapons should be sent back to Italy. On 11 February 1933 the British and French governments delivered an exceedingly strongly worded note to Vienna giving the Austrian government two weeks to agree to a full investigation of the affair in which Austrian officials would be placed under oath.[8] The Anglo-French note was so harsh that it provoked an instant reaction in Austrian public opinion and even some Social Democrats were outraged. The *Giornale d'Italia* published a skilful attack on the French government, written at the express command of Mussolini, that argued that this was typical of the bully-boy tactics of the French government against helpless little states.[9] Even the German government was prepared to give its support to Austria, and there was much talk in the German press of 'rape' and 'assault'. Dollfuss was encouraged by this massive reaction both at home and abroad against the Anglo-French ultimatum, and quickly realised that it had misfired. The French and the British also did not wish to see Austria seriously weakened, for an Austro-German conflict was clearly looming on the horizon and the Western powers had no desire to see Austria overrun by Germany. They were therefore prepared to accept an Italian compromise solution, under which it was agree that the weapons should be sent back to Italy. In fact this gentleman's agreement was never respected. The weapons were never returned, although in the summer of 1933 Dollfuss insisted that they had been, and many of them were later smuggled across the border to Hungary.

Although the Dollfuss régime had weathered the storm of the Hirtenberg weapons affair, it still faced chronic difficulties at home. With a majority of only one vote in parliament and acute economic and social problems to tackle in the midst of a mounting political crisis, it seemed to many observers that the régime was unlikely to survive. On 4 March 1933 Dollfuss closed down parliament and began to establish his authoritarian régime, but he was obliged to rely more than ever on Mussolini to give him the support that he lacked at home. On 14 March 1933 Mussolini told the German government that Italy and Germany had a common interest in a strong Dollfuss government, and this line of argument was supported by a similar note from the Hungarian government.[10] The Italians and the Hungarians insisted that if the Nazis pushed too hard in Austria the country would turn more and more to the Social Democrats. Hitler was not interested in pursuing a thoroughly aggressive policy towards Austria at this time, preferring to bide his time and to strengthen Germany's international standing before turning his full attention towards Austria. On the other hand he was certainly not prepared to support Dollfuss, and resolved to keep up pressure on his régime. For Hitler, Austria was part of Germany, Austrian affairs internal domestic concerns of the German Reich. He could never accept Mussolini's desire for an independent Austria, and was convinced that a National Socialist victory in Austria would come as the natural consequence of his own victory in January 1933. Thus he demanded new elections in Austria, which he was certain would result in a major victory for the Nazis. He obviously imagined that the Austrian Nazis would be able to get to power by their own efforts, thus making an Anschluss superfluous. For the moment the motto was *Gleichschaltung* (co-ordination) rather than Anschluss.

In April 1933 Dollfuss visited Mussolini in Rome, in part because he feared that the visit by Göring and Papen, scheduled at this time, might lead to some agreement at Austria's expense. The Italian dictator was emphatic that the National Socialist movement had to be crushed in Austria, and that the only way to do this would be by launching an all-out attack on the Social Democrats. If Dollfuss were to crush 'Marxism' then the wind would be taken out of the Nazis' sails.[11] This was to be the *leitmotiv* of Mussolini's exchanges with Dollfuss for the next seven months. Few were aware of the fact that it rested on a basic fallacy. One of these few was the Catholic journalist, Karl Winter, who was both a friend and a perceptive critic of Dollfuss. On 4 May he wrote directly to Mussolini insisting that he would have to decide between a 'non-Anschluss' or a fascist Austria, because it was impossible to have both. Mussolini had to face the alternative of 'the swastika on the Brenner or democracy in Austria'. This being so, if Mussolini wanted to preserve the independence of Austria, he would have to tolerate the Austrian left which was its best guarantee.[12]

There can be no doubt that Winter's analysis of the situation was absolutely correct, but Dollfuss was deaf to such criticism. There are a number of reasons for this. The Nazis were constantly hostile towards his government, and he thus welcomed Mussolini's support for an attack on his most troublesome political opponents. Dollfuss also tried to separate German foreign policy from the policy of the NSDAP. There was some reason for him to do so. The German Foreign Office was often totally unaware of the activities of Hitler and the party towards Austria, and the professional diplomats in the Wilhelmstrasse were certainly much more sympathetic to Austria than was the party. This confusion and division of labour was typical of the Third Reich, the source of much misunderstanding at the time, and much difficulty to historians eager to unravel the knots in the formulation of policy and in the chain of command. Thus Dollfuss did not think that an attack on the Nazi Party in Austria would necessarily worsen relations with Germany, and he knew that many German diplomats did not consider Austrian affairs to be part of German domestic politics. Dollfuss was also determined to root out Social Democracy. This was a central part of his political programme. To attack National Socialism by attacking Social Democracy was certainly part of the motive for the attack on Marxism, but it was certainly not the only or principal reason. After all, in May 1933 Dollfuss was busy negotiating with Habicht and was ready to offer the Nazis two positions in his cabinet — hardly the stand of a militant anti-Nazi. Never at any point was he prepared to make a similar offer to the Social Democrats. The negotiations failed because of the Nazis' continued insistence on new elections, elections which Dollfuss feared would bring them greatly increased support. There were also many Christian Socials who favoured an alliance with the National Socialists, fearing that Dollfuss was becoming too dependent on the Heimwehr.

Hitler was well aware of all these manoeuvres in Austria. He witnessed Christian Socials negotiating with the Nazis to counter the influence of the Heimwehr, and at the same time members of the Heimwehr negotiating with the Nazis against the Christian Socials. In such a situation all he had to do was to keep up the pressure on Dollfuss and continue to demand new elections, posing as the champion of parliamentary democracy against the tyranny of the Dollfuss dictatorship. In May 1933 Hitler imposed what amounted to a fine of 1,000 marks on any German citizen visiting Austria, which had an immediately damaging effect on the tourist trade that was important to the Austrian economy even before the days of mass tourism. The German Minister of Justice Frank was sent on a deliberately provocative visit to

Austria in the same month and was expelled by the Austrian government. Throughout the months of May and June there were countless similar incidents. Habicht was thrown out of the country, and on 19 June 1933 the National Socialist Party was banned in Austria.[13]

In May Hitler had been optimistic, telling his cabinet that the conflict with Austria would be decided by the end of the summer.[14] By June, with the party forced underground and party headquarters under Habicht moved to Munich, he was less confident. By August even Hitler was keeping Habicht under control and was uncertain about the efficacy of Nazi terrorism in Austria.[15] In June, when the relations between Austria and Germany were particularly strained, Mussolini offered Dollfuss a military alliance under the terms of which Italian troops would march into Austria if it was attacked by Germany. Dollfuss, feeling that the choice was between a German occupation and an Italian occupation, tactfully declined the offer. Mussolini then warned Göring that if Germany threatened the independence of Austria, either by invasion or by a putsch, Italy would be forced to go to its aid. This prompted Hitler to inform Mussolini that 'The Anschluss of Austria is not under consideration by the German government ... We Germans are greatly concerned ... that German-Italian relations should not be strained or hindered by the Austrian question.' The German government, however, would not agree to make a public statement rejecting the Anschluss, and Mussolini quite understandably told Gömbös that as he knew the Germans only too well he was taking their assurances on the Austrian question with a pinch of salt.[16]

This exchange of notes between Rome, Berlin and Vienna points out the dilemma in which Dollfuss had placed himself. Earlier in the year he had warned Suvich that if he did not get the support he needed from Italy he would be forced to approach France and the Little Entente. He had warned that this would mean a political alliance with the Social Democrats, and he had backed up this threat with a curious speech appealing for working-class support. Dollfuss was well aware of the dangers of allowing himself to get stuck between the Nazis and the working class, but his threat to the Italian government was pure bluff for there was no immediate chance of an alliance with France as long as the Hirtenberg affair had not been settled, and Dollfuss had still not totally rejected the idea of a coalition with the Nazis.[17] On the other hand, as became clear in June, he did not want to become too close to Mussolini and was anxious to preserve his freedom of action. He also knew that any agreement with France, Britain or the Little Entente would only be possible if he made concessions to the Social Democrats. The British government expressed its sympathies for Dollfuss's predicament, as can be seen in Anthony Eden's speech in the House of Commons on 21 June, but it also insisted that Dollfuss would have to come to some sort of an agreement with the Social Democrats for otherwise he ran the risk of becoming seriously isolated. Paul-Boncour went even further, saying that as long as Dollfuss pursued a pro-Italian policy he could not expect any support from French socialists.[18] In such a situation Dollfuss was prepared to gamble that in a crisis France and England would not allow Germany to overrun Austria. This was a risky game to play, although it must be added that the odds were considerably more in Austria's favour in 1933 than they were in 1938.

Mussolini continued to press Dollfuss to take firm action against the Social Democrats. On 1 July he wrote to the Austrian Chancellor expressing his support for the Patriotic Front and for his decisive action against the Nazis. But he insisted that fascist reforms were needed in Austria, otherwise the Nazis would get all the credit for being anti-socialist. The Social Democratic Party should be destroyed and socialist Vienna crushed. A fascist Austria would then find powerful allies in Hungary and Italy.[19] Dollfuss replied that he was working with Dr Ender on a new authoritarian constitution and added: 'We are determined ... as soon as conditions allow to take away from the Marxists those positions of power that they still possess.' Vienna could best be brought to heel by cutting off funds and thus starving the gigantic Social Democratic system. Dollfuss excused himself for being somewhat slow in dealing with the socialists by arguing that he had his hands full dealing with the Nazis, and had it not been for them the problem would have probably already been solved. On the Patriotic Front he said that it was based on the leadership principle (*Führerprinzip*) and there was no question that he, Dollfuss, was the leader. Thus the Patriotic Front was seen by Dollfuss as a major step towards the creation of fascism in Austria, and he insisted that his relations with the Heimwehr were excellent and that he had their support for these moves.

If the Italian government was concerned with the slow progress towards fascism and a somewhat dilatory attitude towards the menace of Marxism, the Hungarians were also dissatisfied with Dollfuss. On 13 July Gömbös sent a rather sour note to Mussolini complaining that Austria was not doing its fair share in the economic struggle against the Little Entente, and that if it was serious about wanting the friendship of Hungary it would have to play a far more active role.[20]

Such was the background to Dollfuss's talks with Mussolini held on 19 and 20 August in Riccione. In an *aide de memoire* for his talks with Dollfuss, which was presented to the Austrian delegation, Mussolini demanded a thoroughgoing constitutional reform along fascist lines that would affect the entire political, economic and social structure of the country. After a plebiscitory approval of the constitutional reform the new state should be in operation by 1934.[21] In the course of the discussions Mussolini suggested that a new constitution based on the estates (*ständische Verfassung*) should be ready by September 1933. He wanted an end to the special status of Vienna, calling for the appointment of a commissar for the capital. Taking up Dollfuss's earlier assurances that all was well between him and the Heimwehr, he insisted on a closer co-operation with the Heimwehr and the inclusion of Heimwehr leaders in a new government, for the present government seemed to him to be too much of a survival from the past. A radical break was needed to create a strong, independent and fiercely national Austria. Mussolini reiterated his determination to preserve the independence of Austria and stated that if there was an attack from Bavaria, either by the 'Austrian Legion' of exiled Nazis, or by the Germans, or by a combination of both, then the Italians would come to Austria's aid. Dollfuss found it impossible this time to resist Mussolini's demands for a military convention, and it was agreed that the details should be worked out in the following months.[22]

Mussolini's belief was that a fascist Austria would be able to come to a working agreement with Germany and nothing would stand in the way of the creation of a strong triple alliance of Italy, Austria and Hungary. He complained that Dollfuss had been far too lax in his attitude towards Social Democracy, and he would not accept his excuses for his procrastination. He told Dollfuss that his own relations with Germany were made all the more difficult by having an ally that seemed to do nothing against socialism. Official Nazi propaganda at this time took the line that Dollfuss was hand in glove with the Marxists and that the attack on the Nazi Party in Austria was done to please his allies on the left.

The meeting at Riccione was somewhat humiliating for Dollfuss. In spite of the assurances of support and friendship, he had been obliged to listen to long lectures from Mussolini in which his shortcomings and mistakes had been listed in detail. Such an experience is disconcerting for any politician, but particularly for a man as proud as Dollfuss. It is clear, however, that he took Mussolini's words to heart and stepped up his efforts to create a new authoritarian state.

Shortly after Dollfuss's meeting with Mussolini, Starhemberg travelled to Rome to discuss the Austrian situation with the Duce. Mussolini used the occasion to write to Dollfuss and to give him another push. He said that Starhemberg had reinforced his belief that the Austrian Nazis were simply *malcontenti* who would leave the Nazi Party as soon as the government started on a clearly fascist course and had nothing more to do with liberalism and democracy.[23] Ministers such as Winkler and Schumy were obviously hindering the progress towards fascism and would have to go. Dollfuss had to understand that the Heimwehr was in a difficult situation, for it had to keep a certain distance from the government as long as it was not leading a determined fight against Marxism, for otherwise it would be unable to win over the discontented youths from the Nazis. Once again Starhemberg had scored against Dollfuss by telling Mussolini exactly what he wanted to hear. Starhemberg's major problem was that he had nothing to offer as an alternative to Dollfuss's policy, and he was far too devious and unprincipled to be able to pursue a coherent and forceful course of his own.

Once again Dollfuss swallowed these criticisms and continued with his schemes for the formation of a new state. On 11 September he gave a major public speech at the trotting-racetrack in Vienna, outlining his schemes for constitutional reform. In the course of this speech he said: 'The time of liberal thought, the time of the seduction of the people by Marxism and materialism, the time of the rule of the parties is over ... We want a social, Christian and German state on the basis of the estates and with strong authoritarian leadership.'[24] But such talk was too vague to have much of an impact, and did little more than confirm opinions that were already held either for or against the Chancellor. Dollfuss was again in a difficult quandary. To be too 'German' would be to play into the hands of the Nazis. To be too openly fascist would all too easily stir up strong and traditional anti-Italian feelings in Austria. But to steer a course between the two forms of fascism was likely to alienate him from both.

Three days after the racetrack speech Dollfuss met the Italian ambassador, Preziosi, to discuss the political situation in Austria and relations with Italy. He insisted that his pro-Italian line was in no sense dictated to him by the Heimwehr, and that they were making his task all the more difficult by refusing to give him the support he badly needed. He made it perfectly clear to Preziosi that he was uncertain whether he would be able to control the Heimwehr and rather pathetically asked for the help of the Italian government to force them to support his government. Preziosi felt that this was largely an excuse for the Chancellor's inaction against the Social Democrats. He expressed his dismay that Dollfuss had still done nothing positive against the Marxists, and added that he had little confidence in his friends in the Landbund. Dollfuss then fell back on the argument that he had used with Mussolini in Riccione. He had been held up in his fascist reforms by the activities of the Nazis, and he slyly added that at times it seemed almost as if the Italian government sympathised with the Germans. Somewhat maliciously he argued that the fact that Italy seemed to have so little influence on the German government was harmful to her prestige, and also weakened the case for fascism in Austria.[25]

Thus by September 1933 Austria and Italy were both repeating their well-worn arguments and little progress was being made. The Italian government was becoming increasingly disillusioned with Dollfuss. Mussolini complained that with all his ifs and buts he was a typical old-style Austro-Hungarian civil servant. The Italian military attaché in Vienna, Fabbri, argued that Dollfuss's position was hopeless and the time had come to let someone else have a try. Fey and the ambassador in Rome, Rintelen, were the favourite candidates.[26] For the next few weeks there was very little contact between the Italian and Austrian governments. The Italians were disappointed with their protégé, and Dollfuss was trying once again to come to some working arrangement with the German government.

Towards the end of October 1933 the Austrian ambassador in Berlin, Tauschitz, reported that Neurath was in favour of coming to an agreement with Austria, and that he had the support of a large number of moderates both in the German foreign office and in the general public.[27] Tauschitz talked the matter over with Neurath, but got the perfectly correct impression that the German Foreign Minister was unable to do very much to influence policy towards Austria. Among those who were in favour of improving relations with Austria was the press officer of the NSDAP, Hanfstaengl, who had worked out a nine-point plan on Austro-German relations. These points included demands that Austro-Marxism should not be allowed to represent the Austrian workers and that Austria should remain 'neutral' on the Jewish question. Unfortunately for Hanfstaengl nobody took his plan seriously and Hitler even went as far as to describe it as 'idiotic'.[28]

A week later Hitler told Tauschitz that 'Habicht or no one' would work out an agreement with Austria, and made it perfectly clear that he would not tolerate Hanfstaengl's interference in foreign affairs.[29]

Tauschitz believed that the SA leader, Röhm, was behind a plot to remove Habicht in order to initiate a new policy towards Austria. In any case, he was certain that Habicht was the main obstacle, and that he alone was stopping the cooler heads in the Foreign Office from working out a settlement of outstanding differences between the two countries. This view was also shared by the Austrian government.[30]

These reports from Berlin were hardly encouraging, but Dollfuss continued to believe that it would be possible to drive a wedge between the Nazi Party and the Foreign Office, and the different views of Hanfstaengl and Habicht seemed to indicate that there were also divisions within the party on the Austrian question. Thus Dollfuss was prepared to continue negotiations with both the German Foreign Office and with Habicht. At Geneva at the end of September he agreed to meet Neurath, but the encounter never took place because neither was prepared to make the first move to visit the other.[31] Far more significant were the negotiations between Habicht and the Austrian government.

Through the intermediary of two Greater Germans, Foppa and Langroth, Habicht began to negotiate with Dollfuss.[32] The Greater Germans, who had formed their 'battle alliance' with the National Socialists on 15 May 1933, were in effect the representatives of the illegal party in Austria, and the most useful intermediaries between the Nazis in Munich and the government in Vienna.[33] Dollfuss understandably had little desire to negotiate with Habicht, and would have preferred to talk directly with Hitler or even Hess, but he agreed to allow Foppa and Langroth to act as intermediaries. On 13 October they discussed the whole affair with the Chancellor, and on 20 October they returned to Munich with the good news that Dollfuss was prepared to consider Habicht's proposals. Habicht was delighted and seems to have convinced himself that he was on the verge of success in Austria, feeling that he might be able to emulate, on a smaller scale, his Führer's 'seizure of power' in January. Foppa and Langroth were sent back to Vienna with Habicht's conditions. On 25 October they met Dollfuss. Habicht was prepared to agree that Fey should continue in a new cabinet that would include Nazis, and that the inclusion of the National Socialists in the government would necessarily settle the issue of relations between Austria and Germany. This assurance was extraordinarily vague, but his other proposals were both concrete and unacceptable. Habicht demanded half of the seats in the cabinet for the Nazis and insisted that he should be given the post of Vice-Chancellor in place of Fey. To give greater strength to his arguments, he let it be known that the political truce which he had imposed on the Austrian Nazis would be lifted and that the government could expect a new wave of terror.[34]

Dollfuss, knowing from Tauschitz of the existence of a moderate group in Berlin, decided to end the negotiations with Habicht, but continued the attempt to reach some sort of an agreement with the German government. At about this time Dollfuss received a visit from one Dr Kanzler, a German citizen who appeared to be on a good footing with senior officials in Berlin, including Hess and Bormann. Kanzler had no official position, either in the party or the foreign office, and his claim to be acting purely as a private citizen appears to be true. He was anxious that Germany and Austria should come closer together and that the friction between the two countries should cease. He suggested that a direct meeting between Dollfuss and Hitler would be the best means of solving the problem. Hess had already agreed that such talks would be useful if they were properly prepared. Dollfuss shared this view.[35] Accordingly the head of the political section of the Austrian Chancellory, Hornbostel, along with Hohenlohe-Langenburg, were sent to Berlin to prepare the ground for a meeting between Dollfuss and Hitler. On 30 November the Austrians met Hess, Bormann and Kanzler in Berlin.[36]

Hess's attitude made it plain from the outset that the German government had no serious intentions of negotiating with Dollfuss, and hopes that it would be possible to get around Habicht were dashed. Hess demanded an immediate end to the persecution of the Nazis in Austria and disciplinary action against Starhemberg for behaviour considered to be insulting to Hitler. He then asked the astonished delegation what legitimate right Dollfuss had to speak on behalf of the people of Austria, and he repeated the familiar theme that Austrian affairs were internal German concerns, not matters of foreign policy. Obviously there could be no discussion along these lines, and Hornbostel and Hohenlohe returned to Vienna empty-handed.

Dollfuss's position was thus now weaker than ever. Mussolini was growing increasingly impatient; Hitler refused to talk; Habicht made impossible demands. His support from the Heimwehr seemed dubious, given the ever-increasing tensions between Fey and Starhemberg. Hornbostel reported that Fey was negotiating behind Dollfuss's back with the Nazis through the intermediary of the moderate Count Trautmannsdorff who was close to Neurath and Hanfstaengl.[37] His belief that it would be possible to separate the Nazi

Party from the Foreign Office was proved false. An anti-Nazi policy was construed in Berlin as anti-German, and an anti-German policy would leave Austria hopelessly alone. The Hungarian government, for example, was opposed to an anti-German policy.[38] The Italian government was also concerned that Austria should have tolerably good relations with Germany, and still believed that a violent anti-socialist course would solve the problem of dealing with the Nazis without alienating the German government. On the other hand, relations with Britain and France could only be seriously improved if Dollfuss abandoned his anti-socialist policy, and this he was certainly not prepared to do. His determination to crush Social Democracy was a central and consistent feature of his politics, and through all his tactical twists and turns and his political compromises he never lost sight of that goal.[39]

On 12 December Suvich visited Berlin in an attempt to ease the tensions between Austria and Germany. He had no illusions about the difficulty of the task and had little hope that the visit would produce any concrete results. During the three days he spent in Berlin he met most of the leading personalities of the Third Reich, including Hitler, Göring, Goebbels, Hess, Neurath, von Papen and even Hindenburg. Hitler granted his Jewish visitor two lengthy interviews, flattering him as a 'comrade-in-arms' and as a fellow 'former subject of the Habsburg monarchy'. Hitler professed a lack of interest in the Anschluss, arguing that since Austria was economically so backward it would be an enormous financial burden on Germany and would be constantly in need of substantial subsidies. He argued that both Germany and Italy had an interest in a strong Austria and needed to stop it from joining the Little Entente. But Austria could never be strong until the political situation was clarified, and this was only possible if elections were held so as to give an accurate indication of public opinion. Hitler said that he wanted to see a coalition government of all 'national and right-thinking people', and even praised Dollfuss as a 'German-minded' (*deutschgesinnten*) man and for his determination to fight against Marxism and freemasonry. In a brief moment of weakness during this extraordinary performance Hitler could not help making the remark that it was pointless to negotiate with a man who had no support behind him, but he was quickly back on the track of saying that the precondition for any negotiations would have to be an end to the ban on the Nazi Party and the restoration of constitutional rights.

Suvich was far too experienced a man to be taken in by this nonsense. History does not record whether Suvich remembered

Hitler's remark on page one of *Mein Kampf* that 'the same blood belongs in the same Reich' regardless of the economic cost of an Anschluss. Nor do we know what Suvich's reactions were to witnessing a fascist dictator posing as the champion of constitutional rights and parliamentary democracy, concerned about the state of public opinion. It is certain, however, that he realised that there was no chance of a reconciliation between Hitler and Dollfuss, and he recognised all the familiar arguments even though some were dressed up in rather exotic new clothes. Suvich knew that Hitler was determined to get rid of Dollfuss and he thus made it clear to the Chancellor that the Italian government supported Dollfuss and intended to do everything in its power to strengthen his position. The only point of agreement between Suvich and Hitler was that Austria was far too unimportant to become a bone of contention between Italy and Germany.[40]

Suvich returned from Berlin, after brief visits to Cologne and Munich, with his worst fears about Germany confirmed. He was convinced that if the National Socialists became coalition partners with Dollfuss this would be the first step towards an eventual Anschluss, and he was shocked by the aggressive and bellicose tone of his German hosts. He was struck by the fact that the country was a 'massive armed camp' ready to pursue its goals relentlessly as soon as it felt strong enough.[41] Mussolini shared Suvich's concern. He told the Fascist Grand Council that if Italy could not keep Dollfuss in power the Germans would soon be on the borders of both Italy and Hungary, and that Italy would very likely be forced out of the Balkans. Mussolini had seldom been so open or outspoken in his deep-seated fear of German intentions, and his conviction that Austria was a central question in his foreign policy.

Having been once again rebuffed by Berlin, the Austrian government now began to think of a *démarche* at the League of Nations to gain international support against the threat of Nazism to its independence and sovereignty. The government prepared a lengthy document on Nazi provocations and crimes in Austria, and detailed the support given to these activities by the German government. In Geneva the Austrian delegation prepared the way for the discussion of Austro-German relations with the powers.[42] In London the suave, cultured and popular Austrian ambassador, Franckenstein, was busy drumming up support for Austria. Predictably, Vansittart expressed his wholehearted support for Austria against Germany, adding that Sir John Simon shared his views. Simon told Franckenstein that he was a firm believer in non-aggression pacts, and that he was convinced that Hitler would be bound by them. Franckenstein relayed this astonishing notion to the Ballhausplatz without comment.[43] There were also encouraging signs from Paris that the French government was not prepared to barter away the independence of Austria.

Thus Dollfuss was reasonably sure of French and British support against Germany and was prepared to threaten his northern neighbour that unless the constant provocation by the Nazis stopped he would denounce their activities to the League of Nations. But this was a dangerous game to play. In the middle of January 1934 Tauschitz in Berlin warned that the Nazis were likely to step up their activities in Austria.[44] After all, Hitler would simply deny that he had anything to do with the Austrian Nazis and their activities, just as the German government had even denied the existence of the Austrian Legion, merely saying that there were some men of 'German origin' in the SS and the SA.[45] But other signs were more encouraging. The Austrian ambassador to the League, Pfluegl, reported that there was marked sympathy from France and Britain for the idea of taking the matter to the League, and he added that Baron Aloisi had admitted that he saw no alternative. Of the three countries France appeared to be by far the strongest in its determination to help Austria and to curb Germany.[46]

At the same time as Pfluegl's note arrived in Vienna, a further report from Franckenstein in London indicated that perhaps the British government was not quite as enthusiastic a champion of Austrian independence as he had first thought. Simon had warned Franckenstein in a further conversation that going to the League would be 'difficult' as Germany was not a member. He further told the Austrian ambassador that he had informed the German ambassador that the British government favoured the independence of Austria. This was hardly encouraging news for Franckenstein, who concluded that neither Simon nor Eden were prepared to do much to help Austria. It appeared to him that the French were alone in wanting to mount an attack on all the wrong-doings of the Reich, of which its attitude towards Austria was but one.[47]

Pfluegl, perhaps hoping that his great day was to come, remained optimistic, and insisted that if Germany were to be denounced to the League of Nations it would lead to a serious humiliation of Austria's greatest rival. Faced with mounting evidence from London that the British government was unenthusiastic, to say the least, it was felt in Vienna that Pfluegl was getting a little carried away. This was confirmed by a further report from Franckenstein that the British cabinet was considering making a move to negotiate directly with Berlin on the Austrian question and obviously did not favour using the League of Nations as an international forum to air Austria's grievances.[48]

Further evidence of his excessive optimism came from the Austrian ambassador in Rome, Rintelen, who reported that, contrary to Pfluegl's report, the Italians would do nothing to support an Austrian move in Geneva. Suvich told Rintelen that the most he could do was to tell Neurath that he was going to ask the Austrian government to stop persecuting the Nazis, but he would add that since the Nazis were behaving badly in Austria there was very little that he could do.[49]

With the British at best lukewarm in their support for Austria, and with the Italians positively hostile to any attempt to use the League of Nations, only France seemed to be willing to back an Austrian appeal to the League. In France it was Paul-Boncour who was most in favour of using the League. Hornbostel's roving reporter, the journalist Helmut Hütter, who reported under the pseudonym 'Martin', a widely travelled and well-informed man, reported that the French government was disappointed at the British government's reluctance to use the League of Nations.[50] This impression was confirmed in a report from Tauschitz on a lengthy conversation with François-Poncet who had told him that the French government was behind Austria and believed that the moral effect of the League condemning Germany would be strong and effective.[51] The British government was anxious that this enthusiasm of the French for the League might push the Austrians into what it considered to be hasty action. Thus Vansittart asked Franckenstein to wait for the outcome of the British *démarche* in Berlin before turning to Geneva.[52]

By the end of January 1934 the Austrian government was uncertain how best to deal with the Germans. Pfluegl argued that the British attempt to negotiate directly with Berlin was risky for Austria, for the British might very well do a deal with the Germans behind Austria's back. On the other hand Franckenstein continued to be optimistic, in spite of rather scant evidence, insisting that the British government was sincere in its professions of friendship for Austria, and that it would act in Austria's best interests. Rintelen's reports from Rome were also regarded with a certain suspicion, for there were rumours that he had been negotiating with Habicht in Italy and he was known to have political ambitions that could well colour his dispatches. Rintelen denied these charges, writing that Suvich was sincerely pro-Austrian and that Austria could count on Italy's support against Germany.[53] Thus enthusiasm for taking the whole affair to Geneva began to wane, although the work on the preparation of a dossier on Nazi crimes continued.

At the beginning of February Rintelen had a long interview with Suvich to discuss Austro-German relations.[54] Suvich thought that going to the League was a ridiculous idea (*brutta soluzione*) and used the familiar argument that the only way to deal with the Nazis in Austria was to destroy the basis of their support. Suvich said that there were two types of Austrian Nazi: the Anschluss fanatics and those who were desperately looking for something new. He insisted that the latter type could be won over to the Dollfuss régime by a determined attack on Social Democracy, and with horrible cynicism he suggested that a touch of anti-semitism would not come amiss. A new fascist constitution would complete the work and Austria would be free of the Nazi nuisance.

Shortly after this important interview with Suvich the Austrian government received word from Paris that Mussolini had told the French ambassador in Rome that he would support an Austrian initiative in Geneva, but that he did not think that it would do much good.[55] In London the House of Commons debated the Austrian question, and Vienna was impressed by the strong expressions of support for Austria, although a suggestion by the Labour MP Cocks that one day Germany might attack Austria was regarded as utterly absurd.[56] Franckenstein reported that the Austrian dossier on Nazi crimes had created a strong impression in London, and that he was convinced that the British government would support an Austrian appeal to the League of Nations.[57]

Thus on the eve of 12 February Dollfuss had every reason to believe that the British, French and Italian governments supported his régime. In England and France there were many who disliked his authoritarian régime and his anti-socialist policies, but on the other hand he appeared to be fighting a brave battle against Hitler, and some socialists were even prepared to overlook his domestic political shortcomings simply because he appeared to be one of the few European statesmen who stood up to Hitler; there was even hope that the cause of Austria could be used to help form an anti-Nazi alliance. Few paused to think that such an alliance would be made up of some very curious partners. Dollfuss had made no commitments whatever. He had few real friends but many sympathisers, and, however unpopular his policies might be, he was able to pose as the champion of a small nation threatened by a country whose ambitions caused considerable concern in the capitals of Europe.

While Dollfuss was threatening to expose Germany in front of the League of Nations he was still open to discussions with the Nazis and was careful not to exclude the possibility of a negotiated settlement. His New Year speech to the Austrian people was interpreted in Germany as an attempt to leave the way open for such talks with the Nazis.[58] Habicht's visit to Rome in December was a matter of grave concern to Dollfuss, for he feared that a deal might be made behind his back, and also because he was uncertain of Rintelen's loyalty.[59] Dollfuss was anxious to have the opportunity to talk directly with both Suvich and Habicht to make certain that they were not planning a new policy at his expense. It is doubtful that he expected anything else from these visits, for he must have known that Suvich would want to know why he had not lived up to the agreements made at Riccione four months previously, and there was no reason to believe that Habicht would change his tune.

Hitler agreed that Habicht should go to Vienna on 8 January, ten days before Suvich's announced visit. The German Foreign Office was unhappy about this move, but Hitler saw it as a useful step. It meant that Dollfuss finally accepted the fact that the problem was a 'party question' and that he would have to deal with Habicht, not with the Foreign Office with its cautious and conservative approach to foreign policy. The German Foreign Office wanted to postpone the visit partly because they disapproved, and partly because they felt that if it had to take place there should at least be sufficient time to prepare the ground. They therefore suggested that Habicht should go to Vienna after Suvich. Dollfuss, however, was particularly anxious to see Habicht before Suvich. He knew what to expect from Suvich and hoped that Habicht might give him some excuses for failing to honour the Riccione agreements.[60]

On 3 January 1934 Tauschitz told the Austrian government that Habicht was prepared to come to Vienna.[61] The ambassador suggested that he should travel by plane, and spoke quite highly of Habicht's companion on the trip, the Prince of Waldeck and Pyrmont, in spite of his unfortunate habit of strutting around at diplomatic receptions in his SS uniform. It is clear from Tauschitz's dispatches to Vienna that although he was a competent traditional diplomat he had little understanding of how the National Socialists operated, and perhaps it should be said in his defence, neither did Neurath. It might have seemed to them that Hitler's more moderate attitude to the Austrian question was due to the restraining influence of the Wilhelmstrasse, but in fact Hitler was prepared to postpone the

Anschluss simply because the foreign political situation was very sensitive, and he did not wish to risk outright confrontation with Italy over Austria. Habicht was of course delighted that there was no longer any question that he was the only man to speak on behalf of the Führer on the Austrian question, and he was convinced that he was on the eve of a great personal triumph.

Dollfuss had kept his negotiations with Berlin over the Habicht visit secret from the Heimwehr because at that time relations between the Nazis and the Heimwehr were particularly strained. He imagined that it would be possible to smuggle Habicht and his entourage into Vienna by plane, have lengthy and intricate discussions, and then send them back to Berlin without anyone among his Heimwehr cabinet colleagues knowing anything about it. Surprisingly Dollfuss very nearly got away with it, for it was not until the evening of 7 January, the day before Habicht was due to arrive, that the Heimwehr leaders got wind of his plans. Their reaction was immediate and violent. Fey told Dollfuss that he would have Habicht and his gang immediately arrested if he dared to set foot on Austrian soil. Starhemberg said that he could no longer support Dollfuss if Habicht came to Vienna. There was even a hint of a Heimwehr putsch if Dollfuss persisted with his scheme. The Heimwehr's patrons, the Italian government, were equally enraged when they heard of the plan. They knew perfectly well that Dollfuss was trying to come to some sort of an agreement with the Nazis before Suvich arrived, so that he could have an excuse for not fulfilling his promises to the Italian government. In this situation Dollfuss had no alternative but to cancel the visit, giving as a rather shallow excuse acts of violence by the Nazis in Austria on 6 and 7 January.[62] Habicht had already taken off from Munich when Hitler ordered him to return. He was furious, blaming the abortion of the mission on Starhemberg and on the weak-kneed diplomats.[63] Neurath asked Tauschitz pathetically: 'Where do we go from here?'[64] In Vienna, Dollfuss announced a further crackdown on the National Socialists, a task that he entrusted to the willing hands of Fey as Minister of Security.

The role of the Italian government in this whole affair is obscure.[65] It is hard to believe, although it is possible, that Dollfuss tried to conceal his negotiations with Berlin from the Italians. It is possible that he tipped them off that he might meet Habicht, but that he did not give a date, so that the Italians could assume that it would happen after the Suvich visit. Nor is it clear what precise relations existed between the Italian government and the Heimwehr. Morreale, the press secretary at the Italian embassy in Vienna, was the contact man between Suvich and Starhemberg, and did not always inform his ambassador, Preziosi, what was afoot. It was Morreale who protested to Dollfuss over the Habicht visit on 7 January, so that it is just possible that he knew nothing of the visit until the very last moment, and then joined forces with Starhemberg to make sure that the visit was cancelled.[66]

Dollfuss's *faux pas* over the Habicht affair placed the Italians in an even stronger bargaining position for the forthcoming Suvich visit. Having failed to come to terms with Berlin and having estranged himself from his only ally it is hardly surprising that he stepped up the initiative at Geneva to bring Nazi activities to the attention of the League of Nations. The day before Suvich arrived in Vienna, on 17 January, the Austrians presented the German government with the dossier on Nazi interference in Austria, with the warning that if it did not cease forthwith they would regretfully have to take the matter to the League.[67] Although the Italian government made supportive noises for foreign consumption, it was opposed to the idea of appealing to the League and was convinced that its own solution was more realistic.

Suvich stayed in Vienna from 18 to 20 January.[68] Relations between Dollfuss and his visitor were very strained. Suvich was angry at Dollfuss's duplicity, his negotiations with Berlin and his appeal to Britain and France for support. He treated the Chancellor to a stern lecture on his failure to live up to the Riccione agreements. He repeated the Italian position in forceful language. Dollfuss should destroy Marxism, smash the Social Democrats in Vienna and in the provincial parliaments, replace party politics with the Patriotic Front which should be the sole political body in the country and promulgate an anti-parliamentary, authoritarian and corporatist constitution. Only by these means could Austria be given a new sense of purpose and direction, and the disaffected youth be won away from the lure of National Socialism. This new Austria would be a worthy partner in a triple alliance between Italy, Hungary and Austria which would be both political and economic in character, and Suvich suggested that such an alliance could be negotiated at a summit conference to be held in Rome in March.

Dollfuss was very angry at this treatment, the more so as it was at the hands of a man whom he described as 'a one-time deserter from the Austro-Hungarian army'. But there was little he could do but listen to Suvich's homily. Even the social side of the visit was a disaster. An

Austrian Nazi had managed to place a musical-box in the Chancellory that went off in the middle of an official reception playing the Horst Wessel song.[69]

Knowing perfectly well that Dollfuss was an unwilling listener, and having little reason to suppose that he would suddenly change his course, Suvich concentrated his efforts in Vienna on Fey whom he saw as a possible strong man, maybe even a successor to Dollfuss. He urged Fey to keep up constant pressure on the Chancellor to make sure that the Riccione agreements were implemented. Fey was delighted to pose as a crusader against socialism and democracy, and Suvich told the Hungarian ambassador in Vienna that Fey would see to it that the government would live up to its commitments.[70]

It was clear after the failure of the Habicht visit, and the threat of taking Germany to the League of Nations, that the National Socialists would step up their terror campaign in Austria. The pastoral letter of the Austrian bishops at Christmas in 1933 had condemned National Socialism and triggered off a violent reaction in the German press. The normally rather moderate *Börsenzeitung* argued that Germany should renounce the concordat with Rome after this slanderous attack.[71] The party newspaper, the *Völkische Beobachter*, described the letter as 'an open attempt to sabotage the domestic peace of Germany'.[72] The letter had such an impact in Germany that the *Völkische Beobachter* returned to it a week later, in a bitter attack on the Austrian bishops.[73] In Germany it was felt that one way to attack the Austrian government was to attack the church, because it was known that the régime was strongly influenced by Catholic Social teaching. In Austria there was a growing uneasiness that some churchmen might be sympathetic to the Nazis, among them the cardinal archbishop of Vienna, Innitzer.[74] The result of this propaganda offensive against the main ideological support of Dollfuss's régime was that the church became a trifle uncertain of how it stood in relation to the fascists, National Socialists and the Dollfussites. All shared a common loathing of socialism, but there were uncertainties as to how Austria would, and should, proceed.

A week after Suvich had visited Vienna, Habicht made a major speech on Bavarian radio in which he attempted to explain the situation to the people of Austria. The speech was relatively moderate in tone. Habicht acknowledged the fact that Dollfuss had made an effort to come to a working agreement with Germany, but that he had been forced into an anti-Nazi position by the Heimwehr. Fey was thus painted as the real villain, appointed Minister of Security in order to do the dirty work. It would be impossible, in Habicht's view, for the Austrian government to deal with the Nazis, and therefore they would be forced to go to the League of Nations, a course of action which Habicht thought was hardly likely to be successful.[75]

The attitude of the German government towards Austria in January 1934 indicated that it thought that Dollfuss's régime was extemely weak and unlikely to survive. By keeping up the pressure, either by attacks on the church or through Habicht's speeches from Munich, speeches which the Austrian government took very seriously, it was hoped that they could contribute to the impending domestic political crisis by which the Nazis were almost certain to profit. At the end of January Dollfuss had a frank and remarkable conversation with the German ambassador, Rieth.[76] Rieth began to talk about the position of Austrian Social Democracy, and Dollfuss immediately stepped in with the remark that he intended to destroy Marxism in Austria once and for all. He continued by saying that the destruction of Marxism would create a certain parallel between the régimes in Austria and Germany and that these similarities could perhaps form the basis for the improvement of relations between the two countries. Dr Rieth, who appears to have been poorly briefed on National Socialist policy towards Austria, remarked that a strong line against the Social Democrats would hardly suit the Nazis because they feared that once the Chancellor had successfully dealt with his red opponents he would turn against his brown ones with renewed strength.[77]

This extraordinary remark by the German ambassador must certainly have strengthened Dollfuss's determination to act as soon as possible against the Social Democrats. On 5 February the cabinet held a special meeting on Austro-German relations.[78] The familiar arguments that had been detailed in the dossier for the League of Nations were repeated. The somewhat exaggerated effects of the 1,000-mark fine on German tourists to Austria, the constant anti-Austrian propaganda kept up by the German government and the Nazi Party, the smuggling of weapons and ammunition across the border to arm Austrian Nazis and the frequent acts of terror and violence, were all discussed. Fey argued for a strong and determined policy against the Nazis, saying that any sign of weakness would be a 'nail in Austria's coffin'. In his view even illegal methods were justified. Neustädter-Stürmer, the Minister of Social Affairs who also came from the ranks of the Heimatschutz, expressed his concern that an anti-Nazi line should not involve any deals with France or Britain, both of which countries he assumed favoured the Social Democrats. He added that

France could only bluff, because in the end it would have to support Austria against Germany.

Dollfuss argued that the best way to attack the Nazis was to go for the Social Democrats.[79] He told the ministers of a conversation that he had had with the French ambassador who was concerned that there might be an attempted coup by the Heimatschutz. The Chancellor had told him that this was out of the question, but that an insurrection by the left was very much on the cards. Dollfuss insisted that the Nazis were terrified that the government might attack the Social Democrats because the menacing attitude of the left was the best possible propaganda for the National Socialists. The French ambassador agreed that an attack on the left would be the best way of undermining the Nazis. Neustädter-Stürmer was satisfied with this answer, but none of the ministers stopped to ask Dollfuss what he meant by the 'menacing attitude' of the Social Democrats.

By February the government was becoming increasingly concerned with the activities of the Nazis. Dollfuss's régime was extremely shaky with its narrow basis of support. The Nazis were keeping up a steady terror and propaganda campaign which was having a marked effect. Many well-informed people were deeply concerned about the future of Austria. In Berlin the French ambassador, François-Poncet, told Tauschitz that he was an Austrophile and that in his view Austria was the most important question for the German government at the moment, and that once Austria fell Czechoslovakia would be next on the list.[80] *The Times* correspondent in Berlin, Stimson, told a senior official in the Tyrol that the British government was not fully aware of the gravity of the situation in Austria, and that Franckenstein had not done enough to convince Sir John Simon of the danger of the threat from Germany. He felt that the British government thought that Austrian complaints were peevish and exaggerated. Stimson stressed the extraordinary brutality of the Nazi régime and the acute economic crisis facing the country due to its unwillingness to increase exports and achieve a satisfactory balance of trade. It was absurd and dangerous to think of Hitler as a man of peace who would keep his word. In Stimson's view, Hitler would annex Austria and violate his treaty with Poland at the earliest possible opportunity, and Britain and France would do nothing in the event of an Anschluss.[81] The Italian ambassador in Berlin, Cerruti, an expert on Austrian and Hungarian affairs, was convinced that Germany would soon be able to annex Austria by peaceful means, and he agreed with François-Poncet that Hitler would then turn his attention to Czechoslovakia. At the beginning of February Cerruti visited Rome where he reported that, in his opinion, Italy had failed in its attempt to frustrate German ambitions in Austria.[82] Suvich felt that Austria had reached a 'critical point', Mussolini thought that the situation was 'difficult, but not hopeless'.

At the end of January Hitler gave a speech to the Reichstag to celebrate his anniversary in office.[83] Turning to Austrian affairs he announced that Austria was German and that the 'German idea' could not stop at the frontier. Dollfuss could not survive without the support of the Social Democrats and was being pushed by Britain, France and Czechoslovakia to reach an agreement with the Nazis. As Dollfuss had no support among the people he would have to come to terms with the Marxists. The fact that the Social Democrats had announced their willingness to support Dollfuss against 'national fascism' was skilfully used by Nazi propagandists to create the impression that Dollfuss was hand in glove with the socialists. At the same time the Nazis posed as the champions of human rights and democracy in Austria. The press thundered on about 'this unrestrained and sadistic gang of desperados, a small group of traitors paid by foreigners and Jews', and the 'hangman system'.[84]

Hitler's speech and the Nazi press campaign gave Dollfuss more reasons to pursue his anti-socialist course, and he was more convinced than ever that he could destroy the Nazis by destroying the Social Democrats. Among all the warnings about the danger from Germany, some of which were of remarkable perspicacity, and in spite of the dwindling support for Dollfuss's régime, hardly a voice was raised pointing out the folly of the assumption that it would be possible to combat Nazism by attacking the left. Almost the only person to consistently point this out was Hornbostel's informant, Helmut Hütter.

It seems that Hütter first heard of the idea that Dollfuss should go for the left before attacking the Nazis during a visit to London in June 1933 when he visited Wickham Steed who told him that the Czechs had advised the Austrian government to do this, although they said that the left should not be hit too hard.[85] Hütter simply relayed this information to Hornbostel without giving the matter much thought, and it was not until he returned to his native Carinthia in September that he began to get seriously concerned about the problem of Social Democracy. Although Carinthia was far from being a centre of radical Social Democracy, and played virtually no part in the fighting in February 1934, he saw that there was a growing frustration and an increasing determination to act. Local Social Democrats felt that the party should negotiate some form of agreement with Dollfuss, and as the Chancellor was trapped between the Nazis and the Social Democrats, he was almost bound to accept such an offer.[86]

With mounting Nazi terror Hütter became convinced that Germany might attack Austria at any time. He pointed out that Austria had no proper border defences and would easily be overrun by the German army. In this situation it was vital not to alienate the workers, who were the only really reliable opposition to the Nazis, for everyone else was tainted by compromise and collusion. At the Labour Party Congress in October Fritz Adler told his audience that the working class was the strongest support of the independence of Austria and the best guarantee against National Socialism. Hütter clearly thought that this was a good point, but Hornbostel thought that it was absurd.[87]

Hütter felt that it was necessary to come to an agreement with the moderate leaders of the Social Democratic Party, thus forcing the radicals in the rank and file to either toe the party line or resign to form a new party. Clearly such a policy would not be possible if the government were determined to pursue a policy of 'anti-Marxist measures'. At the beginning of November Hütter discussed the situation with the Social Democrat moderate, Robert Danneberg, who complained that the government's policies were causing an alarming and dangerous radicalisation of the working class, and who feared that if this continued an explosion was likely to occur. He said: 'In February we shall see if the government wants to pursue a policy of an open *coup d'état*, or if it is prepared to respect the provisions of the constitution with respect to the budget.'[88]

If Dollfuss continued with his own form of fascistic government there was no reason at all why the workers should defend it against Hitler. A number of workers told Hütter that if one was to have fascism in Austria, why not have it under Hitler rather than Dollfuss?[89] As long as the working class was opposed to Dollfuss, opposition to Hitler was bound to be a second priority. He remained convinced that the party should be split rather than outlawed, and that the moderates could easily be won over to the 'Austrian side'.[90]

With Rome constantly demanding the destruction of Social Democracy, with mounting evidence that Berlin was worried about the prospect of Dollfuss winning popular support for an anti-Marxist crusade, and with the British and French governments showing little concern for the future of democracy in Austria, the government was in no frame of mind to listen to Hütter's warnings. It was willingly persuaded to follow a policy which was to reach its fulfilment in February 1934.

Notes

1. Jens Petersen, *Hitler-Mussolini. Die Entstehung der Achse Berlin-Rom 1933-1936* (Tübingen 1973), p. 81.

2. Jürgen Gehl, *Austria, Germany, and the Anschluss 1931-1938* (Oxford 1963), p. 41.

3. Baron Aloisi, *Journal* (Paris 1957), 14 January 1933.

4. Petersen, *Hitler-Mussolini*, p. 80.

5. Ibid., p. 84.

6. Ibid., p. 94.

7. Dieter Ross, *Hitler und Dollfuss: Die deutsche Oesterreich Politik 1933-1934* (Hamburg 1966), p. 15.

8. For the text of the Anglo-French note see: *DDF*, II, p. 283; the Little Entente's note is in *DDF*, II, pp. 259. A comparison of the two notes is instructive.

9. Petersen, *Hitler-Mussolini*, p. 98.

10. Ross, *Hitler und Dollfuss*, p. 18.

11. Petersen, *Hitler-Mussolini*, p. 189.

12. Ibid., p. 189.

13. Ross, *Hitler und Dollfuss*, pp. 29-55; G.Otruba, 'Hitler's Tausend-Mark-Sperre' in *Festschrift Ludwig Jedlicka* argues that the measure had little effect.

14. Petersen, *Hitler-Mussolini*, p. 191.

15. Ross, *Hitler und Dollfuss*, p. 71.

16. Petersen, *Hitler-Mussolini*, pp. 195-6.

17. See the interesting memorandum of the Bundesrat member Josef Pleyl. *AVA*, Zl. Pr. IV — 2606/ 1934, Box 13.

18. Gehl, *Anschluss*, pp. 60-1.

19. *NPA*, Fasz. 477.

20. Ibid.

21. Ibid. Mussolini spoke of 'il projetto di reforma della constituzione austriaca, reforma su basi *fasciste* dal punto di vista politico, economico, sociale'.

22. Ibid.

23. Ibid. Mussolini to Dollfuss, 9 September 1933. Austria should abandon the 'morta gora del liberalismo e della democrazia'.

24. Lajos Kerekes, *Abenddämmerung einer Demokratie* (Vienna 1966), p. 158.

25. *NPA*, Fasz. 105.

26. Petersen, *Hitler-Mussolini*, p. 285.

27. *NPA*, Fasz. 466.

28. Ross, *Hitler und Dollfuss*, p. 114.

29. *NPA*, Fasz. 466.

30. Ibid.

31. G.D. C, vol. 1, no. 405.

32. Franz Langroth, *Kampf um Oesterreich* (Wels 1951), pp. 120-32.

33. See the article by Ackerl in *Vom Justizpalast zum Heldenplatz* (Vienna 1975), p. 121.

34. G.D. C vol. II, no. 35.

35. *NPA*, Fasz. 466.

36. Ibid.

37. Ibid.

38. *NPA*, Fasz. 257. See 'Martin' (Helmut Hütter) to Hornbostel, 8 September 1933. Among other problems the Hungarians also desired to get back the Burgenland from Austria.

39. Gehl in his excellent book argues that Dollfuss was simply a tactician trying to establish an equilibrium in a highly unstable political situation. Although he was exceptionally flexible, it is mistaken to see Dollfuss as a man totally without political principles.

40. G.D. C, vol. II, no. 126.

41. Petersen, *Hitler-Mussolini*, p. 291.

42. *NPA*, Fasz. 466.

43. Ibid.

44. Ibid.

45. Ibid.

46. Ibid.

47. Ibid.

48. Ibid. A marginal comment reads 'Optimistic!!!'

49. Ibid.

50. Ibid.

51. Ibid.

52. Ibid.

53. Ibid.

54. Ibid.

55. Ibid.

56. House of Commons Debate, 6 February 1934.

57. *NPA*, Fasz. 466.

58. *Frankfurter Zeitung*, 1 January 1934. This was one of the most intelligent and best-informed papers in Germany.

59. G.D. II, no. 143.

60. Gehl *Anschluss*, pp. 74-7; Ross, *Hitler und Dollfuss*, pp. 140-57.

61. *NPA*, Fasz. 466.

62. Ibid; Franz Winkler, *Die Diktatur in Oesterreich* (Zürich 1935), pp. 86-8.

63. *NPA*, Fasz. 466.

64. Ibid.

65. Petersen, *Hitler-Mussolini*, p. 293.

66. Petersen suggests that the Italians might have known of an intended visit by Habicht, but did not know the precise date. When they knew for certain that the meeting would take place before the Suvich visit they acted immediately. This is plausible, but without any evidence it is merely a hypothesis.

67. G.D. II, no. 188.

68. Petersen, *Hitler-Mussolini*, p. 294, for the best account of the visit.

69. *NPA*, Fasz. 114.

70. Ludwig Jedlicka, 'Neue Forschungsergebnisse zum 12 February 1934', *Oesterreich in Geschichte und Literatur*, 2 (1964).

71. *Börsenzeitung*, 28 December 1933.

72. *Völkische Beobachter*, 28 December 1933.

73. Ibid., 4 January 1934.

74. *NPA*, Fasz. 1006. Innitzer was a friend of a prominent Nazi, Dr Ammende, who in turn was a close associate of Rosenberg. As scholars are denied access to the diocesan archives in Vienna it is impossible to examine the role of the church. One is led to the obvious conclusion that the church authorities have something to hide.

75. Ibid., Fasz. 466.

76. Ibid.

77. It is interesting that Hitler did not receive Rieth until after 12 February, thus showing his comparative lack of interest in Austrian affairs at this time. Hans-Adolf Jacobsen, *Nationalsozialistische Aussenpolitik 1933-1938* (Berlin 1968), p. 409.

78. *AVA*, Ministerrat Protokolle, 918-23, Karton 170.
79. Ibid.
80. *NPA*, Fasz. 12.
81. Ibid., Fasz. 107.
82. Petersen, *Hitler-Mussolini*, p. 296.
83. *NPA*, Fasz. 477.
84. Ibid., Fasz. 105 for press clippings.
85. Ibid., Fasz. 1006.
86. Ibid.
87. Ibid.
88. Ibid. Why Danneberg said 'February' is obscure.
89. Ibid.
90. Ibid.

8   THE PATRIOTIC FRONT

In March 1933 Dollfuss gave a speech in Innsbruck in the course of a local election campaign in which he said: 'Thus I believe that today and for the next while we are in a decisive period...when party differences no longer have a place. I call upon our Christian and German people in the alpine provinces, old and young, to form an Austrian Patriotic Front.'[1] For the first time the phrase 'Patriotic Front' was introduced to the Austrian public, although it was still a vague and nebulous concept, an expression for the desire for political and national unity rather than a concrete programme. Dollfuss appealed to the 'revolutionary idea of patriotism' and called for unconditional support for the task that lay ahead to form an effective government in the place of the parliamentary régime that had ceased to exist when parliament had been closed on 4 March 1933.

The response to this speech was encouraging. The Ballhausplatz was flooded with letters of support. A special office, the Heimatdienst, was formed to deal with this mail and to co-ordinate effective propaganda. The office was closely associated with the Heimwehr, and its chief, Pankraz Kruckenhauser, was a Nazi who sabotaged the work of his own department. It is thus hardly surprising that in spite of an initial response which might, with care, have been effectively exploited, the idea of a Patriotic Front failed to win widespread public approval and support.

Kruckenhauser was replaced in August 1933 but the Heimatdienst remained a somewhat ineffective propaganda institution, unable to match either the Social Democratic, Communist or Nazi propagandists in skill and experience. Dollfuss gave a large number of public speeches in which he stressed his government's rejection of 'red and brown socialism' and its determination to uphold true Austrian values. The military band of the Deutschmeister, Fanny Starhemberg's Women's Organisation, the weekly newsreel *Austria in Pictures and in Sound*, the Union of Christian Employees and the Wehrbund (army league) were all roped in to play their part in a massive effort to win support for the 'Austrian idea'.

173

There was a certain amount of curiosity and even enthusiasm for these displays of patriotic fervour, but this potential was never developed. Part of the problem was that not even Dollfuss really knew what the Patriotic Front was supposed to be. It was agreed that it was not a trade union, and that it was not a political party, but its positive qualities remained obscure. In August 1933 the Employment Organisation (DO — *Dienststellenorganisation*) was formed, forcing all white-collar workers in government departments, or in companies that were closely associated with the government, to join the Patriotic Front via the DO. Protests against this move were silenced with the remark that only true patriots could possibly be good civil servants, but this answer could not hide the fact that membership of the DO was compulsory in spite of protests to the contrary.[2]

It was hoped that the Patriotic Front could be organised on the basis of cells (*Sprengel*) under a Sprengelführer, or leader. Each cell would have ten members, the ten Sprengelführer would form a group under a Gruppenführer and so on, by tens, up to a national leader. This ambitious scheme, based on the organisation schemes of the Patriotic Front's opponents on the left and on the right, was never fully realised. Organisation at the grass-roots level was very weak, members being forced into the Patriotic Front either by the DO, or through the equivalent Works Organisation (BO — *Betriebsorganisation*) which was designed to replace the Social Democratic unions. With no genuine enthusiasm for the Patriotic Front among the working class and the petty bourgeoisie, force and persuasion were the only effective ways of getting members. With the high level of unemployment it was possible to face employees with the choice of either joining the Patriotic Front or losing their jobs. It took a brave man of strong political convictions to refuse such blackmail. But even in this policy there was confusion, as Neustädter-Stürmer pointed out at a cabinet meeting in July 1933. The government could not decide whether to adopt a policy of persuasion or to emulate the example of Italy and Germany and simply use force. A mixture of the two policies was bound to fail. In October Fey announced a policy under which government contracts would only be given to 'patriotic' firms, and these firms could only employ members of the Patriotic Front. This became law on 23 January 1934. But such measures created a great deal of ill feeling towards the Patriotic Front, and were not harsh enough to create an atmosphere of resignation in the face of a measure that might have been accepted as harsh but necessary by the politically uncommitted.

In an attempt to counter the 'heathen swastika' the Patriotic Front adopted its own symbol, the cross potent (*Kruckenkreuz*), the symbol of the holy sepulchre and the Kingdom of Jerusalem, also of King Arthur and his knights, and a particular favourite of Seipel's. For Dollfuss it was the symbol of the crusade for a new Austria, of the 'knightly ideals of mediaeval chivalry' of the 'highest ideals of the high middle ages', the 'cross created by the sons of the north', and a 'uniquely Germanic cross'.[3] In these outbursts there is a characteristic blend of a reactionary and sentimental hankering after the distant past, typical of ultra movements, and a fervent belief in the power of symbols and imagery to inspire and unite a political movement.

It was hoped that the Patriotic Front would replace the political activity of the parties as parliament had been closed, the Communist Party and the Nazis banned in the following months, and the Social Democrats clearly next in line as soon as a suitable opportunity presented itself. The Christian Social Party devoted most of its efforts to winning supporters for the Patriotic Front. But the attitude of the party faithful to this new role was mixed. Many were so enthusiastic for the end of party politics that they were quite happy to see what amounted to the destruction of their own party. The argument ran that Dollfuss was no longer a Christian Social, he was a true Austrian, and some of his followers were prepared to follow this romantic path. But others were uncertain. They wished to preserve the party, at least as a security against the National Socialists, who certainly had not lost their belief in the efficacy of party politics, even though their final aim was to destroy the other political parties, and, as the experience of Germany was to show, to destroy themselves. Many Christian Socials were also understandably concerned about the vagueness of the Patriotic Front's programme that seemed to have nothing much to offer but empty slogans. Part of this was sour grapes, for the end of party politics also meant the end of comfortable political appointments for the party leadership. Dollfuss needed the support of the Christian Social Party in order to build up the Patriotic Front, but once the Patriotic Front was strong enough there would be little further use for the party. The Christian Social Party itself had always been something of a mixed bag. There was a liberal wing that opposed Dollfuss's authoritarian government and wished to return to parliamentary democracy. Others felt that the Patriotic Front was simply the Christian Social Party under a new name, but many of these were to soon become disillusioned. The powerful role of the Heimwehr both in the Patriotic Front and in the government, and the growing influence of fascist ideology, were matters of grave concern. Talk of 'dictatorship' and of the 'un-Christian Patriotic Front' were frequent and symptomatic complaints by the Christian Social faithful, the first by the democratic wing, the second by the politicised Catholics. A third group, which was sympathetic to the Heimwehr and supported a fascistic course for Austria, had no striking leaders but had considerable support among the rank and file. In general the Christian Social Party followed Dollfuss, often with a certain degree of reluctance and without any great enthusiasm, largely because there seemed to them to be no valid alternative. They were uncertain where they were going, but they were certainly dissatisfied with things as they were.

The main problem for the Patriotic Front seemed to be the attitude of the Heimwehr. They saw the Patriotic Front as a challenge to their own position, and claimed a monopoly of authoritarian and 'truly Austrian' ideas. If the Chancellor wished to build an authoritarian and fascistic Austria, then why not do so on the basis of a proven movement rather than risk the formation of a new and somewhat dubious organisation without traditions, roots or enthusiastic support? After Dollfuss's famous speech at the trotting-racetrack, in which he sketched the outline of the new authoritarian state, Starhemberg issued an order to the Heimatschutz that no member should attend meetings of the Patriotic Front in uniform, and that the Heimatschutz would not take part in any manifestations of the Patriotic Front. Members were not allowed to join the Patriotic Front, make propaganda for it or wear its insignia. This order was partly the result of the strained relations between Starhemberg and Dollfuss, but it was also because the Heimwehr was uncertain quite what the Patriotic Front involved. Thus the order was as much a question of 'wait and see' as it was an outright rejection of the new organisation. With the new government of September 1933, which was clearly authoritarian and a distinct break with the old parliamentary régime, the Heimwehr became more favourably disposed towards the Patriotic Front. At the end of September the provincial leaders of the Heimwehr announced that their movement would give it its undivided support. In October Starhemberg accepted an appointment in the leadership of the Patriotic Front. But this did not end the problems of the relationship between the Patriotic Front and the Heimwehr. Many members of the Heimwehr were concerned that their organisation would simply become absorbed by the Patriotic Front, and negotiations with Dollfuss were complicated by the rivalry between Starhemberg and Fey, the latter wanting to keep his distance from the Patriotic Front.

For Starhemberg the agreement between the Heimwehr and the Patriotic Front was 'a further step along the way to the success and realisation of the fundamental ideas of a special fascist idea of the state in Austria'.[4] This statement is a clear indication of Starhemberg's position. The Patriotic Front could become the instrument of creating a fascist Austria, as his often reluctant supporter, Mussolini, wanted and as Dollfuss intended. Fey, with his closer association with the Nazis, was unwilling to let the Heimwehr become the armed wing of the Patriotic Front, and wished to preserve its relative independence in order to give it greater bargaining power.

Relations between the Landbund, with its curious blend of antiquated liberalism and belief in the organisation of the state according to the estates, and the Patriotic Front were also very strained. The Landbund, which had long called for a society according to the estates, but with a degree of parliamentary democracy to distinguish it from authoritarian and fascist variations of this same nebulous theme, felt that the Patriotic Front was usurping its ideas. The Landbund therefore hoped to counter the move towards the creation of a fascistic state by the formation of a 'National Front of the Estates' (*nationale ständische Front*) under the then Vice-Chancellor, Winkler. Winkler hoped that he could counter the influence of the Heimwehr with its fascist ideology, and strengthen his own political position within the cabinet. Dollfuss suggested that Winkler should amalgamate the 100,000 members of his Front with the Patriotic Front. At first Winkler was tempted, thinking that his membership was large enough to counter the influence of the Heimwehr within the Patriotic Front. But after Riccione, and the beginnings of a distinctly fascistic course in Austrian politics, Winkler was one of the very few politicians not on the left who realised that it was absurd to pretend that one could combat National Socialism by creating an Austro-fascism.[5] From September 1933 Winkler's Front was outspokenly critical of the Heimwehr and the new course. In the ensuing struggle the Heimwehr was triumphant. With the support of Mussolini, its control of key government positions and its closeness to Dollfuss's own position, it could easily outmanoeuvre the Landbund and its affiliates.

The Landbund was now hopelessly isolated. In February 1934 the Landbund leader Pistor told the Social Democrat Witternigg that Dollfuss had betrayed the Landbund and that he would support a move by the Social Democrats to recall parliament. Witternigg replied that the Landbund had turned down so many offers by the Social Democrats for joint action in the past that he could hardly take this move seriously. He then put forward the highly dubious suggestion that as Dollfuss had borrowed money from France, and had promised to be democratic, there was no danger that the Social Democratic Party would be disbanded.[6] In this exchange there can be no doubt that Pistor was more perspicacious than Witternigg, but the Land-bund, like so many political organisations in Austria at that time, had no clear programme and was a collection of often contradictory tendencies. While one group was sending out feelers to the Social Democrats, another was intriguing with the Nazis in Munich. Soon after 12 February the organisation was disbanded.

Thus the Patriotic Front was never able to win the hearts and minds of Austrians as Dollfuss had hoped. It soon degenerated into a system of coercion and favouritism that attracted opportunists and careerists, not the selfless and dedicated patriots to whom the Chancellor so frequently appealed. Joining the Front made all the difference if one wished to get a tobacco concession, or sell lottery tickets; failure to do so might mean the loss of one's job in the civil service, or of an important government contract. There were many people who were prepared to say 'yes to Austria' as Schuschnigg demanded, but very few would give an unqualified 'yes' to the Austria of Dollfuss and the Patriotic Front. By February 1934 Austria was going headlong towards its own form of fascistic state, the Patriotic Front having fallen completely into the hands of those who wished to put into effect the reforms suggested by Mussolini at Riccione. Indeed, many leaders of the Patriotic Front were pushing Dollfuss to establish a fully autho-ritarian régime.

Although the 12 February seemed to be a triumph for the Patriotic Front and the most significant step towards the creation of the new Austria of which there had been so much talk, it was Fey and the Heimatschutz who appeared as the immediate heroes, and the National Socialists the long-range winners. The Patriotic Front played little part in the events. The Front's automobile association offered its members vehicles as alternative transport to the Vienna tramways that had been closed down by the strike. The DOs and the BOs by their very existence helped to frustrate any attempt to call a general strike. The leadership had to admit that it had played no part in the glorious struggle against Marxism, for this was the task of the executive, but it comforted itself in the belief that it had done much to create the moral climate in which such a crusade was possible.

The ideology of the Patriotic Front was based on the ideas of political Catholicism which had always found strong support in Austria.[7] Political Catholicism itself resulted from violent reactions to the political revolution in France and the industrial revolution in England, twin revolutions which overthrew traditional European values. The Catholic church rejected the idea of the rights of man as an attack on man's obligations to God, and also despised *laissez-faire* liberalism for its lack of concern for the downtrodden and the under-privileged. The church insisted on the divine nature of the state's authority which obliged it to show real concern for the welfare of the citizens. According to Pope Leo XIII, liberalism, by refusing to accept the notion of a society based on the rights and duties of the individual according to his place in society, had opened the door to the grim materialistic totalitarianism of socialism. The church offered two answers to the modern predicament: social reform, which involved the restoration of the old organic order based on hierarchy, and social politics, which was concerned with reforms within the existing system. In Leo XIII's encyclical *Rerum Novarum* of 1918 the emphasis was firmly on social politics, although many Austrian Catholic thinkers, the most prominent being Karl Vogelsang, continued to stress the paramount importance of social reform.

Unlike many Catholic conservatives Vogelsang was a supporter of Lueger, for he detested the liberal state not only for its denial of a higher moral law but also for its inability to protect its weaker members against rapacious capitalism. He believed that society should be organised according to the Stände 'estates', but this remained a hopelessly vague notion that was never given any concrete expression. With its idealisation of the community spirit which was supposed to have existed in the Middle Ages, the ideology of the Ständestaat was essentially an expression of the aspirations of the artisans and small businessmen who were threatened by modern industrial capitalism dressed up as concern for the working class.[8] Thus in the Korneuburger oath there was an attack on 'liberal-Jewish high capitalism' as well as 'bolshevism', although the former was the sour-grapes anti-capitalism of the little man, whereas the anti-socialist component of the programme was far more genuine and menacing.

Ignaz Seipel's political ideas were equally vague and subject to frequent changes. In his book *Nation and State*, published in 1916, Seipel seemed to be on the liberal wing of political Catholicism, emphasising the distinction between the state and society and insisting that as the state was not an absolute it could only make limited demands on the individual. This liberalism took on alarming proportions in the eyes of many conservative Catholics when he argued in favour of accepting the new republic, but then much to their relief he was to become one of the republic's most outspoken and violent critics. Seipel tried to get out of this apparent contradiction by talking about 'true democracy', a concept that remained deliberately vague and could mean almost anything. True democracy was to be based on the twin principles of piety and authority. The political parties, lacking piety and engaged in constant wrangles that undermined the authority of the state, were thus clearly undemocratic. True democracy involved the abolition of liberal democracy, but it was never clear what was to take its place.

In spite of uncertainties about what the Ständestaat or true democracy really involved, there was general agreement in the Catholic camp on certain fundamental principles. There was no question that the enemy was on the left, and all factions were united in a violent anti-socialism. They were also against liberal democracy on the grounds that it was based on individualism which destroyed traditional values, undermined the sense of community and led to a selfish materialism. Similarly, the political parties were condemned on the grounds that they made it impossible to rule by consensus. Lastly, they demanded strong and firm government which was impossible as long as the executive was hamstrung by the deadlock between the Christian Socials and the Social Democrats.

With the onset of the depression the Vatican turned its attention once again to the social question, and in 1931, forty years after *Rerum Novarum*, Pius XI published his encyclical *Quadragesimo Anno*. As its title suggests, the new encyclical was based on the earlier document, reaffirming the basic notion of human solidarity as a means of overcoming the social problem. Pius XI repeated Leo XIII's belief that the division of society into a small group of the wealthy and a vast mass of the poor could not be overcome by either socialism or liberalism, the former because it offers 'a remedy much more disastrous than the evil it is designed to cure' and the latter because it had proved incapable of solving the social question.[9] Once more the need for social justice, for the protection of the 'sacred rights of working men', and for co-operation between the classes was emphasised. As a means towards these ends the Pope stressed the need for Christian trade unions, and also for associations of employers. He was anxious to defend the church against the charge that it sided with the wealthier classes against the proletariat, and thus insisted that property had both an individual and a social character, giving particular weight to the obligations of the latter. Although private ownership is 'ordained by nature itself...wealth...must be so distributed amongst the various individuals and classes of society that the common good of all...be thereby promoted'.[10] To achieve this the state may have to exercise its right to adjust ownership to meet the needs of the public good, but the usual method would be to ensure that workers received a just wage, a wage which should take into consideration the needs of individual families. In a just society both capital and labour should get their fair share, but the Pope was quick to point out that the notion of fairness was singularly hard to define.

Individualism, according to the encyclical, had led to the destruction of the social fabric. The aim of Catholic Social policy should thus be to restore to social life the organic form that had been lost. The class struggle should be replaced by co-operation between the various ranks of society. Quoting Ephesians iv 16 the Pope argued that the ideal society was one in which 'The whole body being compacted and fitly joined together, by what every joint supplieth, according to the operation in the measure of every part, maketh increase of the body, into the edifying of itself in charity.' This ideal in practice was remarkably similar to Italian fascism. Corporations should be founded in which both employers and employees were represented, strikes and lock-outs should be banned, and if no agreement could be reached between the two sides the state would have to intervene.

There was no doubt in the Pope's mind that the principal evil of the modern world was socialism, but the encyclical is also outspoken in its attacks on the monopolistic accumulation of wealth, which was the result of free competition and which led to repression, injustice and war.[11] As a result free competition died, to be replaced by economic dictatorship. It was thus hardly surprising that the working class turned in such numbers to socialism for a solution to their problems. The encyclical repeated the assertion of Leo XIII that socialism and Christianity are irreconcilable, and insisted that only if society returns to Christian principles could the social problem be solved.

The encyclical is thus a vague and ambiguous document. The attack on socialism is clear and outspoken. Criticisms of the abuses of modern capitalist society are both frequent and forceful. The suggested remedies are much less precise, and the relative importance of corporative and democratic elements is never clearly delineated. On the one hand there are unmistakably positive references to the organisational model of Italian fascism, and yet on the other hand it is implied that the ideal corporate structure should be based on free self-

governing professional bodies that could lead to a degree of democratisation of the workplace. In Austria, the *Quadragesimo Anno* was
interpreted in the most authoritarian manner possible. Dollfuss deliberately used the encyclical as a justification for his own fascistic
policies, and within the Christian Social party there was an increasing
demand for an authoritarian régime based on the estates which, it was
argued, was fully in accordance with the teaching of the church. The
Austrian bishops were so blinded by their hatred of Social Democracy
that they did nothing to protest against this clearly one-sided interpretation of the encyclical. It was the common determination to
destroy socialism that bound all the movements of the right together,
and the *Quadragesimo Anno* gave the Catholics an admirable excuse
to join the crusade. Thus it was a simple task for Dollfuss to combine
the teaching of the encyclical with the fascism of the Heimwehr as can
be so vividly seen in his speech at the trotting-racetrack in September
1933.

The alliance between the Christian Socials and the Heimwehr with
its authoritarian and anti-socialist policies was most attractive to many
industrialists who longed for the opportunity to destroy any vestiges of
industrial democracy and to crush the unions, thus establishing their
unchallenged control over the economic sphere. But the new alliance
was certainly not merely an expression of the political aspirations of
the economic elite. As the depression deepened the call for a new
society and an end to the old corrupt and inefficient system found an
enthusiastic echo among the people at large. However vague and
contradictory the arguments, the promise of a radical solution and the
heady mixture of anti-socialism and anti-capitalism became increasingly tempting to those whose position seemed hopeless. But at the
same time the siren call of the National Socialists was attracting an
ever-increasing number, particularly from the Greater German bourgeoisie, the urban middle classes and ring-wing intellectuals. The
anti-democratic right was thus divided into two hostile camps, the one
appealing to the traditions of the church and of Austrian nationalism,
the other to the dynamism of the 'New Germany' and the intoxication
of radical fascism.

The formation of the Patriotic Front in May 1933 was thus an
attempt to cement the alliance between the Christian Socials and the
Heimwehr, to provide a forceful alternative to Nazism, and to provide
mass support for the movement. From the outset this was a marriage of
convenience that lacked cohesion and a sense of common purpose. In
the long run it could not possibly match the Nazis as a radical move-

ment directed towards clearly perceived political aims. The Patriotic Front was a mixture of Heimwehr fascists, Christian romantics, Austrian nationalists, Nazi sympathisers, anti-socialist autocrats and even those who had a lingering affection for parliamentary democracy. Its mass support was questionable, and there seemed to be little hope of welding all these elements together to form a genuine alternative to National Socialism. There were many who called for a policy of the firm hand, but firmness alone at this stage was not enough.

The response of the Social Democrats to these developments was confused. From March 1933 the party became seriously divided between those who demanded action, fearing that Austria was going headlong towards fascism, and the moderates who felt that the Dollfuss régime was the lesser evil that should be given some support for fear that otherwise the Nazis would come to power. March was a dramatic month. On 1 March the railwaymen's strike had been broken, army units taking over the railway stations. Three days later parliament was closed down on a technicality, and the following day the Christian Socials announced that they intended to rule without parliament and establish an authoritarian state. On 7 March the government began its new authoritarian policy, using as a basis the war emergency laws of 1917. The freedom of the press was drastically restricted, political demonstrations were rigorously controlled and frequently forbidden. On 15 March the Social Democrats and Greater Germans tried to reopen the parliamentary session, but were stopped by the police. The following day the Schutzbund was forbidden in the Tyrol. On 25 March the government decided to steer a harshly anti-socialist course, and at the end of the month the Schutzbund was banned.

This rapid series of events appeared to many Social Democrats to be alarmingly similar to events in Germany during the previous year. Many militants demanded action before it was too late. There were frequent articles in the party press during March which stressed the gravity of the situation, and provided ample arguments for the militants. The party headquarters were flooded with resolutions from Social Democratic groups throughout Austria, and from individual party members, demanding action.[12] Within the Schutzbund, even before the formal ban on the organisation, there was widespread disappointment that the order had not been given to fight in defence of democracy.[13] The inaction of the party leadership resulted in some of the younger members of the party and of the Schutzbund joining the Nazis who were unquestionably more militant. The party could afford to lose the hotheads and adventurers whose motives for political activity were excitement and adventure rather than commitment and understanding, but it failed to appreciate the degree to which the rank and file were losing their enthusiasm, and were falling into the kind of resignation that had paralysed the party in Germany. In the Tyrol the party was bitterly disappointed that the leadership had done little when the Schutzbund was banned, particularly as there was a clear realisation that this was part of deliberate strategy designed to destroy the party.[14] It is clear that in the Tyrol there were many Social Democrats who were ready to make any sacrifice to avoid sharing the fate of their German comrades. Feelings ran high in the Tyrol, not simply because it was here that the Schutzbund was first banned, but also because, being a border province, the people were well aware of the reality of German fascism, and because the Nazi Party was particularly strong and menacing there.

As the Schutzbund was forced onto the defensive, and then outlawed, the contrast between it and the Heimwehr became all the more pronounced and added to the demoralisation of the movement. The Heimwehr was better equipped and better paid than the Schutzbund and it enjoyed the support and the sympathy of the authorities. To the militants, only decisive action could counteract this slow erosion of enthusiasm and confidence and the remorseless progress of fascism. As early as 12 March, the local party organisation in Ferlach wrote a detailed letter to party headquarters, arguing that the government was clearly determined to establish a '100% dictatorship'. The mood in the party was one of 'enough is enough' and the local membership had reached the conclusion that the time had come to act. 'Every proletarian today must be on the alert and show the absolute, clear and unflinching will to use all means to seize state power.'

Such ideas were by no means simply isolated outbursts of frustration, they were indicative of a profound malaise within the party. The example of German Social Democracy which had submitted to fascism without a struggle was a terrible warning that few could ignore. Most Austrian socialists were determined that the same thing should not happen in their country. In response to each of Dollfuss's authoritarian moves, demands came from local organisations for action.[15] In the course of the summer there was a certain cooling of passions. Perhaps the banning of the National Socialists in June strengthened the hands of those in the party leadership who constantly argued that Dollfuss was better than Hitler, a point of view that was fiercely rebutted by the militants with the argument that the German party's policy of the lesser evil had led them to disaster, and that fascism should be combated in any of its many forms.

With the clear associations between Dollfuss and Mussolini, the Riccione meetings were in late August, and with the racetrack speech in September, there was renewed militancy within the party. The argument that Dollfuss was not as bad as Hitler could now be answered by pointing out that he was rapidly becoming a mini-Mussolini. The threat of an authoritarian, anti-parliamentary and fascistic constitution was now very real. Between 14 and 16 October an extraordinary party conference was held in Vienna to discuss strategy in the face of the mounting danger of fascism. As a clear sign that things had changed, the protocol of the conference had to be shown to the State Secretary for Security in person.[16] The details of the conference were not allowed to be published in the press.[17]

The three main aims of the conference, according to advance publicity, were to delete the demand for an Anschluss from the party programme, which in spite of the fact that the Nazis had come to power in Germany was still formally on the programme, to elect a new party directorate and to create a 60-member party council that would mediate between the directorate and the congress.[18] The real purpose of the congress, however, was to try to placate the left opposition and unify the party behind a leadership that was losing credibility.

The left opposition set the tone of the conference from the beginning.[19] There were demands for a general strike in defence of democracy, as was provided for in the Linz programme that was still the official programme of the party. Others went further, calling for a defensive war against the authoritarian moves of the government. There were frequent attacks on the leadership's theory of the lesser evil, and an insistence that this policy had been a disaster in Germany. There was general agreement that no further compromises should be made with the government and that the time had come for the party finally to take a stand.

This feeling of discontent and frustration was not reserved to the far left. Manfred Ackermann, a leader of the white-collar workers who was not a member of the left opposition, pointed out that under certain circumstances it was correct for a party to wait and watch for further developments, but that it was imperative for the party leadership to have a precise and carefully worked-out plan in the case of violent upheaval. At the moment the party seemed to be waiting for the spontaneous activity of the masses, while at the same time being scared of the consequences of such action. Ackermann's speech, in spite of its moderate language and careful phrasing, was a devastating criticism of the leadership's policies. The gist of the argument was that the party was following a policy of wait and see, not out of careful tactical considerations, as the bolsheviks had done before the October Revolution, but because they had no policy at all, and were afraid of the radicalism of the rank and file. As Friedrich Adler had said during his trial in 1917: 'I have come to the conclusion that a revolution in Austria will only take place against the will of the party leadership, and that the party leadership is a brake on revolutionary activity.'[20]

Otto Bauer's speech to the conference was a skilful attempt to reach a compromise, but a compromise was hardly what was needed in October 1933. He began with a rejection of the Anschluss idea, a point on which there could be no possible disagreement. He then tried to paint an optimistic picture of the problems facing the Dollfuss government. The fact that the Landbund was no longer in the government was taken as a sign of a severe split within the bourgeois camp. This was evidence that a significant part of the bourgeoisie, particularly on the land, was disenchanted with Dollfuss's fascistic methods, and Bauer suggested that it might be possible to form an alliance with the disenchanted peasantry and thus strengthen the anti-fascist front. In reply to those at the conference who were calling for an all-out struggle against Austrian fascism he quoted Engels' famous passage in the introduction to the 1895 edition of *Civil War in France* warning about the tremendous difficulty of armed insurrection in modern states.

Bauer tried to interpret the demand for a determined, and if necessary violent, anti-fascist struggle as a demand for an immediate socialist revolution. This to him was tantamount to a putsch by the party leadership which was bound to either fail or degenerate into dictatorship. What was needed was a struggle fired by the 'fundamental passions of the people'. He insisted that there were four instances when the party was duty-bound to fight. If the independent rights of Vienna were attacked and a federal commissar was appointed to rule the capital. If there was an attack on the rights and independence of the trade unions. If there was a direct attack on the party. And finally, if there was an end to the equal ballot and the promulgation of a new constitution. He refused to discuss whether or not the party had followed the right policy on 15 March, which had been a clear and obvious attack on parliamentary democracy, and yet the party had done nothing. He repeated his old argument that the best that could be hoped for under the present circumstances was a bourgeois democracy, because a socialist Austria could not possibly hope to survive when it was surrounded by so many hostile states.

This speech avoided many of the key issues and failed to satisfy the opposition. In a sense it was something of a self-fulfilling prophecy, typical of Austro-Marxism. On the one hand he urged caution and stressed the need to avoid any precipitate action, on the other hand he called for the united and passionate efforts of the masses without which no militant policy could hope to succeed. Yet Bauer's speech was calculated to dampen the passion and the determination of the masses and thus justify the inaction of the party leadership. By talking about the possibility of a socialist revolution in Austria he was deliberately avoiding the central question of how best to combat fascism. As such, the speech, in the final analysis, was an admission that Bauer's tactics had failed in March, and was an attempt to justify the party's inaction rather than to tackle the immediate and pressing problem of what to do in the next few months. Not until after February 1934 was Bauer to admit this terrible mistake, but it is greatly to his credit that he did so. It was one thing to have four conditions under which the party was prepared to fight, it was quite another thing to work out how to organise that fight, especially when the leadership had virtually admitted that a fight was impossible.[21]

Bauer's speech failed to satisfy the radicals. The delegation from Bruck-an-der-Mur called for a general strike in the event of the creation of new provincial assemblies, or assemblies based on the estates, as seemed to be threatened in the forthcoming constitutional changes. The Rothneusidel delegation condemned the 'wait and see' policy of the leadership and insisted that the time had come for action. The mood of the Viennese delegates was also militant. Vienna-Neubau insisted on a general strike in defence of the Linz programme's demand that democracy should be defended at all costs. Vienna-Alsergrund demanded the end of all emergency legislation against the working class and the abolition of fascist paramilitary organisations. Vienna-Favoriten spoke out against the leadership's 'wait and see' policy. Vienna-Ottakring called for harsh measures against the Nazis. Vienna-Hernal suggested a hard line against the government, and said that force would have to be used if any further inroads were made into the liberties of Austrian people. Vienna-Inner City said that the time had come for the party to go on the offensive. Vienna-Döbling attacked the policy of the lesser evil. The delegation from Wollersdorf was more concerned with economic conditions and suggested mass action to stop any further reduction in the workers' real wages, or any worsening of working conditions. The provincial party of Lower Austria, a province that failed to respond in February 1934, condemned the party leadership for having lost sight of the aim of the socialist movement which is the creation of a socialist society, and suggested that this was because the party leadership was too old and should be replaced by younger and more active people.

There were a considerable number of delegates from foreign parties at the conference, even though it was an extraordinary conference, and these delegates gave strong support to the leadership. Smith, representing the British Labour Party, expressed the solidarity of the Trades Union Congress and the Labour Party for the Austrian socialists, and talked in glowing terms of the leadership. From France, Leon Blum was more concerned about foreign politics, saying that there was a very real danger that Germany and Italy would settle their differences, and that when this happened Austria would almost certainly go fascist, and then there would be a serious danger of war. Albarda from Holland, Stivin from Czechoslovakia and Grimm from Switzerland gave conventional speeches of solidarity, but Vandervelde, speaking for the Socialist International, warned against the policy of the lesser evil which, in a remarkable analogy, he compared to eating an artichoke — leaf after leaf goes until there is nothing left. The faded hero of the left, Friedrich Adler, defended the fatalism of the right by attacking what he believed to be the fatalism of the left in their apparent belief that fascism was inevitable. Adler argued that Dollfuss and his crew knew nothing about politics and appealed for unity which alone would save the party from a common danger.

During the conference the left did most of the talking and won most of the debating points. Among the outstanding and most energetic of the left was Ernst Fischer, a young editor of the *Arbeiter-Zeitung* who was to join the Communist Party after the failure of the February uprising and who was beginning his career as a leading Marxist intellectual. Fischer's short book, *Crisis of Youth*, had been a considerable success, and he was already the unofficial spokesman of the left.[22] But the silent majority continued to support the leadership, and the left was defeated, thus adding to the frustration and sense of powerlessness of the militants, who were still convinced that, unless something drastic were done, Austria would go the same way as Italy and Germany. Outwardly unity was preserved and the leadership was unshaken, but within the party there was severe malaise.

Bauer's 'four points' which the party was prepared to defend with all the power at its command were amplified in a six-point resolution on tactics. Since the government took the party's willingness to negotiate — a willingness that was reaffirmed at the conference — as a sign of weakness, the party made the following six demands: parliament should be reconvened; an anti-inflationary policy should be put into effect, and jobs found immediately for 200,000 workers; the freedom of assembly and association should be restored; unemployment insurance benefits should be increased; there should be freedom of the press and of assembly for all democratic parties; all fascist paramilitary organisations should be disarmed and disbanded. If any of the Heimwehr's demands for constitutional change were met there would be a general strike.

In a sense the four points on fundamentals and the six points on tactics were a concession to the left and a means of maintaining the unity of the party, but it can be argued that they were a serious tactical mistake. Critics pointed out that by listing the conditions under which the party was prepared to fight it was in effect allowing the government to do anything short of these things. Given the overwhelming evidence that Dollfuss was slowly chipping away at the foundations of the democratic state, this policy was bound to fail.[23] The Austro-Marxist sheep was being dressed up as a militant wolf, but this failed to impress Dollfuss and his government.

The party conference was the first clear indication of the growing strength of the left opposition within the party. Until then it was possible to dismiss the left as a group of young hotheads who would sooner or later see reason, but their performance at the conference showed that the left had wide support and that it was a coherent expression of a deeply felt disenchantment with the leadership and its policies. The left was to grow in strength and influence between October and February and then many were to join the Communist Party. The movement had started among the Social Democratic youth in the Jungfront, which in April 1933 had passed a resolution calling for action and condemning the party leadership. The resolution was couched in violent language: 'We are not willing through loyalty to the party leadership to become criminals and deliver up our youth to the serfdom and slavery of fascism.' The resolution also attacked the salaries of party functionaries and their lack of accountability to the rank and file.[24] In August 1933 there was a call from the 19th district in Vienna for the amalgamation of the Second and Third Internationals on the grounds that 'the unconditional support of bourgeois democracy leads inevitably to fascism'. What was needed was a united front against fascism.[25]

The leadership was hardly perturbed by such outbursts. The first could be attributed to the impatience of youth, the second to a minor local victory for the Communist Party and its persistent call for a united front against fascism. It was not realised that the party was becoming seriously divided, that the leadership was losing touch with the mood of the rank and file, and that such occasional outbursts could not be easily disregarded.

At the end of October the Czechoslovakian Social Democrats held their party conference, and the chairman of the party emphasised the tremendous importance of Austria, assuring the Austrian comrades of the complete solidarity of the party. The Austrian government was particularly concerned with the attitude of the Czech party, and watched the conference closely. Gömbös was also worried about the activities of the Schutzbund in Czechoslovakia, activities that were highly alarming to the local bourgeoisie whom Gömbös and the Austrian government hoped to used to drive the Schutzbund out of Czechoslovakia. The Czech Communist newspaper *Rudý Večerník* said that the Austrian Social Democrats were trying to get the Western powers to intervene, a point of view that was shared by the Austrian government.[26] Indeed this was a constant theme of the Austrian government that the Social Democrats were the marionettes of the Western powers, a view that had been derided by Leon Blum in his speech to the conference in Vienna, and that they could not therefore possibly claim to be able to speak on behalf of the Austrian people.

In spite of the six-point resolution on tactics at the party conference, the Social Democrats had to submit to a series of humiliating restrictions on their freedom of expression in November. The Socialist International called for a day of remembrance for the German Revolution of 9 November 1918, but the Viennese police would not permit any demonstrations or meetings. Two days later a procession to the grave of Viktor Adler was banned. On 12 November a march of solidarity for Austrian independence by the party was forbidden. The next day a torchlight parade for the mayor of Vienna, Karl Seitz, was also banned.[27]

The party was so obsessed with the danger of Nazism that it tended to overlook the danger that came from the Dollfuss government. Thus the party spent a lot of time collecting detailed information on individual Nazis. An entire section of party headquarters was devoted to the examination of the political affiliations of various prominent figures, and to the uncovering of Nazi agents within the party and the

Schutzbund. The party showed little concern for the Heimatschutz or for the Dollfuss government which it seemed to feel was genuinely anti-Nazi. The party was thus so committed to the policy of the lesser evil, that it could do nothing but make empty protests as its rights and freedoms were slowly whittled away. By concentrating their efforts against the greatest of evils, militant German fascism, the leadership overlooked the lesser but often equally serious evils, and forgot its commitment to democracy that had been reaffirmed at the extraordinary conference in October.[28]

By January 1934 it was clear that the policy outlined at the extraordinary conference had failed. The provincial executive of Lower Austria, the most consistent mouthpiece of the right wing, argued that the proletariat was so badly hit by the economic crisis and unemployment that it could not possibly use the general strike as a weapon, and that the congress's provisions for a general strike to meet the threat of fundamental constitutional change were useless. Since March 1933 the party could not use parliament as a forum. Being unable to use the strike, or parliamentary means, the only possible course of action was to negotiate with the government. The provincial executive suggested that the party should agree to grant the government emergency powers to deal with the present crisis, and that it should accept the idea of the influence of the estates (*berufsständische Einrichtungen*) in a new constitution, and in return the government should agree to the restoration of certain fundamental rights such as the right of assembly.[29]

There was no doubt that the party was failing to live up to the resolutions made at the congress. On 1 January Dollfuss introduced a new budget which was not presented to parliament and was thus clearly unconstitutional. The democratically elected workers' councils (*Arbeiterkammer*), in which the Social Democratic unions had a clear majority, were destroyed. In the Vienna workers' council there had been 111 Free Trade unionists, ten Christian Socials, ten Greater Germans and three Communists. In the new 'Organisational Commission' (*Verwaltungskommission*), which had a mere eleven members, only four came from the trade unions.[30] The Nazis began a fresh wave of terror on New Year's Day, but the Heimwehr also began to step up its anti-socialist activities in emulation of the Italian fascists on whom they were increasingly dependent. At the beginning of February, the Heimwehr smashed the type in a Social Democratic printing shop in Innsbruck. A socialist journalist was beaten up in Rattenberg, the Heimwehr attempting to give him the classic fascist castor-oil treatment. The unfortunate journalist was given five days' arrest for insulting a policeman who seems to have been sympathetic to his assailants.[31]

On 20 January the *Arbeiter-Zeitung* was banned for printing an article on the South Tyrol which was felt to be insulting to the Italian government and to Suvich, as well as being unnecessarily critical of the Dollfuss government.[32] A few days later it was announced that all schoolteachers had to join the Patriotic Front in the province of Carinthia, and that all schoolchildren were to wear the Front's badge. The party insisted that members were not allowed to join the Patriotic Front, so that Social Democratic teachers were faced with the choice of losing their jobs or resigning from the party, a clear violation of their democratic rights of association which the conference had sworn to defend.[33]

On 23 January the federal leadership of the party met to discuss the political situation. In a lengthy speech, Oehm, who represented the Tyrol, gave a thoughtful summary of the dilemma facing the party, an analysis that was quickly denounced by Julius Deutsch as being hopelessly pessimistic.[34] Oehm reported that the trade unionists complained that they were rapidly losing members, and that they were unable to call an effective strike because of the economic situation. The workers were becoming increasingly resigned. Most of them were unable to see the difference between the party and the unions, and were often quick to blame the party leadership for the shortcomings of the unions. The rank and file had little respect or sympathy for the Social Democratic members of parliament who continued to draw their salaries even though parliament had been closed down, and who seemed to show an extraordinary apathy in such critical times. The party conference had called for a determined and united defence of the constitution, but as so many of the fundamental rights guaranteed by the constitution had already been lost, this looked like empty posturing. For Oehm the party had three possible courses of action. It could take a militant line which would have as its first aim the restoration of the constitution. It could capitulate completely to Dollfuss, or it could negotiate to see what could be saved. As the party leadership would not accept a militant line, and as the rank and file were in no mood to capitulate, the only possible course of action was to negotiate with the government. To the charge of pessimism Oehm replied that he had been charged with the same failing in the early 1920s when he had warned that the Volkswehr was unlikely to survive, and Deutsch had dismissed his arguments then. In his defence Oehm quoted the *Manchester Guardian* which had said of the German Social Democrats that they thought it was better to be defeated legally than to be illegally victorious, and that the Austrian socialists were following meekly along the same path.

Part of the reason for this extraordinary lack of concern by the party leadership in the face of the constant and determined attack by the government on basic constitutional rights, was its belief that Dollfuss's régime was primarily concerned with the destruction of National Socialism in Austria. At the beginning of January 1934 party headquarters had written that the government's attacks on National Socialism meant that it would no longer be able to attack the Social Democratic Party as it has done before.[35] The leadership was convinced that if it came to a showdown between Dollfuss and the Social Democrats the Nazis would be the winners. This analysis was perfectly correct, but there was one fatal flaw in the argument. Dollfuss believed the exact opposite.

Political meetings were banned between 1 December 1933 and 15 January 1934 in Dollfuss's 'Christmas truce'. A six-week period in which political passions could cool off suited the party leadership which was convinced that it was aimed largely against the National Socialists. But there was also an uneasy feeling that the Christmas truce might be extended indefinitely, and the party stressed the importance of 'careful preparation for the time when normal means of communication (press, meetings, etc.) are no longer possible'. This document was seized by the police after 12 February and used as evidence that the uprising had been carefully prepared. Whether the police seriously believed this ridiculous piece of evidence is not recorded.[36]

In these circumstances it is hardly surprising that the left wing of the party grew increasingly strong and outspoken. This was a matter of particular concern to the party leadership, because since parliament had been closed down in March 1933 the party had lost 32 per cent of its membership.[37] The strength of the leadership rested on the support of the ordinary rank and file, but this was slowly withering away so as to offer greater opportunities to the militants effectively to attack the leadership. There were two main groupings on the left, the Trotskyite 'Revolutionary Opposition within the Social Democratic Party of German Austria' (*Revolutionären Opposition in der Sozialdemokratischen Arbeiterpartei Deutschösterreichs*) and the 'Social Democratic Left' (*Linken innerhalb der Sozialdemokratischen Partei*) whose position was close to that of the Communist Party, much to the latter's disgust, and whose members mostly joined the Communists after 12 February. The leadership was more concerned about the Trotskyites, even though they were a smaller group with little organisational ability and no outstanding spokesmen. This is largely because the Trotskyites were erratic and unpredictable, their ideas quite foreign to the traditions of Austro-Marxism, whereas the left opposition spoke a language that could be understood. The Trotskyites denounced the Soviet Union as a degenerate and bureaucratised state and said of the Austrian Communist Party: 'It is a rickety child brought up by Moscow with a well-filled milk bottle.' Their aim was 'proletarian revolution', but they had little idea how to achieve this goal, and contented themselves with wild talk of using the sewage system to blow up public buildings in Vienna.[38] The Trotskyites were so heartily disliked in the party that some right-wingers like Hans Jiricek were convinced that the whole February debacle was due to the sinister and provocative behaviour of this small group.

The left opposition was a much more serious organisation that had made a real impact during the 1933 conference, and grew steadily in influence in the following weeks. Their programme was outlined in the typewritten 'Theses of the Left' that was circulated at the conference, and copied frequently afterwards. The left argued that the time had come for the Austrian proletariat to step up the class war and to engage in revolutionary activity in order to destroy the old order. They attacked the ideas of the fathers of Austro-Marxism, Kautsky, Hilferding and Renner, for their belief that history would of its own accord achieve socialism without human interference. Fascism had been able to succeed in Europe because Social Democratic parties were more concerned with preserving the old order than with fighting a revolution. A reformist leadership was thus a severe hindrance to the anti-fascist struggle. In an acute economic crisis such as Europe was experiencing the bourgeoisie was no longer able to rule on its own because it was unable to make any concessions to the working class. Parliamentary democracy, based on the principle of concessions, could no longer function. The Dollfuss régime was already the 'first step to fascism', and yet the leadership of the party offered no resistance whatever to it, and was thus betraying the Linz programme and the cause of democracy. The reformist leadership was in fact supporting these 'agents of Italian fascism' because they thought that they were better than the German fascists. Such a policy was bound to lead to disastrous failure, and the only possible policy was to direct the united efforts of the working class to the destruction of the government and the ending of all emergency laws. The victory of the working class in Austria would not lead to the intervention of any of the European powers, as the leadership argued, because there was a widespread fear of war, and intervention in Austria would be too great a risk. On the contrary the victory of the working class in Austria would be a tremendous boost to the working class in Central Europe and a massive setback to fascism. Thus the left called for a two-front struggle, against fascism and against the reformist leadership.[39]

The party was uncertain what to do with the left opposition. In late January the party in Graz asked Vienna what should be done. In Graz, Ernst Fischer's brother Otto was the outspoken and courageous leader of the left, supported by Willi Scholz. Otto Fischer was a member of the provincial executive and no one could doubt his sincerity, his devotion to the cause of socialism and his humanity. In the fighting in February he was to lose a leg, and was only able to escape summary execution by pretending to be insane and then escaping from hospital to go to the Soviet Union once he had been fitted with an artificial leg.[40] No one wished to expel Otto Fischer or Willi Scholz from the party, but they were at a loss to know what to do, and appealed to the national leadership for advice.[41]

On 27 January the party's national council (*Parteirat*) met in Vienna to discuss the problem of opposition tendencies within the party. The police were highly alarmed, reporting that such well-known militants as Koloman Wallisch and Otto Fischer (who incidentally was suspected of having murdered an SA man) were headed for Vienna, and that the Schutzbund had been put on the alert. There were rumours that a large shipment of weapons was due to arrive from Czechoslovakia and that workers' councils were to be formed and the unemployed organised.[42] In fact the meeting was something of an anticlimax. It was decided that unity was the first essential at this time of fascist threat, and that therefore there should be no fractions within the party.[43] The militants left Vienna more depressed and frustrated than ever. As a small concession to the left, the party announced the following day that Dollfuss could hardly expect the workers to co-operate, as he had suggested in his speech on 18 January calling for a united effort of all classes to create a new Austria, if at the same time he persisted in taking away all their rights.[44]

In the following days leading Social Democrats appealed to the rank and file for moderation. At the Hotel Schwarzer Adler in Klagenfurt, Maria Hautmann (Wiener Neustadt) and Falle

(Klagenfurt) addressed some 700 party members, calling upon the audience to support the government against brown terror and against the excesses of green fascism.[45] Oskar Helmer, who for several years had been in favour of a coalition with the bourgeois parties and who was a leading representative of the party in Lower Austria, along with the mayor of Klagenfurt, called for an agreement with the Christian Socials in order to stop the fascists. Mark Siegelberg, the parliamentary correspondent of the *Arbeiter-Zeitung*, relayed this offer to Dollfuss on 9 February, but the Chancellor replied that the situation was not serious and that he did not feel obliged to make any concessions.[46]

In spite of these offers of support, and in spite of the fact that all terrorist activities were either proved to be by the Nazis or those guilty could not be found, and in no case could they be shown to have been committed by members of the Social Democratic or Communist parties, the government continued to insist that the Social Democrats could not be trusted, that their offers of co-operation were insincere, and that their help was not needed.[47] Indeed it was argued that it was precisely because the leadership was so conciliatory that the party was so dangerous. In February there was an unconfirmed report that the rank and file were prepared to ignore the party leadership and to go on the offensive. The leadership had allowed the prohibition of the Schutzbund, the restriction of civil liberties and the denial of constitutional rights, and thus could no longer be trusted. Terrorist groups were to be formed, and workers who refused to join would be shot.[48]

The attitude of the party can best be seen in the 'situation reports' (*Lageberichte*) of the party secretariat.[49] Whereas the leadership was arguing that the Christmas truce showed that the government was serious in its attack on National Socialism, the situation reports show clearly that they knew perfectly well that this was not the case, and that the government was using the truce to slowly destroy the liberties of the working class. The factory committees in all government enterprises were replaced by the harmless committees of the Patriotic Front. The social insurance system was modified and cutbacks in government expenditure on the social services were imminent. The workers' councils were under constant attack. Passing the budget by emergency decree was a clear violation of the constitution. The reintroduction of the death sentence, and its use against a poor devil who was clearly demented, merely to show how tough the government was and to warn its opponents, was another unpleasant example of the new policy. In December the Heimwehr leaders had laid down their conditions for their continued support of the government and the Patriotic Front. These included the end of party politics, the abolition of the Social Democratic Party, the appointment of a government commissar for Vienna, the end of provincial autonomy (*Gleichschaltung*), and the appointment of Fey to the Ministries of War and Security. Although the Heimwehr did not immediately get its way, it must have been obvious to the party that the government's coalition partner was determined to implement a programme that was a deliberate and calculated attack on the four points that the party congress had declared to be considered adequate cause for the utmost resistance, yet the leadership did nothing to prepare for the struggle which seemed almost inevitable.

Even the appeal by the government for support against Nazi terror was a mistake, according to the situation reports, for it made the National Socialists seem even more threatening and dangerous. The party was very concerned about the number of open Nazi sympathisers in the police and the auxiliary forces (*Hilfskorps*) and began to get seriously worried that the Nazis might have infiltrated the army thus making it unreliable in the event of a civil war involving the Nazi Party. The Heimwehr leader, Alberti, had been found by the police in the middle of a meeting with the Nazis, a meeting which included the dreadful Prince of Waldeck-Pyrmont, an official German diplomat and member of the SS. Starhemberg promptly fired Alberti and his second-in-command, Kubacsek. Alberti countered by claiming that he was acting on Starhemberg's instructions, resulting in a further loss of face for the Heimwehr and giving further evidence that there was sympathy within the government camp for the Nazis.

Cardinal Innitzer issued a pastoral letter giving the church's support to Dollfuss's régime and the proposed constitutional changes. There was no criticism of the proposed changes in the bourgeois press, changes which included giving all power to the President and the council of state which would be appointed by the President. Provincial governments would be appointed by the council of state. Representatives of the estates would meet in professional councils (*Ständekammern*) which in turn would elect representatives to economic councils (*Wirtschaftskammern*). A cultural council (*Kulturkammer*) would be elected by priests, university professors and carefully selected intellectuals. Since such a constitution would clearly be opposed by the Social Democrats and by the Nazis it would be promulgated by decree.

On 18 January Dollfuss gave a speech appealing to the 'decent workers' to support the new system, but the speech had little effect as it coincided with the banning of the *Arbeiter-Zeitung*, a newspaper that all workers, 'decent' or otherwise, respected and supported. In February the situation report argued that Dollfuss's policies simply showed that it was impossible to fight fascism with authoritarian means. Only democracy could offer an effective antidote to fascism. The government's propaganda against Nazism was useless because at the same time it was strangling the press, dismissing civil servants who did not support the government, diminishing the rights of the workers and failing to master the economic crisis. The Führer ideology of Hitler could not be countered by the Führer ideology of Dollfuss.

The confusion of the party in the face of the complete bankruptcy of its policy can best be seen in the resolution of the party council at the end of January. The party asked, almost wistfully, how it was possible for the party to support a system which brought mass unemployment, the erosion of workers' rights and the threat of constitutional changes which, although vague, were clearly undemocratic. The party was prepared to defend Austrian independence to the last man, and would join forces with anyone in the fight against Nazism. At the same time the party warned that any putsch attempt by the Heimwehr would be resisted to the utmost. Dollfuss could afford to ignore these threats, and set about methodically building his particular brand of fascistic state. The Social Democrats had accepted defeat after defeat, and there was little reason for the government to believe that they would offer much more than token resistance as their remaining rights were taken away.

The concern about the Nazis by the Social Democrats was quite understandable, the more so as the government seemed unwilling to take any effective action. At the cabinet meeting on 30 June 1933 Fey argued that the ban on the Nazi Party, which had gone into force on 19 June after a terrorist attack on Christian Social gymnasts, would lead to even more audacious terrorist attacks by the party.[50] Dollfuss agreed, and was particularly concerned that reports of such outbreaks of violence should not be published in the press for fear that they might influence the tourist trade. It is difficult to believe that this was Dollfuss's true motive. The 1,000-mark fine imposed on German tourists the previous month had a catastrophic effect on tourism, and it is doubtful if a few bombs would have made much of a difference. Probably Dollfuss wanted to use this as an excuse so that the Nazis would not get any further publicity, and the government would appear to be firmly in control of the situation.

Bombings and outbursts of terror continued throughout most of

1933, but the government was not seriously worried about the military effectiveness of the movement. A secret report prepared for the government on the problems of internal security at the end of the year estimated the total strength of the SS and SA in Austria to be between thirty and forty thousand men. It was assumed that the firm line taken by the government had led to a loss of membership. Since Germany was in a delicate international situation it was unlikely to make any drastic moves in foreign policy for some time to come, and for this reason would not support an attempt by the Austrian Nazis to over-throw the government by force. The Nazis would certainly not support a general strike called by the Social Democrats to defend the constitu-tion, but on the other hand they would probably take the opportunity offered by such a strike to make life as difficult as possible for the government. This was likely to be the main thrust of Nazi policy for the next few months, to keep constantly aggravating the domestic political situation in order to exploit every possibility to embarrass the govern-ment and keep up the morale of the outlawed party.[51]

During the week in which the Habicht visit was being prepared, Nazi terror activities reached a new peak. There was an almost endless series of incidents, mostly involving small bombs. The department of public security devoted all its attention to the National Socialists, and hardly a single incident was reported which involved members of the Social Democratic Party. On 8 January many Jewish stores were attacked in Vienna and there was a further wave of bombings to protest the cancelling of the Habicht visit. In the following weeks there were constant bombings and Nazi attacks on Social Democratic meetings, attacks which the Social Democrats did nothing to counter. There were also mounting rumours that the Austrian Legion was becoming increasingly restless and was ready to move into Austria in the event of a major civil unrest. Until 12 February the Nazis continued to throw their bombs, smash property, paint slogans and hurl stink bombs with growing enthusiasm. Units of the SS and the SA visited Austria, thinly disguised as German ski excursions, to encour-age their Austrian comrades into further action. Effective counter-measures against such activity are difficult at the best of times; in 1934 they were made all the more difficult by the sympathy that many policemen, customs officials and civil servants showed towards the National Socialist movement.[52]

Notes

1. Irmgard Bärnthaler, *Die Vaterländische Front* (Vienna 1971), p. 12.

2. Ibid., p. 21.

3. Ibid., p. 28.

4. Interview of Starhemberg to AP and Reuter, *Wiener Neueste Nachrichten*, 14 October 1933.

5. Franz Winkler, *Die Diktatur in Oesterreich 1934-1938* (Paris 1938), where this argument is developed in detail. His position was most confused. As a pro-German he had supported negotiations with the Nazis. His anti-fascism was the result of a strong dislike for the Heimwehr rather than any profound respect for democratic principles.

6. *AVA*, Bundeskanzleramt Inneres 1934, 22/gen. 4883.

7. Alfred Diamant, *Austrian Catholics and the First Republic* (Princeton 1960), for a good summary of these ideas.

8. Ibid., p. 63.

9. *Quadragesimo Anno: Encyclical Letter of his Holiness Pope Pius XI*, para. 10.

10. Ibid., para. 56 and 57.

11. Ibid., para. 108.

12. *AVA*, Sozialdemokratisches Parteiarchiv, Parteistellen 175a.

13. Ibid., report from the Leoben party secretariat, 27 March 1933.

14. Ibid., letter from Murzzuschlag, 16 March 1933.

15. Ibid., letter from Lettner, a Social Democratic leader in Traisen, Lower Austria.

16. *VGA*, Lode 16, Mappe 33.

17. Ibid., Lode 16.

18. C.A. Gulick, *Austria from Habsburg to Hitler* (2 vols., Berkeley 1948), vol. 1, p. 1212.

19. *AVA*, Zl. Pr. IV — 2606/1934, Karton 5.

20. Quoted in Norbert Leser, *Zwischen Reformismus und Bolschewismus. Der Austromarxismus als Theorie und Praxis* (Vienna 1968), p. 479.

21. *AVA*, Sozialdemokratisches Parteiarchiv, Parteistellen 175a.

22. Ruth von Mayenburg, *Blaues Blut und rote Fahnen* (Vienna 1969), p. 95.

23. Gulick, *Habsburg to Hitler*, vol. 1, p. 1213.

24. *AVA*, Parteistellen 191.

25. Ibid., Parteistellen 123.

26. NPA Fasz. 839.

27. *AVA*, Parteistellen 191.

28. Ibid., Parteistellen 35.

29. Ibid., Zl. Pr. IV — 2606/1934 Karton 5.

30. Ibid., Parteistellen 175a.

31. Ibid., Parteistellen 191.

32. Ibid., Parteistellen 123.

33. Ibid.

34. Ibid.

35. Ibid.

36. Ibid., Parteistellen 16.

37. Ibid., Zl. Pr. IV — 2606/1934, Karton 6.

38. Ibid.

39. Ibid.

40. This incredible tale is told by Mayenburg, *Blaues Blut*, pp. 119 and 139.

41. *AVA*, Parteistellen 123.

42. Ibid., Bundeskanzleramt Inneres 4885.

43. Ibid., Parteistellen 35.

44. Ibid., Parteistellen 191.

45. Ibid., Bundeskanzleramt Inneres 4885.

46. *VGA*, Lode 17, Mappe 1.
47. *AVA*, Bundeskanzleramt Inneres 4885.
48. Ibid., Polizeidirektion Wien, Zl. Pr. IV — 2606/1934, Karton 1.
49. Ibid., Parteistellen 162.
50. Ibid., Bundeskanzleramt Inneres 4885.
51. *KA* Int. Zl. 890 — 1/33.
52. *AVA*, Bundeskanzleramt Inneres 4885.

9 THE FIGHTING ON 12 FEBRUARY 1934

At 3.30 a.m. on 12 February 1934, a telephone girl in Linz overheard a curious conversation. A Mr Alois Jalkotzy from the 13th district of Vienna (telephone number R31-9-44) called a number in Linz and gave the following message: 'Uncle Otto's and Auntie's condition will be decided tomorrow. The latter says wait. Don't do anything for the time being.'[1] The girl recognised the voice at the other end of the line as being that of Richard Bernaschek, the party secretary of Upper Austria and leader of the local Schutzbund, a man well known for his militant views.[2] It did not need much imagination to work out that 'Uncle Otto' was Otto Bauer, and that 'Auntie' was the Social Democratic Party. The girl, who obviously had little sympathy for the Social Democrats, and a strong sense of her obligations as a civil servant, decided to inform the police.

The police decided to act quickly. At 7.00 a.m. they broke into Bernaschek's office in the Hotel Schiff in Linz. As they entered the room he yelled, 'Get your guns!' He was placed under arrest and his office searched. Soon the police's worst suspicions were confirmed. A copy of a letter was discovered, dated 11 February and addressed to the party leadership in Vienna. According to this letter Bernaschek had held a meeting with five of his most trusted Schutzbund members to discuss the political situation and the course of action that should be taken.[3] After a lengthy debate it was decided that the Upper Austrian Schutzbund had had enough and were determined to take decisive action if any further weapons searches or harrassments of the Schutzbund or the party were to take place. It was agreed to place the Schutzbund on armed alert immediately, and that if there were any further searches for weapons by the police, or if any officer of the Schutzbund or the party should be arrested, this should be met with armed resistance. Any such action in Linz should be taken by the Vienna Schutzbund as a signal to go on the offensive, and if they failed to do so they would earn the contempt of the labour movement.

Bernaschek and his companions were convinced that if the Social Democrats continued to be so passive, and if they refused to hit back, Austria would go the same way as Germany.

The letter was sent immediately by special courier to Vienna. The courier was Alois Jalkotzy, a Vienna city councillor and chairman of the Social Democratic children's society. Jalkotzy had been in Linz on party business, and had attended Bernaschek's meeting. As a moderate, he had tried to calm down those whom he considered to be hotheads, and tried in vain to persuade the meeting that the situation was not nearly so critical as they feared. However, Jalkotzy agreed to deliver the letter to Bauer that evening as soon as he returned to Vienna. He had to wait some time before he could discuss the matter with Otto Bauer, because Bauer and his wife had gone to the cinema to watch Greta Garbo and did not get home until after midnight. Bauer was predictably outraged by the letter. He was determined to continue with the party policy of trying to keep up a dialogue with the government and to stand by the four points of the extraordinary party congress. He was well aware of the mounting opposition to the party executive but he stood firm.[4] Jalkotzy can hardly have been surprised, and was certainly not disappointed, by Bauer's reaction and the message that he was asked to send to Linz ordering Bernaschek to toe the party line and not to precipitate a civil war.

In Linz the weather was seasonally unpleasant, rain mixed with snow, the temperature around zero centrigrade, but most men's minds were on other things. It was carnival time. That Bernaschek was in no spirit for carnival was understandable. Rumours had reached him that the police were planning a razzia on the Hotel Schiff in the Linzer Landstrasse, the Social Democratic headquarters, and also an armoury for the Schutzbund. These rumours were well founded. The security chief for Upper Austria, Hans Hammerstein-Equord, ·had ordered a raid on the Hotel Schiff on 9 February but the action had been postponed until Monday morning, 12 February. Bernaschek had placed a guard in the Hotel Schiff from the night of 10 February of about fifty men, and for two days watch was kept throughout the night.

There is evidence that Bernaschek wanted to provoke an incident that would trigger off armed resistance to the government which he felt was long overdue, and that he hoped such an incident would occur on 12, 13 or 14 February.[5] The fact that he had placed a guard in the Hotel Schiff on the night of the 10th, and the fact that he did not wait for an answer from Vienna before ordering the Schutzbund to offer

armed resistance if the Hotel Schiff were searched, is strong supporting evidence. He expected that a search would take place during
official working hours, that is to say after 9.00 a.m., as appears to have
been the case in previous incidents. At 4.00 a.m. he eventually fell
asleep in his office. A reinforcement of the guard was ordered for 9.00.
At 7.00 a shipment of weapons for the Schutzbund was expected to
arrive at the Hotel.

Shortly after 6.00, a detachment of 23 policemen under the
direction of Chief Commissar Dr Hofer assembled at police headquarters in the Mozartstrasse. At 6.45 he informed the army of his
intention of raiding the Hotel Schiff and asked that one company of
infantry be placed on the alert in case of an incident. Hofer did not
imagine for one moment that there would be any trouble, but he felt it
wise to be cautious.

Just before 7.00, guards at the Hotel Schiff spotted the police in the
street. Bernaschek was immediately awoken. His reaction to the news
was extraordinary. He locked himself in his office, crouched on the
ground and made a telephone call to the leader of the Christian Social
Party of Upper Austria, Josef Schlegel. Schlegel was fast asleep at the
time, but seemingly unaware of the gravity of the situation promised
that he would look into the matter and see what could be done to stop
an incident happening. Having made this call as Bernaschek the
faithful party member, Bernaschek the militant socialist took over. He
made a second call to the workers' council in Linz where his faithful
lieutenants were waiting for orders. He ordered the mobilisation of the
Schutzbund, the calling of a general strike, and that Steyr and Vienna
should be informed. Immediately afterwards the police broke down
the door, a brief scuffle took place, and Bernaschek was dragged off
before a shot was fired.

It is not clear who fired the first shot, but soon there was fierce
fighting inside the Hotel Schiff. The Schutzbund used their machine-
guns. The police proved to be the better marksmen, but they were
hopelessly outnumbered. Hofer ordered his men to wait for reinforcements to arrive. The army had in fact taken Hofer's request for
support very seriously. Brigade command had placed the entire Linz
garrison on alert. All officers were ordered to report immediately to
their regiments, and all troops were confined to barracks. As soon as
the news of the Hotel Schiff incident reached brigade headquarters
the garrisons in Steyr, Wels and other major centres in Upper Austria
were placed on the alert. The 5th Company of the 7th Alpine Jäger
Regiment under the command of Major Schusta was sent to help out

Hofer and his policemen. Schusta was an excellent officer, had been highly decorated during the war, and was a cool-headed and intelligent man. His company arrived at the Hotel Schiff at 8.45 a.m. Schusta was determined not to risk the lives of his men in a foolhardy attempt to take the Hotel Schiff by storm, and therefore placed them in positions around the hotel from whence they could fire into the building. The Schutzbund, however, even though their leaders had been arrested, proved to be a determined and effective opponent. The Jäger were kept under constant and well-aimed fire, and were unable to make any progress. Schusta therefore decided to call up reinforcements.

The machine-gun company that arrived quickly on the scene was put into action, and the ring around the Hotel Schiff began to close. A sniper managed to put the Schutzbund's key machine-gun out of action and morale in the hotel began to collapse. Schusta kept up relentless pressure. The Schutzbund asked for mediators. Hofer demanded unconditional surrender. Shortly afterwards the Schutzbund men left the hotel and surrendered to the police. Schusta's action was a model of its kind. Only one man was killed — the Schutzbund machine-gunner, an unfortunate cabinet-maker who had had no great enthusiasm for the whole affair and had almost stayed at home. Schusta had only one man wounded who had uncautiously poked his head over the parapet of the Café Zentral. The police also had only one man seriously wounded in the initial fighting.

News of the fighting in Linz reached Vienna at about eight in the morning. As the party headquarters in the Rechte Wienzeile had already been seized on 8 February, an emergency meeting was held in the apartment of Julius Deutsch's sister, Helene Popper, in the Gumpendorferstrasse in the 6th district. It is impossible to reconstruct exactly what happened at that meeting, and there is considerable uncertainty as to who attended it. By the time Deutsch arrived he was told that those present had agreed by a majority of one vote to call a general strike and to mobilise the Schutzbund. It would seem that during the debate Schorsch, the secretary of the federation of Free Trade unions, was the most outspoken in favour of a general strike, and that he was strongly supported by Bauer. König, the head of the railway workers' union, opposed the strike, for his union had been badly defeated in their recent strike. Helmer, the leading Lower Austrian right-winger, also argued against the strike and called for negotiations with the government. Körner, realising that there was little enthusiasm for a general strike, and knowing that the

Schutzbund was poorly trained, opposed the mobilisation of the party army. Deutsch agreed that the Schutzbund could only be effective if the general strike was a success. The party leaders knew by this time that many of the workers in Vienna were determined to go on strike whatever they said, and this included the electricity workers. It was almost certainly this factor which tipped the balance in favour of supporting a strike. The leadership was thus uncertain what to do, and was forced into action by Bernaschek's escapade in Linz and by the militant attitude of the Vienna workers.[6]

The emergency executive committee having agreed to the defensive mobilisation of the Schutzbund, Bauer and Deutsch established themselves in the Georg-Washington-Hof in the 10th district, forming an impromptu headquarters in case of any fighting. By 10.30 they had warned the Schutzbund to be prepared for action, at 12.30 they issued orders to arm the Schutzbund, and half an hour later gave the order to fight. But by this time the leadership was once again trailing behind events, and confirming what had already taken place.

At the cabinet meeting held on the morning of 12 February to discuss these events, Fey was the main speaker.[7] He insisted that over the past few months there had been steadily mounting evidence that the Social Democrats were planning an armed uprising. The hoards of weapons belonging to the Schutzbund that had been seized by the police in the past weeks had recently been augmented by fresh supplies, mainly from Czechoslovakia, but for foreign political reasons Austria had been obliged to postpone the final reckoning with the Social Democrats and concentrate on the search for weapons.

Fey's opening remarks were highly questionable. He could just as well have argued that the Heimwehr was planning an armed uprising, especially as an attempt at a putsch had already been made in Styria, and the mere fact that the Schutzbund was armed did not mean that it was seeking the first possible opportunity to unleash a civil war. The government knew the Schutzbund's position perfectly well after the extraordinary conference of the party in 1933, in which a government agent had kept the minutes, and was well aware of the fact that the Schutzbund would only fight in defence of certain basic constitutional rights. Nor was it true that the weapons came largely from Czechoslovakia. The bulk of the Schutzbund's weapons came from government surplus stock when the Austro-Hungarian army had been disbanded in 1918. Mention of Czechoslovakia was largely to imply that the Social Democrats were in league with the Little Entente and the agents of a foreign power, and thus could not claim to be true patriotic Austrians. The struggle on 12 February was thus a struggle of Austria against a foreign ideology and an alien movement.

Fey's account of the events that led to the fighting was equally dubious. He said that a telephone call between Linz and Vienna had been overheard and that on the basis of an earlier report which gave additional weight to the significance of the call from Linz the police were ordered to investigate the Hotel Schiff there. Apart from the fact that the telephone call came from Vienna and not from Linz, the raid on the hotel had been ordered for several days beforehand and had been postponed largely because of the carnival celebrations in the city.

Fey then gave a brief account of the fighting. He reported that the Social Democrats had already managed to establish positions in the Southern railway station (*Südbahnhalle*), the steam baths and the Urfahr district in Linz. It was also clear that they wanted to seize the weapons factory, the Steyr works. He mentioned the fighting in Bruck-an-der-Mur and Eggenberg, and placed particular emphasis on Bruck as an important railway junction. He did not show much concern about Vienna as the army was able to maintain complete control over the inner city. His main argument was that the government should act quickly and decisively. Courts martial should be established and summary executions meted out on any offenders.

The main concern of both Dollfuss and Schuschnigg was that the Heimatschutz was not entirely reliable and might not necessarily follow the instructions of the government. For Dollfuss the following days would be the big test of the Heimatschutz, and if it lived up to the government's expectations then a clear distinction would be made between the Heimatschutz and the Nazis. Fey, although he was a prominent figure in the Heimwehr, made no comment, and must have realised that this discussion was an open criticism of the Heimwehr and its dealings with the Nazis. The Chancellor saw the events of 12 February as an ideal chance to make the various political groupings show their true colours. He said: 'The time has come to make far-reaching decisions by the government to clarify the general political situation.' The war emergency law would be put into full operation in order to carry out these basic changes. Vienna would in future be directly ruled by the federal government and would lose its special status. Schuschnigg agreed that this was essential, and that it would be carried out even if it was necessary to break the law in order to do so.

There was also full agreement that the Social Democratic Party should be outlawed, but it was realised that very careful attention would have to be paid to the wording of a decree to this effect so that all aspects of the party's activities were affected. Richard Schmitz, who later on during the Cabinet meeting was to be appointed federal commissar for Vienna, argued that many people joined the Social Democratic Party because it was a vast organisation which provided employment for a large number of people at a time when it was exceedingly difficult to get a job. These people were opposed to the radical faction within the party, but Schmitz feared that if the party were banned they might very well join the ranks of the radicals and that the socialist movement, although outlawed, might be more dangerous than ever. Schuschnigg dismissed this argument saying that the pro-government side would be given such a tremendous boost of morale that it could well afford to run such a risk. There was thus general agreement that the Social Democratic Party should be outlawed, the only lingering doubts were about how it should be done and whether or not it was strictly legal. But these were doubts that did not trouble the Chancellor. The cabinet was quickly adjourned and did not meet again until after the fighting was over.

At 11.46 a.m. on 12 February the electric current in Vienna failed. The trams came to a halt and the traffic lights went out. Everyone knew that this action by electricity workers was the signal for a general strike. In point of fact the Social Democratic Party leadership had decided three days previously to change the signal for a general strike. It was now agreed that the news of the arrest of the mayor of Vienna, Karl Seitz, which would be broadcast from the transmitter in the town hall by a special unit of the Schutzbund, should be the new signal to be followed by the mobilisation of all Schutzbund units throughout the city.[8] This new plan was not yet widely known, and thus there were many misunderstandings from the very outset as to what was to be expected.

Orders from headquarters to the Schutzbund units frequently did not arrive so that there was considerable confusion in the various districts and a complete lack of co-ordinated effort, a fact that made the task of the executive forces much easier. In the militant working-class districts, however, determined efforts were made to fight the decisive battle for which so many had been waiting for so long. Floridsdorf, Ottakring, Simmering and Döbling were the best organised and most aggressive. Fighting actually began before the electricity had been switched off and even before headquarters had issued the order to arm the Schutzbund. The first shot was fired at 11.10 in Simmering when the Schutzbund mounted a concentrated attack on the police station. The police were forced to withdraw and by 11.45 the Schutzbund began to take over control of all the railways that ran through Simmering.[9]

The first shots mentioned in the official police report were at 1.05 p.m. in Ottakring when the police tried to disband an assembly of the Schutzbund at the Sandleitenhof community centre.[10] The police were forced to give up the attempt and to wait for reinforcements. In Margareten the Schutzbund went into action at 3.00 and was successful in establishing a strong defensive position that made it exceedingly difficult for the executive forces to move men and material through a strategically important sector. In the course of the afternoon a bicycle battalion of the Feldjäger brought in heavy machine-guns and was thus able to dislodge the Schutzbund from their barricades at the Reumannhof.

At first all was quiet in the two districts where the heaviest fighting was to take place, Floridsdorf and Döbling. In Döbling the Schutzbund concentrated in the massive building which was immediately to become the symbol of the fighting in February, the gigantic workers' housing project Karl-Marx-Hof. At 6.50 the Schutzbund opened fire on the police station at the Heiligenstadt station from the Karl-Marx-Hof, and the police had to call up support from the army to prevent it falling into the workers' hands.

Floridsdorf was of immense strategic importance to the Schutzbund for it was from this district that the three bridges across the Danube could be controlled. The Schutzbund regiment 'Karl Marx' in Floridsdorf was considered an elite force, and its commander, Heinz Roscher, a man of exceptional courage and military ability. In Floridsdorf the Schutzbund was mobilised slowly and carefully and all unnecessary heroics were avoided. It was not until the following day that fighting actually began. The position of the Floridsdorf workers was made considerably more difficult because the executive forces had arrested all the Schutzbund and party leaders in Brigittenau, the district on the other side of the Danube, and the Schutzbund arsenal was so carefully hidden that the rank and file were unable to get hold of any weapons.

Another isolated area of militancy was the Ankerbrot bakery in Favoriten, an area that otherwise saw little fighting. The management closed down the bakery shortly after the power was cut off. Many of the workers retired to a local pub to discuss what should be done. It was decided to take over the factory, the largest bakery in Vienna, and therefore of considerable importance if the fighting was to continue for some time, running it as a workers' co-operative and as a fortress in an area that as yet had shown little enthusiasm for the Social Democrats. The Schutzbund placed a machine-gun on the roof of the factory, and was able to fight off a unit of the Heimwehr that tried to storm it on the following day. The workers had to abandon the factory on 13 February when army units were called in. In spite of determined fighting the workers were no match for the army.[11]

By the evening of 12 February it was clear that the position of the Schutzbund in Vienna was hopeless. They were fighting in isolated positions with no support from outside the city against a well-armed and determined enemy. In spite of some exceptional acts of courage and often considerable military skill it was clear that it was only a matter of time before the executive gained full control of the city. The government, however, was determined to crush the uprising quickly and violently, in large part to show their determination to smash Marxism once and for all. Now the government had the chance that it was looking for and was determined to use it to the full.

The official government position was that while the government, the police and the army were engaged in a heroic struggle against Nazism and terrorism, and was determined to preserve the independence of Austria against Germany, the Social Democrats had planned a putsch. The government even went as far as to announce that Dollfuss had offered the Social Democrats a partnership in the government, but that this had been turned down. Apart from the fact that the exact reverse was true, such an offer would have been singularly naïve had Dollfuss really believed that the Social Democrats were such sinister and unpatriotic revolutionaries.[12]

Martial law was proclaimed almost as soon as the shooting began. Active support for the 'putsch' was to be punishable by death. There were to be no assemblies in the streets, and everyone was to be home by 10.00 p.m. with the doors locked. To close the cafes was considered to be too much of a sacrifice, even at such a time of national peril, and they were allowed to stay open until 10.00.[13]

The major issue on 12 February was whether or not artillery should be used in the city, particularly against workers' housing. Such was the public reaction against the use of artillery that the government deliberately obscured the circumstances surrounding its use, and an accurate historical reconstruction of precisely what happened is impossible. It seems most likely that it was the Minister of War, General Schönburg-Hartenstein, who first suggested using artillery on the grounds that it would be be quickest way of dealing with the situation. Fey was enthusiastic. Legend has it that Dollfuss only wanted to use tear gas, but was told that the army did not have any because of the prohibition of gas under the terms of the Treaty of Saint-Germain, and it was only then that he agreed to the use of explosives. From the papers of the War Ministry we learn that the army did have tear gas and Dollfuss knew it, so that this version of events is hardly convincing.[14] The artillery was brought into position and first used in the evening of 12 February.[15]

The Schutzbund was determined to continue the fight, and in the course of the afternoon of 12 February, and throughout the night, organised their troops and prepared defensive positions. It was not until the early morning of 13 February that the Schutzbund was fully organised in Meidling, and barricades continued to be built during the course of the day. The railway that joins Vienna to Baden was heavily defended by the Schutzbund and in spite of very determined efforts by the police to dislodge them they remained in their positions. In Floridsdorf the mobilisation of the Schutzbund was not completed until the evening of 12 February.

At half past midnight the Floridsdorf Schutzbund opened fire on the police from the Goethehof. Shortly after 7.00 a.m. they attacked the main police station, the Nordbahnhof and the gasworks. Effective barricades were set up throughout the district. The police were unable to do anything against massive machine-gun fire from carefully selected positions. Among the most effectively defended positions was the main fire station where the Schutzbund was commanded by the engineer Georg Weissel, a left-wing militant and one of the greatest popular heroes of February. The plan was to seize all the police stations in the district and take control of all major public buildings. This was largely successful, although some buildings, such as the main police station, could not be captured.

As the fire station was close to the main police station the executive was determined to capture it so that Weissel's men could not support the efforts of the tramway workers to seize the police station. Weissel had too few men to defend the fire station effectively and his position was hopeless, in large part because the chief fireman on duty had betrayed Weissel's plans to the fire chief of Vienna, who, although himself a Social Democrat, passed them on to the chief of police. Weissel could thus only count on a small number of firemen to stand by him, and his plan to support the attack on the main police station was known to the executive.[16] Once Weissel had been captured the attack on the police station had to be abandoned, the attackers taking up defensive positions.

Although the Schutzbund had failed to capture the main police station and had lost the fire station, they were still in effective control of the district and the police had to to call upon the army to send in troops, for the police had suffered heavy losses and were seriously worried that they might be forced to abandon Floridsdorf to the Schutzbund. The fact that there had been very little activity by the Schutzbund in Brigittenau and Leopoldstadt, the adjoining districts to Floridsdorf, made it very easy for the army to reach the district.

At 10.15 a.m. the army began its operations against the Schlingerhof, a large housing complex in the centre of Floridsdorf. In spite of artillery fire and the use of two armoured vehicles the executive made very slow progress against a determined opponent. The executive were first able to enter the Schlingerhof at 11.45, but it was not until 4.30 in the afternoon that a part of the building was firmly in their hands and 350 prisoners taken. Four of the prisoners were shortly afterwards killed when a unit of the Heimwehr fired at the truck that was driving them away. Other attempts on the part of the executive to dislodge the Schutzbund from their positions failed, the attackers suffering severe losses.

During the night fresh units of troops were brought to Floridsdorf, including three new artillery batteries. At 6.00 a.m. a fresh attack began, but the executive found that resistance was as determined as ever, and progress was very slow. It was not until the early afternoon that the Schlingerhof eventually fell entirely into the hands of the executive. Workers' houses in Kagran were also difficult to capture, for on 13 February the Schutzbund had taken the tramway depot and built effective barricades with snowploughs.[17]

Artillery fire was so heavy that the Schutzbund was in an impossible position. The gasworks had to be abandoned when it seemed likely that the artillery might shell the gasometers. By the late evening of 14 February the executive was in effective control of Floridsdorf, but sporadic fighting continued until 16 February, and a systematic search of all houses continued for a further five days. One Schutzbund unit of 65 men decided to march across the Czechoslovak border. After fifteen hours of dangerous and exhausting march they reached their goal.[18]

In Ottakring the fighting had been fierce from the afternoon of 12 February. It was concentrated on the community centre and the surrounding area which had been heavily barricaded. At about 12.15 a.m. on 13 February the artillery began to bombard the community centre, an attack on the building having been repulsed. The bombardment continued throughout the night. At 3.20 in the morning Fey visited the area and personally ordered further reinforcements from the army. At 7.25 the artillery fire was increased and at 8.30 a fresh attack mounted on the building, in the presence of the Vice-Chancellor. Much to their surprise the executive found the building empty. The 150 to 200 Schutzbund members, who had returned fire until the very last moment, had left the building in an orderly manner and had taken up new positions in other parts of the district. The government's news release spoke of a number of prisoners taken at the Ottakring community centre, but this was pure propaganda. The official army report of the fighting in Vienna, which is on the whole remarkable for its objectivity, makes it clear that no prisoners were taken. After the fall of this key building there was sporadic fighting in Ottakring, but the main centre of resistance had been destroyed.

Simmering, where the first shots had been fired, proved to be one of the most difficult areas to bring under the control of the executive. The Schutzbund managed to seize all the police stations in the district and to besiege the main police station where many of the local police had taken refuge. The Schutzbund fought skilfully, changing their defensive positions so as to outwit the reinforcements that were brought in, and always conscious of their obligation to their comrades in Meidling and Favoriten in their choice of positions to defend. Reinforcements brought into the area on 13 February at Fey's orders were able to control the main working-class housing projects after heavy fighting, but on the following day the Schutzbund launched a counter-attack which was at first partially successful. But against such odds there was little that could be achieved, and by the late evening of 14 February Simmering was securely in the hands of the executive.

The action which had become by far the best known, and which is almost symbolic of the 12 February, was the bombardment of the Karl-Marx-Hof in Döbling. The Karl-Marx-Hof is an immense housing complex, running almost one kilometre along the Heiligenstädter Strasse in the 19th district. The Schutzbund had been relatively slow to mobilise in Döbling, and in fact the police had already searched the Karl-Marx-Hof and the community centre which was to be the assembly point of the Schutzbund before the first shots were fired. After some sporadic street fighting the Schutzbund mounted an attack on the Heiligenstadt station of the Franz Josef railway. After a fierce battle the police were forced to abandon the station and joined a unit of the Heimwehr that was fighting in another part of the station. After reinforcements were called up, the police were able to force the Schutzbund out of the station, but a subsequent attack on the Karl-Marx-Hof was beaten back.

The Schutzbund was in a very strong position in the Karl-Marx-Hof and the police realised that they needed the help of the army if they were to dislodge them. At 11.30 p.m. army reinforcements arrived, a company of infantry and a battery of artillery. The artillery was placed near the sports fields of the Hohe Warte from whence the Karl-Marx-Hof was an easy target. The bombardment began at 1.00 a.m. on 13 February, and shortly afterwards an attack was mounted that was successfully beaten back by the Schutzbund. More artillery and armoured vehicles were called up, and at 4.00 Fey visited the scene and agreed that an intensive bombardment was needed in order to prepare the way for a further assault.

In the early morning of 13 February some workers left the Karl-Marx-Hof to go to work, even though many of them had been fighting during the night. Those who stayed behind protested but the reply was: 'It's OK for you, you're unemployed anyway.'[19] This anecdote shows all too clearly how the morale of the Schutzbund was affected by the high level of unemployment. Men were prepared to risk their lives fighting, but they were not prepared to risk their jobs. In such a situation the morale of the Schutzbund was truly remarkable.

The attack on the Karl-Marx-Hof began at 9.45 in the morning. Under the cover of howitzer fire and heavy machine-guns, and using armoured vehicles, the executive was able to reach the heavy iron gate of the main entrance to the complex which they blew open. The executive now had command of the main courtyard, but fierce fighting continued from apartment to apartment and the Schutzbund were far from abandoning their positions. At this point new orders came for the troops, and the two armoured police vehicles were withdrawn. The situation in Floridsdorf had become so serious that the troops were needed there. The Schutzbund immediately took advantage of this situation and went over to the offensive. By the early afternoon they had begun to fire at the Heiligenstadt station once again.

At 9.15 p.m. fighting in the Karl-Marx-Hof reached a fresh peak. Army reinforcements were brought back, this time they included two whole battalions of infantry and three artillery batteries, one of which was heavy artillery. Although the situation of the Schutzbund was now hopeless, the executive did not risk a fresh assault on the building. On 15 February at 11.30 p.m., after Dollfuss had issued an ultimatum, the Schutzbund surrendered. The executive, fearing that this might be a trap, waited until further reinforcements arrived before beginning a systematic search of the building. By the time they began their search the Schutzbund members had left with their weapons through the sewers. Not a single Schutzbund member was captured.

By the evening of 14-15 February the fighting had virtually ceased in Vienna. An outburst of gunfire on the night of 15-16th turned out to be two drunken Schutzbund members letting their guns off into the air. An attack on the police station at Atzgersdorf that evening, which was unsuccessful, seems to have been the last of the fighting in the capital.[20] On 16th the university was reopened, but only for students taking exams and for doctoral candidates. It was assumed that those who were about to become 'Herr Doktor' would have higher things in mind than civil war.

There was considerable concern at the outset of the fighting that the workers might take over key factories or start destroying industrial property. At 3.00 p.m. on 12 February the industrialist, Julius Meinl, demanded protection for his factory, the largest food-processing plant in Vienna. He was told that if he wished to have the workers driven out by artillery fire he was welcome.[21] Meinl had thus to accept the fact that it was better to risk a short period of workers' control than the destruction of expensive plant by artillery fire. It was precisely this point that made the recapture of the Ankerbrot bakery all the more difficult. The bakery continued to operate under workers' control providing bread for the Schutzbund, and was thus of considerable importance to the insurgents. But the management of the factory would not allow artillery to be used because the damage caused was likely to be considerable.[22] Dollfuss calmly suggested that gas should be used against the electricity works in Simmering so that the workers would not be able to wreck the machinery. That the Chancellor could make such a suggestion at 8.00 a.m. on 13 February is further proof that the army did indeed have gas. The suggestion was rejected on the grounds that it would create a most unfortunate international incident. The use of artillery against civilians was not going to make Austria popular throughout the world. The use of gas, which was expressly forbidden by international treaty, and was universally viewed with horror, was likely to cause even more serious repercussions.[23]

At 9.15 a.m. on 14 February the Industrial Association (*Hauptverband der Industrie*) reported that most factories were working normally. Only the Ankerbrot bakery and the *Apollowerke*, which made candles, were in the hands of the workers. From

Fischamond it was reported that the workers had gone home as they were made so nervous by the persistent sound of artillery fire that they were unable to work.[24] The high level of unemployment and the lack of any industrial strategy by the Social Democrats resulted in most workers reporting for work and few efforts to augment the military struggle in the streets with a political struggle for control of the factories. Only in the instance of the Ankerbrot factory did something like a spontaneous workers' council emerge. The industrialists were able to sleep peacefully. The damage that was done, and it was extensive, was to workers' housing. Only at the Mautner-Markhof factory in Simmering, where mines were used against machine-gun posts, was there any serious damage to industrial property.[25] The Ankerbrot workers were to pay a heavy price for their militancy. A large number of serious charges were laid against them, and many were to serve long sentences.[26]

As the fighting on 12 February was seen by the government as the result of a long and carefully prepared plot, it is not unnatural that a number of alarming rumours were allowed to circulate and were readily believed. The most popular was the belief that a special commando corps of the Schutzbund would work its way through the sewage system and blow up all prominent public buildings and barracks. Such a belief was pure fantasy.[27] The Schutzbund did have an extensive knowledge of the Vienna sewage system, and was able to use it to good advantage, such as in the retreat from the Karl-Marx-Hof and in the skilful movement of forces in Floridsdorf. After the fighting was over the Schutzbund used underground passageways to hide members who were sought by the police, and in some instances small hospitals were improvised in which the wounded were treated by sympathetic doctors.

Another such rumour began at 8.30 a.m. on 14 February, when it was suggested that as a final desperate action the Schutzbund had poisoned the drinking water in the city. The government ordered frequent checks to make sure that this was not true. The results were negative.[28]

The failure to control the railway system was a major setback to the Schutzbund. It is clear that they were well aware of the importance of the railways, and railway stations were always one of the first objects of attack in districts where there was serious fighting. As late as 5.45 p.m. on 14 February the executive were unable to run a train from the Franz Josef station to Nussdorf. The line ran past the Karl-Marx-Hof and came under heavy machine-gun fire.[29] Armoured trains were quickly improvised by protecting goods wagons with sandbags, although the engines were not protected, and were used in the fighting in Floridsdorf. Most serious of all was the fact that the eastern railway, running to Budapest, was completely in the hands of the executive. Ammunition was sent from Hegyeshalom on the Hungarian border to Vienna.[30] The executive had no trouble at all in getting supplies to the troops.

Although by the evening of the 13th the police reported that the 'Schutzbund has lost its head and is without leaders. Wild rumours are circulating that are completely contradictory,' the government was concerned about rumours that support might come to Vienna from Czechoslovakia. In the early morning of 14 February there were rumours of troop movements across the Czechoslovakian border. At 10.00 a.m. the police heard a report that Bauer and Deutsch, who were now in Czechoslovakia, had written a letter saying that they had left the country in order to get military help from Czechoslovakia. Shortly before 6.00 p.m. there were reports of a mysterious aeroplane flying over Vienna dropping leaflets saying : 'Hang on, we are coming to help.' It has not been possible to find out where this plane came from, or indeed whether it ever really existed. Shortly after this incident fresh rumours of troop movements from Czechoslovakia reached police headquarters.[31] Even after the fighting was over, rumours of help from the north continued, but they were no longer taken very seriously. There is no doubt that the Schutzbund was not expecting help from abroad, and it is doubtful whether these rumours had any effect, one way or the other, on its morale.

The government was also somewhat concerned about the attitude of the Nazis during the fighting in Vienna. At 3.00 p.m. on 12 February the police reported that the Nazis were quiet.[32] On 14 February General von Tlaskal, the leader of the Patriotic Front in the 6th district, reported that the local Nazis were full of admiration for the courage and audacity of the Schutzbund and were boasting that when their orders came from the Third Reich they would be even more courageous.[33] The attitude of the party was one of strict neutrality in the fighting, but there are reports of individual Nazis who were longing to have a crack at the 'Marxists' joining the Patriotic Front. For the time being individuals were in a quandary, but skilful propaganda by the party against both Dollfuss and the Social Democrats frustrated Dollfuss's plan of winning support from the Nazis by destroying the left. For a brief moment some members wavered, but party discipline held, and in the long run the Nazis were to gain immensely from the events of 12 February. Rumours of an invasion from Germany also circulated but were not taken seriously in Vienna. More significant were reports on 15 February that the Nazis were trying to buy weapons from the Schutzbund. In some instances it appears that they were successful.[34]

There is some uncertainty about the number of dead and wounded in the fighting in Vienna. In the report to the public prosecutor by the police chief of Vienna on 27 February, in which material was sent to build up a case against the Schutzbund, it is stated that 24 policemen, 1 detective, 19 volunteers and 4 soldiers had been killed in the fighting.[35] These figures are clearly too low, and were revised by the police chief on 3 March in a further letter to the public prosecutor in which it is claimed that on the government side 147 men were killed along with 125 civilians.[36] These figures coincide with those from the Vienna hospitals on 16 February which mention 147 dead, of whom 13 were from the police, and 373 wounded. No mention is made of civilian casualties.[37] In a further report of 16 October it was claimed that the executive had lost 55 dead and 251 wounded; the Schutzbund, civilians and 'right-wingers' 131 dead and 358 wounded.[38] The official report of the army on events in February 1934 talks of 118 dead on the Social Democratic side, of whom 17 were women, and 279 wounded, of whom 62 were women and 5 children.[39] The journalist George Gedeye, whose account of events in Vienna is well informed if flavoured with a certain journalistic hyperbole, estimated that the left had about 1,500 to 2,000 dead, and that there were many women and children among them. He also estimated that there were 5,000 wounded in the underground hospitals alone.[40]

From these figures it would seem that the executive lost about 150 men. This figure appears in a number of reports, and there is no obvious reason why it should be made to appear smaller than was the case. Such a figure is reasonable given the intensity of the fighting and the much better equipment of the executive, and their extensive use of artillery and armoured vehicles. The official statistics on the Schutzbund killed and wounded are all obviously far too low. They cannot have been lower than those of the executive, and we know of a large number of cases of innocent civilians who were killed in the artillery fire. On the other hand Gedeye's figures would seem to be a little too high. In these circumstances an accurate estimate of the number of dead on the left is impossible.

Meanwhile, in Linz, Bernaschek's men in the workers' council did their duty. Throughout Linz the Schutzbund was alerted and the fighting was by no means confined to the Hotel Schiff. Artillery destined for the hotel could not reach its destination because of heavy fire from side streets. One of the barracks, the Fabrikskaserne, was held in check for a while by a group of some fifty determined Schutzbündler. There was also fierce fighting on the railway bridge across the Danube, a key strategic point in the city. Another group met at the Jägermayerhof inn with the intention of seizing the Linz radio transmitter and the water tower. The army was able to contain the Schutzbund in the Jägermayerhof, but as the inn was situated in a high position with a wide field of fire, fighting lasted all day before the Schutzbund finally surrendered. The army lost six men in this action, but most of the Schutzbund members were able to escape capture by retreating through the woods under the cover of darkness.

In the docks some 250 workers erected barricades and formed a powerful defensive position. An attempt was made to send a group to relieve their comrades in the Hotel Schiff, but this failed as the army managed to keep them in their position. Another group of Schutzbündler, almost 150 men, was unable to join the workers in the docks. In the evening the army began an artillery barrage on the docks, and the workers were forced to surrender.

In the east of the city, the working-class district, the fighting was centred around the Zur Eisernen Hand inn, a point where six roads met. The Schutzbund had placed machine-guns at strategic points around this crossroads. A number of the executive were killed in the attempt to gain control of this area. It was not until the artillery was brought into action and after an extensive exchange of fire that the Schutzbund was forced to give up this key position in the late evening of 12 February. In many other areas on the periphery of the city there was isolated fighting.

In spite of the determined efforts of the Schutzbund in Linz there was never any serious danger of the executive losing control of the situation. As in Vienna they had no co-ordinated plan which alone could have made such an uprising successful. There was an understanding of the strategic importance of the Danube bridge, the Zur Eisernen Hand and the Jägermayerhof, but these efforts were not co-ordinated. Isolated displays of courage and military skill were not enough. The official military report on the fighting insists that there was a serious shortage of troops in Linz and that had the fighting been much more extensive they could have been in serious trouble. The Schutzbund leadership turned down the suggestion by militants that all the main roads to Linz should be barricaded, and that the railway tracks should be torn up, so that the executive would be unable to get any supplies into the city. The Schutzbund felt isolated from the rest of the working class and knew that their position was hopeless. In such a situation it is perhaps understandable that the moderates were unwilling to do excessive damage to public property. Like Erich Mühsam's revolutionary lamplighter, they felt that the breaking of lamps was going too far.

News of the fighting at the Hotel Schiff took some time to reach the workers in Steyr, the second largest city in Upper Austria. At 11.15 a.m. a general strike was called, workers left their jobs and the Schutzbund went into action. The army and the police had already been alerted at 8.00 and the police had begun to search for arms and were thus able to stop a large number of Schutzbündler from getting their weapons. In some cases Schutzbund leaders refused to hand out weapons to their men feeling that they would be acting against the wishes of the party leadership in Vienna. Nevertheless the Schutzbund was soon in a powerful position in Ennsleithen, a working-class suburb in a commanding position across the river Enns from the centre of the city. The Steyr factory was in the hands of the workers, the police were driven back after an attempt to gain control of the factory, and its managing director Wilhelm Herbst was shot in the course of this action. A railway viaduct was blown up and a major road bridge defended against the executive. The first attempt by the army to attack Ennsleithen was decisively beaten back; their commander, Captain Fasching, was seriously wounded, and the troops were completely demoralised.

Ennsleithen was extremely difficult to attack. There were no main roads from the centre of the city and icy conditions made an attack all the more difficult. Gustav Moser, a close associate of Bernaschek, head of the works council at the Steyr factory and a militant socialist, played an important part in the defence of Ennsleithen particularly by keeping up morale. In the night of 12-13 February the Schutzbund strengthened their positions in Ennsleithen. The artillery only fired six rounds into the area during the night, largely because it was impossible to aim in the dark, although the army's official report claims humanitarian reasons for not firing.

The attack on Ennsleithen, planned for the morning of 13 February, had to be postponed. The army came under attack from small Schutzbund units from areas around Steyr, and the men in Ennsleithen kept up heavy machine-gun fire. The attack began at 2.00 p.m., by which time Ennsleithen had been under heavy artillery and mortar fire and was completely surrounded by the army. Many houses were completely destroyed by the artillery. It was not until 5.45 that the army was able to gain control of Ennsleithen and begin silencing isolated pockets of resistance. Starhemberg and the Heimwehr played no part in the attack. They arrived in Ennsleithen as glorious victors once the fighting was over.

There are two major reasons why the Schutzbund was defeated at Ennsleithen even though the action was long and difficult for the army. The effect of the artillery fire was demoralising and the damage done considerable. The other major difficulty was complete lack of communications between the men in Ennsleithen and other Schutzbund units in Steyr. Both these factors were of tremendous importance in the fighting in February. Workers in hastily improvised defensive positions and relying on machine-guns on towers and roof-tops were helpless against an enemy determined to use artillery with scant regard to civilian life or damage done to buildings. Isolated units of the Schutzbund, whether in Vienna, Linz or Bruck, without a proper command structure and without an adequate communications network, could do little against a highly trained professional army.

Another scene of serious fighting in Upper Austria was Holzleithen. Holzleithen is a small community in the mining area of Upper Austria. Today it is pleasant wooded countryside with traditional inns providing refreshment for hikers. In February 1934 it was the scene of the most hectic fighting. The Schutzbund leader in the coal district was Ferdinand Fageth, a close associate of Bernaschek and a man of considerable energy who took his position as local leader seriously. It is said that during the fighting he insisted on wearing a sword as a symbol of his rank.[41]

The Schutzbund went into action as soon as the news arrived from Linz. The local Heimwehr headquarters at the Kaiserwirt inn was besieged. The nearby railway tunnel was heavily guarded so as to stop the transportation of men and materials into the area. The army decided that the first step should be to clear the tunnel. At 1.00 p.m. a lieutenant and 30 men were sent by special train to drive off the Schutzbund. They immediately came under heavy fire and were forced to take up a defensive position. An attempt to attack the Schutzbund position from the rear failed owing to the deep snow and incessant fire from Schutzbund detachments. The lieutenant there-fore decided to negotiate with the Schutzbund. The talks led nowhere. The army demanded the right to drive their train through the tunnel; the Schutzbund thought that the army should withdraw. Tempers got short and the lieutenant nearly got shot by an outraged Schutzbündler. The lieutenant withdrew and waited for the arrival of reinforcements. A second company of Alpenjäger arrived too late in the day to make another attempt to dislodge the Schutzbund from the tunnel.

In the course of the evening further reinforcements were brought up to Holzleithen. It was decided that the village itself should be taken and the Schutzbund centre in the workers' hall (*Arbeiterheim*) was to be the main object of the attack. The attackers had an extremely difficult time moving forward in thick snow, and they were under almost constant fire from units of the Schutzbund. Eventually they reached Holzleithen.

The subsequent events are a shameful episode in the history of the Austrian army and one of most shocking incidents in the February fighting. The Schutzbund position at the railway station was extremely well defended and the army could make no progress against it. It was then decided to use Schutzbündler prisoners as hostages. They were forced to march towards the station at gunpoint. The workers in the station would not of course shoot at their comrades, and were thus forced to retreat.

Far worse than the above incident was the sequel to the capture of the workers' hall. The defenders of the hall had hoisted the white flag. The Alpenjäger stormed into the building, seized six men at random, lined them up against the cinema screen in the lecture hall, which was also used as dining room, and shot them. Although 54 shots were fired one man survived, although paralysed by a shot in the backbone. None of the men were armed at the time of their capture. Three of them were medical orderlies. It appears that no officer was present at the killing. There was no official investigation of the case, and no soldiers were punished. The official excuses — that shots were fired after the white flag had been hoisted and that a medical orderly had fired a gun — are of doubtful authenticity, and in any case are no excuse for executions of this sort. Some time later Chancellor Schuschnigg expressed his regrets at the incident.[42]

The miners in the district had shown little solidarity with the Schutzbund. On 12 February only 91 miners failed to report for work. Although the miners were among the most determined and formed the elite of the Social Democratic forces, the rank and file were largely made up of the unemployed or the retired.[43] On 14 February, however, not a single man reported for work in spite of high unemployment and the risk of instant dismissal. News of the murders in

Holzleithen shocked the miners into action. But things were quickly back to normal. By 15 February only 25 per cent of the workers stayed off the job. Within a few days the protest was abandoned.

In the Styrian industrial town of Bruck-an-der-Mur a general strike was called at midday on 12 February. It began in the Felten and Guilleaume works and spread to the railway and electricity works, the paper factory and many of the other industrial enterprises. As elsewhere in Austria the response to the call for a general strike was lukewarm. The police reported that the shift was changed at the Felten works without incident and that the factory was continuing to function more or less as normal.[44] The gendarmerie was immediately alerted and concentrated on protecting those workers who wished to break the strike. The Schutzbund reacted immediately. At 1.15 p.m. a unit of the Schutzbund attacked the gendarmerie barracks, killed the guard at the gate, but was soon beaten back to the main square of the town once the gendarmerie were able to return the fire.

It was at this point, at about 1.30, that the party secretary for Styria, Koloman Wallisch, arrived in Bruck.[45] Wallisch was a Hungarian who had played a role in the Hungarian Soviet Republic and had subsequently moved to Austria. He was a militant, and was among the handful of senior officials of the party who played an active role in the fighting in February. The leader of the Bruck Schutzbund, Sepp Linhardt, had been killed in the attack on the gendarmerie. Wallisch now took over command of the town where for a long time he had been party secretary.

The Felten works soon became the scene of fierce fighting. The Schutzbund encircled the building and kept up a heavy fire on the gendarmerie who had been sent to protect the workers and now found themselves besieged. The gendarmerie was forced to retreat into the management building where they were subjected to continuous fire. At 7.00 p.m. the Schutzbund sent an envoy to the gendarmerie warning them that if they did not leave the Felten works within ten minutes they would blow up the management building. Inspector Knauz refused to accept these terms. The Schutzbund failed in the attempt to blow up the building, the gendarmerie warding off the attackers with well-aimed fire. In the early morning of 13 February the army appeared on the scene and relieved the gendarmerie.

Another centre of the fighting was the Forestry School in which 65 men of the Heimatschutz and 41 men of the Sturmscharen had their headquarters. At 1.25 p.m., when only 20 men were in the building, it was suddenly attacked by the Schutzbund. The Heimatschutz was trapped inside the building, and unable to get any support from the gendarmerie that was still fighting off the attackers on their barracks.

Wallisch was well aware of the need for support from outside if Bruck was to continue fighting; he also realised the importance of cutting off the railway lines leading to the town. Throughout most of 12 February the trains ran normally in Bruck, and it was not until 10.00 p.m. that the Schutzbund seized the station, and one hour later that the railway was brought to a standstill. Wallisch was successful in rounding up Schutzbündler from surrounding villages, and these men he used to establish a strong position on the Schlossberg, a hill that dominates the town.

Yet in spite of these precautions the army was able to enter the town during the night of 12 February. A battalion of Alpenjäger had a difficult time crossing the countless barriers that the Schutzbund had improvised along the streets leading to the centre of the town, and they came under frequent heavy fire. In the early morning of 13 February further troops reached the town. At 4.45 a.m. they began a bombardment of the Schlossberg with artillery and mortar fire. Wallisch's plan was to attack the army from the rear whilst they were preparing their attack on the Schlossberg, but this strategy misfired. The defenders of the Schlossberg were unable to hold out long enough against a vastly superior force. Once the army had dislodged the Schutzbund from the Schlossberg they were soon able to relieve the gendarmerie barracks and the Felten works.

At this point the commander of the Heimatschutz at the Forestry School decided to fight his way out of the building. The Schutzbund, already seriously weakened by their sudden reverse of fortune, were taken by surprise and forced to abandon their positions. The Heimatschutz under Fuchsjäger immediately joined forces with the army commanded by Lieutenant-Colonel Moltini and took part in the mopping-up operations in Bruck.

By 6.00 a.m. on 13 February the army was effectively in command of the situation, but Wallisch was determined not to give up the fight. At first he hoped to march towards Graz, putting Leoben and Donawitz into the hands of the workers on the way to the provincial capital. But it soon became obvious that such a endeavour was bound to fail given the strength of the army. Wallisch therefore decided to retreat with about 400 ill-equipped and exhausted men to the Hochalm in the direction of the Yugoslav border. Wallisch's men were soon utterly exhausted after marching through thick snow, and in an impassioned speech he told anyone who was unable to continue the march to leave.

One of the men who left Wallisch, an officer of the Schutzbund, appears to have betrayed him to the gendarmerie.[46] Until that moment that gendarmerie had no idea where he was, and he was reported to have vanished without a trace.[47] The gendarmerie were quick to see the propaganda value of Wallisch's retreat to the mountains and the fact that a large number of his men had left him. As soon as they got the information on 14 February they began to spread the news abroad.

The first contact between the gendarmerie and the Wallisch group was made in the early morning of 14 February. Ten men who had already left Wallisch were surrounded and captured, one man committing suicide rather than be taken prisoner.[48] Shortly afterwards another 20 Schutzbündler were captured. From information gained from these prisoners the gendarmerie learned that Wallisch, with about 50 men, was resting in a house nearby. A small detachment of the gendarmerie approached the house but came under such heavy fire that they were forcd to wait for reinforcements. By the time it was possible to launch an attack on the house from three sides, Wallisch had left. Only three men who remained behind in the house were taken prisoner.

Further reinforcements of the gendarmerie were brought up and the hunt for Wallisch continued. Progress was slow owing to heavy snow conditions, but in the course of 14 February contact was once again made with him. There was a brisk exchange of fire. Two of Wallisch's men were captured, one man was killed on each side. The gendarmerie forced the prisoners out in front of them so that Wallisch's men had to hold their fire, but the Schutzbund was well situated in a sheltered wood, the weather was extremely bad, and the gendarmerie would not risk an attack.[49] They preferred to wait for the machine-guns to be brought up before risking an assault. By the time the guns had arrived and the assault prepared, Wallisch had already left his position.

Wallisch now hoped to cross the 1,195-metre high Iron Pass, but the weather conditions were so bad that this proved to be impossible. The group disbanded, each man trying to make his own way home. Wallisch was able to hide in the barn of an isolated farmhouse where his wife, Paula, joined him on 16 February. It was arranged that a car should meet him and drive him to Yugoslavia. Meanwhile the gendarmerie sent out ski patrols to find Wallisch. A systematic search of farms, barns and huts turned up a number of exhausted and half-frozen Schutzbündler, but the leader could not be found.

Wallisch and his wife made contact with the car and began the journey to Yugoslavia. A driver for Austrian Railways saw a brown car on the road from Admont to Liezen in which he thought he spotted Koloman Wallisch. Greedy for the handsome reward offered by the government for information leading to his arrest, he reported this to the gendarmerie. A car was immediately sent out in pursuit. About three kilometres outside Liezen the brown car was found abandoned in a ditch, having skidded off the road. After an intensive search of the area, Wallisch and his wife were found in a small village by the name of Reittal. They offered no resistance to their arrest.

Immediately after his arrest on 18 February Wallisch was taken to Liezen where his statement was made. In the afternoon he was taken to Leoben. On 19 February he appeared before a court martial and was condemned to death. A butcher from Vienna was brought in to hang him. He died at 10.40 that night. The butcher bowed to his corpse and said: 'Herr Wallisch, that was a very special pleasure.'[50] Immediately Wallisch became one of the great heroes and martyrs of February, his summary execution providing ample propaganda material against the Dollfuss government, his courage and determination in a hopeless situation becoming symbolic of the struggle of the Austrian workers against the destruction of their rights and freedoms.

In the capital of Styria the appeal for a general strike was no more successful than in Bruck. There were isolated strikes in some factories, but all the public utilities functioned as normal. The Schutzbund was poorly organised and mobilisation was very slow. The police quickly seized the main Social Democratic centres including party head-quarters and the newspaper press. The Schutzbund did not go into action until the afternoon of 12 February when a series of isolated fights between the police and the Social Democrats broke out. An attempt by the Schutzbund to capture the main railway building failed, and the executive was quick to secure the main public build-ings, the bridges across the river Mur and the Schlossberg, a hill which dominates the entire city. The workers therefore tried to strengthen their position in the industrial area, taking over many of the main factories, including the Humanic factory, famous for its ski boots. But soon it became apparent that the workers were trapped in this area. Attempts to gain control of the railway line failed and trains continued to move in and out of the city.

In this situation the military could afford to wait until the artillery arrived. In the evening of 12 February the artillery was in position. With no help from outside, and trapped in the industrial area, the workers had no chance. It was only a matter of time before they were forced to surrender.

One of the major factors in the defeat of the Schutzbund in 1934, particularly in Vienna, was the failure of Lower Austria to respond to the call for a general strike and for action against the government. Lower Austria had a long history of socialist militancy. Towns like Wiener Neustadt were traditional centres of the Austrians labour movement. The Schutzbund in Lower Austria was well organised and well armed. It is true that some of the prominent leaders in Lower Austria, such as Josef Püchler of Wiener Neustadt, the leader of the local Schutzbund nicknamed 'Radikalinski', had been arrested prior to 12 February. In Püchler's case it was 10 February when he was picked up on a charge of drunkenness. The authorities feared that his arrest might trigger off protests among the local Social Democrats, and local military units were placed on the alert.

The party secretary for Lower Austria was a right-winger who adopted a 'wait and see' attitude on 12 February and from the outset began negotiations with the authorities, who refused to talk to him and had him arrested on the spot. There were isolated outbursts of violence in some centres, particularly in Wiener Neustadt, when small units of the Schutzbund hastily grabbed weapons and explosives and went into action. But such acts were spontaneous and unco-ordinated. There was no central direction, no strategy, merely anger and frustration. It was thus relatively easy for the executive to control the situation, and troops could be sent from Lower Austria to areas where they were badly needed, particularly to Vienna and Styria. Trains with military supplies and men, including ammunition from Hungary, were able to pass through Lower Austria without difficulty. Even units of the Schutzbund that were close to Vienna, in places such as Neumödling or Ebergassing, were unable to give any support to their comrades in Vienna, either because they lacked weapons or because of faulty tactics.

Throughout most of the rest of Austria there was very little response to events in Vienna and Linz. In Salzburg, where the party was dominated by the right wing, it was decided to call a conference of party leaders to discuss the situation. The police quickly seized the opportunity to arrest the entire leadership of the party and the

Schutzbund. Isolated acts of violence following these arrests caused the authorities little concern.

In Carinthia the party leadership opposed the use of force by the party; the vice-provincial secretary and the mayor of Klagenfurt both resigned from the party in protest and appealed to the party not to resort to violence. With very few exceptions this appeal was respected. Similarly, the party leadership in Vorarlberg condemned the fighting as 'criminal' and all was quiet. As in the case of Lower Austria, troops from these provinces could be sent to other areas and used against the militant workers whose actions the local party leadership denounced.

The greatest weakness of the Schutzbund in February was the lack of a determined and effective leadership. The party had tried to hold back the militants and wished to avoid a showdown with the government, in part because it feared that the beneficiaries of such a struggle would be the Nazis. In many parts of the country the leadership of the party was either indifferent or hostile to the actions of the Schutzbund in Linz and Vienna. Some leaders allowed themselves to be arrested in their offices, others, like the Salzburg group, made it even easier for the police by holding a well-publicised meeting. In Vienna the leadership of the party was unable to control and direct the fighting so as to ensure maximum effect. By Monday evening Deutsch and Bauer realised that the situation was hopeless, and that it was only a matter of time before the Schutzbund would be forced to give up.[51] Bauer left Vienna and escaped to Czechoslovakia on 13 February, Deutsch followed the next day.

To see the actions of the party leadership solely as 'cowardly capitulation' is one sided.[52] The Schutzbund commandant of 15th district, Eduard Korbel, suddenly realised that as a member of a masonic pacifist sect he could not condone violence and therefore handed his entire sector over to the authorities. But such disgraceful behaviour was untypical. The problem for the party was that Bernaschek in Linz had acted without the authority of the party leadership and was trying to force Otto Bauer into a course of action which he did not approve. Thus the February revolt was not only against the Dollfuss régime, it was also against the party line which the militants were convinced was weak-kneed and bound to lead to the steady growth of fascism in Austria. Many party leaders were caught between their loyalty to the party line and their belief that this policy was correct, and solidarity with the fighting workers. Neither Bauer nor Deutsch were cowards. Their policy was mistaken, and they must bear a heavy responsibility for the defeat of the party. But they showed their solidarity with the workers of Vienna, they did not run away as the government insisted, they only left when in their judgement the situation was hopeless. They also had the intellectual courage to admit their mistakes and to accept full responsibility as leaders for the failure of the revolt.[53] There were individual acts of cowardice and of bad faith in the party leadership, but the basic reason for the attitude of uncertainty and hesitation lies in the fundamental contradiction within Austro-Marxism between its apparently revolutionary rhetoric and its timid reformist practice. The February revolt occurred at a time when the party and the Schutzbund was far less well prepared than the executive. The party was divided as to what to do in the face of the mounting threat of fascism, and had no adequate military plan to deal with an eventual confrontation between the Schutzbund and the executive.

The executive thus held most of the trumps. The army and the police were better trained and better equipped than the Schutzbund. Numerically they were greatly superior. The Schutzbund had already lost many valuable stocks of arms and ammunition in the frequent raids before 12 February. Similarly, many of the Social Democratic leaders had been arrested before the fighting began. A general strike would have certainly made the task of the executive much more difficult. Had the railway system not worked almost without interruption it would have been possible to move men and munitions quickly into areas where they were most needed, and the revolt would certainly have lasted longer, perhaps giving the Schutzbund a chance to strengthen their positions. When Julius Deutsch saw the trains puffing in and out of Vienna on the evening of 12 February he realised that the fight was lost.

The failure of the general strike meant that the bourgeois press continued to publish, and the government was able to use its propaganda machine to the full. The radio, the press and leaflets were all used to report the victories, sometimes imagined, of the executive, and also to issue dire warnings and threats to the Social Democrats. Thus Schuschnigg announced on the radio that Bauer and Deutsch had fled from Vienna, leaving their comrades in the lurch, at a time when both of them were busy at headquarters. Later on, Fey announced that they had arrived in Prague when they were in fact both still in Vienna. Fey's claim that they had run away with the party funds was also a fabrication. Bauer left with 105 shillings, Deutsch had even less.[54] There can be little doubt that this propaganda was effective, the more so because the Social Democrats were unable to counter it. They had failed to capture the radio transmitters, and in many parts of Austria their own press had been seized. Thus the propaganda effect of the shelling of workers' homes in Vienna only caused local resentment and militancy, it could only be used abroad to win sympathy for a cause that had already been lost. John Heartfield and the *Arbeiter Illustrierte Zeitung* were in Prague, not in Vienna.

The government acted quickly, firmly, and in some instances extremely cruelly, against an opponent that was weak and divided. They had at last found the excuse they were looking for to destroy 'Marxism' and they seized it immediately. But the victory was soon to turn sour. By destroying Social Democracy they had also destroyed the one possible defence against Nazism, and their policy was to prove to be based on false premises, wishful thinking and a complete lack of understanding of the objective situation in Austria. The attempt to combat fascism with a fascistic policy was bound to lead to failure. But for the moment the government basked in its triumph, convinced that it had won a great victory.

Notes

1. *AVA*, Bundeskanzleramt Inneres 1934, 22/gen. 4885. The versions in *Oesterreich — Brandherd Europas* (Zurich 1934), p. 279 and Arnold Reisberg, *Februar 1934. Hintergründe und Folgen* (Vienna 1974), p. 1, are inaccurate, but the gist of the story is correct.

2. Inez Kykal and Karl R.Stadler, *Richard Bernaschek. Odyssee eines Rebellen* (Vienna 1976). A useful biography of an extraordinary man.

3. One of the five was Gustl Moser, later a member of the Central Committee of the Communist Party. See his account of the meeting in *Volksstimme*, 2 February 1964.

4. Otto Bauer, *Der Aufstand der österreichischen Arbeiter. Seine Ursachen und seine Wirkung* (Prague 1934), p. 13.

5. *AVA*, Bundeskanzleramt Inneres 4885.

6. See the accounts in C.A. Gulick, *From Habsburg to Hitler* (2 vols., Berkeley 1948), vol. 1, p. 1281; Reisberg, *Februar 1934*, p. 7; Everhard Holtmann, *Zwischen Unterdrückung und Befriedung. Sozialistische Arbeiterbewegung und autoritäres Regime in Oesterreich 1933-1938* (Munich 1978), p. 175.

7. *AVA*, Ministerrat Protokolle 922.

8. Kurt Peball, *Die Kämpfe in Wien im Februar 1934* (Vienna 1974), p. 21.

9. *AVA*, Polizeidirektion Wien, Akten Februar 1934, Zl. Pr. IV — 2606/1934 Karton 1. The attack on the police station is not mentioned in the official police reports, possibly because the police did not put on a very creditable performance even though they had been alerted at 11.00 a.m.

10. Ibid., Karton 10.

11. Ibid., Karton 6 (Waffen und Munitionen).

12. *VGA*, Lode 17, Mappe 1.

13. Ibid.

14. Reisberg, *Februar 1934*, p. 17.

15. *AVA*, Polizeidirektion Wien, Karton 1.

16. See the article on Georg Weissel by Joseph J. Simon in: Norbert Leser (ed.), *Werk und Widerhall. Grosse Gestalten des österreichischen Sozialismus* (Vienna 1964).

17. *AVA*, Polizeidirektion Wien, Karton 10.

18. On the drama of Floridsdorf see Friedrich Wolf, *Floridsdorf. Ein Schauspiel von den Februarkämpfen der Wiener Arbeiter* (Zürich 1935); Hilde Abel, *Victory was Slain* (New York 1941), is a very inferior novel on the same theme.

19. Reisberg, *Februar 1934*, p. 17.

20. *AVA*, Polizeidirektion Wien, Karton 10.

21. Ibid.

22. Ibid.

23. Ibid.

24. Ibid.

25. Ibid.

26. Ibid.

27. Ibid.

28. Ibid.

29. Ibid.

30. L. Kerekes, *Abenddämmerung einer Demokratie* (Vienna 1966), p. 182.

31. *AVA*, Polizeidirektion Wien, Karton 10.

32. Ibid.

33. Ibid.

34. Ibid.

35. Ibid., Karton 1.

36. Ibid.

37. Ibid.

38. Ibid.

39. *Der Februar-Aufruhr 1934. Das Eingreifen des österr. Bundesheeres zu seiner Niederwerfung. Im Auftrag des BM für Landesverteidigung*, manuscript, Vienna 1935, p. 144.

40. G.E.R. Gedeye, *Fallen Bastions* (London 1939), p. 116.

41. Litschel, *1934*, p. 78.

42. It is almost certain that the famous photograph of the execution is a forgery — reproduced in Reisberg, *Februar 1934*, p. 224.

43. Litschel, *1934*, p. 79.

44. *Gendarmeriebericht*, p. 21.

45. Paula Wallisch, *Ein Held stirbt* (Graz 1964), although uncritical, is the best biography.

46. Reisberg, *Februar 1934*, p. 51.

47. *AVA*, Bundeskanzleramt Inneres 4885.

48. *Gendarmariebericht*, p. 30.

49. Ibid., p. 32.

50. Reisberg, *Februar 1934*, p. 51.

51. Julius Deutsch, *Ein weiter Weg. Lebenserinnerungen* (Vienna 1960), p. 215.

52. Reisberg, *Februar 1934*, p. 59.

53. Otto Bauer, *Der Aufstand der österreichischen Arbeiter* (Prague 1934).

54. Ibid., p. 23.

10 THE AFTERMATH OF FEBRUARY

Once it became clear that the government was firmly in control of the situation, it also became obvious that the victory over the Social Democrats was not the universal panacea that Dollfuss had hoped. Schuschnigg as Minister of Justice argued strongly against showing any mercy to those who had been condemned to death by the courts martial, insisting that it was necessary to act swiftly and harshly against the 'bestial' Social Democrats who were thought to be responsible for such dreadful crimes as hacking wounded men to pieces in Styria. But on the other hand, even Schuschnigg had to admit that Austria could not ignore international public opinion, particularly the strong reactions in Britain and Switzerland, and agreed that martial law should be lifted as soon as possible and that some mercy would have to be shown. Thus from the very outset the government was painfully aware of the restraints placed on its anti-socialist policies.[1]

It was also apparent that the idea that the best way to deal with the Nazis was to attack the socialists was a dreadful mistake. At the beginning of March the security director for Syria reported that the Social Democrats were understandably depressed and demoralised after the defeat of the party, but that this had given the Nazis a new sense of confidence and they were becoming increasingly active and dangerous.[2] Vorarlberg reported that the Nazis were behaving well and respecting the law and strongly supported the actions of the government against the 'Marxists', but there was no indication that any of the Nazis were leaving the party to support the Patriotic Front.[3] Salzburg reported that a number of Social Democrats and Communists had joined the National Socialists, having become totally disillusioned with their parties after 12 February.[4] The Tyrol also reported that the Nazis were gaining members from disillusioned Social Democrats, but the security director had the impression that the Nazis were losing support in an area that was one of the great Nazi strongholds in Austria.[5]

The government was particularly concerned about the activities of the Social Democrats in Czechoslovakia. The formation of the Social Democratic Foreign Office (ALÖS) in Brno in March and the publication of a shortened version of the *Arbeiter-Zeitung* was regarded as a particular danger. All post addressed to the ALÖS was opened by the secret police and carefully analysed.[6] Constant rumours circulated that the Social Democrats were preparing for a second round and that they would attack at any moment. These reports were carefully investigated, even though they were clearly at variance with the news from the provinces.[7]

The government tried to deal with the Social Democrats not only with sticks but also with the offer of a modest carrot. In March Prince Hubertus Loewenstein wrote an article in the *Spectator* in which he sensibly argued that it was only with the help of the working class that Austria could be defended against Nazi Germany. Thus the persecution of the Social Democrats would have to cease. The prince hoped that the Free Workers' Association (*Freier Arbeiterbund*) of Dr Zeinitzer of Klagenfurt, who had been a member of the Social Democratic Party, and the Freedom League (*Freiheitsbund*) of the Liberal Christian Social Leopold Kunschak, a man who had chaired the party in the early 1920s, was a specialist on labour policy and an opponent of the Heimwehr, would help to reconcile the workers to the Dollfuss government.[8] Kunschak had little support within his own party and was bitterly opposed by the Heimwehr for his conciliatory attitude towards the workers and his belief in parliamentary democracy. He had never accepted the horror stories about the 'Marxists' and had little sympathy for Dollfuss's constitutional experiments. The Free Workers' Association was a more active, popular and dynamic organisation. With its aim of reconciling the workers to the new state and its lofty appeals for an end to the class struggle, it was attractive to the government and given some support.[9]

In spite of a flood of letters in support of the association, and reports from some provinces that the workers were reconciled to the failure of the party on 12 February and favoured the new non-political unions suggested by the government, the attempt to win the working class over to the Dollfuss régime was a total failure.[10] Workers were forced into the new unions where they promptly formed opposition groups, and very few were reconciled to a system that denied their basic political rights and in which their material conditions of life steadily declined.

An accurate picture of the government's thinking about the effects of 12 February is extremely difficult to reconstruct. Reports on political activity were usually sent to the office of General Ronge, a frustratingly shadowy figure on whom virtually no information is available, and whose papers have disappeared. Without knowing the precise role and the attitude of Ronge, it is difficult to assess how far the reports to the government were vetted to suit his own ambitions.[11] The picture that emerges, however, is reasonably clear and consistent. The Social Democratic Party had suffered a shattering blow, but this had not had the desired effect. The party was not dead but had been radicalised by the experience of defeat. It had lost members, but these gravitated towards the Nazis; thus the government's plan to kill two birds with one stone was a failure. The government was also alarmed by the growth of the Communist Party which, with its powerful ally in the Soviet Union, was felt to be a potential danger.[12] The government was also worried about the effect of recent events on the police and the army. A number of senior policemen, particularly in Vienna, were openly sympathetic to the Nazis, and were sending reports of events in Austria to the Nazi Party headquarters in Munich. Nazis were also very active in the army where they attracted the younger officers, the senior officers with their monarchical ideas also being unsympathetic to the republic. Some of the rank-and-file policemen thought that the 12 February had been deliberately provoked by the government and thus were sympathetic to the workers.[13]

A matter of particular concern was the possibility of an alliance between the Nazis and the left against the government. There were persistent rumours reaching the government to this effect. One popular argument to support this theory was that the left-wing Social Democrats, Communists and Nazis were all radical opponents of the régime, and that socialists thought that the Nazis were in some sense on the left. Furthermore, it was argued in some circles that fascism was a necessary stage through which capitalist society had to pass and that it would be followed by socialism.[14] In April there were reports from Styria that the Nazis and the Social Democrats were planning common actions and that the Nazis were prepared to get Bernaschek out of jail.[15] Even the normally well-informed Hütter, Hornbostel's roving informant, told his boss that in mid-June the Revolutionary Socialists and the Nazis had signed a pact in Laibach in which it was agreed to depose Dollfuss and establish an anti-Catholic and anti-Italian régime.[16]

Dollfuss and his government had little understanding of National Socialism or Social Democracy, and it is thus possible that they might have been taken in by these extraordinary reports. One thing the government refused to admit was that they had made a serious miscalculation in February. Hütter, as early as 20 February, reported that he had met Don Sturzo at G. P. Gooch's house in London where he had said that the Heimwehr had been pushed by Mussolini, and that the Social Democrats had been deliberately provoked. The defeat of Social Democracy would lead to the victory of the NSDAP in Austria. Italian fascism would thus be directly responsible for Hitler's victory in Austria.[17] This view Hornbostel dismissed as 'wicked' (*übel*). Within four years it was to prove absolutely correct. There was a gradual realisation in government circles that the big card had been played, but that little had been won. After February Dollfuss, and then Schuschnigg, had nothing to offer but the increasingly slender possibility of a régime surviving with virtually no popular support, no positive achievements and a determined and powerful enemy in Germany.

If 12 February brought little relief to the Dollfuss government at home it also did little to improve Austria's foreign political position. Mussolini was anxious to 'settle the Austrian question', as he told the German ambassador, his aim being a three-power trade agreement between Italy, Austria and Hungary.[18] The German Foreign Office was highly alarmed at Italy's policies, but the ambassadors in both Vienna and Budapest reported that neither Austria nor Hungary wished to bind themselves too closely to Italy and both governments were concerned to maintain good relations with Germany.

In the middle of March, with the maximum of publicity, the Austrians and Hungarians went to Rome to put the finishing touches to Mussolini's schemes. The situation was favourable. In France, Barthou was thinking in terms of an alliance with Italy and the Soviet Union to contain Germany, and much preferred an Austria closely allied to Italy than an Anschluss. The British government, although conscious of public opinion's disgust with the Dollfuss régime, tacitly supported Mussolini. The Germans seemed to have suffered a temporary setback in Austria, the Nazis having been ousted from their position as principal anti-Marxists. But Mussolini found considerable resistance both from the Hungarians and the Austrians.

The Hungarian government was anxious to preserve its freedom of action and did not wish to break off its relations with Germany. Gömbös told Mussolini: 'Hungary must follow its own policies in the Carpathian basin, south of the Danube it needs the support of Italy, north of the Danube of Germany.'[19] Gömbös was prepared to make considerable concessions in the economic sphere, but not to give up his idea of a three-pronged Hungarian policy. Dollfuss refused to make any concessions either politically or economically, and it was only at the last moment that he gave way and accepted the proposed pact.

The resulting 'Roman Protocols', signed on 17 March, were in three sections. The first protocol was a declaration of intent that the three states would co-operate with one another as such co-operation would form the best basis for relations between the signatories and other states. It was agreed that the independence and rights of individual states should be respected. It was agreed that meetings should be held whenever necessary to discuss matters of common concern and interest. Gömbös absolutely refused to guarantee the independence of Austria as the Italians wished, so that the vague talk of the respect for the independence of states was an empty formula, particularly when coming from such determined revisionist powers as Hungary and Italy. Italy's position was somewhat strengthened by an agreement that there should be consultations before any major political decisions were taken, but here again the phrasing was deliberately vague. In the two protocols dealing with economic affairs preference was given to Austrian industry and to Hungarian grain. Italy guaranteed an increased import of Hungarian grain and gave Austria preferential railway tariffs to Trieste, hoping to divert goods away from Hamburg and Bremen.[20]

The Germans were furious about the Roman Protocols, realising that Mussolini had scored a major success over them on the Danube. Austria was now closer than ever to Italy and had found further support for its independence. But the reaction to the protocols was a trifle excessive. *The Times* wrote that they showed that Italy had no territorial ambitions against Austria, as if this had ever been the point at issue. Benes announced that he was prepared to join in the pact if there was a general guarantee of territorial integrity and a further guarantee that the Habsburgs would not be restored.[21] Italy appeared to various commentators and diplomats no longer to be a revisionist power but a champion of the European settlement. Hungary now seemed to be the troublemaker, and the major revisionist power on the Danube.

The Austrian government did not exaggerate the significance of the Roman Protocols. Dollfuss was well aware of Hungarian reservations and he was also determined to maintain his independence and not to become the puppet of Mussolini. No one thought of the possibility of a *rapprochement* between Berlin and Rome which would destroy the whole basis of the Chancellor's policy. Once Italy and Germany settled their differences the axis, as one wit put it, would be the spit on which Austria would be roasted brown.

Meanwhile at home the persecution of the Social Democrats continued. Central to the prosecution's case against those involved in the fighting in February was the contention that the revolt had been the result of careful planning and preparation by a small group of fanatics, and that it was not the 'uprising of the Austrian workers' as Otto Bauer claimed. The Dollfuss government still hoped to integrate the working class into its corporatist state and thus the argument that it had been misled by sinister and unscrupulous figures was politically convenient.

The evidence produced in support of this contention was slight, and often bordered on the ridiculous. It was argued that the working-class housing in Vienna, such as the huge complex of the Karl-Marx-Hof, had been deliberately designed for military purposes. These buildings, that were regarded as among the finest examples of public housing in the world, were now made out to be armed fortresses. Balconies on which working-class families enjoyed fresh air in privacy turned out to be skilfully disguised machine-gun nests. Courtyards in which children played were designed, it was suggested, as centres of a murderous crossfire, should the enemy enter the complex. Massive gateways were clearly designed to keep out the invaders, not to shut off the noise of the traffic. The sewage system had been designed not to meet the requirements of such large concentrations of people, but to allow military supplies to be brought in and out of these fortresses unobserved by government forces.[22]

In government circles these fantasies were widely believed, but an extensive search for evidence was fruitless. No police agent, no architect's draughtsman, no town planner or building contractor could be found who could provide a shred of evidence to substantiate these wild rumours which continued to circulate. The most solid piece of evidence was a telephone call from a retired major of the German army, Fell, who arrived in Vienna on 12 February to report on events for his paper, the *Berliner Lokalanzeiger*. At 11.30 p.m. on 13 February he telephoned from his hotel to Dönhoff in Berlin telling him that he had evidence that the Social Democrats had been systematically planning the uprising for some time. They had managed to build workers' housing projects at strategic points throughout the city that were made of shellproof ferro-concrete. All the homes in Ottakring were designed with forty machine-gun emplacements. Major Fell felt that the government would have a difficult time defeating an enemy that appeared to be entrenched in such invincible positions.[23] In spite of the fact that the ferro-concrete provided virtually no protection against artillery shells, as countless contemporary photographs show, and although the Schutzbund had few machine-guns, none of which were placed on the balconies, which provided very little cover, the pointless search of guilty architects and city planners continued.

Equally popular were the stories that the sewage system in Vienna had been developed by dedicated socialists determined to build an underground network through which the Schutzbund could move men and materials to strategic points throughout the city and special pioneer squads could blow up public buildings. As these rumours persisted the head of the works council (*Betriebsrat*) of the sewage workers, Paul Gajdorusz, was arrested as early as 15 January. Questioned by the police he admitted that the Schutzbund leader, Alexander Eifler, had told him to appoint two trustworthy men in each district of Vienna. But in spite of further 'reliable' reports that public buildings would soon be destroyed, the police could find no evidence, and Gajdorusz's statement was hardly sufficient proof of a sinister conspiracy. Curiously enough, in spite of this obsession with the sewage works, the police never found out that the Schutzbund was using the system as a hiding place and as a field hospital.[24] Ten days after the fighting stopped in Vienna the police investigated a report from the sewing woman of an architect who heard from a dentist's cook that her fiancé had said that although the Social Democrats had been defeated they were hiding underground and would soon blow up the Chancellory.[25] The atmosphere was such that no rumour was too silly not to be followed up by the police, creating an atmosphere in which petty jealousies and vindictiveness could all too easily be used against neighbours and relatives, and spite could parade as patriotism.

The central argument used by the state in its prosecution of those involved in the fighting in February was that it was a carefully planned and premeditated revolt. This case proved to be exceedingly hard to uphold. Many of the leaders of the party and particularly of the Schutzbund had been arrested before 12 February, and other leaders like Bauer and Deutsch had managed to escape. The only major figure to be captured was Koloman Wallisch and he had been immediately executed so there was little benefit from his trial as far as establishing a case for conspiracy was concerned. On 7 March the state prosecutor's office in Graz wrote to Vienna asking for clear proof that there was a planned uprising by the Social Democrats on 12 February. The Ministry of Justice was unable to provide a satisfactory answer to this request.[26] After extensive research the police reported to the Chancellor on 21 May 1934 that as yet they could find no evidence whatsoever that a plan existed for a Social Democratic revolt.[27] Similar rumours that the Social Democratic headquarters were scenes of luxurious debauchery were also discredited. Frequent attempts were made to discredit the leadership of the party by suggesting that they lived lives of splendid comfort at the expense of the working men. At the insistence of a schoolteacher the workers' club at Ottakring was raided on 7 March. The police report is charmingly laconic: 'In spite of repeated searches of the Ottakring workers' club we have been unable to find champagne, gourmet foods or ladies silk underwear.'[28] The schoolteacher was bitterly disappointed that Dollfuss was unable to broadcast the result of this political panty-raid.

There was general agreement that a tramway strike in Vienna would be the signal for a general strike, but there was no evidence whatever that it was also the signal for an armed uprising.[29] It could not be denied that the Schutzbund had stores of weapons, but it was difficult to prove from this that it was planning a revolution. If this were true then the same would have to be said of the Heimwehr. The prosecution had to prove that a decision had been made, prior to 12 February 1934, to use arms to overthrow the government. This was impossible, because no such decision had been made.

In the attempt to prove that a conspiracy existed the police cross-examined a number of key figures in the party and their families and associates in a series of interviews that are an invaluable source of information on the attitude of the party just prior to 12 February.

Dr Robert Danneberg, a leading moderate intellectual, had been a member of the party executive (*Vorstand*) since 1919 when he was 34 years old. He was an expert on constitutional questions and economic affairs but was almost entirely ignorant of the activities of the Schutzbund. He denied that the Social Democrats were looking for outside help and was a strong advocate of compromise with the government. He told the police that the Christmas truce had made it virtually impossible for the workers to discuss politics with their representatives, with the result that the moderate leadership might have lost a chance to exercise a restraining influence on more militant elements within the party. Danneberg knew nothing of any discussions of a general strike. He had spent the day of 12 February in his office, where he was arrested. He was convinced that the fighting in Linz had triggered off the whole affair and that most Social Democrats were taken completely by surprise by what had happened. That was certainly true in his case.[30]

Dr Wilhelm Ellenbogen was a member of the older generation of the party (he was born in 1863) and had been elected to the council formed at the October congress of the party in 1933. He told the police that the workers were prepared to fight under certain circumstances which had been outlined in the four points of the extraordinary conference. He also told the police that socialists from France, Czechoslovakia, Holland, England, Hungary and Sweden had promised their solidarity with the Austrian workers, but that this promise certainly did not involve the sending of direct aid or military support. Ellenbogen was not a member of the Schutzbund and knew little of its activities. He felt that the fighting on 12 February was the result of years of frustration for the workers, and insisted that the party had not encouraged the fighting nor had it called the strike.[31] Ellenbogen had gone to his office on 12 February, and when he heard of the strike he went to the parliament building to find out what was happening. Getting no useful information he decided to go home, and then, like a good Viennese, he went to his cafe where he was promptly arrested.

The police decided that Helmer, Popp, Schneeberger, Schneidmadl, Renner, Scherf, Körner, Danneberg, Sticka, Petzner and possibly Püchler formed the nucleus of a 'peaceful' group within the party who believed that a compromise with the government was possible, felt that law and order was the first priority, and even after the 12 February still believed that conciliation was desirable.[32] Oskar Helmer, the leading spokesman of the group, was a printer by trade and the deputy provincial leader of the party in Lower Austria. He had consistently been in favour of compromise, and had even been prepared to support Dollfuss's emergency legislation. He had done everything in his power to stop the fighting in Linz spreading to Vienna, and had still been trying to find some compromise solution when he had been arrested by the police. Helmer told the police that the rank and file of the party had been pressing the party and the unions to take action, but that the party leadership had been determined to avoid bloodshed at all costs. The party wanted a broad coalition of all democratic forces to defend the constitution against the National Socialists — as if the Nazis were the only enemies of the constitution — and looked for a solution to the economic crisis. The greatest fear of the party was that if the government forced the party to take action by violating one of the four fundamental principles laid down at the conference in October 1933 it would give the National Socialists the chance they were looking for. In other words, the party desperately hoped that a confrontation could be avoided and that compromise might be possible, because any further disruption would be greatly to the advantage of the Nazis. Helmer's greatest concern was that the moderate policy of the party might alienate the young militants who might then turn to the Nazis for excitement and adventure. He seems to have been genuinely dismayed that Dollfuss failed to see that the Social Democrats were his best allies in a struggle against National Socialism. His theme against the radicals within the party was that if the Social Democrats were to resort to violence and to use the same methods as the Nazis the result would be the certain victory of the Nazis. Violence and terror could best be countered by moral example and rational discourse.

Helmer, and those who shared his ideas, favoured the defence of the existing state and realised that a return to normal parliamentary government was not possible under existing circumstances. They saw the need for emergency decrees and were prepared to accept Dollfuss's 'professional organisations' (*Berufsständische Einrichtungen*) and the proposed plebiscites, provided that they did not become 'compulsory fascist organisations'. The fact that many such organisations were already *de facto* both compulsory and fascistic shows the extraordinary naîvety of the Helmer group.[33]

The police had no reason to doubt these revelations, which must have come as a surprise to some of them. Documentary evidence was produced to support their testimony. Letters showed that the Social Democrats were anxious to appear 'as Austrian as Dollfuss' and were determined to join with the Chancellor in an attack on the menace of National Socialism. Talk of 'Dollfuss fascism' by the left was condemned, for in spite of the many differences between the position of the Social Democratic Party and the government, it was felt that Dollfuss was a valuable ally in the anti-fascist struggle.[34]

Karl Renner, who was 63 in 1934, had been Chancellor in 1918 and had signed the Treaty of Saint-Germain, was the older statesman of the party and the most prominent spokesman of the right wing. He had consistently argued in favour of compromise and civil peace, and had tried to reach an agreement with Dollfuss. When the Christian Social politician Kollman told Renner, at the end of January, that the government refused to consider any compromise agreement, Renner did not give up hope, and replied rather lamely that his suggestions should simply be regarded as the basis for further discussion.[35] He told President Miklas that he would no longer be able to see him because their discussions were making his position in the party extremely difficult. He was greatly encouraged by Dollfuss's speech on 18 January appealing to the 'honest workers' which he believed to be a sign that the Chancellor was considering a coalition of the bourgeois parties to defend the state against Nazism. Renner pointed out to the police that although the *Arbeiter-Zeitung* had been banned on 20 and 21 January the party had decided to do nothing until the party council met on 28 January at which meeting, after a long and difficult debate, it was agreed that the party should continue to compromise with the government. He pointed out that the party no longer supported the Anschluss, so there was no disagreement with the Christian Socials on that question, and wanted a peaceful solution to the problems of the Danube. He admitted that he was prepared to support a general strike if the provincial parliaments were disbanded, but although there was ample evidence that this might happen, Renner did not believe that it was likely. His main concern seems to have been that the moderate policies of the party were alienating young Social Democrats, who were leaving the party to join either the Nazis or the Communists. The implication of Renner's testimony was thus that the party was a supporter, although a critical supporter, of much of Dollfuss's policy, and was a useful organisation for stopping youth falling into the clutches of the radicals on the right and on the left.

Perhaps the most self-serving of the testimonies given to the police was by Heinrich Schneidmadl, a prominent party leader from Lower Austria. He blamed the entire affair on Otto Bauer and the Schutz-bund, even going as far as to claim that Bauer did not believe that it was possible to reach any compromise or agreement with the government and that violence would ultimately be necessary. Schneidmadl went on to claim that Bauer's opponents had argued that such a violent revolutionary course would ruin the economy and that an Austrian workers' state surrounded by Italy, Germany and Hungary would not be able to survive. Thus he had the effrontery to use Bauer's own arguments at the October conference, words that were well known by the police, in order to implicate his party leader in an

attempt to overthrow the government by force. The police reaction
to this astonishing and disgraceful testimony is unfortunately not
recorded. Schneidmadl said that he had always opposed the Schutzbund and the arming of the workers, and had therefore not been upset
by the Schwechat affair in which the police had seized a large number
of the Schutzbund's weapons. He expressed the extraordinary belief
that the Social Democratic Party, although it had been disbanded,
would continue to support the government.[36]

Karl Seitz, the mayor of Vienna, had also believed in the possibility
of compromise with the Dollfuss government, even after parliament
had been closed down in March 1933. He had refused to believe that
the government was working on a new constitution based on the estates
until he had seen an outline of the proposals. When questioned
whether there had been a conference between Otto Bauer, Major
Eifler and local Schutzbund leaders at party headquarters on the
Wienzeile in Vienna to discuss the possibility of armed revolt following
the Schwechat affair, Seitz replied that he did not know, and he
defended Bauer by saying that it was unlikely that he would do such a
thing. Seitz insisted that as a pacifist he was in no way involved in the
activities of the Schutzbund.

Less well-known figures in the party gave further evidence that the
uprising on 12 February was not a planned attempt to seize state
power. Paul Richter, the editor of *Der Sozialdemokrat* and a member
of the executive committee of the party, along with Seitz, Bauer,
Deutsch and Danneberg, was informed of the events in Linz by telephone and went at once to party headquarters on the Rechte
Wienzeile where he was soon afterwards arrested. He was convinced
that the strike was entirely spontaneous and knew nothing of the
activities of the Schutzbund. Alber Sever, a member of the Lower
Austria compromise group, said that none of the four points that were
agreed upon at the conference in 1933 applied in February 1934 and
that the party had not reacted after the Schwechat affair so there was
no reason to suppose that it would react so violently to a similar
incident. Sever, whose wife had been killed by a piece of shrapnel
during the fighting, condemned the violence and professed to know
nothing of what had happened on 12 February.

Paul Speiser, another member of the executive committee of the
party and a member of the Vienna city council, also thought that
Bauer was a radical, although he knew nothing about the meeting
between Bauer and Eifler on 24 January that the police felt was the key
to the conspiracy theory. Speiser seems to have been completely

unaware of what was going on, and clearly knew nothing of the events that led up to the fighting on 12 February. When pushed by his interrogators he admitted that he felt that the party had lost control of the workers and that he did know something about suggestions for a general strike. This he could hardly deny, having been present at the party conference in October 1933. Another city councillor, Anton Weber, was regarded as being particularly suspicious because he had asked for the plans of some underground garages in the course of his work for the city. This was taken as clear evidence that the garages were going to be used by the Schutzbund to hide weapons. Weber skilfully used an offensive approach to the interview, pointing out that on 11 February Fey had made a speech in which he had said that the 'job' would begin tomorrow, and that the arrest of the workers' representative (*Vertrauensmann*) of the Fiat works, Stockhammer, had created an extremely tense situation. Weber also denied any knowledge of a meeting between Bauer and Eifler and implied throughout his cross-examination that the whole affair had been provoked by Fey and his associates. Another member of the executive, and the President of the Vienna Landtag, vigorously defended Bauer against charges of radicalism.

The major piece of evidence against Bauer and in support of the idea of a conspiracy was given by one Josef Sispela. He claimed that Otto Bauer, Eifler, Rudolf Löw, Freytag and Svatoch (acting as deputy for Stockhammer), along with Franz Musil and Kirchenberger, met in the building of the *Arbeiter-Zeitung* on 24 January. He claimed that Bauer had talked excitedly about the imminence of a fascist coup and said that if the party were attacked in any way the city hall of Vienna should be seized by the Schutzbund. Eifler suggested that the best course of action was to arm the Schutzbund, place it on the alert and wait to see the result of a general strike. Eifler then outlined his plan of encircling the inner city. When Eifler was arrested it was suggested that Sispela should take over command of the Schutzbund, apparently on the rather curious grounds that he hated Körner. Sispela also denounced Karl Süss for stealing weapons from the *OeWA* works and giving them to the Schutzbund. In April 1935 during the Schutzbund trial, at which Sispela was one of the key accused, he realised that he was not going to get any benefit from denouncing his comrades, and withdrew the testimony he had given during these preliminary hearings with the police. He was given a ten-year prison sentence.[37] Sispela did not claim to have been present at the meeting on 24 January so he was relying on hearsay evidence, and his testimony leaves the strong impression that he hoped that by giving evidence against Bauer and Eifler he would be treated leniently by the authorities. If this is so, he was to be bitterly disappointed.

Neither Eifler nor Löw were helpful witnesses. Löw admitted that Deutsch had bought weapons for the Schutzbund in Czechoslovakia, but how this had been done he was unable to say. Eifler said that he knew that weapons had been purchased abroad, but simply insisted that the Schutzbund had always acted in self-defence. Both denied the famous meeting of 24 January. Apart from Sispela's testimony, the only evidence the police could obtain against Bauer was even more suspect. A manual worker, Leopold Bergmann, had taken up Dollfuss's offer of clemency to all those who would step forward and give themselves up to the police on 14 February. Bergmann said that he had been ordered to alert the Schutzbund in Vienna because there had been shooting in Linz. He then said that a despatch rider from the Schutzbund headquarters had given the following order: 'Everyone arm themselves and get into the streets, everyone shoot.' When Bergmann asked who had given this peculiar order he was told that it came directly from Bauer. Bergmann said that his own unit was unable to get in touch with anyone at party headquarters or at the headquarters of the Schutzbund in order to confirm this order. He said that no one knew what to do and that the situation was hopeless. Everyone was annoyed with the party and Bergmann vented his fury by tearing up his membership card.

As far as the authorities were concerned, these preliminary interviews offered virtually nothing on which a treason trial against the ringleaders of the supposed revolt could be based. It was established beyond doubt that the Schutzbund was armed, but in this sense it was no different from the Heimwehr and other paramilitary organisations that the government was prepared to tolerate or even support. It had to be proved that these weapons were not designed for self-defence, as the Social Democrats claimed, but were to be used in an armed revolution and that on 24 January the party leadership and the Schutzbund agreed that this armed revolt should take place in the near future. As 16 of the 21 defendants at the Schutzbund trial had been arrested before 12 February, and as three of the remaining five were admitted by the court to have been passive, the entire case rested on a conspiracy that had been hatched on 24 January, at which time a previous decision to use force against the government was confirmed. The government knew perfectly well that the Social Democratic leadership had constantly tried to negotiate with the government, and that the

Schutzbund would not attempt a revolution without the consent of the party leadership. There was clear evidence that Bernaschek in Linz had acted against the express orders of the party leadership and that the Austrian workers were convinced that they were fighting a justified struggle in defence of their freedom. With no evidence for a planned uprising, for no such plan existed, and with ample evidence that the party was determined to avoid a fight at all costs through fear that the Nazis would benefit the most from such a confrontation, the government had no case. The Schutzbund trial in 1935 was an attempt to justify the government's actions in the eyes of world opinion and to reap revenge on the Social Democrats. It merely served to discredit the Austrian government. Liberal opinion was outraged by the sentences. In the end the government had to admit defeat. By Christmas 1935, in spite of sentences of up to 18 years (for Eifler), all the prisoners had been released. But the government got no credit for this hypocritical magnanimity.

With the outbreak of fighting the Social Democratic Party and all its affiliated organisations were banned and its property confiscated. Otto Bauer complained bitterly that the banning of the Workers' Abstinence League of Austria ended an organisation that had 'warned thousands of proletarians of the dangers of alcoholism and thus saved the dignity and happiness of thousands of families'.[38] Other equally useful or politically neutral organisations were also banned, including the Workers' Cremation Society — 'The Flame' — and the Association of Workers' Mandolin and Zither Clubs in Austria, to say nothing of the Friends of Children who organised day-care centres.[39] All Social Democratic bookstores and libraries were closed.[40]

A party of this size which had been vigorously active in all kinds of sporting and cultural activities had accumulated a vast amount of property. It owned a large number of buildings and sportsgrounds as well as libraries, furniture and office equipment. On 15 February it was all declared confiscated, along with the property belonging to the trade unions, and Dollfuss personally ordered that this property should henceforth be used 'for purposes of public security'. This meant, in effect, that it was handed over to Fey to dispose of as he thought fit.[41]

There followed a rather unseemly rush to grab this confiscated property. The small children were thrown out of the Home of the Childrens' Friends in the Tivoligasse, and the Heimatschutz moved in. The Patriotic Front, the police, the Heimwehr, and the Catholic German Students Association were all given substantial amounts of property. The archive in which the bulk of the research for this book was done was rather reluctantly given to the National Archives from this vast pool of property. It was furnished with party furniture, and the typewriters had also once been in the service of the party.[42]

It was suggested that party members should be forced to pay for the repairs needed to damaged buildings. As it was rumoured that the party had moved all its money abroad, and that this money was being used to line the pockets of unscrupulous leaders who had fled the scene of battle and were now living comfortably off the sacrifices of the misled workers, it could hardly be suggested that the party had sufficient funds left over to rebuild damaged housing. Some officials even suggested that Mayor Seitz should pay for the damage himself, but Seitz promptly replied that all his property belonged to his wife.[43]

The vast majority of those who were arrested and tried immediately after the fighting were unskilled workers and casual labourers. Usually those who were arrested with guns in their possession were given four months' hard labour, and those who had been seen to shoot at anything were given between twelve and fifteen months' hard labour. The police complained bitterly that the sentences were too light, that the defence lawyers were often Social Democrats who used the trials to make political propaganda, and that many of the jurors were atheists.[44] It was agreed that any leaders of the party or the Schutzbund, any prominent agitators or radicals, journalists or lawyers who defended leftists should be sent to concentration camps, the best known being at Wöllersdorf near Wiener Neustadt (which is now a monument to the victims of 12 February), and kept there pending a future trial. Among those sent to concentration camps were members of parliament, members of the city council and local representative bodies, and some prominent journalists such as Paul Deutsch of the *Arbeiter-Zeitung* and Helmuth Leipen of *Der Abend*. Anyone who worked for the city of Vienna, in whatever capacity, who was even suspected of having taken part in the fighting, even though they might have been arrested and subsequently set free, was instantly suspended and subjected to disciplinary action.[45]

Some of the charges were absurdly trivial. One Franziska Studeny spent eleven weeks in jail and was then tried on the grounds that she had been a member of the Social Democratic Party and had served coffee and tea to some members of the Schutzbund. For this she was sentenced to 28 days in jail.[46] Koloman Wallisch's wife, Paula, was tried in Leoben on a similar charge of preparing tea and bread for members of the Schutzbund.[47]

The administration of justice after 12 February was an extraordinary mixture of savage cruelty and sloppiness bordering on indifference. Thus the first man to be executed by the special courts was Karl Münichreiter, a minor figure in the Schutzbund who had been severely wounded in the hip and the shoulder in the fighting at the Amalien school. The judge said that Münichreiter, who was still in hospital, would only have to stand trial if the court physician declared that he was fit to do so. The physician decided that he was not severely ill in the legal sense of the term, and could therefore stand trial. It is quite clear that Münichreiter was indeed severely wounded, and would not have been made to stand trial under normal circumstances. Subsequent reports that the wounds were only superficial are a complete contradiction of the court records. Schuschnigg, as Minister of Justice, wanted him speedily executed 'pour encourager les autres' and Münichreiter was summarily dragged off to the gallows. On the other hand Karl Kautsky (not to be confused with his famous namesake), who was jailed for his activities on 12 February, asked permission to be released from jail in order to take the waters at Bad Gastein. His request was promptly granted.[48] Indeed this approach was the most popular and successful way of being released from prison. A sympathetic lawyer and doctor would draw a frightful picture of the state of their client's liver or heart, and the authorities opened the prison doors.[49]

The reasons for these contradictory attitudes are highly complex. From March 1933 the Dollfuss régime had steadily reduced the independence of the judiciary, had interfered with legal norms and had gone to considerable pains to ensure that the courts had 'reliable' juries.[50] By 12 February 1934 this process had not been completed, but on 10 January 1934 a law was passed which made it possible for the government to dismiss judges, so that it was able to place considerable pressure upon them to make the kind of judgements that it expected. The judges tended to be sympathetic to the Greater German position, so they were not enthusiastic supporters of the Dollfuss government by any means, although they were very sensitive to the pressure placed upon them. Thus the judge in the Weissel case, Hanel, agreed to sign a petition to the Minister of Justice asking for clemency. In his petition he wrote that Weissel had 'defended himself like a hero'. When it was pointed out to him that this would cost him his job he changed the word 'hero' to 'man'.[51]

Minister of Justice Schuschnigg argued that the government had to act swiftly and harshly so as to set an example. The example that was set was a singularly unpleasant foretaste of the fascistic state that Dollfuss and his associates were planning. At 11.00 p.m. on 14 February Dollfuss announced on the radio that anyone who gave themselves up to the police could count on lenient treatment. The director of public security was told that only 'responsible leaders' should be brought before the courts martial. In fact men who had surrendered in good faith and who were in no sense leaders of the Schutzbund were still hauled up in front of the courts, the judges arguing that 'pardon' could only be granted by the government and could not be applied by the courts themselves. 'Pardon' could thus mean that instead of summary execution the accused was given a 20-year jail sentence.[52]

Evidence against Schutzbündler frequently took the form of 'confessions' extracted from prisoners by torture and violence, and no efforts were made to investigate the frequent accusations of police brutality. Once such a confession was made it was taken as hard evidence that could not be challenged or withdrawn. In the case of the trial of Koloman Wallisch in Leoben, the evidence that he was largely responsible for the fighting around Bruck-an-der-Mur was presented to the court by police officers, who read the testimony of witnesses that they had interviewed. The witnesses themselves did not appear in court, nor did the court allow the evidence to be challenged.[53] As Wallisch was executed after the fighting had stopped, Schuschnigg's argument that such harshness was necessary to ensure a rapid end to the revolt could not apply. Wallisch was executed in the late evening of 19 February. On 29 February the government ended the state of martial law and the death sentence for rebellion.

Most of the initial arrests were based on the highly dubious thesis that there was a vast conspiracy by the Social Democratic Party and the Schutzbund to overthrow the state. On this basis there were 7,823 arrests in Vienna alone. As there was no evidence that such a conspiracy existed, it proved very difficult to get as many convictions as the government hoped. There were very few executions, many death sentences being commuted to long prison sentences. Those executed were Josef Ahrer, Anton Bulgair, Josef Gerl, Johann Hois, Karl Münichreiter, Viktor Rauchenberger, Josef Stanek, Emil Swoboda, Koloman Wallisch and Georg Weissel.[54]

Of those executed Georg Weissel became a martyr. He was the commander of the Floridsdorf fire brigade, an educated man with his engineer's diploma and a member of the left opposition. Although there was no evidence whatsoever that he had actually fired a shot himself, he accepted full responsibility for everything that had been done by the men under his command.[55] When the police arrived and he realised that further fighting was useless, he had ordered his men to surrender. In court Weissel gave an extraordinary display of personal courage and loyalty to his comrades. His only request was that he should be shot rather than hanged. The court strongly supported this plea in its submission to the government and implied that the man should be pardoned. The judge argued that Weissel had fought bravely during the war, had admitted his crime, was a brave and a decent man, and was married with a four-year-old child. Schuschnigg's refusal to consider commuting the death sentence was a vindictive act of political justice against a fine man. Like Münichreiter and Wallisch, Weissel was a well-known member of the left opposition, and as such was a marked man. His political stance was his death warrant; he was hanged.

The cult of Georg Weissel which soon developed was deliberately encouraged by the Social Democrats of Vienna as a means of protesting against the Dollfuss government. Postcards of Weissel hanging from the gallows sold briskly, providing his widow with a modest income.[56] The police in Simmering were particularly worried that his grave in the local cemetery was becoming a pilgrimage spot — it was covered with wreaths, each one a silent and perfectly legal slap in the face of the government.[57] One Katharina Erasmus, who described herself as a 'religious socialist', was sent to jail for 42 days for complaining that the wreaths on Weissel's grave had been mutilated, an extraordinary charge that was made possible by an emergency law of June 1933.[58]

Once Schuschnigg's deterrence theory of summary executions could no longer be maintained, a number of death sentences were commuted to long prison sentences.[59] As the conspiracy theory could not withstand close examination without further evidence being produced, a large number of prisoners were released. The courts were not wholly reliable instruments of the government, and many lawyers were concerned about the arrest of a number of defence lawyers whose only offence was to sympathise with their clients. But there can be little doubt that a major factor in the government's more lenient attitude was the reaction of foreign countries, particularly Britain, France and Czechoslovakia, to events in Austria. Particularly important to the Austrians was the attitude of the British government. Neither Britain nor her allies had any sympathy for the Social Democrats, and felt that the Austrian government was perfectly justified in taking all necessary measures against the Schutzbund in February, but the British government was concerned that the violent reaction of the Dollfuss régime might be the first step in the establishment of an outright fascist régime. Thus, on the evening of 12 February, Sir John Simon sent a telegram to Mussolini telling him that the British government would not be able to support an outright dictatorship by Dollfuss because this would be quite unacceptable to British public opinion, and the same was likely to be true in France. Simon also warned Mussolini not to give any direct support to an effort to establish a fascist or semi-fascist state in Austria.[60] Pressure from London, Paris and Prague, largely through demonstrations of public outrage and the strong reactions of influential newspapers, did much to force the government to modify its policy and to make magnanimous gestures of generosity towards the prisoners.

Charges that conditions at the Wöllersdorf concentration camp, where many of the Social Democrats were imprisoned, were inhumane were investigated by the Red Cross. In October 1934 a delegation of the Austrian Red Cross inspected the camp and was positively lyrical in its descriptions of the conditions there. The following month the *Revue International de la Croix-Rouge* of Geneva gave a favourable report of conditions at Wöllersdorf.[61] Wöllersdorf also became a symbol of 12 February. To democrats it was the concentration camp of a fascistic régime, the symbol of the loss of personal freedom and the trampling of democratic rights. To others it was proof that the Dollfuss régime was not so bad after all. Wöllersdorf was not Dachau and even if Dollfuss had been a trifle ruthless, the Social Democrats got what they had been asking for.

The attitude of the German government to these events was also somewhat confused. The immediate reaction of the German press to 12 February was that it was the result of Starhemberg's efforts to overthrow the remnants of the constitution and establish the 'dictatorship of the Heimwehr'. Fey's repressive actions had been the direct cause of the revolt which also showed that the Austrian workers had lost faith in their leaders. The National Socialists, of course, refused to support the socialists and were as determined as ever to fight both the régime and the 'Marxists', hoping that those workers who felt betrayed by their leaders would join the struggle.[62] Tauschitz reported from Berlin that a special meeting of newspaper editors was held in the propaganda ministry to tell them how to deal with the Austrian situation. In spite of earlier articles which stressed the roles of Starhemberg, Fey and the Heimwehr it was now ordered that the blame should be placed on

Dollfuss. As the Nazi régime had consistently blamed Dollfuss for being soft on the Marxists it was obviously no longer possible to continue this line of argument without the Nazis running a real risk of losing support in Austria. Thus the campaign had to be directed against the Chancellor so as to undermine the effects of his anti-socialist course which threatened to weaken the Nazi position in Austria.[63] In an interview to the enthusiastically pro-fascist *Daily Mail*, Goebbels remarked smugly that it was Austria and not Germany that was suffering under a repressive dictatorship, and that no houses had been bombed or small and innocent children massacred in January 1933.[64]

The first German radio reports announced that Dollfuss was the prisoner of Starhemberg and Fey.[65] Broadcasting from Munich, Habicht said that the struggle between Dollfuss and the Social Democrats was the 'clash between foreign powers on German territory' thus implying that Italy and the Western powers were the motive forces between the two sides. The Nazis had nothing whatever to do with the whole affair. In an indirect appeal for support from the working class, Habicht said that Dollfuss would now be crushed between 'the mill-stones of the Social Democrats and the National Socialists', for he was now left completely without support. Habicht appealed directly to the 'good and courageous workers', who had been misled by the leaders of the Social Democratic Party, to join the Nazis in the struggle against Dollfuss and for revenge for his 'bloody carnival'.[66]

In a second talk on 19 February Habicht drew a distinction between Italian fascism, Austrian fascism and National Socialism. Without talking directly about Italian fascism he spoke of the 'fascist-author-itarian ideas of the south' which he implied were distinct from National Socialism. 'Fascism', for Habicht, was something foreign and un-German. Austro-fascism ruled by force, National Socialism by conviction. Again he appealed to the 'good German workers' for support.[67]

The Austrian government was obviously most concerned about Habicht's speeches and was worried that they might have a consider-able effect. It was determined to take every possible diplomatic step to get them stopped. Habicht argued that a 'bolshevik revolution' encouraged by a curious combination of France, Czechoslovakia and the Soviet Union had been allowed to take place and that the Dollfuss government, supported by the Catholic church, had done nothing to prevent this uprising.[68] In spite of the constant demands of the Nazis, the government had failed to disarm the Schutzbund and had thus allowed the terrible bloodshed in which good German lives had been lost.[69] Of course, the Austrian government was unable to stop Habicht, and the German press and radio thundered on about the dreadful tyranny of Austria compared to the peaceful contentment of National Socialist Germany, with one *Volk* united happily in a common purpose.

The Austrian ambassador in Paris reported on 12 February that the French Foreign Minister was somewhat alarmed that events in Austria might lead to an alliance between the Nazis and the Social Democrats, but the ambassador was able to persuade him that this curious idea was mistaken, and pointed out that Dollfuss had been waiting for a long time to attack the Social Democrats and that the outcome was greatly to the benefit of France because it would weaken the Nazis.[70] In subsequent exchanges it became clear that the Doumergue government in France was strongly in favour of Dollfuss's actions against the Social Democrats.[71]

The Italian government was of course delighted that Dollfuss had at last acted. Mussolini was convinced that Dollfuss's position was greatly strengthened. Suvich felt that Dollfuss was in such a strong position that it was no longer necessary to appeal to the League of Nations against Nazi interference in the internal affairs of Austria.[72] Italy wanted to avoid at all costs the embarrassing strain on Italo-German relations that would be bound to result from an Austrian *démarche* in Geneva. The Vatican had no such second thoughts. The church was delighted with Dollfuss and sang his praise extravagantly in the *Osservatore Romano*.[73]

The Hungarian government was also pleased. Gömbös was somewhat upset with Dollfuss because he had refused an invitation to attend the Budapest Opera ball on 1 February. Kanya had reported that Dollfuss said that he might be able to visit Budapest a week later, but that he sounded unenthusiastic. He also said that he felt that Dollfuss's talk about 'Nazi terror' was overdone.[74] Gömbös got his own back by awarding Fey the Hungarian service medal first class for his heroic actions against the rebels on 12 February. He told the Austrian ambassador that he was delighted about what had happened in Austria, and made particularly unpleasant remarks about Körner who had been his instructor at the Austro-Hungarian war academy, saying that he hoped he would get what he deserved.[75] A protest by the small Hungarian Social Democratic Party in parliament on 21 February had little effect, for the party had no real political power and its pronouncements could be ignored by Gömbös's authoritarian government.

Reactions in Britain were more complex and of greater importance to the Austrian government, and were also reported in much greater detail by the ambassador, Franckenstein. Communist demonstrations against the 'infamous Dollfuss dictatorship' and the collection of funds by the TUC for Austrian Social Democrats — actions condemned by the Conservative MP, Major H.A. Procter, as incitement to civil war and interference in the internal affairs of another state — were taken as signs of strong rejection by British public opinion of the Dollfuss government's actions.[76] The attitude of the British press was mixed. The *Economist* blamed the Heimwehr, but not Dollfuss, for 12 February and wrote that Austria had fallen back into barbarity. The *Daily Herald* paid its tribute to the 'Vienna Martyrs'. The *Morning Post* argued that the fact that there was no general strike proved that the workers did not support the Social Democratic Party, and the uprising was largely the fault of armed bands of Marxist rowdies. The *Manchester Guardian* pointed out that events in Austria had strengthened Mussolini's hand and had shown the weakness and indecision of France and Britain. *The Times* came up with the extraordinary story that Dollfuss was in Hungary during the fighting and therefore could not have had anything to do with it; other papers, regarding *The Times* as infallible, repeated this wholly inaccurate story. Garvin, writing in the *Observer*, said that Dollfuss had become a dictator against his will and suggested that fascism was more civilised than barbaric National Socialism.

The reaction of the British press, which was on the whole poorly informed, slipshod and lacking in analysis, was an adequate reflection of the party political attitude to events in Austria. Franckenstein reported that the Conservatives had a 'complete understanding' of the situation, whereas the Liberals and Labour were very much opposed.[77] Franckenstein complained that British intellectuals had no idea how radical Otto Bauer was, and failed to realise the fantastic waste of money by the city council of Vienna. He very sensibly suggested that moderate Social Democratic leaders who were well known abroad, such as Renner, should be treated leniently as the British were strongly affected by humanitarian considerations.

Not all Conservatives were happy about events in Austria. Walter Runciman and Sir Austen Chamberlain pointed out that relations with Britain were bound to be strained because of the friendship between leading Labour politicians and the Austrian Social Democrats. Others, like L.S. Amery, were strongly in favour of Dollfuss and saw him as the saviour of Austria from the threat of bolshevik revolution.[78] By the end of February *The Times* had bought the official government line that the socialists had been aiming at a violent overthrow of the government, and that the workers' housing projects in Vienna had been specially built as armed fortresses for use in a civil war.

Franckenstein was particularly concerned with what he felt to be 'tendentious reports on prisoners and their conditions' in the British press. Sir Arthur Willert, the press chief of the Foreign Office, a man who sympathised with Dollfuss, gave Franckenstein some helpful advice on how to improve Austria's image. The ambassador talked to a number of leading editors, including Ewer of the *Daily Herald*, but although he was given a polite reception his efforts do not seem to have had much effect. Liberals and the left were strongly opposed to Dollfuss, whereas most Conservatives supported him. The Austrian government was concerned that there was so little sympathy for Dollfuss in Britain and that public opinion was clearly opposed to the harsh treatment of the Social Democrats after the failure of the uprising. This fact had a considerable influence on moderating government policy in the following months.

The Soviet press was of course united in its condemnation of Dollfuss and his government and scathing about the treachery of the Social Democratic leadership. At the beginning of March *Isvestia* published a series of articles by Ilya Ehrenburg under the title 'The Civil War in Austria'.[79] The articles were written in a somewhat tiresomely dramatic style: 'On 12 February it was cold and grey in Vienna', or 'The Social Democratic flag had already become a pale and dirty pinkish grey but in the streets of Vienna it became red once more, coloured by the blood of workers.' However, the articles made some telling points. Ehrenburg realised that the failure of the Social Democrats could not simply be reduced to the treachery of the Social Democratic leadership, although he was bitterly scathing about Korbel who had betrayed the workers of the 13th district to the police, and the demoralising effect of mass unemployment on party militancy was properly stressed.[80] He also pointed out that most of the militants were young men, and at one point he talks about the 'revolution of youth'. He also stressed the leading role played by the left opposition in the uprising, mentioning men like Münichreiter and Weissel as leading examples. Ehrenburg had a good journalist's nose for anecdote. Thus we have Herr Krupka of the Vienna Society for the Protection of Animals making a public protest against the mistreatment of animals in Spain whilst the fighting was still raging in the streets, and making Fey the honorary president of the society. There is the chief rabbi, Dr David Feuchtwang, thanking God for the glorious victory over the workers and calling for a collection from pious Jews for the families of the 'fallen heroes'. On a more serious level Ehrenburg felt that the Social Democrats had failed because there had been too many 'pacifists, Tolstoyites and vegetarians' in the party. He also argued that an Anschluss was now just a matter of time, for the German Nazis were getting bored with persecuting 'Jewish dentists and liberal actors' and were looking for something better to do.

The events of 12 February 1934 made it impossible for Britain and France to achieve a moral victory over Nazi Germany by giving full support for the Austrian *démarche* at Geneva. Dollfuss had played his last card against the Nazis, and if it failed there was nothing for him to fall back on. The most that could be salvaged from the wreckage was the Three Power Declaration of 17 February in which Britain, France and Italy announced that they were 'unanimously convinced of the necessity of preserving the integrity of Austria according to existing treaties'.[81] This was hardly the kind of language likely to restrain Hitler. Dollfuss had to hope that he could defeat the Nazis at home and that his gamble would pay off. He could hope for little help from outside.

In spite of the bloodshed, the repression and the progress towards the creation of Dollfuss's fascistic state, the Austrian labour movement could not be destroyed. Many prominent Social Democrats who stayed in the country, among them Renner and Seitz, felt that any sort of underground organisation was pointless and bound to fail. With Bauer and Deutsch in Czechoslovakia and many militant leaders in jail, it was the middle and lower echelons of the party leadership that formed the new illegal party called the Revolutionary Socialists, a title that showed that the party faithful had moved markedly to the left as a result of the experiences of February.[82] In Prague Bauer and Deutsch formed the Foreign Office of the Austrian Socialists and continued to publish the *Arbeiter-Zeitung* and the theoretical journal *Der Kampf*.

The Revolutionary Socialists were closely affiliated with the Second International, and the correspondence between the Central Committee and the secretary of the International, Friedrich Adler, gives a vivid impression of the attitude of the party.[83] The party was grateful to the International for its solidarity and help for the victims of February, but it clearly disagreed with the International's reformist

policies. It argued that the lessons of February were that 'all democratic and reformist illusions' had been destroyed, and that the fascist
violence could only be met by violence. The aim of the party was to
establish the revolutionary dictatorship of the proletariat in order that
the capitalist system might be destroyed. It called for the closest
possible co-operation with the Communist Party in spite of the
differences between the Second and Third Internationals. At the very
least there should be a 'non-aggression pact' between the two. In
August 1933 the International had agreed at its conference in Paris
that fascism could only be destroyed by the armed strength of the
proletariat, but this remained a rather vague formula, a gesture of
frustration at the spectacular failure of the German Social Democrats
to do anything to halt fascism. Friedrich Adler sympathised with the
Revolutionary Socialists, but insisted that a careful discussion of
tactics was necessary. He felt that the destruction of illusions, be they
democratic, reformist, socialist or revolutionary, was always a good
thing, but he was afraid that the Revolutionary Socialists might,
through sheer frustration, go on an anti-democratic course and thus
neglect the democratic anti-fascist forces. Adler pointed out that
Marx in his addresses to the First International had always insisted on
democracy as an essential ingredient of socialism and begged the
Revolutionary Socialists not to allow their revolutionary zeal to lead
them to forget their commitment to democracy. He also agreed that
unity with the Communists was highly desirable, but that this was
exceedingly difficult as the Communists were constantly attacking the
Second International as 'social fascists'. Adler argued that the anti-
democratic thrust of the theory of social fascism was a serious
hindrance to the anti-fascist struggle, and that the Communists were
suffering from 'revolutionary illusions'. Quoting Rosa Luxemburg,
without acknowledgement, Adler reminded the Revolutionary Socialists that reform and revolution were not alternatives, there was a need
for both tactics.

The analysis of the Revolutionary Socialists was similar to that of
the Communists. In March 1934 Dimitrov argued that the mistake
that had been made in February was the 'result of the harmful
influence of Social Democracy' that led to a false belief that defence
against fascist attack was enough. An armed revolution by the
proletariat was the only antidote to a fascist offensive. Dimitrov
insisted that Bauer was talking nonsense when he spoke of the 'uprising
of the Austrian workers'; there had been no uprising, merely a defensive action. The failure of the February struggle was due entirely to the

'capitulationist and defeatist attitude towards the fight' that had led to
the demoralisation of the Schutzbund. The Austrian workers should
have taken over the leadership of the struggle themselves, along with
the Communists, and this would have led to victory.[84] Friedrich Adler
was right to condemn such talk as 'revolutionary optimism', for
Dimitrov's spontaneitist ideas were wildly un-Leninist in their emphasis on the possibility of a new leadership suddenly emerging in the heat
of battle. Indeed this is very much what had happened in Austria. The
'capitulationist and defeatist' leadership had been taken by surprise
and had played no active role in the fighting. The militants had taken
over, but it was impossible to co-ordinate the efforts of the individual
units without a carefully prepared plan.

Revolutionary optimism formed a common bond between the
Revolutionary Socialists and the Communists. But the Communists
were deeply suspicious of the Social Democratic left, denouncing the
entire group as part of a sinister manoeuvre to fool the workers and to
win them over to the cause of social fascism. Ernst Fischer, who joined
the party almost immediately after the February debacle, was singled
out as a particularly devious and untrustworthy character.[85] The
Communist slogan 'From Bloody February to Red October' had a
strong appeal, and even Otto Bauer, who had never been overenthu-
siastic about bourgeois democracy, announced that Austrian fascism
had destroyed the workers' faith in democracy so that revolutionary
dictatorship was now the only possible strategy.[86] The leftward move
among Austrian socialists can clearly be seen in the marked increase in
membership of the Communist Party. According to the minutes of the
party congress in September 1934, which was held in a suburb of
Prague, membership had increased from 4,000 to 16,000, a remarkable performance for an illegal party.[87] This success gave the party a
greater sense of confidence and a certain flexibility. The erstwhile
social fascist and deadly enemy of the Austrian proletariat, Ernst
Fischer, was elected to the Central Committee, and a major step was
taken towards dropping the disastrous notion of social fascism as the
party began to realise the need for an anti-fascist front among widely
different political groupings which could not be simply denounced as
agents of fascism.

Revolutionary Socialists such as Oscar Pollak and Otto Leichter,
the latter the author of the best contemporary account of 12 February,
were thus ready and willing to co-operate with a Communist Party
that shared a common and somewhat romantic dream of a Red
October, the possibility of which it is hard to believe anyone took

seriously. Within the Revolutionary Socialists was a less romantic group who felt that a long and painful struggle lay ahead, that the National Socialists were a greater danger in the long run than the Dollfuss supporters, that a revolution was a very distant prospect, and that the Communist Party had not undergone such a fundamental change in its policy towards the 'social fascists'.[88]

With a repressive régime and constant surveillance of militants it was difficult even for those who believed passionately in the need for common action to achieve very much. On the first anniversary of 12 February, Social Democrats, members of the Schutzbund and Communists organised joint demonstrations. Where possible lights were turned out between seven and ten on the night of 12 February. Pubs and cinemas were empty. There were mass visits to the graves of prominent figures such as Georg Weissel, and in some instances the trams in major cities were sabotaged.[89] On the whole the state security officials were unconcerned. They did not think that violence was likely to occur, but they were ready for such an eventuality. The February manifestations in 1935 were the result of an agreement between the Revolutionary Socialists, the Schutzbund and the Communists in January, a prefiguration of the popular front that was to become official Communist policy after the Sixth Congress of the Communist International later that year.[90]

State security officials were somewhat concerned about the Revolutionary Socialists, for they realised that the nucleus of the new party would be formed by relatively new people who were not necessarily known to the police, who would therefore find it rather difficult to discover what was going on.[91] Particularly troublesome to the government was the foreign propaganda of the Revolutionary Socialists, which was particularly successful. The plight of the Austrian workers became a popular cause in liberal circles in the Western democracies. Films and plays about 12 February drew sizeable audiences. Demands for the release of prisoners came from people who could not possibly be described as socialists, but whose consciences had been aroused by the skilful propaganda efforts of the underground party. Tourists were frequently given propaganda leaflets which seem to have had some effect, for they certainly were a source of worry to the authorities.[92] The government appeared to be almost helpless in the face of this constant criticism, and was unable to do much apart from issue denials of the charges, which merely confirmed the opinions of its critics.

In November of 1934 the Second International and the International Trades Union Congress met in Paris to discuss the events of 12 February.[93] The conference concluded that a major problem was that the Schutzbund lacked leadership, was only supported by a small group of activists, and that the vast mass of the party membership had stayed neutral. In a general historical sketch the report pointed out that the party had been in opposition since 1920 and after 1927 had been faced with the determined opposition of the strongly anti-Marxist 'bourgeois bloc'. Its remaining centres of strength had been in Vienna, the provinces (except for the Tyrol and Vorarlberg) and in local administration. The rank and file of the party had been disorientated by the lack of a coherent and consequential party programme, and by internal bickering and dissent. Its foreign policy had been particularly unfortunate. First it had been an outspoken champion of the Anschluss and then, with the triumph of fascism in Germany, this had to be hastily dropped from the party programme. Because of its belief in the need for an Anschluss the party had not been able to form satisfactory relations with France and the Little Entente. On 15 March 1933, when parliament had been closed down, the party leadership did nothing, although the rank and file were ready to act. There had been a total lack of preparation for a civil war, even though it seemed to many to be imminent, and no emergency plans had been formed to deal with the possibility that many leaders would be arrested. The Lower Austrian leaders, Schneidmadl, Helmer, Petznek and Popp, came under particular criticism for attempting to negotiate an agreement with the Christian Socials behind the back of the party leadership. But the leadership was also blamed for not disciplining the Lower Austrians for this extraordinary breach of loyalty. Lower Austria was also blamed for doing nothing during the fighting in February, and for allowing government troops and munitions to pass without any difficulty.

The February fighting had been doomed to failure because of the fact that there had been no general strike. Such strikes as there were had often harmed the Social Democrats as much as the government. Thus party placards could not be printed because the printers were on strike. Particularly harmful had been the failure of the railwaymen to strike, but on the other hand the reluctance of the workers to strike, or the Schutzbund to fight, was due in large part to the pusillanimous behaviour of the party leadership which lasted for such a long time that it was hardly surprising that the rank and file failed to react strongly and with determination. The conference concluded with the resolution that the basic lesson of 12 February was that in the face of fascism an offensive and not a defensive strategy was needed, but once again the details of such an offensive strategy were conveniently omitted.

There was little chance of a successful offensive strategy, given the situation in Austria. The police had managed to infiltrate the Revolutionary Socialists and had their leaders, as well as those of the Communist Party, under close observation. A meeting between the Revolutionary Socialists and the Communists in which a common strategy was being discussed was broken up by the police, and the leaders of both parties were arrested at the meeting and in the following days. Among those arrested was the present Chancellor of Austria, Bruno Kreisky, who spoke strongly during his trial in favour of a popular front in Austria. Most of those arrested were sent to the Wöllersdorf concentration camp. The illegal party continued its struggle but had strictly limited opportunities for action. Demonstrations on 12 February and 1 May continued as part of a united effort of Revolutionary Socialists and Communists along with units of the Schutzbund. Opposition groups were formed within the organisations of the Patriotic Front, particularly within its trade union organisation. The government kept up constant pressure against all socialist organisations. There were frequent arrests and constant surveillance. It was not until 4 March 1938 that Schuschnigg suddenly began negotiations with labour leaders in an attempt to gain their support against Hitler's ultimatum to Austria. Although it was a difficult choice for many to vote for Schuschnigg's referendum, the Revolutionary Socialists initially adopting the slogan 'First Freedom, Then Yes!', the Communists being in favour of the referendum from the beginning. It was finally agreed that all should vote in favour. The opportunity never came. On 12 March 1938 'Operation Otto' began, and Austria was invaded. Having jailed and exiled all those who were the most determined opponents of Nazi fascism, Schuschnigg was left without support and the 'free, German, independent, social, Christian and united Austria' for which he claimed to stand ceased to exist.

On 12 February 1974 the left-wing press of Austria took the opportunity to assess the lessons of events that had happened forty years before. Many different conclusions were drawn. *Der Privatang-estellte*, a monthly journal for white-collar workers, argued that 12 February showed the need for capital and labour to co-operate in a common effort for the common good and to avoid confrontation and class struggle. If capital and labour did not at least agree to differ then things could all too easily get out of hand.[94] *Arbeit und Wirtschaft* took a very different view. In this version, 12 February was a deliberately planned and carefully executed attack on the Austrian working class. The fundamental error by the Social Democrats had been that they had not changed the basis of Austrian society in 1918 so that 12 February was the price that was paid for the failure to stage a revolution after the war.[95] Other papers were content to give factual accounts of events leading up to 12 February.[96] Some used the opportunity to sing the praises of Social Democracy.[97] *Die Presse* argued that celebration of 12 February was largely an excuse to look away from the boredom and the materialism of contemporary Social Democracy to a romantic and idealised version of the heroic past. This overlooked the fact of the terrible fanaticism of Social Democracy in 1934 and simply served the monopolisation of history by left-wing elements.[98]

In 1974 the politicians had little of interest to say about 12 February beyond the reiteration of pious platitudes about democracy and freedom, the need for toleration and co-operation, and appeals to idealism and a sense of common destiny. Of far more value was a conference of Austrian historians that discussed the events of 12 February with a vigour and passion that showed that these events were of far greater significance than the politicians dared admit.[99] Their work shows that it is only through painstaking and scientific analysis can the true meaning and significance of the past be captured, and without such effort the past can all too easily become a convenient source of empty slogans and misleading clichés which do nothing to help confront and overcome the challenges and problems of the present.

Notes

1. *AVA*, Ministerrat Protokolle 923, when these problems were discussed at some length.
2. Ibid., Bundeskanzleramt Inneres 1934, 22/gen. 4883.
3. Ibid.
4. Ibid.
5. Ibid. For further details of the Tyrol see Gerhard Oberkofler, *Februar 1934. Die historische Entwicklung am Beispiel Tirols* (Innsbruck 1974).
6. Ibid.
7. *AVA*, Ministerrat Protokolle 935.
8. *Spectator*, 30 March 1934.
9. *NPA*, Fasz. 257.
10. *AVA*, Bundeskanzleramt Inneres 4883.
11. Ibid. Ronge worked in Abteilung 2 of the Ministry of War, a section that was supposed to deal with mobilisation plans and thus could not come under parliamentary

scrutiny. In fact he was the head of the army's anti-socialist section which worked closely with the police. He was also in close contact with the Heimwehr. There is some evidence to suggest that Ronge was expecting a Social Democratic coup. See the Körner papers in ibid Zl. Pr. IV 2606 — 1934.

12. Ibid., Bundeskanzleramt Inneres 4888.

13. Ibid.

14. *NPA*, Fasz. 281.

15. *AVA*, Bundeskanzleramt Inneres 4888.

16. *NPA*, Fasz. 257.

17. Ibid., Fasz. 114.

18. Jens Petersen, *Hitler-Mussolini. Die Entstehung der Achse Berlin-Rom 1933-1936* (Tübingen 1973) p. 313; Mussolini to Hassel, 18 February 1934.

19. *Allianz Hitler-Horthy-Mussolini* (Budapest 1966), p. 115.

20. Text of the protocols in *Survey of International Affairs 1934* (London 1935), p. 499.

21. *NPA*, Fasz. 654.

22. For plans and photographs see J. Schlandt, 'Die Wiener Superblocks', *Werk*, 4 (1970).

23. *AVA*, Bundeskanzleramt Inneres 4885.

24. Ibid., Zl. Pr. IV — 2606/1934, Karton 6.

25. Ibid., Bundeskanzleramt Inneres 113486-125424.

26. Ibid., Zl. Pr. IV — 2606/1934, Karton 5.

27. Ibid.

28. Ibid.

29. Ibid., Karton 10.

30. Ibid., Polizeidirektion Wien, Akten Februar 1934, Zl. Pr. IV — 2606/1934, Karton 1.

31. Ibid.

32. Ibid.

33. See Chapter 8 for further details.

34. *AVA*, Zl. Pr. IV: 2606/1934, Nr. 1.

35. Ibid.

36. Ibid.

37. C.A. Gulick, *Austria from Habsburg to Hitler* (2 vols., Berkeley 1948), vol. 1., p. 1345.

38. Otto Bauer, *Der Aufstand der österreichischen Arbeiter* (Prague 1934), p. 4.

39. *AVA*, Bundeskanzleramt Inneres 4883.

40. Ibid., Bundeskanzleramt Inneres 4884.

41. Ibid., Zl. Pr. IV — 2606/1934, Karton 5.

42. Ibid., Bundeskanzleramt Inneres 4888.

43. Ibid., Bundeskanzleramt Inneres 4886.

44. Ibid., Zl. Pr. IV — 2606/1934, Karton 6.

45. Ibid.

46. Ibid.

47. Ibid.

48. Ibid.

49. Ibid.

50. Everhard Holtmann, 'Politische Tendenzjustiz während des Februaraufstands 1934' in Ludwig Jedlicka and Rudolf Neck, *Das Jahr 1934: 12. Februar* (Vienna 1975), pp. 45-57.

51. See the comment by Kann in *Das Jahr 1934: 12. Februar*, p. 156.

52. Holtmann, *'Politische'*, p. 48. Gulick, *Habsburg to Hitler*, vol. 1, p. 1857 for Schuschnigg's version.

53. Transcript of the Wallisch trial in *Dokumentationsarchiv des österreichischen Widerstandes* 6979.

54. *AVA*, Bundeskanzleramt Inneres 113486-125424.
55. *Neue Kronen Zeitung*, 10 February 1974. *AVA*, Zl. 2837 — Pr./1934.
56. *AVA*, Zl. Pr. IV — 2606/1934, Karton 5.
57. Ibid., Karton 6.
58. Ibid.
59. Ibid., Bundeskanzleramt Zl. 2837 — Pr./1934.
60. *Documents on British Foreign Policy*, 2nd series, vol. VI, p. 403.
61. *NPA*, Fasz. 280.
62. *Völkische Beobachter*, 13 February 1934.
63. *NPA*, Fasz. 12. The *Berliner Tageblatt, Vossische Zeitung* and the *Kölner Zeitung* still blamed the 'Austro-Marxists'.
64. *Daily Mail*, 18 February 1934.
65. *NPA*, Fasz. 466.
66. Ibid., Fasz. 477.
67. Ibid., Fasz. 105.
68. Ibid.
69. Ibid.
70. Ibid., Fasz. 466.
71. Ibid., Fasz. 59.
72. Ibid., Fasz. 466.
73. *Osservatore Romano*, 20 February 1934.
74. *NPA*, Fasz. 20.
75. Ibid.
76. Ibid., Fasz. 48.
77. Ibid.
78. Ibid.
79. *Isvestia*, 6 March 1934. This is a truly remarkable piece of 'instant journalism'.
80. According to the Social Democratic exile press, Korbel was murdered. This charge was studiously ignored in the Austrian press. *NPA*, Fasz. 280. Also *Sozialdemokrat*, 8 April 1934.
81. *Survey of International Affairs 1934* (London 1935), p. 455.
82. Walter Wisshaupt, *Wir kommen wieder! Eine Geschichte der Revolutionären Sozialisten Oesterreichs 1934-1938* (Vienna 1967).
83. *NPA*, Fasz. 292.
84. *Geschichte der KPÖ*, p. 155.
85. *AVA*, Bundeskanzleramt Inneres, 1934, 22/gen, 4884.
86. *Der Kampf*, May 1934.
87. *Geschichte der KPÖ*, p. 158.
88. The spokesman for this group was Joseph Buttinger. See his book, *Am Beispiel Oesterreichs. Ein geschichtlicher Beitrag zur Krise der sozialistischen Bewegung* (Cologne 1953).
89. *NPA*, Fasz. 293.
90. 'Wir kommen wieder!' in *Die Rote Fahne*, 24 January 1935.
91. *NPA*, Fasz. 293.
92. Ibid.
93. Ibid.
94. Rudolf Häuser, 'Ursachen und Wirkungen', *Der Privatangestellte*, 2 (1974).
95. Josef Hindels, 'Niemals vergessen', *Arbeit und Wirtschaft*, 28 February 1974.
96. See *Wochenpresse*, 6 February 1974.
97. Fritz Klenner, 'Blutiger Februar', *Solidarität*, February 1974.
98. Otto Schulmeister, 'Niemals vergessen!', *Die Presse*, 9-10 February 1974.
99. Jedlicka and Neck *Das Jahr 1934: 12. Februar*.

11 *AUSTRO-FASCISM*

A party that had such a strong tradition of theoretical discussion, and which could draw on the living tradition of Austro-Marxism, was bound, when faced with the dangers of fascism both at home and abroad, to attempt a theoretical analysis of fascism. Curiously enough the results were rather meagre. Some of the finest minds of contemporary socialism seemed incapable of reaching a concrete analysis of the most powerful and menacing political movement of the day. Without an adequate understanding of the true nature of fascism the party was unable to develop an adequate defensive strategy, and was outmanoeuvred by a ruthless opponent. The Austrian Social Democrats were certainly not unique in their failure to analyse fascism, in many ways their achievements were greater than most of the other parties, and they never made the dreadful blunder of the Communist International with its disastrous theory of 'social fascism'.[1] In spite of many shortcomings the Austrian Social Democrats made some important contributions to the the theory of fascism, and their efforts were certainly not inferior to those of other parties. During the period of the rise of fascism, theory lagged disastrously behind practice, and it was only when fascism triumphed in Germany that the left was forced to rethink its position. By then it was too late.

In November 1922 Julius Braunthal published a short article entitled 'The Fascist Putsch' in the party's theoretical journal *Der Kampf*.[2] Written immediately after the March on Rome it is hardly surprising that Braunthal was unable to offer more than a few comments on Italian fascism and had neither the time nor the space to expand them into a full-blown theory. He saw fascism as a successful attempt by the propertied classes to upset the 'equilibrium of class forces' between the economic power of the bourgeoisie and the political power of the working class by violent means.[3] But the bourgeoisie was unable to rule on its own. It employed a gang of thugs to crush the working class who in turn seized political power. These modern condottieri were content to leave economic power in the hands of the bourgeoisie. Fascism was thus a form of political gangsterism, an extremely violent form of class domination.

Like most socialist intellectuals of the time Braunthal overlooked one essential ingredient of fascism: its mass appeal. The mass support given to fascist parties was a source of exceptional strength, a fact over-looked by talk of condottieri. No anti-fascist strategy could be effective that did not take into account and carefully analyse the nature of the popular support given to fascism. Braunthal realised that there was more than the 'dictatorship of capitalism' involved, and he understood the complex and often contradictory relationship between the fascist leadership and the representatives of the bourgeoisie, but he seriously underestimated the grass-roots support for fascism. For a party that was determined to preserve and strengthen democratic freedoms, and which counted on mass support to achieve democratic socialism, this was a fateful oversight.

Braunthal was intellectually very close to Otto Bauer, and it is hardly surprising that Bauer's first comments on fascism should be very close to those of the editor of the *Arbeiter-Zeitung*.[4] Bauer was profoundly influenced by Marx's writings on Bonapartism which formed the basis of his theory of the modern state and of fascism.[5] It was from these pieces that Bauer developed his theory of equilibrium and the independence of executive authority. The conclusions he reached were sometimes a little bizarre. Convinced that there was an equilibrium of class forces in the early years of the republic, Bauer concluded that Austria had ceased to be a class state.[6] Such an extra-ordinary gaffe by a Marxist theorist earned him the justified criticism of both the liberal Hans Kelsen and the Social Democrat Otto Leichter.[7] For Bauer, post-war Europe was characterised by a high degree of class co-operation, and where this did not exist open dicta-torship was practiced. He made no distinction between fascism and Soviet Communism, both he saw as dictatorships of small cliques that did not represent particular class interests, inasmuch as the practice of political domination was concerned, but he was careful to point out that there were many distinctions between the two systems.[8] Bauer condemned both fascism and Communism as 'totalitarian dictator-ships' but, unlike later theorists, he did not regard them as identical.

Bauer's reading of Marx's texts was somewhat superficial, and certainly lacked the insight of the major exponent of the theory of Bonapartism, August Thalheimer. For Bauer, the theory was a useful political weapon, a Marxist critique of Soviet practice and a means of explaining fascism. It also served as a means of justifying the party's policies in post-war Austria. He failed to develop Marx's comments on the popular support given to Bonapartism, and he made no attempt to analyse its class composition. The result was a certain muddle-headedness and lack of precision. Much the same is true of his theory of capitalist domination in bourgeois democracies, according to which the capitalist class rules, but does not govern.[9] The big bourgeoisie continues to control the economy, but is obliged to leave the running of governments to the majority parties. These parties remained under a high degree of ideological influence from the big bourgeoisie and were directly or indirectly economically dependent. It was thus still possible to talk of bourgeois rule, but not of bourgeois dictatorship. This analysis provided the theoretical justification for the party's support of a coalition with the bourgeois parties after 1918, and predictably prompted angry criticism from the left without satisfying the thoroughgoing reformism of the right.

With the temporary improvement of the economy after the Geneva Treaty in 1924 there seemed to be less of a threat of right-wing extremism in Austria. At the party conference at Linz, fascism was only mentioned at one point in the programme, although in an important context. It was argued that as the struggle between bourgeoisie and proletariat grows more intense the working class might well be able to win over to its side the marginal elements of both the working class and the bourgeoisie, to create a state of equilibrium. But as the proletariat grows in strength and confidence within the limits of the bourgeois state, the bourgeoisie might become increasingly anxious and fearful that it could no longer exercise dominance. At this point the bourgeoisie might be tempted to resort to monarchist restoration or fascist dictatorship. Thus the proletariat must make certain that it has a firm footing in the army and police and that it has its own effective military force. Then comes the most controversial passage in the whole Linz programme:

If, in spite of all these efforts by the Social Democratic Workers' Party, a counter-revolution by the bourgeoisie should be successful in destroying democracy, then the working class can only seize state power by means of a civil war...If the bourgeoisie resists the social revolution, which will be the task of the control of the state by the working class, by a planned sabotage of economic life, by violent resistance, by conspiracy with foreign counter-revolutionary forces, then the working class will be obliged to use dictatorial methods to destroy the resistance of the bourgeoisie.[10]

In the following years the right was to quote parts of this passage, suitably out of context, to show that the Social Democrats were striving to establish a dictatorship in Austria on the bolshevik model. A number of delegates at Linz had objected to the use of the word 'dictatorship' in the programme, on the grounds that it would be used by the right to equate Social Democracy with Soviet Communism.[11] Given the ambiguity of the term 'dictatorship of the proletariat', and its practical application in the Soviet Union, which to many was hardly an attractive prospect, such criticisms were well justified. It could hardly be expected of Social Democracy's enemies that they would accept the argument that dictatorship would only be a temporary measure, which was in no way contradictory to the principles of democracy, even though this was undoubtedly the genuine and profound belief of the vast majority of the party.

The Linz programme thus hardly contains a theory of fascism. The passage on the seizing of state power comes directly from Bauer, and is in accordance with his theory of Bonapartism, but lacks any theoretical dimension or practical analysis. There was some talk at the conference of fascism 'lying in wait everywhere' and of the anti-capitalist longings of the rural population, but they were made *en passant*, and far more time was spent in criticisms of bolshevism than in serious discussion of the problem of fascism.[12] The conference made the serious mistake of assuming that the Austrian bourgeoisie would in fact be content to continue sharing political power along the lines of the balance of power theory, and that somehow Austria was completely different from other European countries, and that an examination of the political situation in Italy or Hungary was thus hardly appropriate. Within a year, 15 July was to show how wrong they were.

Otto Bauer made brief reference to the question of fascism at the Vienna Party Congress in 1929. Up until that time the main threat seemed still to come from monarchist reactionaries rather than from an Austrian form of fascism. But now the reality of a growing fascistic movement could not be denied. He claimed that the Heimwehr was the creation of the bourgeois parties and that it was financed by big industry, but he did realise that this movement had a certain independent momentum that meant that it was not in every case merely a puppet in the hands of big capital. Bauer never analysed how far the Heimwehr was a kind of sorcerer's apprentice, and his remarks on fascism at the conference were rather superficial. It is somewhat surprising that Bauer, the leading theoretician of Austro-Marxism, should show such little interest in fascism. Johann Hirsh had already published an important article on the sociology of Austro-fascism in *Der Kampf*.[13] Wilhelm Ellenbogen's articles in the same journal and Julius Deutsch's collection of essays on fascism in Europe show that the intellectuals in the party were becoming increasingly concerned about the dangers of fascism, which were bound to become more acute as the world entered a period of severe economic disruption.[14]

Deutsch's view of fascism was extraordinarily complacent. Fascism in his view was little more than the violent defence of the capitalist system against the demands of the propertyless workers and peasants.[15] Fascists were therefore 'the paid mercenaries of capital'.[16] They could thus be simply combated by democratic defence. As the Schutzbund was larger than the Heimwehr there was no possible cause for alarm. The 'quiet confidence' of the Schutzbund was such that fascism presented no real danger in Austria.[17] In a second book published in the same year Deutsch offered a slightly more serious discussion of fascism.[18] He was puzzled by the fact that Italian fascism had started out as a form of social revolutionary movement but had ended up as the willing instrument of capitalist domination. Deutsch offered no satisfactory explanation for this fact, and merely suggested that it was because of a violent reaction against the radicalisation of the peasants' organisation, the Fedaterra, and the occupation of the factories in 1920.[19] Deutsch warned that although the working class talked a lot about revolution and the dictatorship of the proletariat, it was quite unprepared for violence of any kind, and fascist violence in particular. Blind faith in the efficacy of the general strike was not enough, the proletariat needed its own military organisation. The fatal weakness of Deutsch's analysis was that he saw fascism purely in military terms. Thus fascism is perceived as an army rather than a party, as mercenaries paid by landowners and industrialists.[20] Starting from this premiss, Deutsch found it hardly necessary to define fascism. Statements such as 'Austrian fascism is nothing but reaction', or 'National Socialism is a psycho-pathological condition' are not very enlightening.[21] He did, however, suggest that fascism was a reaction to the failed revolutions of the immediate post-war period when the left was destroyed.[22] He also made the important point that fascism was only possible at a certain stage in the class struggle, and that it could not exist in a backward country where there was no developed proletariat. Even in Spain he saw that the struggle of the extreme right was against liberalism rather than the working class.[23]

Deutsch's analysis of fascism served to stengthen his views on the organisation of the Schutzbund, and his writing on fascism contains many oblique attacks on General Körner. He warned against the mistake of arming the people, which only leads to a mass of individual actions. He used the example of the abortive 'March Action' of 1921 by the German Communists as proof of this assertion. In spite of the anti-militarism of the working class they would have to submit to strict discipline and rigorous training in order to combat the fascists from whom they could learn a lot.[24] For Deutsch the perfect example of an anti-fascist organisation was the Schutzbund, which other countries should emulate. Anti-fascism was thus a technical military question rather than a political strategy. Complacently believing that Austria had found the answer to the challenge of fascism, Deutsch found it hardly necessary to define it in any depth. From Deutsch, who had little repute as a thinker, this is perhaps understandable, but that Bauer should share these views is remarkable. Blind faith in the Schutzbund was not merely a military mistake, it was also a political blunder that blocked the way to a true understanding of the forces at work in Austrian politics. Within the party it was the Schutzbund that was most concerned about the question of fascism, for it was to be in the front line of the struggle, but little was achieved beyond a few empirical observations and self-congratulatory posturings.

In spite of the alarming advances of National Socialism in Germany the Austrian Social Democrats continued to show little interest in fascism as a topic worthy of serious discussion. The Heimwehr still seemed to be relatively weak, the failure of the Pfrimer putsch in September 1931 was not taken as a warning of things to come, but rather as further evidence of the weakness of the Heimwehr. But by the spring of 1932 it was no longer possible to ignore the growing danger from the extreme right. The National Socialists seemed to be rapidly overtaking the Heimwehr, and in Vienna had polled almost as many vote as the Christian Socials.[25] Bauer began to take a rather more serious look at the problem of fascism.[26] At last he examined the social basis of the mass support for fascism which he saw as coming from petty bourgeois elements that were economically and socially threatened, and also from certain sections of the unemployed and youth. He also saw that the anti-capitalist rhetoric of the fascist parties could not be ignored, and that it was an essential part of a system that could not simply be seen in Deutsch's terms of the 'mercenaries of capital'. Bauer argued that as the crisis grew worse the capitalists would be tempted to use the fascist bands in order to destroy the economic power of the working class as organised in the unions.[27] This in turn gave the working class the opportunity to fight the decisive battle between socialism and fascism; but once again Bauer side-stepped the issue by insisting that this decision would not be made in Austria but in the 'big wide world'. Unlikely to have to put his ideas into practice, he could afford this rhetoric. The choice still seemed to be between capitalism and socialism, not democracy and fascism. This made a concerted anti-fascist effort by a broad cross-section of society very difficult to achieve, for the uncommitted were hardly likely to be attracted by the apparently radical alternatives presented.

Bauer's mature writings on fascism date from 1932, when he made an important speech to the party congress. When Hitler became Chancellor in January 1933 and the Austrian parliament was closed the following March, fascism had to be the concern of every socialist. The ideas that Bauer was developing at this time were later summed up in two major writings, published in 1936 and 1938.[28] Although it is true that Bauer had learnt much from the painful experience of February 1934, his later writings are based in large part on the Bonapartist theory that he had sketched as early as 1924 and on articles and speeches given before 12 February. By now he had perceived the important distinction between fascism as a social move-ment on the way to the seizure of state power, and fascism as a mode of political domination. He was one of the first socialist intellectuals to realise that there was an essential contradiction between these two phases. The early fascist movements were relatively autonomous orga-nisations which the capitalist class found useful in order to control and eventually crush the working class. The fascist dictatorship, however, becomes 'the executive organ of the needs, interests and will of the capitalist class'.[29]

Fascism starts as armed bands of uprooted ex-servicemen, fired by a petty bourgeois anti-capitalism and a fanatical hatred of the working class. In the course of a sustained economic depression these paramilitary organisations are joined by disgruntled petty bourgeois elements both from the urban areas and the land. Gradually the capitalists realise that they can use this movement for their own inter-ests, and direct their energies against the working class.[30] The same economic crisis that strengthens the fascists also weakens the working class, but the bourgeois parties also find that they are losing mass support to the extreme right. They are thus less and less able to use the instruments of state power to crush the working class, and are tempted to make use of the fascist militias. With a bourgeoisie unable effec-tively to rule in its own interests, and with the working class severely weakened by the economic crisis, there exists a certain stalemate between the two great antagonistic classes of modern industrial society. The fascists are able to gain power precisely because of this relative weakness of the two main classes.

Fascism in power no longer represents the interests of the petty bourgeoisie which forms its mass following. It becomes an open dictatorship over all classes, including the bourgeoisie. But at the same time it secures and strengthens the economic hegemony of the capitalist class. Thus fascism in power often finds itself in conflict with its own rank and file, and uses violent methods to overcome conflicts within the capitalist elite. The fascist leaders are forced to purge the movement of the radicals who are demanding a 'social revolution' as a reward for their past efforts. The régime tries to find a way out of these increasing social tensions by forced armaments and eventually war. Bauer argued that such a policy would create further problems, and give rise to the opposition of all those who had little interest in an economy based on armaments and who were unwilling to risk the uncertainties of war, but he believed that the officer corps, the heavy industrialists and the landowning aristocracy were still in such a position of power that Europe would soon be faced with the ghastly prospect of another war, unless a proletarian revolution put an end to the fascist nightmare.

These ideas were a fairly simple application of the Marxist theory of Bonapartism to the changed conditions of contemporary Europe, but, without a careful analysis of those changed conditions, the theory lacked depth, concerning itself only with the surface appearance of political phenomena. Bauer paid no attention at all to the critical changes in capitalist economies that were essential preconditions for fascism. There are passages in his book *Between Two World Wars?* which suggest that the development of monopoly capitalism leads to the increased exploitation of the working class and to imperialist wars in the mad search for new markets and sources of raw materials. Monopoly capitalism also tends to increase the tendency for state intervention in the economy, particularly in states like Germany where there was no strong liberal tradition. This situation was further exacerbated by the fervent nationalism of the 'new arrivals', such as Germany and Japan.[31] None of these themes were developed, so that his theory of fascism was still lacking in firm objective foundations.

Otto Bauer died on 5 July 1938, and on that very day was still writing on the theory of fascism. A book based on his last writings was published shortly after his death, and it contains an important chapter on fascism.[32] In this final version Bauer sees fascism resulting directly from imperialist rivalries grounded in the development of monopoly capitalism. The modern capitalist state is marked by a high degree of state intervention, a characteristic that had long been of central interest to the Austro-Marxists, and this tendency had been greatly strengthened by the war and subsequent depression.[33] In a situation of extreme crisis it is thus possible for the beleaguered bourgeoisie to look for a solution in a totalitarian state. In Italy and Germany there were three main reasons for the fascist seizure of power. Both countries had their national aspirations frustrated by the peace settlement and were determined to revise that decision. Both suffered from acute political crises in the post-war years in the course of which neither revolution nor counter-revolution resulted in any significant changes in the social structure, half-measures merely serving to heighten the already intense contradictions within the system. Lastly, in both Italy and Germany, severe economic crises had further intensified the social and political tensions to a critical point.

The fascist state is marked by the highest degree of étatism. The state regulates prices, wages, consumption and production, exports and imports, profits, wages, credit and the appropriation of resources and wealth. Its twin aims are autarchy and rearmament. The main thrust of its ideology is 'anti-Marxism'. At home it destroys the labour movement and establishes an exploitative system against which the workers have no defence. The whole system is held together by propaganda and terror. Owing to the relative success of fascist régimes, particularly in overcoming unemployment, they managed to win the grudging support of at least a section of the working class, and yet Bauer was convinced that it was the working class alone who could overcome fascism. Even within the fascist movement there were many who were frustrated by the failure of the régime to implement the fascist social revolution, and they were only partly placated by the anti-capitalist rhetoric of the anti-semitic campaigns. Lastly, there were elements within the bourgeoisie, mainly those who had not benefited directly from the policy of autarchy, who were in varying degrees dissatisfied with the régime. Bauer hoped, although on what grounds it is hard to imagine, that these three groups might join together in an anti-fascist revolution.

In these last writings Bauer stressed the imperialistic nature of fascism. Writing immediately after the Anschluss this is hardly surprising, and once he began to talk of imperialism, as a good Austro-Marxist he was bound to pay closer attention to the economic background. Hilferding's theory of imperialism now appeared more useful to him than Marx's theory of Bonapartism, and talk of the equilibrium of class forces is no longer heard. Unlike the Communist theory of fascism, Bauer does not see fascism as a form of monopoly capitalist dictatorship, but rather as a dictatorship over the economy, a notion that is highly problematical and which can hardly be upheld in so simple a form.[34] The strength of this last essay is in its insistence on the mass basis of fascism, on the severe contradictions within the system, and on the historical background to the failure of bourgeois democracy. Bauer certainly did not produce a final and thoroughly convincing theory of fascism, but he opened up many fruitful avenues for further research.

It was not until this late stage that Bauer became fully aware of the distinction between fascism and régimes such as that of Dollfuss. Dollfuss's state was semi-fascist, clearly modelled on the example of Italy, but he had no mass support and his régime was only superficially similar to full fascism.[35] Bauer was never a man to refuse to admit his mistakes, and he was convinced now that the success of semi-fascism and the collapse of the republic was due in no small measure to the failure of the Social Democrats to secure fundamental reforms in the years immediately after the war. The theory of equilibrium of the class forces had thus been a dangerous illusion.

Karl Renner, the outstanding spokesman of the right wing of the party, also wrote about fascism, but neither at the same length nor as thoughtfully as Bauer. His main interest was in the nature of the mass following of fascist movements. In 1932 he wrote that the bulk of Nazi supporters were petty bourgeois, and that the movement had little appeal to either the propertied classes or the proletariat.[36] There were, however, important proletarian sectors that were attracted to fascism. The proletariat proper remained faithful to socialism, but opportunists and blacklegs who betrayed their proletarian origins in the desperate hope of finding employment at a time of acute economic crisis, those who had been cast down into the ranks of the proletariat but who refused to accept proletarian class consciousness, and the growing mass of white-collar workers, were all easily tempted by fascist appeals. These elements were radicalised into violent action by the effects of the depression, but Renner imagined that once in power the movement would start to disintegrate as Hitler would purge the party of radical elements.[37] Renner returned to the problem of fascism after the war, but added little to these earlier comments. The anti-Communist element of Renner's thought was by now more pronounced than ever, and he was prepared to argue that Western fascism was a necessary response to Russian Communism.[38] He felt that fascism and Stalinism were identical in their forms of political domination, even though the goals of the régimes might be quite different. Both régimes were forms of counter-revolution caused by the failure of the working class in 1918-19 to transform society. Renner did not deny that the banks and the industrial magnates of Germany had betrayed democracy and had turned to the Nazis to destroy the labour movement, but his main objection to Communist theories of fascism was that he believed that once in power a dictatorship of the party elite was established which was in no sense the mindless executive of the wishes of the capitalist elite, but a régime that relentlessly pursued its own goals by a policy of divide and rule and by the ruthless repression of all dissent. Renner's main contribution was his insistence on the importance of the mass party, but beyond that he made little real contribution to the understanding of fascism, and his writings on the topic are of considerably less interest than those of Otto Bauer.

From the left of the party Max Adler made some interesting comments on fascism, although taken together they hardly add up to a coherent theory. From Marx's writings on Bonapartism, Adler became interested in the idea of the state appearing to become divorced from all links with class to become the common property of society as a whole, but as a true Marxist he argued that this was an illusion, and the 'classlessness' of the state existed only in the minds of those who believed it. Adler had little interest in defining fascism, to him it was any form of attack on democracy and the working class that could be loosely defined as 'anti-Marxism'.[39] This imprecise and unthinking use of language was not untypical of left-wing writing on fascism in the interwar period, Communists being particularly guilty of lumping all kinds of separate movements together under the general heading of fascism. After Hitler gained power in Germany, Adler stressed the anti-capitalist longings of the Nazi rank and file and came to the conclusion this disillusionment with modern capitalism by the petty bourgeoisie could be exploited by the socialist movement.[40] This extraordinary optimism, based on a misunderstanding of the nature and extent of petty bourgeois anti-capitalism, was also shared by Trotsky, but there is no evidence that Max Adler was in any way influenced by Trotsky's writings on fascism.[41] For Adler, the fascist followers had no will of their own, they were misled and manipulated by the capitalists who employed the fascists to do their dirty work for them. If this was indeed the case, then there was some hope that the lost sheep could be brought into the socialist fold.

This dangerous illusion was shared by Otto Bauer. Commenting on the results of the local elections on 24 April 1932 he wrote:

> The broad petit bourgeois and proletarian masses, which previously followed the old bourgeois parties, have become enraged as a result of the crisis and are now on the move. But they can be won over to our side. If we appear to the masses as guilty partners in the bourgeois world we will simply push them towards fascism, and thus increase the danger of fascism. The more powerfully we express the feeling of rebellion which has taken hold of the masses, and the more sharply we align ourselves against the capitalist world, and the more daringly we lead the battle against capital, against its governments and parties, against its entire economic, political and ideological system, and the more daringly we show the great aim of the socialist revolution to the masses as a task worth fighting for, the greater the section of the mobilised masses that will be attracted to us.[42]

But Bauer was far too intelligent a politician to mistake this vague anti-capitalist longing for a desire to create the socialist society. Bauer later realised that it had been a mistake to demand new elections and thus overthrow the Buresch government and pave the way for Dollfuss, and that this political error was based in large part on a faulty understanding of the dynamics of fascism.

Looking back at Austro-Marxist writings on fascism, it is clear that it was not until Hitler's triumph in January 1933 that the party began to take the fascist menace seriously. Even though Bauer studied the writings of Italian exiles he tended to think of fascism as a uniquely Italian affair, and considered Mussolini's epigones in Austria and Germany as cranks and neurotics. The elections on 24 April 1932 made the Nazis the third largest party in Austria. In less than a year Hitler was Chancellor of Germany. Fascism could no longer be dismissed as a matter of a handful of misguided provincials that could be easily controlled by the Schutzbund. After January 1933 the party presses produced a flood of pamphlets and articles on fascism, but by now it was almost too late.

It is perhaps surprising that a party that was renowned for its theoretical brilliance should have failed so badly when it came to an understanding of fascism, and seriously underestimated the danger it posed to Austrian democracy. Theory failed to guide practice, limping sadly behind, all too often used to justify hasty decisions by the party leadership. At times there was an unreal sense of optimism. In 1920 Bauer had said that Austria could not hope to survive as a socialist oasis in capitalist Central Europe, but by 1932 he was arguing, with even less justification, that it could become a democratic island in a fascist ocean. Others viewed the future with a growing sense of doom, their will paralysed by a feeling of the inevitability of defeat. It was only after the disaster of 12 February that the Austro-Marxists were able to make some contribution to the analysis of fascism. As was so often the case with the party, theory and practice were badly out of step, and the price paid for this failure was cruelly high.

After the closing of parliament on 15 March 1933 the Dollfuss government began to establish an authoritarian régime, modelled in part on Mussolini's Italy, which many observers, not only socialists, promptly labelled 'Austro-fascism'. This was soon to set off a seemingly endless debate on how 'fascist' was 'Austro-fascism', a debate only rivalled by the longer-lasting discussion of how 'Marxist' was 'Austro-Marxism'. The results of these debates were very meagre, for the underlying motive was in almost every case to apportion blame for the fighting of 12 February, and not to discover the real nature of the régime. Deeply felt political resentments prevented an objective analysis of the Dollfuss government, and it is only recently that scholars have been able to write more dispassionately on the subject.[43]

There has also been some uncertainty as to the relevant component parts of Austro-fascism. Some scholars argue that the Heimwehr, with its obvious links to Fascist Italy and its pronounced fascist style, was the pure form of Austrian fascism. Others prefer to see Austrian fascism as a series of fascist movements which include the Heimwehr and the Austrian Nazis.[44] A further question is whether in addition to the fascist movements there was also a fascist system in Austria in the years between February 1934 and the Anschluss. This immediately leads to two further questions, both of which are singularly difficult to answer: the precise nature of fascism, and the extent to which the Austrian state approximated that definition.

On one issue there can be no disagreement. The régime begun by Dollfuss and completed by Schuschnigg was an outright rejection of the liberal democratic tradition.[45] After March 1933 the parliamentary system was destroyed, individual freedoms were drastically curtailed, the labour movement was brutally suppressed, the executive power of the government was freed from traditional restraints, and steps were taken to reorganise society along strictly hierarchical and authoritarian lines. Unlike the régimes in Italy and Germany, the Austrian system was never fully totalitarian, pockets of limited individual freedom survived, and not all opposition voices were brutally silenced. The régime had no ideology of its own, borrowing it from reactionary Catholic Social philosophy, particularly from the encyclical *Quadragesimo Anno*, but this also acted as a restraint on the inhuman excesses of fully-fledged fascism, with its total lack of respect for human life and the rights and needs of the disadvantaged and the weak.

Austro-fascism also lacked the pseudo-revolutionary mass party that is an essential characteristic of fascism. The Christian Social Party could never be converted into a radicalised mass party, and the attempt to create mass support for the régime with the formation of the Patriotic Front was largely a failure. The Front might have looked impressive at mass rallies and marches, but it lacked a cohesive ideology and a sense of common purpose. Heimwehr radicals, clerical conservatives and romantic Austrian nationalists formed an uneasy alliance, with the Heimwehr and the clericals openly struggling to gain the upper hand. The Heimwehr gave the Front its momentum, but it was never able to gain full control. The Front also lacked the leadership and the dynamism to hold heterogeneous elements together, an acute problem even in such parties as the Italian Fascists and the Nazis, and thus it could not provide that additional strength that would have made possible the formation of a truly totalitarian régime. The Front was merely a useful means of control.

As early as 1934 Palmiro Togliatti, in his perceptive and original *Lessons on Fascism*, had argued that it was a mistake to confuse the radical transformation of bourgeois institutions, such as the formation of a presidential régime, with fascism.[46] On the other hand the precise demarcation lines between an authoritarian bourgeois state, the totalitarian state and fascism are very hard to draw. The Austrian government, particularly after the Enabling Act of 30 April 1934, possessed the legal prerequisites for the foundation of an authoritarian régime, but how far its political practice corresponded to that of typical totalitarian régimes has still to be fully researched.

Historians have not yet examined in detail the economic and social history of Austria from 1934 to 1938, so that it is still too early to say with any real conviction whether the relationships between the capitalist elite and the holders of political power were similar to those in the fascist states, and whether the social system approximated to that of fascism. Certainly the proposed Ständestaat was based in large measure on Italian fascism, even though it was presented in terms of Catholic Social philosophy, but precisely how this state worked in practice has still to be thoroughly investigated.

One obvious characteristic of fascism is the excessive emphasis on military values, a strident militarism and a willingness to fight an imperialist war. Rearmament, the militarisation of society and thorough preparation for war were fundamental ingredients of fascist policy. Dollfuss and the Heimwehr were ever eager to strut around in uniforms and praise military virtues, but then so was a significant sector of the Social Democrats. That Austria was contemplating an aggressive war, perhaps as an ally of another power, has never been seriously suggested. The Patriotic Front praised the military virtues of discipline and self-sacrifice, but there were none of the loud praises of war and condemnations of peace that are such striking components of fascist rhetoric. Austria was saved the horrors of a programme of forced rearmament that was eventually to lead to the militarisation of the labour force in Germany, where terror was soon to become almost a mode of production. The Dollfuss and Schuschnigg governments protected agriculture, which resulted in high living costs, but they did not force industry to attempt to achieve economic autarchy, thus disrupting an economy in the pursuit of rapid rearmament which was to create such an impasse that war seemed to offer the only possible salvation.

The most striking similarity between Austria and the fascist states is the régime's militant anti-Marxism. The outlawing of the Communist Party, the crushing of Social Democracy after 12 February, the virtual ban on stikes, and the reorganisation of the working-class institutions in the new state, were all typical of fascist practice. But the Austrian workers were never as ruthlessly persecuted as their comrades in Italy and Germany.[47] The labour movement was still far from moribund in 1938 when delegates offered Schuschnigg support in a stand against Nazi Germany. The régime never consistently attacked the labour movement, and at times was forced by economic and foreign political considerations to modify its policies. These policies were thus marked by both persecution and appeasement

Austro-fascism was thus not the fully-fledged fascism of Italy or Germany. Otto Bauer's expression, 'half-fascist authoritarian corporate state', although something of a mouthful, is as good a description as any. The prefix 'Austro' is a diminutive.[48] It was not until 1938 that Austria became fully fascist, and then not because of the inner dynamics of the system, but because of the military, economic and political dominance of Nazi Germany.

Notes

1. Gerhard Botz, 'Austro-Marxist Interpretations of Fascism', *Journal of Contemporary History*, 11 October 1976. For a more general discussion see Martin Kitchen, *Fascism* (London 1976).

2. Julius Braunthal, 'Der Putsch der Faschisten', *Der Kampf*, 22 (November 1922).

3. On the 'equilibrium of class forces', an essential dogma of Austro-Marxism, see Otto Bauer, 'Das Gleichgewicht der Klassenkräfte', *Der Kampf*, 17 (February 1924); also his *Die östereichische Revolution* (Vienna 1923).

4. Botz suggests that Braunthal's article was written in collaboration with Bauer, although he gives no real evidence for this. Botz, 'Interpretations', p. 132.

5. Karl Marx, *18th Brumaire of Louis Bonaparte*, and *The Civil War in France*. See also Kitchen, *Fascism*, Ch. 7.

6. Bauer, *Revolution*, p. 246.

7. Both in *Der Kampf*, 17 (1924), pp. 50-6 and 179-87.

8. Otto Bauer, *Zwischen zwei Weltkriegen?* (Vienna 1937), p. 187.

9. Otto Bauer, 'Kapitalherrschaft in der Demokratie', *Der Kampf*, 21 (August-September 1928).

10. *Protokoll des Parteitages 1926*, p. 176.

11. Norbert Leser, *Zwischen Reformismus und Bolschewismus. Der Austromarxismus als Theorie und Praxis* (Vienna 1969), p. 394.

12. See the later comments of Bauer in *Zwischen zwei Weltkriegen?*, p. 342.

13. Johann Hirsch, 'Zur Soziologie des Austrofaschismus', *Der Kampf*, 22 (May 1929).

14. Julius Deutsch (ed.), *Der Faschismus in Europa* (Vienna 1929).

15. Ibid., p. 3.

16. Ibid., p. 4.

17. Ibid., p. 52.

18. Julius Deutsch, *Antifaschismus! Proletarische Wehrhaftigkeit im Kampfe gegen den Faschismus* (Vienna 1926).

19. Ibid., p. 13.

20. Ibid., p. 31.

21. Ibid., pp. 35 and 42.

22. Ibid., p. 45.

23. Ibid., p. 58.

24. Ibid., p. 86.

25. Gerhard Botz, 'Genesis und Inhalt der Faschismustheorien Otto Bauers', *International Review of Social Hisory*, XIX, Part 1 (1974), p. 38.

26. Otto Bauer, 'Der 24. April', *Der Kampf*, 25 (1932).

27. Leser, *Reformismus*, p. 454.

28. Bauer, *Zwischen zwei Weltkriegen?* and 'Der Faschismus', reprinted in *Die Zukunft* (Vienna 1948), pp. 33-41.

29. Bauer, *Zwischen zwei Weltkriegen?*, p. 130.

30. There is nothing strikingly original in this view. Giovanni Zibordi, *Critica socialista del fascismo* (Bologna 1922), was almost certainly known to Bauer, who spoke Italian.

31. Bauer, *Zwischen zwei Weltkriegen?*, pp. 70, 72, 77, 214 and 220.

32. Otto Bauer, *Die illegale Partei* (Paris 1939).

33. Hilferding's writings on organised capitalism are reprinted in H.A. Winkler (ed), *Organisierter Kapitalismus* (Göttingen 1975).

34. Kitchen, *Fascism*, Ch. 5.

35. Otto Bauer, 'Der Faschismus', *Der Sozialistische Kampf — La lutte socialiste*, 4 (July 1938) (reprint of part of Die illegale Partei).

36. Karl Renner, *Novemberverbrecher? Die Anklagen der Hitler-Bewegung gegen die 'Novemberverbrecher wegen nationalen Verrats* (Vienna 1932), pp. 89-92.

37. This forecast, shared by Bauer and Adler, was not as far from the mark as has often been suggested. Once in power a serious split developed between the Nazi 'left' and Hitler which resulted in the 'Röhm putsch' of 1934.

38. Karl Renner, *Wandlungen der modernen Gesellschaft* (Vienna 1953), p. 65.

39. Max Adler's writings on fascism include 'Faschismus und Koalitionsgesinnung', *Der Klassenkampf*, 3, 20 (1929); 'Das österreichische Beispiel und der Faschismus', *Der Klassenkampf*, 4, 5 (1930); 'Was ist Antimarxismus?', *Der Klassenkampf*, 4, 22 (1930); 'Wandlungen der Arbeiterklasse', *Der Kampf*, 26, 8-9 and 10 (1933).

40. Adler, 'Wandlungen der Arbeiterklasse'.

41. For a discussion of Adler's thought see Leser, *Reformismus*, pp. 513-61. For Trotsky's theory of fascism see Martin Kitchen, 'Trotsky's Theory of Fascism', *Social Praxis* (1975).

42. Quoted in Leser, *Reformismus*, p. 457.

43. Grete Klingenstein, 'Bemerkungen zum Problem des Faschismus in Oesterreich', *Oesterreich in Geschichte und Literatur*, 1 (1970).

44. F.L. Carsten, *Faschismus in Oesterreich*, is an excellent example of this approach.

45. This does not imply that Dollfuss from the very outset had a clear idea of exactly what he wanted to do. John Rath, 'The First Austrian Republic — totalitarian, fascist, authoritarian, or what?' in Rudolf Neck and Adam Wandruszka, *Beiträge zur Zeitgeschichte: Festschrift Ludwig Jedlicka* (St Pölten 1976), p. 174, makes the amazing remark that Dollfuss simply wanted to make democracy 'more efficient'. Quite what he means by this remains obscure.

46. Palmiro Togliatti, *Lezioni sul fascismo* (Rome 1970).

47. See Everhard Holtmann, *Zwischen Unterdrückung und Befriedung. Sozialistische Arbeiterbewegung und autoritäres Regime in Oesterreich 1933-1938* (Munich 1978), for a thoughtful analysis of the labour movement in Austria in this period.

48. Gerhard Botz, 'Die Ausschaltung des Nationalrates und die Anfänge der Diktatur Dollfuss in Urteil der Geschichtsschreibung von 1933 bis 1973' in *40 Jahre danach. Der 4. März 1933 im Urteil von Zeitgenossen und Historikern* (Vienna 1973).

12 CONCLUSION

The events of 12 February 1934 were a sudden and violent response to an immediate situation in Linz, but the outcome was determined by factors which had been slowly developing. The Social Democrats, forced into action by their comrades in Linz, were singularly ill prepared. They had long been paralysed by the fatalism of Austro-Marxist ideology, by a principled rejection of violence, and by a belief in the policy of the 'lesser evil'. The official policy of the party was acceptable to many, for the social consequences of the depression, particularly in a country with an economy as weak as Austria's, were such that few were willing to risk a radical policy. The *radikalinskis* were either men with nothing to lose, those who had suffered months of unemployment and saw no hope of any improvement, or those who were convinced that Austria was going the same way as Germany and that it was madness to support Dollfuss as the only barrier against National Socialism.

The hopelessness of the Social Democrats in the face of a growing fascist threat was symptomatic of the collapse of party politics in the Austrian republic. Their greatest rivals, the Christian Socials, by attacking the principles of party politics, were condemning their own party to eventual extinction. The Greater Germans collapsed to become little more than hangers-on of the Nazis. The Communists were a small sect, and up to 12 February were totally lacking in popular support.

Few Austrians were convinced supporters of parliamentary democracy, but there was considerable confusion as to what should take its place. The Heimwehr was determined to destroy democracy, possibly by a dramatic 'March on Vienna', but had no idea what this would involve. Some admired the Italian fascists, others the Nazis, and a third group dreamed of some form of Austrian fascism but could offer no concrete plans for this new society. The Christian Socials, with their vision of an 'authoritarian Christian state of the estates', were equally vague. They could appeal to the traditions of Catholic Social theory and to the papal encyclical *Quadragesimo Anno*, but these sources were also susceptible to many different interpretations and did not provide a practical guide to political action. The Social Democrats, for all their talk of 'socialism' and 'dictatorship of the proletariat', were equally at a loss to provide practical proposals for a way out of current difficulties. In such an atmosphere it is hardly surprising that violence took the place of reasoned dialogue, or that ill-digested utopian panaceas replaced pragmatic politics.

Dollfuss, however vague his dreams of a future society might have been, and however flexible his tactics, was determined to destroy Social Democracy. 'Anti-Marxism' was the guiding principle of his politics. Many Social Democrats longed for a compromise, probably a majority of the party, but Dollfuss would not even consider such proposals. His entire policy was based on a fatal fallacy. He believed that by destroying 'Marxism' in Austria he would also destroy the basis of the support given to the Austrian Nazis. The experiences of Papen in Germany, who suffered from a similar delusion, seemed to escape the notice of the Austrian Chancellor. At the same time he hoped that by defeating Nazism and by defeating Austrian independence he would be able to win over the working class to support his régime. On both counts 12 February 1934 was a miserable failure. The defeat of Social Democracy strengthened rather than weakened the Nazi Pary and destroyed the greatest anti-fascist force in the country. The violence and brutality of February was such that the working class could never be reconciled to the régime. Some disillusioned radicals joined the Nazis, there was a mass exodus to the Communist Party, and others continued to work within the reorganised illegal party, radicalised by the experiences of February, their 'democratic illusions' shattered.

Austro-fascism was not created in February 1934, although this was a key date in the creation of the new state. Long before February Dollfuss had begun the systematic destruction of democratic freedoms and the abolition of legal rights, and had started to lay the basis for the authoritarian state. Lacking mass support, without an aggressive imperialist foreign policy, borrowing its ideology from the Catholic church and reluctant to indulge in the bestial brutality of the fascist régimes of Italy and Germany, Austro-fascist domination was distinct from the typical fascist régimes. The fact that Austro-fascism is so hard to define partly explains why the Social Democrats were incapable of accurate analysis of the dynamics of the Dollfuss régime. The hopes for a compromise with the government by the right were as unrealistic as the utopian dreams of the left. The party was held together by a mixture of radical rhetoric and timid practice and thus became an easy victim for a ruthless opponent. By 12 February 1934 the party had already suffered a series of crippling political defeats and was in danger of falling apart under the pressure of conflicting views on future policy. Its military policy was hopelessly inadequate and its rank and file frustrated and demoralised.

The government seized the opportunity that was offered, and had little difficulty in crushing its greatest opponent. But the victory was Pyrrhic. The defeat of Social Democracy did not lead to any increase in support for the Patriotic Front which merely attracted cynical opportunists and careerists. The Nazi Party continued to grow in strength and belligerence, and the government had lost its only valuable ally against the Nazi threat. In 1938 the Social Democrats were still prepared to defend Austria and to support Schuschnigg, but by this time it was too late.

It may seem that the men of the Schutzbund died in vain, for their deaths failed to unite the European left which continued its suicidal bickering until the Nazis were on the point of overrunning the whole of Europe. But the lessons of February are clear. Democracy is a terribly fragile system that demands constant vigilance and determined support. It is not enough merely to defend it against encroachments by its bitterest enemies, it must be constantly extended and strengthened. Concessions to opponents are doomed to failure. It is only through the extension of democracy that people can lead fuller, richer and more truly human lives. The men of 12 February were often confused and misled, but they all knew deep within them that their struggle was for a decent, just and humane society. It is for this reason that they should never be forgotten.

BIBLIOGRAPHY

Archival Sources

Oesterreichisches Staatsarchiv, Allgemeines Verwaltungsarchiv (AVA)

Polizeidirektion Wien, Akten Februar 1934, Zl. Pr. IV — 2606/1934, Karton 1-16.
Bundeskanzleramt Inneres 1934, 22/gen.: 4883; 4884; 4885; 4886; 4887; 4888
Ministerrat Protokolle: 708; 743; 888; 918-23; 934; 935; 951
Sozialdemokratische Parteiarchiv, Parteistellen: 34; 35; 106; 123; 162; 175a; 191
Die Bundesgendarmerie in den Tagen des Aufstandes Februar und Juli 1934. B/839.

Haus- Hof- und Staatsarchiv, Neues Politisches Archiv (NPA)

Fasz. 12; 48; 59; 84; 89; 104; 105; 106; 107; 114; 257; 278; 280; 281; 292; 293; 312; 313; 465; 466; 477; 654; 839; 840; 1006
Kriegsarchiv (KA)
Int. Zl. 890 - 1/33
2 - 3/2 4491/34

Verein für die Geschichte der Arbeiterbewegung (VGA)

Lode 16, Mappe 33; 34
Lode 17, Mappe 1; 2; 2b; 2c

Secondary Sources

Abel, Hilde *Victory was Slain* (New York 1941)
Ackerl, Isabella 'Die Grossdeutsche Volkspartei 1920 bis 1934 — Versuch einer Parteigeschichte' (unpublished PhD thesis, Vienna 1967)

Adam, Ingrid 'Zum 12. Februar 1934', *Oesterreich in Geschichte und Literatur*, 8 (January 1964)

Adler, Max 'Faschismus und Koalitionsgesinnung', *Der Klassenkampf*, 3, 20 (1929)

____ 'Das österreichische Beispiel und der Faschismus', *Der Klassenkampf*, 4, 5 (1930)

____ 'Was ist Antimarxismus?', *Der Klassenkampf*, 4, 22 (1930)

____ 'Wandlungen der Arbeiterklasse', *Der Kampf*, 26, 8/9 and 10 (1933)

Aloisi, Baron Pompeo *Journal*, Mario Toscano (ed.) (Paris 1957)

Andics, Helmut *Der Staat der keiner wollte, Oesterreich 1918-1938* (Vienna 1962)

Ausch, Karl *Als die Banken fielen* (Frankfurt 1968)

Bärnthaler, Irmgard *Die Vaterländische Front* (Vienna 1971)

Basch, A. and Dvoracek, J. *Austria and its Economic Existence* (Prague 1925)

Bauer, Eugen *Oesterreich eine Lehre für Alle* (Prague 1934)

Bauer, Otto *Nationalitätenfrage und die Sozialdemokratie* (Vienna 1907)

____ *Die österreichische Revolution* (Vienna 1923)

____ *Die Wirtschaftskrise in Oesterreich. Ihre Ursachen, ihre Heilung* (Vienna 1925)

____ *Der Aufstand der österreichischen Arbeiter* (Prague 1934)

____ *Zwischen zwei Weltkriegen?* (Bratislava 1936)

____ *Die illegale Partei* (Paris 1939)

____ 'Das Gleichgewicht der Klassenkräfte', *Der Kampf*, 17 (February 1924)

____ 'Kapitalherrschaft in der Demokratie', *Der Kampf* (August/ September 1928)

Bayer, Hans *Strukturwandlungen der österreichischen Volkswirtschaft nach dem Kriege* (Vienna 1929)

Benedikt, Heinrich *Geschichte der Republik Oesterreich* (Munich 1954)

Berger, Paul *Faschismus und Nationalsozialismus* (Vienna 1934)

Berghahn, V.R. *Militarismus* (Cologne 1975)

Bernaschek, Richard *Die Tragödie der österreichischen Sozialdemokratie* (Prague 1934)

Borkenau, Franz *Austria and After* (London 1938)

Born, Karl Erich *Die deutsche Bankenkrise 1931* (Munich 1967)

Bottomore, Tom and Goode, Patrick (eds.) *Austro-Marxism* (Oxford 1978)

Botz, Gerhard *Gewalt in der Politik* (Munich 1976)

_____ 'Austro-Marxist Interpretations of Fascism', *Journal of Contemporary History*, 11 (October 1976)

_____ 'Genesis und Inhalt der Faschismustheorien Otto Bauers', *International Review of Social History*, XIX (1974)

Botz, Gerhard, Hautmann, Hans and Konrad, Helmut *Geschichte und Gesellschaft. Festschrift für Karl R. Stadler zum 60. Geburtstag* (Vienna 1974)

Bracher, K-D. *Die deutsche Diktatur* (Cologne 1969)

Brandstotter, Rudolf 'Dr. Walter Riehl und die Geschichte der nationalsozialistischen Bewegung in Oesterreich' (unpublished PhD thesis, Vienna 1969)

Braunthal, Julius 'Der Putsch der Faschisten', *Der Kampf*, 22 (November 1922)

Brügel, Ludwig *Geschichte der österreichischen Arbeiterbewegung* (5 vols., Vienna 1922-5)

Brusatti, Alois *Oesterreichs Wirtschaftspolitik vom Josefinismus zum Ständestaat* (Vienna 1965)

Busshoff, Heinrich *Das Dollfuss-Regime in Oesterreich* (Berlin 1968)

_____ 'Berufsständisches Gedankengut zu Beginn der dreissiger Jahre in Deutschland und Oesterreich', *Zeitschrift für Politik*, 13 (1966)

Buttinger, Joseph *Am Beispiel Oesterreichs* (Cologne 1953)

Camp, Richard L. *The Papal Ideology of Social Reform* (Leiden 1969)

Carsten, F. L. *Faschismus in Oesterreich. Von Schönerer zu Hitler* (Vienna 1977)

_____ *Revolution in Central Europe 1918-1919* (Berkeley 1972)

Ciller, A. *Vorläufer des Nationalsozialismus* (Vienna 1932)

Collotti, E. 'La sconfitta socialista del 1934 e l'opposizione antifascista in Austria fino al 1938', *Rivista Storica del Socialismo*, vol. 6 (Milan 1963)

Czeike, Felix 'Wirtschafts- und Sozialpolitik der Gemeinde Wien in der Ersten Republik (1919-1934)' *Wiener Schriften*, vols. 6 and 11 (Vienna 1958-9)

Czernetz, Karl '12. Februar 1934 — Februar 1964', *Die Zukunft*, 3 (1964)

Danneberg, Robert *Wirtschaftskrise, Faschismus und Arbeiterklasse* (Vienna 1932)

Deutsch, Julius *Ein Weiter Weg. Lebenserinnerungen* (Vienna 1960)

_____ *Der Faschismus in Europa* (Vienna 1929)

_____ *Putsch oder Revolution?* (Karlsbad 1934)

_____ *Antifaschismus! Proletarische Wehrhaftigkeit im Kampfe gegen den Faschismus* (Vienna 1926)

_____ *Aus Oesterreichs Revolution* (Vienna 1923)

_____ *Alexander Eifler, Ein Soldat der Freiheit* (Vienna 1947)

_____ *Wer rüstet zum Bürgerkrieg?* (Vienna 1923)

_____ *Die Faschistengefahr* (Vienna 1923)

Diamant, Alfred *Austrian Catholics and the First Republic* (Princeton 1960)

Die österreichische Sozialdemokratie im Spiegel ihrer Programme (Vienna 1964)

Documents Diplomatiques Français 1932-1939, 2e. Série (Paris 1963)

Documents on British Foreign Policy 1919-1939 (London 1947 ff.)

Documents on German Foreign Policy 1918-1945 series C (1933-7) (London 1957 ff.)

Dokumente zum Wiener Schutzbundprozess (Karlsbad 1935)

Duczynska, Ilona *Der demokratische Bolschewik. Zur Theorie und Praxis der Gewalt* (Munich 1975)

Ehrenburg, Ilja *Der Bürgerkrieg in Oesterreich* (Prague 1934)

Ehrlich, Otto *Kann Oesterreich geholfen werden?* (Vienna 1927)

Eichstädt, Ulrich *Von Dollfuss zu Hitler* (Wiesbaden 1955)

Ellenbogen, Wilhelm 'Der österreichsiche Faschismus und wir', *Der Kampf* (June 1933)

Fischer, Ernst *An Opposing Man* (London 1974)

Fraenkel-Verkade, E. *Correspondentie van Mr. M.M. Rost van Tonningen*, (Gravenhage 1967)

Franzen, Hans *Die deutsch-österreichischen Wirtschaftsbeziehungen in der Nachkriegszeit* (Cologne 1928)

Freund, Rudolf *Die Genfer Protokolle. Ihre Geschichte und Bedeutung für das Staatsleben Deutsch-Oesterreichs* (Berlin 1924)

Frisch, Hans von *Die Gewaltherrschaft in Oesterreich 1933-1938* (Leipzig 1938)

Frishchauer, Margrit 'Auseinandersetzungen und Kontakte zwischen Sozialdemokraten und Kommunisten 1927-1934' (unpublished PhD thesis, Vienna 1976)

Fürnberg, Friedl *Geschichte der Kommunistischen Partei Oesterreichs 1918-1955. Kurzer Abriss* (Vienna 1977)

Gebert, Erich *Flammenzeichen. Oesterreichs Wirtschaftsschicksal* (Vienna 1927)

Gedeye, G.E.R. *Fallen Bastions* (London 1939)

Gehl, Jürgen *Austria, Germany, and the Anschluss 1931-1938* (Oxford 1963)

Gerdenitsch, Josef 'Das Wiener Arsenal in der ersten Republik' (unpublished PhD thesis, Vienna 1967)

Goldinger, Walter *Geschichte der Republik Oesterreich* (Munich 1962)

Gulick, C.A. *Austria from Habsburg to Hitler* (2 vols., Berkeley 1948)

Haas, Karl 'Zur Wehrpolitik der österreichischen Sozialdemokratie in der Ersten Republik', *Truppendienst*, 2 (1973)

Haber, Franz *Die osterreichische Wirtschaftsbilanz* (Munich 1927)

Hannak, Jacques *Karl Renner und seine Zeit* (Vienna 1965)

Hartlieb, Wladimir von *Parole: Das Reich* (Vienna 1939)

Hautmann, Hans *Die Verlorene Räterepublik. Am Beispiel der Kommunistischen Partei Deutschlands* (Vienna 1971)

_____ *Die Anfänge der Linksradikalen Bewegung und der Kommunistischen Partei Deutschösterreichs 1916-1919* (Vienna 1970)

_____ 'Die Kriegslinke in der Sozialdemokratischen Partei Oesterreichs zwischen 1914 und 1918', *Die Zukunft*, 13/14 (Vienna, July 1971)

_____ and Kropf, Rudolf *Die österreichische Arbeiterbewegung vom Vormärz bis 1945* (Vienna 1974)

Hertz, Friedrich *Ist Oesterreich wirtschaftlich lebensfähig?* (Vienna 1921)

Hirsch, Johann 'Zur Soziologie des Austrofaschismus', *Der Kampf*, 22 (May 1929)

Holtmann, Everhard *Zwischen Unterdrückung und Befriedung. Sozialistische Arbeiterbewegung und autoritäres Regime in Oesterreich 1933-1938* (Munich 1978)

Holzbauer, Wilhelm 'Die Wiener Gemeindebauten der ersten Republik', *Zeitgeschichte*, 1 (October 1973)

Höper, Gerhard *Oesterreichs Weg zum Anschluss* (Berlin 1928)

Huber, W. and Schwerdtfeger, J. *Frieden, Gewalt, Sozialismus — Studien zur Geschichte der sozialistischen Arbeiterbewegung* (Stuttgart 1976)

Huemer, P. *Sektionschef Robert Hecht und die Zerstörung der österreichischen Demokratie* (Vienna 1975)

Jacobsen, Hans-Adolf *Nationalsozialistische Aussenpolitik 1933-1938* (Berlin 1968)

Jedlicka, Ludwig *Ein Heer im Schatten der Parteien* (Graz 1955)

_____ 'Heer und Staat in Oesterreich 1918-1938', *Bücherschau der Weltkriegsbücherei*, vol. 28 (1956)

_____ 'Neue Forschungsergebnisse zum 12. Februar 1934', *Oesterreich in Geschichte und Literatur*, 2 (1964)

_____ 'Die Jahre 1933-1935 in der osterreichischen Innenpolitik

Veröffentlichungen des Verbands österreichischer Geschichtsvereine, 15 (1965)

―――― 'Die österreichische Innenpolitik 1934-1955', *Oesterreich in Geschichte und Literatur*, 6 (June 1962)

―――― and Neck, Rudolf *Das Jahr 1934: 25. Juli* (Vienna 1975)

―――― *Das Jahr 1934: 12. Februar* (Vienna 1975)

―――― *Oesterreich 1927 bis 1938* (Munich 1973)

―――― *Vom Justizpalast zum Heldenplatz* (Vienna 1975)

Kallbrunner, Hermann *Der Wiederaufbau der Landwirtschaft Oesterreichs* (Vienna 1926)

Katsoulis, Ilias *Sozialismus und Staat* (Meisenheim/Glan 1975)

Kautsky, B. *Löhne und Gehälter* (Vienna 1926)

Kelsen, Hans *Marx oder Lassalle — Wandlungen in der politischen Theorie des Marxismus* (Leipzig 1924)

Kerekes, Lajos *Abenddämmerung einer Demokratie* (Vienna 1966)

―――― 'Neauer Aktenfund zu den Beziehungen zwischen Hitler und Dollfuss im Jahre 1933', *Acta Historica Academiae Scientiarum Hungaricae*, 18 (1972)

―――― 'Akten zu den geheimen Verbindungen zwischen der Bethlen-Regierung und der österreichischen Heimwehrbewegung', *Acta Historica Academiae Scientiarum Hungaricae*, 11, 2 (1965)

―――― 'Italien, Ungarn und die österreichische Heimwehrbewegung 1928-1931', *Oesterreich in Geschichte und Literatur*, IX (1965)

Keri, Paul *Soldat der Revolution. Koloman Wallisch* (Prague 1934)

Kienböck, Viktor *Das österreichische Sanierungswerk* (Stuttgart 1925)

Kitchen, Martin *Fascism* (London 1976)

―――― 'Friedrich Engels' Theory of War', *Military Affairs*, XLI, no. 3 (October 1977)

―――― 'Trotsky's Theory of Fascism', *Social Praxis* (1975)

Kleinwächter, F.G. *Der deutsch-österreichische Mensch und der Anschluss* (Vienna 1926)

Klemperer, Klemens von *Ignaz Seipel — Christian Statesman in a Time of Crisis* (Princeton 1972)

Klingenstein, Grete *Die Anleihe von Lausanne* (Vienna 1965)

―――― 'Bemerkungen zum Problem des Faschismus in Oesterreich', *Oesterreich in Geschichte und Literatur*, 1 (1970)

Kluge, U. 'Das Dilemma einer Demokratie', *Neue Politische Literatur*, 2 (1978)

Kniesche, Herbert *Die grossdeutsche Wirtschaftseinheit* (Leipzig 1929)

Kodre, Helfried 'Die stilistische Entwicklung der Wiener Gemeindebauten', *Der Aufbau*, 9 (1964)

Kun, Bela *Die Februarkämpfe in Oesterreich und ihre Lehren*
(Moscow 1934)

Kuppe, Rudolf *Karl Lueger und seine Zeit* (Vienna 1933)

Kurella, Alfred *Mussolini ohne Maske* (Berlin 1931)

Kykal, Inez and Stadler, Karl R. *Richard Bernaschek. Odyssee eines
Rebellen* (Vienna 1976)

Langoth, Franz *Kampf um Oesterreich* (Wels 1951)

Layton, W.T. and Rist, Charles *Die Wirtschaftslage Oesterreichs*
(Vienna 1925)

Leser, Norbert 'Der Austromarxismus als Strömung des marxistischen
Zentrums', *VIII. Linzer Konferenz der Historiker der Arbeiterbewegung* (Linz 1972)

_____ 'Austro-Marxism: A Reappraisal', *Journal of Contemporary
History*, 11 (July 1976)

_____ *Zwischen Reformismus und Bolschevismus. Der Austromarxismus als Theorie und Praxis* (Vienna 1968)

Leser, Norbert (ed.) *Werk und Widerhall* (Vienna 1964)

Litschel, Rudolf Walter *1934 — Das Jahr der Irrungen* (Linz, n.d.)

Mayenburg, Ruth von *Blaues Blut und rote Fahnen* (Vienna 1969)

Mayer, Hans (ed.) *Hundert Jahre österreichische Wirtschaftsentwick-
lung 1848-1948* (Vienna 1949)

Mitteracker, Hermann *Zur Geschichte der Kommunistischen Partei
Oesterreichs* (Vienna 1959)

Mommsen, Hans (ed.) *Industrielles System und politische
Entwicklung in der Weimarer Republik* (Düsseldorf 1974)

Neck, Rudolf and Wandruszka, Adam *Beiträge zur Zeitgeschichte.
Festschrift für Ludwig Jedlicka* (St Pölten 1976)

_____ *Die Ereignisse des 15. Juli 1927* (Vienna 1979)

Oesterreich — Brandherd Europas (Zürich 1934)

Otruba, Gustav *Oesterreichs Wirtschaft im 20. Jahrhundert* (Vienna
1968)

Peball, Kurt *Die Kämpfe in Wien im Februar 1934* (Vienna 1974)

'Pertinax' (Otto Leichter) *Oesterreich 1934 — Geschichte einer
Konterrevolution* (Zürich 1935)

Petersen, Jens *Hitler-Mussolini. Die Entstehung der Achse Berlin-
Rom 1933-1936* (Tübingen 1973)

Ratzenhofer, E. 'Die Niederwerfung der Februarrevolte 12-15 Februar 1934', *Militärwissenschaftliche Mitteilungen* (1934)

Reisberg, Arnold *Februar 1934: Hintergründe und Folgen* (Vienna 1974)

Renner, Karl *Novemberverbrecher? Die Anklagen der Hitler-Bewegung gegen die 'Novemberverbrecher' wegen nationalen Verrats* (Vienna 1932)

_____ *Wandlungen der modernen Gesellschaft* (Vienna 1953)

_____ *Oesterreich von der Ersten zur Zweiten Republik* (Vienna 1953)

Roscher, Heinz *Die Februarkämpfe in Floridsdorf* (Moscow 1935)

Rosdolsky, Roman *Studien über revolutionäre Taktik — Der österreichische Januarstreik 1918* (Berlin 1973)

Ross, Dieter *Hitler und Dollfuss: Die deutsche Oesterreich-Politik 1933-1934* (Hamburg 1966)

Rothschild, Kurt W. 'Wurzeln und Triebkräfte der Entwicklung der österreichischen Wirtschaftsstruktur' in W. Weber (ed.), *Osterreichs Wirtschaftsstruktur gestern -heute -morgen*, vol. 1 (Berlin 1961)

_____ 'Staatengrösse und Lebensfähigkeit. Das österreichsiche Beispiel', *Zeitschrift für Nationalökonomie*, 19 (1959)

_____ *Austria's Economic Development between the Two Wars* (London 1947)

Sailer, K.H. *Mussolini-Dollfuss, geheimer Briefwechsel* (Vienna 1949)

Sandkühler, Jörg and Vega, Rafael de la (eds.) *Austromarxismus. Texte zu Ideologie und Klassenkampf* (Frankfurt 1970)

Scheffer, Egon *Oesterreichs wirtschaftliche Sendung* (Leipzig 1927)

Scheu, Friedrich *Der Weg ins Ungewisse* (Vienna 1972)

Schilder, Siegmund *Der Streit um die wirtschaftliche Lebensfähigkeit Oesterreichs* (Stuttgart 1926)

Schlandt, Joachim 'Die Wiener Superblocks', *Werk*, 4 (1970)

Schneidmadl, Heinrich *Über Dollfuss zu Hitler* (Vienna 1964)

Seghers, Anna 'Der letzte Weg des Koloman Wallisch' in *Aufstellen eines Maschinengewehrs im Wohnzimmer der Frau Kamptschik* (Berlin 1970)

_____ *Der Weg durch den Februar* (Berlin 1951)

Seipel, Ignaz *Der Kampf um die österreichische Verfassung* (Vienna 1930)

Slavik, Gerhard *Der Aussenhandel und die Handelspolitik Oesterreichs 1918-1928* (Klagenfurt 1928)

Spitzmüller, Alexander *...und hat auch Ursach' es zu lieben* (Vienna 1955)

Starhemberg, Ernst Rudiger Prince *Between Hitler and Mussolini* (London 1942)

Staudinger, Anton 'Die österreichische Wehrgesetzgebung 1918-1938', *Oesterreichische Militärische Zeitschrift*, pp. 151-5, 219-24 (1971)

_____ 'Bemühungen Carl Vaugoins um Suprematie der Christlich-sozialen Partei in Oesterreich (1930-1933)', *Mitteilungen des österreichischen Staatsarchiv*, vol. 23 (1970) (Vienna 1971)

_____ 'Die sozialdemokratische Grenzländerkonferenz vom 15. September 1933 in Salzburg — Ein sozialdemokratisches Angebot militärischer Kooperation mit der Regierung Dollfuss gegen den Nationalsozialismus' in *Festschrift für Franz Luidl*, vol. 3 (Vienna 1971)

Steiner, Herbert 'Die KPÖ und der Februar 1934', *Weg und Ziel* (1964)

_____ 'Die Kommunistische Partei Oesterreichs von 1918 bis 1933. Bibliographische Bemerkungen', *Marburger Abhandlungen zur Politischen Wissenschaft*, vol. 11 (Meisenheim/Glan 1968)

_____ 'Auseinandersetzungen innerhalb der Sozialdemokratie vor dem 12. Februar 1934', *Weg und Ziel*, 2 (1973)

Stolper, Gustav *Deutsch-Oesterreich als Sozial- und Wirtschaftsproblem* (Munich 1921)

Sweet, Paul R. 'Democracy and Counter-Revolution in Austria', *Journal of Modern History* (March 1950)

Tautscher, Anton and Kübler, Ernst *Die Lebensfähigkeit Oesterreichs* (Vienna 1946)

Tober, Helmut 'Alexander Eifler, vom Monarchisten zum Republikaner' (unpublished PhD thesis, Vienna 1966)

Trebitsch *Der 15. Juli und seine rechte Lehre* (Vienna 1927)

Trotzki, Leo *Oesterreich 1929-1933* (Prague 1934)

Vierzig Jahre Danach: Der 4. März 1933 im Urteil von Zeitgenossen und Historikern (Vienna 1973)

Vlcek, Christine 'Der Republikanische Schutzbund in Oesterreich. Geschichte, Aufbau und Organisation' (unpublished PhD thesis, Vienna 1971)

Wallisch, Paula *Ein Held stirbt* (Graz 1964)

Warren, J.C.P. 'The Political Career and influence of Georg Ritter von Schönerer', (unpublished PhD thesis, London 1963)

Weissel, Erwin *Die Ohnmacht des Sieges* (Vienna 1976)

Whiteside, Andrew G. *Austrian National Socialism before 1918* (the Hague 1962)

_____ The Socialism of Fools — Georg Ritter von Schönerer and

Austrian Pan-Germanism (Berkeley 1975)

Winkler, Franz *Die Diktatur in Oesterreich* (Zürich 1935)

'Wieser, Georg' (Otto Leichter) *Ein Staat stirbt. Oesterreich 1934-1938* (Paris 1938)

Wolf, Erich Hans *Katastrophenwirtschaft. Geburt und Ende Oesterreichs 1918-1938* (Zurich 1939)

Wolf, Friedrich *Floridsdorf* (Zürich 1935)

Wunderer, Otto 'Der italienische Faschismus in der Analyse der österreichischen sozialdemokratischen Partei 1922-1933' (unpublished PhD thesis, Vienna 1974)

Zibordi, Giovanni *Critica socialista del fascismo* (Bologna 1922)

INDEX